W9-AXF-716
DISCARDED

761.209
H58i

92768

DATE DUE

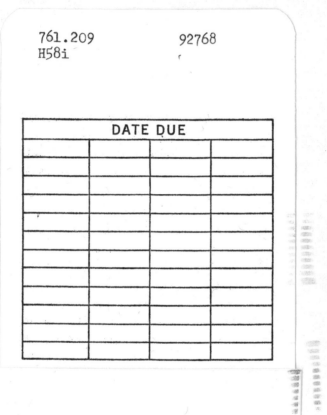

AN INTRODUCTION TO A

HISTORY OF WOODCUT

WITH A DETAILED SURVEY OF WORK DONE IN

THE FIFTEENTH CENTURY

BY

ARTHUR M. HIND

Late Keeper of Prints and Drawings in the British Museum

WITH FRONTISPIECE AND 483 ILLUSTRATIONS IN THE TEXT

IN TWO VOLUMES

VOL. I

DOVER PUBLICATIONS, INC. NEW YORK

CARL A. RUDISILL LIBRARY
LENOIR RHYNE COLLEGE

Published in Canada by General Publishing Company, Ltd., 30 Lesmill Road, Don Mills, Toronto, Ontario.

Published in the United Kingdom by Constable and Company, Ltd., 10 Orange Street, London WC 2.

761.209
H58i
92768
Mar. 1975

This Dover edition, first published in 1963, is an unabridged and unaltered republication of the work first published by the Houghton Mifflin Company in 1935. In the original edition the frontispiece of the first volume was reproduced in collotype.

International Standard Book Number: 0-486-20952-0

Library of Congress Catalog Card Number: 63-5621

Manufactured in the United States of America

Dover Publications, Inc.
180 Varick Street
New York 14, N. Y.

TO

CAMPBELL DODGSON
MASTER OF THE HISTORY OF WOODCUT

AND TO

A. L. H.
FOR FRIENDSHIP

PREFACE

THE hopes expressed in the preface to the third edition of my *History of Engraving and Etching* (1923) that I should be able to compass a History of Woodcut have practically disappeared. Years of work have been spent on the beginnings of this task, and in a detailed examination of xv-century work, and I am now induced to publish the results of these researches rather than continue such labours over the later centuries with the dwindling hope of eventually producing a General History. I become more loth with years to attempt such a work without the intensive study which each period claims before generalisations can be ventured with confidence.

Though the work I offer is complete in itself, I regard it in the nature of a challenge to some other student to continue on the same basis through the xvi century (more than enough in itself for a long volume), and from the xvii to the end of the xix century (which might be covered by a third volume), leaving the xx Century, its achievement and promise, to an epilogue. With my official duties, and the complete illustrated catalogue of Early Italian Engravings which I have in hand, I cannot hope to advance further in the field myself.

I still hope that my predecessor as Keeper of Prints and Drawings at the British Museum, Mr. Campbell Dodgson, may find leisure to undertake the xvi century, with Dürer as its *fons et origo*, for no one has comparable knowledge and material. His official catalogues would thus find their coping stone in a more general survey. My dedication to him implies a great debt throughout many years of official service, as well as a valued friendship. He has, moreover, given me great help in reading the present work in proof.

Apart from the detailed and critical study which must chiefly touch the special student, I have a lurking hope that the wealth of illustration which my publishers have allowed me may offer some pleasure to the artist and amateur, especially to those interested in book-illustration, for no period is richer in beauty in this respect than the xv century.

Most of the illustrations have been reproduced from originals in the British Museum, and here I owe much to the skill and patience of Mr. Donald Macbeth. For the remainder, numerous photographs have been supplied me by other museums (and I would acknowledge various gifts from the Pierpont Morgan Library, and the helpfulness of the Fogg Art

Museum, Harvard, and the John Rylands Library, Manchester), while in certain cases I have been permitted to reproduce from published series. On this score my thanks are due to Prince d'Essling for Figs. 104, 200 and 261 (taken from his father's *Livres à Figures vénitiens*); to Herr Paul Heitz for Figs. 42, 63, 75, 82 and 84 (taken from his series of *Einblattdrucke*); to Herr Karl Hiersemann, through the good offices of the Director of the Deutsches Buchmuseum, for Figs. 111, 112, 116, 166 (taken from Schramm's *Bilderschmuck der Frühdrucke*); to Hofrat Dr. A. Weixlgärtner and the Gesellschaft für Vervielfältigende Kunst, Vienna, for Figs. 39, 41, 55, 61 and 86 (taken from the facsimiles of woodcuts and metal-cuts of the Albertina, edited by Haberditzl and Stix); to M. Paul Lemoisne for Figs. 50, 51, 52, 70 and 71 (taken from his edition of the woodcuts in the *Bibliothèque Nationale*); to the Director of the Official Publications of the Imprimerie Nationale, Paris, for Figs. 348, 357, 363, 386 and 391 (taken from Claudin, *Historie de l'Imprimerie en France*); to Dr. A. Ruppel and the Gutenberg Gesellschaft, Mainz, for Fig. 124 (taken from Schottenloher, *Die Liturgischen Druckwerke des E. Ratdolt*); to Hofrat Dr. F. Winkler for Figs. 145 and 146 (taken from articles by Dr. Roemer in the *Jahrbuch der Preuss. Kunstsammlungen*); to the Verlag der Münchner Drucke for Fig. 268. (taken from M. J. Husung, *Drucker- und Verlegerzeichen Italiens*); to M. Émile Protat of Macon for Fig. 32; to M. Pierre Gusman for Fig. 384 (taken from *Byblis*); to Messrs. Maggs Bros. for Fig. 483 (taken from Don Manuel's work on Portuguese woodcuts); to the Trustees of the Pierpont Morgan Library for Figs. 148 and 371 (taken from their *Catalogue of Early Printed Books*, 1907); to Mr. Wilfred Merton for Fig. 301 (taken from an original edition in his possession); and to Mr. Dyson Perrins for Figs. 33 and 298 (taken from the *Catalogue of the Early Italian Printed Books* in his library).

I have not tampered with photographic facsimile, except to the extent of removing certain library stamps which happened to disfigure the woodcuts, and omitting pen- or brush-work in a few subjects which seemed best rendered by line-blocks, even though it demanded some sacrifice. Only in the case of the collotype frontispiece did I feel justified in making up any defective lines in the woodcut (which are often useful indications of the condition of the block in certain editions), and here only in two breaks in the border-line which impaired the harmony of the subject.

Those who have helped me in the course of the work are too numerous to mention, and I can only extend a general word of thanks to many colleagues at home and in European and American museums and libraries.

But I would express special gratitude to my colleague and friend Victor Scholderer for constant advice in regard to the books with which he is so conversant, and which form the background to a large part of the present work. Nor would I omit to mention the help of another colleague, Mr. A. F. Johnson, on various bibliographical questions, and the kindness of Dr. Fritz Saxl, Director of the Warburg Library, in lending me for many months Schreiber's own material of reproduction. In revising my technical chapter I owe much to the criticism of Mr. Noel Rooke, but even so I realise acutely the omissions and shortcomings incidental to a layman's explanation of the various methods of craftsmen.

I realise no less acutely how variable in quality my work as a whole must be, extending as it has done over a long period of years, reflecting the natural zest of one moment and the flagging interest of another. I can only hope that the material offered, even at moments when critical appreciation was dull, may serve some purpose, at least as the basis for a livelier enjoyment of one or another of the many subjects under review.

The background for my work has inevitably been offered by the collection of prints and books in the British Museum. There are few other great collections in which I have not studied the prints, but I cannot claim to have had the leisure for more than occasional research in other libraries for books not found in the British Museum, and as a general rule I have only referred to other libraries and museums in the case of books not represented in the British Museum. In describing books I have attempted throughout to give precise references to editions, for I have often been baffled by the lack of such reference in historical works. But error always lies in wait for the nodding student, and I would be grateful to any who will send me corrections and revisions.

It only remains for me to confess that no work that I have hitherto undertaken has been more exacting; that it has demanded patience and extorted pains for the reward of occasional pleasure. If any of the pleasure I feel in completing a hard task can be shared, I shall be amply rewarded.

A. M. H.

July 1935

CONTENTS

Bibliographies come at the end of each chapter or section, while references to special
books are given in the footnotes. Additions and Corrections to Vols. I. and II.
are given in Vol. I. at p. 265, and space is left for further notes

VOL. I

CHAPTER I

CHAPTER V

VOL. II

CHAPTER VI

CONTENTS

CHAPTER VII

BOOK-ILLUSTRATION AND CONTEMPORARY SINGLE CUTS IN THE NETHERLANDS

CHAPTER VIII

BOOK-ILLUSTRATION AND CONTEMPORARY SINGLE CUTS IN FRANCE AND FRENCH SWITZERLAND

LIST OF ILLUSTRATIONS

Unless otherwise described the reproductions are from books or prints in the British Museum Library or Print Room. The name of a town without further qualification implies the principal collection of prints.

VOLUME I

AN
INTRODUCTION TO A
HISTORY OF WOODCUT

THE most frequent abbreviation used in Volume I., that of S., refers to W. L. Schreiber's catalogues. In the case of single cuts it is to the German edition, *Handbuch des Holz- und Metallschnittes des xv Jahrhunderts*, and in that of the block-books it is to his earlier *Manuel de l'amateur de la gravure sur bois et sur métal au xv⁰ siècle* (Vol. IV.), as this section of the work was still unrevised at the time of Schreiber's death in 1934.

Other references, if not explained in footnotes, will be readily solved by consultation of the General Bibliography, at the end of Chapter II., and the Special Bibliographies at the end of chapter or section.

CHAPTER I

PROCESSES AND MATERIALS

PRINTS may be classed as (1) *relief-prints*, (2) *intaglio-prints*, (3) *surface-prints*, according to whether the black line of the design (i.e. the part inked for printing) on the original block, plate or stone is (i) in relief, (ii) in intaglio (i.e. cut into the surface), (iii) on the surface (i.e. on a level with the rest of the surface).

These divisions correspond roughly to (1) *woodcut and wood-engraving*, (2) *engraving and etching on metal*, (3) *lithography*.

In an earlier volume I dealt with intaglio prints and engraving and etching on metal. The present work is devoted to the history of relief-prints, i.e. woodcut and wood-engraving, and analogous work on metal. A metal plate cut, engraved, or etched in relief is reasonably classed with woodcut and wood-engraving, just as lithography is generally held to include surface-prints from metal plates. In fact the form of the block or plate rather than its substance, and the style of printing used for such a form, offer the best divisions of classes of prints,[1] as the substance itself is by no means invariably evident from the print. The style of printing is generally a safe criterion, though examples may occur where a superficial resemblance causes confusion, e.g. between certain woodcuts and lithographs, and between certain lithographs and crayon-engravings.

I shall often use the term *woodcut*, as on my title-page, as the simplest designation of the whole class of relief-prints, where specific reference to particular prints is not implied.

In printing plates engraved or etched in intaglio, the ink is transferred to the paper not from the surface but from the furrows (the surface of the plate being as a rule wiped clean), and a special double-roller press is required of sufficient power to force the damped paper into the furrows so as to pull out the ink. One of the distinctive qualities of intaglio-prints consists in the strength and brilliance of line, as the ink will stand in relief on the paper according to the depth of the furrow from which it is transferred. Another distinguishing sign of an intaglio-print is its plate-mark, i.e. the indentation in the paper caused by the edge of the plate in the

---

[1] See *paste-prints* (pp. 22, 197) for an exceptional type of print included in the present study.

I

press. This mark is not, however, invariably present as later damping and pressing might have eliminated it, and the paper might of course be cut within the work.

On the other hand a print from a relief block shows little or no mark at its edge as the pressure in printing is so much less,[1] while a lithograph shows no indentation at all, the only difference in the latter case between margin and the white parts of the print consisting in a certain smoothening of the surface of the paper within the area of the subject.

The printing of a woodcut is similar in method to printing from type, the ink being transferred from the surface of the parts in relief. The pressure applied is vertical, on the same principle as the ordinary printing-press, and the power required is considerably less than in the double-roller copper-plate press. The ink is thicker and more sticky than that used in intaglio printing so that it may lie on the surface without flowing into the hollows. Any heavily sized paper, and most hand-made paper, must be damped before printing.

Fig. 1. Jost Amman. The Printer, with the press open.

The essential elements of the press are clearly illustrated in Jost Amman's woodcut of book-printers at work in Schopper's *Panoplia Omnium Artium*, 1568 (fig. 1). The man on the right is inking the type (which might equally be a wood block) laid on what is called the *chase*. He is inking with dabbers (printer's balls), but this process was done later by a roller.[2] The man at his side is placing the paper on the *tympanum*, which is hinged to the chase. Beyond a further hinge, left, is a framework called the *frisket*. Paper is stretched across the frisket and first impressed

---

[1] Marks from pressure on a print from a relief block are chiefly visible when the impression has been taken with the rubber; but these consist in a general indentation of all the lines, and not a mere indentation at the edge of the block corresponding to the plate-mark of an intaglio print.

[2] Inking with dabbers was the usual practice until the xix century. For an early illustration of the form of the dabber, see J. Amman, *Charta Lusoria*, Nuremberg, 1588, sig. B 2, showing printers at work.

on the block to mark the part which is to be printed: this part is then cut out as a hole in the paper on the frisket, so that when folded over the tympanum it only discloses such part of the paper as is to receive the impression, protecting the margins from the ink.

The tympanum protected by frisket is then folded over the block in the chase, and all is ready to be pushed with the *bed* beneath the press. When this is in position, the *platen* is forced by handle and screw on to the back of the tympanum, obtaining the print by vertical pressure.

An illustration of the same form of press, closed, may be seen in the wood-cut dated 1520, attributed to Dürer (P. 286), which served as printer's mark for Jodocus Badius of Assche, whose press was at Paris (fig. 2).

Fig. 2. Albrecht Dürer (?). The Printer, with the press closed.

Before the development of the printing-press, prints were of necessity made by one or another form of hand pressure, and there were two distinct methods.[1] What appears to be the earliest of these followed the common method of printers of pattern blocks on textiles, printing by stamping. The woodcutter would lay his paper on a hard board, and then press, stamp, or hammer his inked block face downwards on to the paper. Lippmann called this type of printing *Press-druck* in contrast with *Pressendruck*, the method of printing with the press.

Many of what appear to be the earliest prints from wood blocks (dating

[1] On the development of the printing of wood blocks see F. Lippmann, Repertorium für Kunstwissenschaft, i. 215; A. M. Hind, Print Collector's Quarterly, xv. 131 (April 1928).

about 1400–40) were probably printed in this way: they show little or no indentation of the paper, the ink is generally deep black of a thick oily [1] consistency, broken in impression and irregular at the edges of the lines.

Lippmann was right in accepting this view as to the method by which the earliest woodcuts were printed. But he went astray in stating that it was the method described by Cennino Cennini. He wrongly interpreted Cennini's article on the printing of textiles (*Il Libro dell' Arte*, Milanesi, cap. 173, *Il modo di lavorare colla forma dipinta in panno*), and Forrer followed his erroneous interpretation against his better reason even to the extent of illustrating a false reconstruction of the method indicated.

Cennini's passage describes the textile as laid across a framework; the block being placed *beneath*, and the rubber being used above. Although he does not mention any basis, it must, I think, be understood that the block was laid on a hard board or table. It was inconceivable to the experienced textile printer with whom I discussed the matter [2] that the block could have been laid on the textile, however the latter was stretched, and rubbed from beneath (as Lippmann interpreted Cennini).

But though Cennini only describes what appears to be a less common method of textile printing (and one certainly less adapted to obtaining the proper register in a repeated design), the other method of hammering the block face downwards must have been in use in his time, and was undoubtedly the precursor of the earliest method of printing wood blocks on paper.

It should be noted that in a print so stamped or hammered, the ink would naturally show a somewhat mottled character with irregular edges; and the centre of the block would generally print less darkly and clearly than the edges. Signs of occasional duplication of certain lines might be indications of the surface of the block having just touched another part of the paper in being put down or taken up (a fault more likely to happen in this process than in the later methods of printing).

The second method of printing by hand is that of *printing with the rubber*.[3] The inked block would be laid on some flat board or table, face upwards, and the paper laid over this and rubbed on the back with a hard

---

[1] Cf. pp. 114, and 125.

[2] Miss Phyllis Barron.

[3] Chinese and Japanese woodcutters have consistently used the method of rubbing their impressions with a pad (or *baren*, as they term it) to the present day. The water-colour they use is applied to the block with a brush. It is this imitation of a brushed, or washed, drawing which gives the Oriental method its special character. In Western work the standard method of producing gradations of tone is by the cutting of additional lines on the block.

pad, a flat piece of wood, a burnisher, or a leather *frotton*, in the manner described by Cennini in relation to textile printing. Indentation of the paper, and irregular marks of polish on the back of the print, are both indications of a rubbed impression. The absence of such indentation or marks on the reverse need not of course imply that the impression was not obtained by rubbing, as the indentation might not be permanent in softer qualities of paper, or might have been eliminated by damping and pressing, while the marks on the reverse might be prevented by the use of a sufficient layer of thicker paper between the rubber and the paper that receives the impression. The indentation is perhaps the reason why the printer of the early block-books, who practised this method, only used one side of the paper. A thinner ink would probably be used in this process than in the first method described, for a thick oily ink would tend to be smudged by rubbing.

Rubbed prints, which appear for the most part in the second and third quarters of the xv century, are generally found in brownish and greyish tones of ink. The brown tones certainly imply an iron-gall ink, which may originally have been darker, if not black, in tone, and become oxidised (like iron rust) in the course of time. The ink which has remained deep black may equally have been made from iron and oak galls, and the permanence of the tone might be explained by the admixture of carbon, or by the prevention of oxidisation by the presence of more oil. Both reasons may account for the deep black of the earliest prints which we have surmised were stamped like textiles.

The ancients appear to have chiefly used inks made of carbon (mixed with gum, etc.), which could be washed out with a sponge and water, though iron-gall ink may also have been known. Theophilus in his *Diversarum Artium Schedula* (written at the turn of the xi and xii centuries) describes iron-gall ink, which from his day became the common form in use.

The woodcutter no doubt availed himself of the *printing-press* used by the printer of books soon after the introduction of printing from movable type. Though some years after this event, it is still of interest to note documentary reference to a press which was in use in a convent at Malines before 1465. It is the reference in the inventory of a deceased Abbess Jacoba van Looz-Hensberge,[1] who died in 1465 at the Bethany Convent, Malines, to *unum instrumentum ad imprimendum scripturas et ymagines . . . cum quatuordecim aliis lapideis printis.*

[1] See Edward Van Even, *L'Ancienne École de Peinture de Louvain*, Brussels and Louvain, 1870, p. 104. Cf. below, p. 84.

Various forms of simple presses for bookbinding and other crafts must have been in use well before the invention of movable type and the introduction of the ordinary printing-press, so that it is impossible to say that the woodcutter only took advantage of such technical aid contemporane-

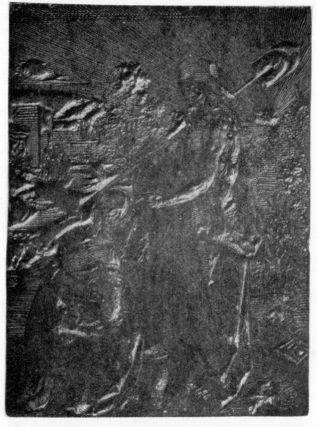

Fig. 3. Albrecht Dürer. Christ appearing to St. Mary Magdalene. The original wood block.

ously with the printer of books, i.e. from about 1450. Nevertheless it may roughly be assumed that the earlier methods of printing by hand pressure became increasingly rare after the development of the ordinary printing-press. But occasional examples of rubbed prints can be quoted quite late in the xv century, e.g. the *Spiegel der Vernunft*, of 1488 (S. 1861, Munich), and modern original wood-engravers constantly pull their proofs by hand.

In woodcut and wood-engraving the design is drawn directly on the surface of the block, and the parts which are to print white are cut away, leaving the black lines or spaces in relief. The appearance of a block after cutting is shown in the reproduction of one of the wood blocks of Dürer's *Little Woodcut Passion*, preserved in the British Museum (fig. 3).

The tool used is either a *knife*, or the *graver* (*burin*). The *knife* is a flat piece of steel with its cutting edge at an acute angle to its back, and set in a handle as illustrated in another of Jost Amman's woodcuts showing the woodcutter at work (fig. 4).[1] It should be noted that the bevel (which is more clearly seen in the accompanying figure 5) is on the left side, i.e. the opposite side to that on the Japanese woodcutter's knife.

Fig. 4. Jost Amman. The Woodcutter.

The *graver*, or *burin*, is a small steel rod, of square or lozenge section, with its point sharpened in an oblique section. The usual shape of the tool and its handle is shown in the

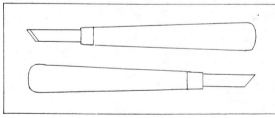

Fig. 5. The Woodcutter's Knife.

illustration (fig. 6). It is practically the same tool that is used in line-engraving on copper, though for wood-engraving the handle is sometimes tilted at a slight angle to the blade. A dry-point by Whistler, the portrait of *Paul Riault* (1860), shows the wood-engraver at work on his block (fig. 7). The handle is held against the palm, or against

[1] For two other illustrations from Schopper's *Panoplia Omnium Artium* see figs. 34 and 35.

the fourth finger, and the graver pushed before the hand, directed by the thumb held near the point of the blade, ploughing up the furrows. The method of holding the tool contrasts with the hold in line-engraving on metal, where the first finger is in advance along the blade.

The wood-engraver also uses a variety of graver which is more nearly triangular in section, and formed in a more or less acute angle according to the delicacy of the line required. This kind of graver is called the *tint-tool*, as it is used in making delicate series of lines to produce a tone or tint (fig. 8, section a).

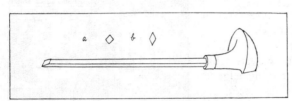

Fig. 6. The Graver, or Burin.

Other forms are the *spit-sticker*, used for curved lines (fig. 8, section b), the *scorper*, or *scauper* (fig. 8, section c), and the *threading-* or *multiple-tool* for producing a series of parallel lines (fig. 8, section d). Gouges are used for clearing away larger spaces of the block in woodcut on the plank, and flat tools, or chisels, serve to clear away parts of the wood outside the lines in relief on the outer parts of the block.[1]

In cutting with the knife the wood used is generally of fairly soft character, e.g. pear, apple, cherry, sycamore, or beech. But there is evidence of the use of boxwood in the xvi century and considerable probability that it was used for delicate work in the late xv century.[2] The cutting is done

---

[1] For some good illustrations see T. H. Fielding, *Art of Engraving*, 1841 and 1844. The British Museum possesses E. Whymper's set of wood-engraving tools. For most technical illustrations the Victoria and Albert Museum has more material. In regard to methods of wood-engraving in the early xix century, a chapter by Thomas Smith (Master at the Slade School) in Herbert Furst, *The Modern Woodcut*, 1923, should be consulted.

[2] Mr. Noel Rooke assures me that the original block of Holbein's *Portrait of Erasmus* (*Erasmus im Gehäus*, Woltmann, No. 206) which is preserved in the Oeffentliche Kunstsammlung, Basle, is of boxwood. Boxwood must have been imported at that date entirely from Turkey, and the supply was probably chiefly available through Venice. This, apart from purely artistic considerations, may have had some influence in determining the delicate linear style of much xv-century illustration in Venice, as the Venetian woodcutters, like Holbein's, may have used box. At present boxwood is also imported from the West Indies, but this variety is inferior to Turkey box in quality.

Early references to the use of box for woodcut are: (1) the colophon verses attributed to the printer Johann Trechsel, presumably of the xv century (see p. 209); (2) Vasari, 1550, who speaks of pear and box in his technical chapter on chiaroscuro woodcut; (3) W. Salmon, *Polygraphice*, London 1672, who speaks of beech and box, to which he adds pear in his edition of

on the plank, i.e. on blocks of a tree sawn along the grain (lengthwise), and planed down (French: *bois de fil*).

Chinese and Japanese woodcut is always on the plank, and a special

Fig. 7. J. A. McN. Whistler. The Wood-engraver (Paul Riault).

kind of cherry has generally been found most suitable for their mode of printing in water-colour. Other woods, which would not be affected by oil

1706; (4) J. Barrow, *Dictionarium Polygraphicum*, London 1735, referring to box and pear; (5) Papillon, *Traité historique et pratique de la gravure en bois*, 1766, ii. pp. 57-63, who speaks of box, service (*cormier*) and pear as the best woods, and apple, cherry and wild-cherry (*mérisier*) as other woods in use.

and printer's ink, are too absorbent of water, which swells the grain and raises the surface in irregular ridges.[1] Non-absorbent blocks, printed with water-colour, would be all the more important when several colour blocks were used, and exact register required. An outstanding distinction between the methods of Oriental and Western woodcut is that gradation of tone is achieved in the former chiefly by the brush and water-colour on the surface of the block, in the latter by cut or engraved lines.

Work with the graver cannot be done on the plank, except in the direction of the grain, so that blocks made from cross-sections of the tree (endgrain, *bois de bout*) are essential. In most wood-engraving boxwood is used,

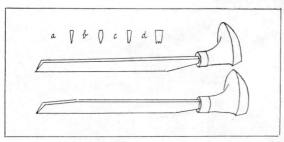

Fig. 8. Varieties of the Graver.

but the earliest examples of graver work on wood were possibly done on end-grain of softer woods. A considerable amount of Dutch xvii-century woodcut, such as that of Christoffel van Sichem II.

(1581–1658), and Dirk de Bray (worked 1651–after 1671), with its admixture of white line, appears at first sight to be graver work, but a careful examination of their white lines renders it more probable that they still used the knife.[2] On the other hand, Papillon[3] speaks of the Dutch manner of using the graver on wood, imitating line-engraving in its crosshatchings of white lines, and refers in this relation to an unnamed frontispiece of a Dutch book of 1729, so that it seems that wood-engraving proper was a common practice at that period. In the passage noted Papillon speaks of the method as unsuited to wood, but in another passage he refers, without expressing disapproval, to the new method of engraving on end-

---

[1] For Japanese processes see T. Tokuno, *Japanese Woodcutting and Woodcut-printing*. Edited by S. R. Koehler, Washington 1894 (Smithsonian Institution). From the Report of the U.S. National Museum for 1892. My own references to Oriental woodcut are only given as a side issue in so far as it explains, or reflects on, the methods used in the West.

[2] With the single cut of the graver the two sides of a white line would be parallel: the white line cut by the knife would require two separate cuts, so that the sides would seldom be exactly parallel.

[3] *Traité historique et pratique de la gravure en bois*, 1766, ii. p. 124.

grain of service and pearwood practised by a certain Foy of Lyon ('graveur de la Ferme et Régie des Cartes).[1]

Further evidence of the practice of engraving on end-grain has been recently offered by M. Pierre Gusman,[2] who describes and reproduces a wood-engraving which appeared in an Armenian book, *Agathangelos*, printed at Constantinople in 1709. The examination of Armenian books in the British Museum, suggested by M. Gusman's notice, has confirmed his opinion, and even if it is impossible to dogmatise as to the character of the wood used, boxwood might reasonably be expected in Eastern Europe.

The books examined include:

Armenia, Church of. *Sermons of the Fathers*. Constantinople 1722 (Arm. 217). *Adoration of the Magi*: rough white-line cut ($4 \times 2\frac{7}{8}$ in.), copied from the cut by C. van Sichem

Fig. 9. Christoffel van Sichem. Adoration of the Magi.

which first appeared in *Der Zielen Lust-Hof* (New Testament Illustrations), Louvain 1629 (B.M. Print Room; see fig. 9), and later in the *Sharakan* (Armenian Hymnal), first edition, Amsterdam, printed by Oskan, 1664, and the *Armenian Bible*, Amsterdam, printed by Oskan, 1666. The *Sharakan* was reprinted at Amsterdam 1685, and at Livorno 1692; the *Armenian Bible* at Constantinople 1705 (with a few of the original blocks).

[1] *Ibid.*, i. p. 337.

[2] *La gravure sur bois*, Paris 1916, p. 246, and figs. 136-38. See also Enrique Mayer, *Prioridad de un artista Santiagues respecto al perfeccionamiento del grabado en Madera*, Santiago 1903, for reference to blocks in this manner printed at Santiago about 1730.

Directorium (Tonatsoyts). Constantinople 1722 (Arm. 165). The same *Adoration of the Magi*, but a different and better block, signed ԴՐ, and other rougher cuts, some signed ԴՐ, several (e.g. the *Transfiguration*) copied from signed cuts by van Sichem in the *Sharakan*.

Nerses Klayetsi. *Yisous Ordi* (Poem on the life of Christ). Constantinople 1724 (Arm. 160). Cuts signed ԴՐ.

Cyril of Jerusalem. *Catechetical Lectures*. Constantinople 1727–28 (Arm. 106). An interesting series of white-line cuts in the manner of 'Agathangelos' (fig. 10). The book also has attractive decorative and figured initials.

Ergaran (Armenian Hymnal). Echmiadzin 1744 (Arm. 172). The *Adoration of the Magi* (signed ԴՐ) and other cuts with the same signature.

Mr. A. G. Ellis, with whom I examined these books, informed me that the signature ԴՐ would correspond to initials *DR* (and in the less frequent form ԳՐ would be *GR*). He did not know to what form of Armenian name this might apply at the period, and thought in consequence that it might be the transliteration of the initials of a European cutter.

Many of the cuts in these Armenian books are accepted by Mr. Noel Rooke as graver work, done either on end-grain or on soft metal.

It is noteworthy that Christoffel van Sichem produced most of the Scriptural cuts for Armenian works printed at Amsterdam, in the *Sharakan* 1664 and the *Armenian Bible* 1666, and that several of his blocks reappeared in the *Armenian Bible* printed at Constantinople in 1705.[1] Moreover, the style of the cuts with the Armenian signature was manifestly based on that of van Sichem, and many of them, as we have noted above, are direct copies from his work.

The thickness of wood blocks is generally about $\frac{7}{8}$ in., i.e. a size which will print conveniently in conjunction with type.[2] Some earlier blocks are considerably thicker, a difference which would not matter if the cuts were

---

[1] Many of the cuts in the *Sharakan* and *Armenian Bible* had appeared earlier in *Der Zielen Lust-Hof* (New Testament Illustrations), Louvain 1629 (B.M. Print Room).

For the van Sichem family see H. F. Wijnmann, *Oud-Holland*, xlvi. (1929), 233. His Christoffel van Sichem ii. (1581–1658) appears to have been chiefly responsible for the woodcuts, but other Christoffels may have participated if new blocks were made after 1658.

[2] For the adaptation of the thickness of blocks to type see p. 288.

designed for separate printing, particularly if the printing were to be done by hand rubbing. Sections of box cannot, of course, be had so

Fig. 10. From Cyril of Jerusalem, *Catechetical Lectures*, Constantinople 1727–28.

large as pieces of the plank, whether of box or other trees, and for larger woodcuts several blocks have to be fitted together.[1] Later impressions from

---

[1] Blocks of sections of box are now seldom to be had exceeding about 5 × 6 in., the tree being considerably used, and seldom left uncut to any great age. Two unusually large blocks of the earlier XIX century, one 7¾ × 9 in., the other 9 × 10 in., are preserved in the British Museum. They were acquired from the wood-engraver Edward Whymper, with a note that 'boxwood of this size could be obtained before 1850'.

such composite blocks often show white gaps where the wood has warped, and the join slightly separated.

A curious method of imitating line-engraving in woodcut was first discussed by Papillon (*Traité*, supplement, p. 74), but I can quote no example of its use before Adolphe Gusman (after 1870), to whom the method occurred independently, and Frédéric Florian (after 1896).[1] Two blocks were used, the first being engraved with the principal lines following the general direction of the design. A proof of this was impressed on the surface of the second block so that the lines showed on the block in the same direction as on the first block. The second block was then engraved with lines crossing the first series of lines. A print taken from the two blocks, properly registered, would show cross-hatchings corresponding in style to a line-engraving. A third block could be added if further complexity of line was required.

Corrections can be made in woodcut by drilling out a portion or portions of the block and plugging it with one or more new pieces of wood, but it is neither so expeditious nor so satisfactory a method of correcting as is possible in engraving or etching on metal.

The word *state* is applied to the stages through which a print passes when changes are made on the block, whether in the subject or in its inscriptions. Additional work would be easy in the case of white-line woodcut, but in the case of the ordinary black-line cut, where the white parts of the design had been cut away, the addition of lines would imply plugging to obtain a new surface. In view of the drawing on the surface of the block (generally used as his guide) the woodcutter will seldom print from his unfinished block, and for this reason as well as on account of the difficulties of adding work in black line and of correcting in general, far fewer states of woodcuts are known than in the case of etchings. To show the condition of an unfinished block, I reproduce a proof of a wood-engraving, *Le Bêcheur*, by J. F. Millet, in which much of the surface, printing black, remains to be cut away (fig. 11).

The work will of course deteriorate in the course of printing, but the rate of such deterioration will depend on various factors, such as hardness of wood and delicacy of line. Later impressions often show breaks in lines, particularly in the isolated border lines, though such things may pass through various stages of repair. In general, wood blocks yield a fairly large number of impressions if printed with care, and are in consequence thoroughly fitted as illustrations for lasting out a moderate-sized edition of a book.

[1] See P. Magnus, *Une pseudo-gravure en taille-douce*, Byblis i. (1922), 178.

In the latter half of the XIX century nearly all 'wood-engravings' were printed not from the original wood blocks but from metal *electrotypes* taken from them, only a limited number of proofs being pulled from the original blocks.[1] Strictly speaking, prints from these electrotypes are

Fig. 11. Le Bêcheur. Woodcut by J. F. Millet. Unfinished.

facsimile reproductions in the same sense that a photogravure of an etching is a reproduction, but as the original block may often have been scarcely used except as the means of producing the more sturdy metal form, and as it is sometimes impossible to say whether the print is from the wood or from an electrotype, a purist attitude in this matter cannot be maintained,

[1] In *electrotypes* metal is precipitated by electricity from its solution on to a mould, and backed up with type-metal before relief-printing. *Stereotypes* from wood blocks (i.e. metal plates cast from moulds) were used in 1832 in the Penny Magazine, as is stated in its preface.

and such prints may reasonably be described in the category of wood-engravings.

Electrotypes are sometimes printed in conjunction with wood blocks on the same page. This was the case in many of the Kelmscott Press books, where the initial letters and borders were invariably printed from the electro-type, and the subject illustrations from the wood. The actual printing of wood in conjunction with metal (whether of other blocks or of type) is no real difficulty, as the same consistency of ink is suitable to both. But the printer has to remember that when blocks are cleaned (with turpentine, etc.), wood takes longer to dry than metal. Electrotypes are naturally of most use in book production for decorative pieces subject to frequent repetition, such as borders and initials, and the extra strength of the metal would be an added reason for their use in borders. The need for some-thing less fragile than wood may have inclined the cutters of the French Books of Hours of the xv and early xvi centuries to use metal for their borders, though perhaps the chief reason in their case was their use of a method of white dotted shading which would be more suited to metal. Certain Basle printers of the early xvi century also used metal blocks for borders and other decorative pieces.

It has generally been stated that casts, corresponding to the modern electrotypes, were never used by the earlier book-illustrators,[1] though there is no *a priori* reason why the well-known methods of casting should not have been applied as an aid to book-illustration. But it has recently been suggested by a very experienced printer,[2] judging from the appearance of the impressions, that the bichrome initials in the Mainz Psalters of 1457 and 1459 were printed not from wood blocks but from metal casts. And small decorative motives were almost certainly multiplied by casts from the xv century onwards.[3]

Nevertheless, in most of the early repetitions of woodcut subjects, it may be generally assumed either that the original blocks were used (sometimes passing from one printer to another, occasionally from one country to

---

[1] E.g. see A. W. Pollard, *The Transference of Woodcuts in the xv and xvi Centuries*, Biblio-graphica II (1896).

[2] Gustav Mori, *Was hat Gutenberg erfunden? Ein Rückblick auf die Frühtechnik des Schrift-gusses*. Beilage zum xix Jahresbericht, Gutenberg Gesellschaft, Mainz 1921.

[3] For earlier suggestions and notes on the subject of casts from wood blocks see C. F. von Rumohr, *Zur Geschichte und Theorie der Formschneidekunst*, Leipzig 1837. Note also the soft-metal cuts in the Spanish 1573 edition of Olivier de la Marche, *Le Chevalier Délibéré*, which are referred to in the article on Juan de Arfe in Thieme-Becker's Lexicon, as either copies or casts (*clichés*) of the original cuts. Cf. Index of Subjects, under *casts*.

another) or that copies were made on other blocks. Very exact copies might be made by methods of transfer, but seldom so exact as not to disclose differences in detail, which would rule out the possibility of a cast. Most of the poorer copies are in reverse, the natural result of the easiest method, i.e. of copying an impression directly on to another block.

Before engraving, the artist will either (1) draw his design on the surface of the block, (2) paste a drawing on paper to the surface of the block, or (3) transfer a drawing on paper to this surface.

The planed surface of the block may be prepared by rubbing with powdered bath-brick slightly moistened (the powder being removed when dry), so that the pencil has a better hold on the block. The drawing may also be done in pen and ink, washed if required with a brush. The surface is sometimes covered with white (e.g. lead-white and gum-water), so that the drawing may show up with greater brilliance.

Various blocks of the xv and xvi centuries are preserved which have drawings on the surface, prepared for the knife, but uncut, e.g. the designs attributed to Dürer for an unpublished edition of Terence, at Basle, and other examples at Vienna and Munich. xix-century examples are offered by several drawings by G. J. Pinwell, Frederick Walker and A. B. Houghton on blocks in the British Museum.

The second method, pasting an actual drawing on to the block, and cutting directly through this, is a regular practice in the East, but less used by Western woodcutters. That it was practised by French woodcutters of the xvi century is proved by a reference to his woodcutters by Philibert de L'Orme in his *Premier Tome de l'Architecture* (Paris 1567).[1]

Finally, the transfer from paper to the surface of the block may be achieved in various ways. Drawings in soft pencil or chalk only require slight damping and pressing on the block. Another of the simplest methods is to cover the back of the drawing with red or black chalk, and laying the paper, drawing upwards, on the block to impress the design on the whitened surface of the block by indenting the lines with some hard point (a 'swallow's quill' is quoted in certain old books on processes).

A print may be transferred by first covering it with gum solution; laying it face downwards on the block; then damping the back and fretting the body of the paper away, leaving the print on the block. This method was no doubt continually practised in old book-illustration to replace worn

---

[1] First noted by W. M. Ivins, Junior, in the Bulletin of the Metropolitan Museum of Art, New York, May 1929, p. 150.

blocks. Distinction between original and repetition is not always easy when this method is used, and the new cutting done with great exactness.

In recent times photography has been considerably used by reproductive wood-engravers for transferring designs. One practical advantage it offers is the ease of altering the scale of the drawing, so that the original designer can draw in whatever size he chooses. The reproductive engraver may count this a gain, but in general I should think it placed too great a temptation before the designer to use conventions in his drawing unfitted to the scale and character of the wood-engraving projected.

In the xix century the engraver working after a painter's design would often be responsible for transforming the drawing into the conventions of his own medium. It is a much debated question how far this was the case with the work of the earlier engravers; whether in the xv century, for example, the woodcutter who used a painter's invention drew it himself in the terms of his own craft on the block, or whether the painter not only invented the design, but made the final drawing on the block for the engraver to follow without deviation in his cutting. The question will be discussed further in various parts of my text,[1] but in general one must be ready to envisage variety of method at all periods.

Design in woodcut may be approached from two opposite points of view: (1) in which the relief is intended for the design itself, i.e. as *black line* showing against a white ground, (2) in which the furrow is regarded as the design, as *white line* showing against a black ground.

Until the time of Thomas Bewick most woodcut followed the black-line method; since his day the white line has been used to a far greater extent in both woodcut and wood-engraving. The black-line method is a negative one in so far as the cutter is concerned, for his business is merely to remove the whites, i.e. the negative parts of the design. This cutting away of the spare wood is implied in one of the French terms for woodcut, *gravure en taille d'épargne*. It is for the most part a facsimile method, i.e. a method in which the cutter follows in detail the lines of the draughtsman's design. Most of the famous early designers of woodcuts, e.g. Dürer and Holbein, left the cutting to others, and in facsimile work of this purely negative kind there is certainly no reason for the artist to do it himself. On the other hand, the white-line method is positive, and requires the original artist's own hand on the block if the full vitality of his design is to be preserved. Thus, as a medium of original expression on wood, the white-line method has much

[1] See Index of Subjects under *designer and cutter*.

in its favour. This does not mean that many of the greatest woodcuts are not

Fig. 12. Urs Graf. Standard-bearer of the Canton of Unterwalden.

in black line—in fact there are far more in black line than in white line—
but it does imply that the greatest woodcuts in black line keep to breadth

and simplicity of treatment, and avoid the complex system of cross-hatching which calls for merely negative drudgery from the cutter.

On the other hand, one of the real dangers that besets white-line cutting is in book-illustration, where too much black surface overbalances the tone of the page of type, and moreover requires such heavy inking that type printed with it may very easily be blurred.

The simplest form of white-line cut may be illustrated in Urs Graf's *Standard-bearer of the Canton of Unterwalden*, dated 1521 (fig. 12). But the process exhibits a variety of grades of intention, from that of pure outline to the rendering of the most complex surfaces of tone, the chief problem of the reproductive wood-engravers of the later xix and early xx century. In its complex forms, white-line engraving is practically a black-line rendering of a design, helped out in its tones and details of texture by the intermixture of white line.

The comparison of a cut from Holbein's *Dance of Death* with a copy by John Bewick (younger brother of Thomas), in which white line is used, may be more illuminating than verbal description (figs. 13 and 14).

The earliest examples of white-line cuts (or rather white-line engravings) are the so-called *dotted prints*, or prints, as they are also called, in the *manière criblée*, or *dotted manner*, which belong chiefly to the second half of the xv century. The material used was a metal plate, but as the printing is from the parts of the plate in relief, it is reasonable to class these prints with woodcuts. The graver was certainly used as well as the knife.

For convenience of printing in relief these plates appear to have been fixed to wood blocks, if this is the correct explanation of the pin-holes seen at the corners of some impressions. Or it may be that the use of a softer metal than copper, adapted to the punches of decorative patterns used in the process, rendered it advisable to fasten the plate to a block before engraving. In some cases the pin-holes may mean no more than that the plate itself has been used as a decorative plaque.

The term *manière criblée* comes from *crible*, the French for a sieve, as many of the prints are characterised by groups of dots, produced by punches resembling a sieve. These dots were used quite indiscriminately in various parts of the design, wherever the artist wished to break up his ground. The *dotted manner* is the usual English term, but the white line is an even more important element in the process than the white dots. Various forms of punches and stamps, their heads lined with different patterns, are also used, to avoid the repeated engraving of a single pattern, and to express various conventional forms in the design (fig. 80).

Dotted work on a black ground is also found in French Books of Hours of the late xv and early xvi centuries, and, as we have already noted, metal is generally the material used. But they are not on that account to be classed with prints in the *manière criblée*, as the design is always in black line, the dots being reserved for the background.

The occasional use of white-line methods in the xvii and xviii centuries, before the introduction of boxwood cut across the grain, may also sometimes point to the use of the graver on soft metal.[1]

It has sometimes been stated that the broadly designed cuts of the early

Fig. 13. Hans Holbein II. The Preacher, from the *Dance of Death*.

Fig. 14. John Bewick. The Preacher. Copy after Holbein.

xv century are on metal, but there is nothing to support the contention. The only blocks known of such black-line woodcuts are wood, and, apart from the appearance of the impressions preserved, the early cutters, carpenters and pattern-block makers as they were, would naturally use wood.

On the other hand, there is clear evidence, in the bending of lines through use, that certain black-line cuts of the late xv century are printed from metal blocks, e.g. in the marks of the printers Antoine Vérard and Richard Pynson,[2] so that we must beware of dogmatic statements.

If absolute proof as to material is wanting in the absence of all but a small proportion of blocks, the different manner in which wood and metal

---

[1] But not invariably, as W. J. Linton asserted. Cf. p. 10.
[2] See pp. 680, and 732, and figs. 415 and 466.

react to the pressure of printing should give some clue, at least if late impressions are known. Metal would bend, where wood might break or fray. But a slightly bent line might only mean a line originally cut out of the straight in the wood.

Plates engraved in the same manner as the white-line metal cuts of the xv century are also sometimes found printed in intaglio. The existence of impressions in relief from the same plates justifies their inclusion in a history of woodcut and relief-prints. A glutinous ink (*paste*) was commonly used so that gold leaf could be attached, and further tints of colour were sometimes added on the impressions. They are generally called *paste-prints* (in German, *Teigdrucke*), and belong entirely to the latter part of the xv or the very early years of the xvi century.

Another rare variety of prints of the same period, in which paste has also been used, has been called *flock-prints*. The velvety surface seems to have been obtained by sprinkling minute shearings of wool on to the damp paste impression, and the textile appearance might be enhanced by preparing the paper with a series of short flicks cut in the surface. The German title for such flock-prints is *Samt-teigdrucke*, the French, *empreintes veloutées*. They are actually ordinary black-line woodcuts printed in relief, and though paste is used, should not be grouped under the more specialised connotation of paste-prints.[1]

Both paste-prints and flock-prints are so imitative of other modes of expression (such as embossed leather, textile- or goldsmith-work) that it is tempting to regard them as craftsmen's proofs done to test the effect of such work. Nevertheless, the preservation of these prints, like most early woodcuts, in the bindings of old books or manuscripts, points on the whole to their being isolated experiments in individual modes, comparable to the original experiments of Blake at a much later period.

The processes of paste-prints and flock-prints are so complex, and the engravers' intention so obscure that further discussion of the technical side is left to the section dealing with the history of the prints themselves.

Occasional woodcuts of the xv century are partially embellished by *tinsel*, i.e. small fragments of thin and sparkling metal, which requires the use of paste or other adhesive. Incrustation of quartz crystals is also found on similar prints.[2]

---

[1] In the xvii century this flock, the waste product in the manufacture of cloth, was used in a similar manner for wall-paper. See C. C. Oman, *Catalogue of Wall-Papers*, Victoria and Albert Museum. London 1929, p. 10.

[2] See p. 171.

Metal plates for relief-printing have occasionally been produced by etching away the negative parts of the subject (*relief-etching*), the design being drawn on the surface with a varnish that would resist the acid. I can refer to no example before the xviii century, for Bouchot's suggestion with regard to the xv-century cut of *St. Veronica* (S. 1719) lacks foundation.[1] William Blake, who used the process, called this kind of work 'woodcut on copper'. He also produced relief-prints with the graver, calling them, in no less arbitrary fashion, 'woodcuts on pewter'.[2] Blake's work in these methods has been referred to in my *History of Engraving and Etching*, but it would be treated even more appropriately under the category of wood-cut. His methods are so individual that they can only be dealt with satis-factorily in a detailed survey of his work.

Linoleum has of recent years been considerably used in place of wood for simple work broadly cut.[3] The material is cheap, and easy to cut, both reasons offering temptations to beginners and amateurs. The process may have certain economic and educational uses, but I do not feel that it possesses sufficient quality of its own to render it more than a weak sub-stitute for the woodcut.

A large number of the earliest woodcuts were coloured by hand. In fact one of the aims of the early woodcutter was to supply a cheap coloured picture, and economy was achieved on one side by multiplying the outline of the design in the press.[4] It was only in the second half of the xv century that the colour itself was achieved by printing.[5]

The process of using several wood blocks in conjunction on one subject to render various tones or colours is called the *chiaroscuro* method, from its imitation of light and dark tones. The French term is *camaïeu* (i.e. cameo, the name given to stones of two layers of colour, such as sardonyx, cut in relief), which by analogy suggests planes of colour. If a black-outline block is used this is called the *key-block*, and would be cut first to give the main lines of the design. Impressions from this block would be transferred to further blocks as a guide in cutting such tone-blocks as might be required. It is seldom that more than two or three tone-blocks would be used in

---

[1] See p. 125.

[2] See Gilchrist, *Life of Blake*, 1880, ii. p. 178.

[3] Allen W. Seaby, *Colour Printing with Linoleum and Wood Blocks*, Leicester (Dryad Handi-crafts), 1925; Claude Flight, *Lino Cutting and Printing*, London, 1934.

[4] For further notes on colour see pp. 167 and 398.

[5] See Index of Subjects under *colour-woodcut*.

chiaroscuro, which is strictly a composition in various tones of one colour (though it also includes allied colours on the same print, e.g. browns, yellows, greens) in contrast to a *colour-woodcut*, which may show any variety of contrasting colours. But it is difficult to fix an absolute border-line between chiaroscuro and colour-woodcut.

Variety in chiaroscuro methods depends to a considerable extent on the less or greater use of the black outline in the key-block, or in its complete elimination.

The printing from several blocks needs care to ensure the corresponding parts of the subject being exactly superposed. In transferring an impression of the key-block to a tone-block, exactly corresponding points in the corners of the respective blocks are marked, and by the use of pins the impressions of the various tones can be pulled with exact register on the paper. In general the printing, as described by Vasari, is in the reverse order to the cutting of the blocks, i.e. the lighter tones being printed first, then the heavier, and finally the outline or key-block. The Japanese method of obtaining register is by the use of notches, a rectangular notch on the right of the block, and a straight notch on the left.

Colour- or tone-prints are also sometimes made by a combination of wood and metal plates, the metal usually serving as the key-plate (e.g. the later chiaroscuro cutters, and George Baxter).

Woodcutters have sometimes combined a blind *embossing* (*gaufrage*) of the paper with their impression. This could be done by pressing the dry paper (after the print had been made) on to a special block, and rubbing it on the back. Embossing has been used considerably in Japanese work, but only occasionally in Europe (e.g. by J. B. Jackson).

Two examples (probably of the latter half of the xv century) are known of paper embossed blind by the impress of a wood or metal relief block, the *Coronation of the Virgin* in the New York Public Library (S. 2863 m) and *St. Denis, St. Emmeram and St. Wolfgang* (Patron Saints of Regensburg), in the Metropolitan Museum, New York (S. 2863 x). Mr. Mabbott has christened this kind of work *seal-prints*.[1] Such prints (rare curiosities of little interest in our history) have sometimes been called stereotype prints, but this use of the word *stereotype*, distinct from its proper application to the cast of a mass of type, is unhappy. Another term that has been applied

[1] See W. L. Schreiber, *Die älteste Stereotyp-Matrize*, Gutenberg Jahrbuch, Mainz, 1927, p. 44; T. O. Mabbott, *Seal-prints and a Seal-paste-print*, Bulletin of New York Public Library, August 1928; T. O. Mabbott, *Paste-prints and Seal-prints*, Metropolitan Museum Studies, February 1932.

to such embossed impressions, e.g. to those of a contemporary French artist, Pierre Roche, is that of *gypsographic prints*.

The question of state has already been discussed in relation to work on the block. Some further notes may be given on prints in general.

Impression is the general term covering any print from a block. Whether it is an early or late impression has no relation to state, which implies alteration of some kind on the block itself. So that it is possible to have a late and worn impression of an early state; or a fine impression of a late state: state, without further qualification, being no guide to the number of impressions printed.

Proof, or proof impression, should strictly be limited to impressions pulled by the artist to prove or test his work, whether before or after completion of the block. The question of *before*, or *after letters* or lettering, will occasionally occur, but not so frequently as in the case of line-engraving.

Counterproof is a print pulled, not from the block, but from a damp impression. The object of a counterproof is to give the artist a print in the same direction as the original block to serve as a guide in the making of additional work. As alterations on the block are less frequent than on copper

Fig. 15. Jost Amman. The Paper-maker.

plates, counterproofs are in consequence rarer in the case of woodcuts than of etchings and engravings.

The average life of a wood block is impossible to estimate in the number of impressions it might yield, for this depends on a variety of factors, i.e. the hardness of the wood, and its freedom from warping; on the quality of the work (broad or delicate in line), and not least on the care of the printer.

Impressions are generally pulled on paper, though vellum has been considerably used, especially in the early period. Occasional woodcuts are printed for their own sake on silk or other textiles. *Prints on textiles*, in which the textile, and not the print, is the important factor (*Zeugdrucke*), are intimately related to our subject in its initial stages, but they will only be studied in so far as they throw light on the development of the early printing of woodcut on paper.

The quality of paper, of which the *water-mark* is the most definite token, is a considerable aid in dating or localising anonymous early woodcuts, and in dating impressions of known masters. But the international trade in paper is an ever-present factor to qualify dogmatic conclusions about locality, and the date of manufacture is only certain as a *terminus a quo.*

Briquet's *Dictionary of Water-marks* [1] (Geneva) is the most valuable reference in this relation up to the end of the XVI century. For later water-marks there is still no corpus of information comparable to Briquet for the earlier period.[2]

The question of the supply of paper and its relation to the beginning of woodcut will be discussed in the historical section, and occasional notes may be given about some of the more important water-marks. How far the quality of paper obtainable at various periods and places reacted on varying styles of cutting is a question that might raise many matters of interest, though it would probably be more fraught with speculation than fact.

The following are some of the commonest forms of inscriptions found on woodcuts and wood-engravings:

Sculpsit (sculp., sc.), sculptor ⎫
Incidit (incid., inc.), incisor ⎬ engraved, cut, engraver, cutter.
Fecit (fec., f.) ⎭

Formis ⎫
Excudit (excud., exc.) ⎬ printed, or published.

Divulgavit: published.

Impressit (imp.): printed.

Pinxit (pinx.), pictor: painted, painter.

Delineavit (delin.), delineator: drew; draughtsman.

Invenit (inv.), inventor ⎫
Composuit ⎬ designed, designer.

Figuravit: drew (generally referring to a drawing made for the engraver, sometimes by the engraver himself, after a painting to be reproduced).

---

[1] *Les Filigranes. Dictionnaire historique des marques de papier . . . jusqu' en 1600.* 4 vols. Paris, London, etc., 1907.

[2] Edward Heawood, late Librarian of the Royal Geographical Society, has published a few papers on the subject, and is making a large collection, part of his material being already deposited in the Department of MSS., British Museum.

Cum privilegio: implying a privilege to publish, and often a special right, corresponding to modern copyright, granted by some political or ecclesiastical authority.

Published according to Act of Parliament: relating to one of the various English Acts of Parliament (from 1735 onwards) dealing with the copyright of engravings. The English copyright law has never made it necessary to deposit an impression of every print (as of every book) in any public institution.

Déposé à la Direction [Générale des Estampes]; *Déposé à la Bibliothèque [Nationale, Royale]*: these and similar inscriptions refer to the custom in France after the Revolution of depositing prints with various State Departments, but it never became compulsory.

BIBLIOGRAPHY

THEOPHILUS (probably identical with a Benedictine monk Rugerus, of Helmershausen, near Paderborn, who worked as a goldsmith at the turn of the XI and XII centuries), *Diversarum Artium Schedula*. Ed. G. E. Lessing, Brunswick 1781; Escalopier, Paris, 1843; R. Hendrie, London, 1847; A. Ilg, Vienna, 1874.

Note cap. xl (on Inks); cap. lxxi, *De opere interrasili*; cap. lxxii, *De opere punctili*. See my historical section on dotted prints, p. 187.

CENNINI, Cennino. *Il Libro dell' Arte, o Trattato della Pittura* (written according to Milanesi before 1437). Ed. G. and C. Milanesi, Florence 1859; Renzo Simi, Lanciano, 1913, and D. V. Thompson, New Haven, U.S.A., 1932; German transl. by A. Ilg, Vienna 1871, and Willibrord Verkade, Strassburg, 1916; English transl. by Mrs. C. J. Herringham (Lady Herringham), London 1899, and by D. V. Thompson, New Haven, U.S.A., 1933; French transl. by V. Mottez, 2nd ed., Paris 1911.

Chapter 173 describes the method of printing on textiles.

[The Italian ed. of Tambroni, 1821 (English transl. by Mrs. Merrifield, London 1844; French transl. by V. Mottez, Paris 1858), lacks certain chapters, including the section referred to.]

VASARI, Giorgio. *Le Vite de' piu eccellenti Pittori, Sculptori e Architetti*, First ed., 1550, and second ed., 1568, *Introduzione*. Cap. xxxv. *De le stampe di legno* (English Edition 'Vasari on Technique' tr. by Louisa S. Maclehose, ed. G. Baldwin Brown, London 1907, p. 281). Deals only with Chiaroscuro woodcut.

SALMON, William. Polygraphice. London 1672.

BARROW, J. Dictionarium Polygraphicum. London 1735.

PAPILLON, J. B. M. Traité historique et pratique de la gravure en bois. 3 vols. Paris 1766.

SAVAGE, William. Practical Hints on Decorative Printing. With illustrations engraved on wood and printed in colours. London 1822.

FIELDING, T. H. Art of Engraving. London 1841 (and 1844).

BLANC, Charles. Grammaire des Arts de Dessin. Paris 1867. (English transl. by K. N. Doggett, Chicago 1874.)

LIPPMANN, F. Über die Anfänge der Formschneidekunst und des Bilddruckes. *Repertorium*, i. (1876), 215.

KOEHLER, S. R. Über die Technik des alten Holzschnittes. *Chronik*, iii. (1890), 82.

BRACQUEMOND, F. Étude sur la gravure sur bois, et la lithographie. Paris 1897.

VINNE, Theodore de. The Printing of Wood-engravings. *Print Collector's Quarterly*, i. (1911), 365.

FLETCHER, F. Morley, and SEABY, A. W. Wood-block printing: a description of the craft of woodcutting and colour printing based on the Japanese practice. London 1916.

BEEDHAM, R. John. Wood-engraving, with an introduction and appendix by Eric Gill. Ditchling 1920.

COLE, Timothy. Considerations on Engraving. New York 1921.

BUSSET, Maurice. La technique moderne de bois gravé et les méthodes anciennes des Xylographes du xvi siècle et des maîtres-graveurs de Yedo. Paris [1925].

BLISS, Douglas Percy. Woodcuts or the Practice of Engraving and Cutting upon Wood. Leicester (Dryad Handicrafts) 1926.

HUBBARD, Hesketh. How to distinguish Prints. Print Society. Woodgreen Common (near Salisbury) 1926.

MORIN-JEAN. Manuel Pratique du Graveur sur Bois. Paris 1926.

ROOKE, Noel. Woodcuts and Wood-engravings. London 1926.

HIND, A. M. On the Printing of Early Woodcuts. *Print Collector's Quarterly*, xv. (1928), 131.

LEIGHTON, Clare. Wood-engraving and Woodcuts. London 1932.

SERVOLINI, Luigi. Tecnica della Xilografia. Milan 1935.

CHAPTER II

A GENERAL HISTORICAL SURVEY OF THE ART FROM THE FIFTEENTH TO THE TWENTIETH CENTURY

THE History of Woodcut and Wood-engraving demands in some ways a more complex treatment than that of Intaglio Engraving and Etching. In dealing with the latter class of work, my chief and almost exclusive consideration was the engraver or the etcher, whether working out his own design on the plate, or reproducing the drawing or painting of another artist. The only important exception to this was my treatment of the book-illustrators of the XVIII and early XIX centuries, where the greater emphasis was laid on the draughtsman.[1]

In woodcut, on the other hand, the first consideration will be the designer, whether he be identical with the cutter or engraver or not.

Woodcut in its simpler forms, i.e. black-line woodcut in general, might be termed a *facsimile* process, being so absolute a transference of the lines or tones of the draughtsman's design that the mechanical factor of cutting the wood (all the more mechanical because of the negative nature of the cutting) might be said to possess no artistic virtue.

Though it is known with fair certainty that Dürer did not make a practice of cutting his own designs (whether he had technical knowledge of the craft or not), and leaving out of consideration the question as to whether he drew on the block itself,[2] or only supplied his cutter with drawings on paper for transfer, nevertheless his usual manner of drawing is so nearly allied in its linear conventions to the style of his woodcuts as to justify our speaking of them as his original woodcuts, without thought of the cutter.

Another kind of woodcut or wood-engraving, where the engraver translates into his own idiom the style of another medium, might be called an *interpretative* method, in contrast with the facsimile process. In this category the cutter would certainly demand more individual consideration.

Apart from the more modern phases of wood-engraving, the reproductive

---

[1] See A. M. Hind, *History of Engraving and Etching*, 1908 (3rd ed. 1923).
[2] As he certainly did if the Terence drawings on the blocks at Basle are his, as is now very generally believed. Cf. p. 332.

line-engraver or etcher has generally been a more independent artist than the woodcutter. The draughtsman seldom finished his design in detail as he intended it to appear on the copper plate. He left his engraver to translate his more expeditious methods of shading in chalk or wash into the formal convention of line-engraving.

The comparative lack of material concerning the woodcutters of the earlier periods, whether they were doing original or facsimile work, is in itself some evidence of the slighter regard in which they were held in contrast with the intaglio engravers. The woodcutter belonged, at least in the early history of the craft, to the same class and guild as the carpenter; he was lower in the hierarchy of craftsmen than the goldsmith to whom the line-engraver was allied, and in view of a constant anonymity it is often impossible to be certain whether he was his own designer or not.

In general it appears to me probable that in the earliest period as well as in the later xv century and during the xvi century, the cutters were a separate class from the designers, and that the designers, as later, were the painters. In the xvi century the designer, or *Reisser* (fig. 34), is often indicated on the print by the sign of a pen, the woodcutter by a knife. There is no reason to think that a practice recognised when the designers' names are known should not have been the traditional practice.[1]

The most important agent in the making of a woodcut is, generally speaking, the designer, and in the case of the facsimile cut essentially the designer. On this assumption, as long as a design is definitely intended for translation into the medium of a block, whether by facsimile or interpretative cutting, its author is of the first importance in our subject. The problem as to whether the designer was also the cutter or engraver must frequently be left unsolved, except by probable answers on the basis of such general inference as we have indicated. As the detailed study in this volume only concerns the xv century, and deals chiefly with anonymous work, there will only be occasional need to attempt individual differentiation of designers and cutters. But wherever it seems possible this attempt will be made by indication in the index against the names of artists quoted.

By minimising the importance of the cutter or engraver, I do not intend to slight the value of original woodcut. It is undoubtedly the ideal combination if the artist's brain and hand can work together throughout the whole process. So long as the work with the knife or graver is not merely mechanical, the chances of realising a living value in the line must thereby be increased. But in black-line woodcut, i.e. in the greater proportion of early

[1] See Index of Subjects, under *designer and cutter*.

woodcuts, the work of cutting is so consistently negative in character (in contrast with the positive of the design), that the process is hardly one to which the original artist would naturally turn. For an engraver's medium into which he can best infuse a personal and vivid expression he will probably choose line-engraving or etching, where the lines he makes on the metal are the positive lines of his design.

The woodcutter only finds this positive expression in the white-line process, the value of which has been most fully realised in modern wood-engraving. Here the lines he cuts are the design itself, and the method offers in consequence as natural a medium for original work as the intaglio processes on metal. But the white-line process has drawbacks, partly in being in its essence a negative way of regarding design (white on black being in some respects a less natural convention than black on white), and partly in the actual weight of the black itself, unless it is broken up sufficiently by the white line. The latter consideration is its chief danger in book-illustration, where too much black overbalances the weight of the type, and where the amount of ink required for the black surfaces implies overloading the accompanying type with ink and risking smudginess on the page. Possibly the value of white line is best realised in the varied possibilities it offers, in combination with black line, in the rendering of tone in reproductive engraving.

Another consideration which complicates a history of woodcut is its intimate connection with the study of printed books, and the difficulty of treating the subject in such a way as to satisfy both artist and bibliographer. As a relief process printed in the same manner as type, woodcut is of all the processes of engraving the one most naturally fitted for book-illustration, only one printing being necessary for both text and figures. A census of the whole history of engraving might perhaps show as large a number of books illustrated with line-engravings as with woodcuts, but in the xv and xvi centuries, the periods distinguished by the finest sense for book-illustration, woodcut is by far the more commonly used for this purpose.

Very few of the line-engravings of the xv and early xvi centuries are known to have been used as book-illustrations,[1] and anonymous work in this medium lacks in consequence one good key to the localisation and date of the artist. With woodcuts, on the other hand, place and date are often fixed by the publication of the book in which they appeared, though the possibility of the blocks being borrowed must be taken into considera-

[1] See my *History of Engraving and Etching*, and Philip Hofer, *Early book-illustrations in the intaglio medium*, Print Collector's Quarterly, xxi. Nos. 3 and 4 (July and October, 1934).

tion. But in spite of this aid, our knowledge of the authors of woodcut illustrations in the xv and xvi centuries is far more meagre than of the line-engravers of the same period. Names, monograms, or marks of the artists appear less frequently on early woodcuts than on line-engravings, and apart from these clues the woodcutters have been less successfully identified or grouped than the line-engravers.

In dealing with woodcut illustrations we at least have definite lines marked out for a survey of the art in relation to the principal towns where the books were published. The printers of the books themselves do not concern us directly except in certain cases where they may have combined the crafts of printing and cutting. But they will inevitably be cited as the most convenient handle for grouping anonymous illustrations. Moreover, some of the early printers have a close relation to the history of wood-cut in so far as they supported workshops of cutters, just as they did of illuminators and rubricators, who may have turned in some cases to cutting.[1] The uniformity in the style of woodcut work done for certain early printers (e.g. Johannes Grüninger of Strassburg) shows the close relations that must have existed between printer and woodcutter.

The intimate relationship between woodcut and the printed book leads one to recognise the influence of a style suited to book-illustration on the development of woodcut and wood-engraving in general. In spite of the numbers of single cuts intended for wall decoration, it is book-illustration on the whole rather than exhibition that has been the strongest governing factor in determining the style of woodcut at various periods.

In the study of book-illustration I shall attempt to give such references as will leave no doubt as to the editions quoted. This should of course be taken for granted in historical or critical studies, but there are, I fear, few students who have not constantly suffered from their omission. I do not propose to refer to the locality of copies of the editions quoted, except in the case of books not in the British Museum, and then not necessarily to the place of more than a single copy. Schreiber's *Manuel de l'Amateur* and the *Gesamtkatalog der Wiegendrucke* (when complete) will provide such additional information.

One term commonly used in reference to book-illustration, i.e. *vignette*, perhaps needs some explanation. The term originated in ornamental work

---

[1] Note the description of Francesco Rosselli, in a Florentine Inventory of 1528, as a *Miniatore e Stampatore* (illuminator and printer), and one who, to judge from his son's inventory, had been in possession of a large stock of copper plates and wood blocks (see p. 534). Cf. also the practice in Italy about 1469–72 of printing outline borders as a basis for illumination (see p. 398).

based on the form of the vine (leaves, tendrils, and grapes) such as was found in the illuminations of medieval MSS. This connotation was transferred in printed book-illustration to any form of decorative details suggested by the usage of earlier marginal illuminations, such as borders, head- and tail-pieces. The earliest use of the term in this meaning to which I can refer occurs in the *Repertoire des Figures* in Jean Dupré's *Horae* of 4th February 1488/89, where it certainly appears to indicate the decorative and pictorial borders, whether or no it includes the occasional larger subjects. It might also be noted that the words *rabeschi e fogliami* (arabesque and leaf patterns) were used by Baldinucci in reference to the decorative parts of woodcut illustration, a genre of work which he stated that Claude Lorrain produced in his youth under an elder brother Jean Gellée. Finally, and more specifically, vignette has been applied to illustrations either without definite border lines, or not completely rectangular in shape.

The term has been occasionally used to denote any book-illustration smaller than the full-page,[1] but this seems to me a loose connotation which should be avoided.

I have referred in my technical introduction to woodcut being naturally fitted for printing in conjunction with type, as both blocks and type are printed from the surface. It has been stated that wood blocks are difficult to print with movable type,[2] but the difficulty appears to lie rather in the care required than in the essence of the combination. Wood blocks, electrotypes and metal type all take ink of the same consistency.[3]

I propose to devote the rest of the present chapter to some general survey of the art of woodcut from its inception to the end of the XIX century, referring to its character, uses and local distribution at the different periods of its history, and ending with a summary of the development of chiaroscuro and colour-woodcut.

The practice of impressing patterns on textiles by wood blocks is in principle entirely analogous to making prints from woodcuts on paper, though the actual methods of printing went through varying developments.

---

[1] E.g. A. W. Pollard, *Early Illustrated Books*, 2nd ed., 1917, p. 95 : 'vignettes, or small cuts worked into the text.'

[2] See Charles Ricketts, in his Preface to a Catalogue of an Exhibition of *Famous Woodcut Illustrations of the XV and early XVI Centuries*, London (about 1897) : 'With the triumph of the great printer the fate of block illustration wavers and hesitates, for wood blocks are to this day difficult to print with movable type ; it is for this reason that some of them were executed, or perhaps merely cast, on metal.'

[3] See p. 16.

Reference has already been made to these textile patterns and the method of their printing, and further details will be given in the succeeding chapter;[1] but the study of *textile-prints* (*Zeugdrucke*) is in reality more strictly related to the history of textiles than to the history of woodcut in our limited sense, so that it will only be introduced here as a side-issue.

Wall-paper designs printed from wood blocks are in a similar category. They could in one sense be rightly included in a history of woodcut, but their study is again rather that of a separate craft in which wood blocks happen to be used as an auxiliary. And in any case there are only occasional examples until well after the period to which I am devoting detailed attention in this volume.[2]

These remarks may suffice to excuse what might from certain points of view be regarded as an arbitrary limitation of my subject, which is concerned with prints from wood blocks, made for their own sake rather than as adjuncts to other crafts.

The origins of woodcut in this sense probably go back to the end of the xiv century, a subject which will be discussed in detail in the succeeding chapter. Whatever the place of origin, it seems fairly certain, if one envisages the art until the end of the xv century, that Germany was the most productive country in Europe. The question of the distribution of the earliest cuts between the neighbouring regions of Germany, Austria, the Netherlands, and France, is one of great obscurity. Italy may have been early in the field, but undoubtedly produced less, and Spain was nearly as late as England in its first adoption of the art towards the end of the xv century.

The application of woodcut and engraving to the multiplication of designs, associated with the discovery of printing, may without exaggeration be regarded as one of the greatest advances ever made in the means of disseminating knowledge and ideas; and since the xv century there has certainly been no advance of comparable importance until the discovery of wireless and the development of broadcasting.

The activities of the early woodcutters were largely divided between the production of playing-cards and the making of pictures of saints and other religious subjects for sale or distribution by the convents.

The history of *playing-cards* is certainly more directly allied to our subject than that of printed wall-papers or textiles, but in their study

---

[1] See pp. 67-72.

[2] Cf. p. 77. See A. V. Sugden and J. L. Edmondson, *History of English Wall-Paper*, 1509–1914. London, 1926; and C. C. Oman, *Catalogue of Wall-papers*, Victoria and Albert Museum, London, 1929.

woodcut is of less moment than the games and packs themselves, which have been made and decorated in a diversity of ways. So I may treat them likewise as a side-issue which demands separate historical treatment.[1]

The first idea of the making of a printed book appears to have come through woodcut in the form of the *block-books*, i.e. books in which text and picture were printed from wood blocks. Most of the important block-books, i.e. the *Apocalypse*, the *Ars Moriendi*, the *Canticum Canticorum*, and the *Speculum Humanae Salvationis*, originated in the Netherlands, though various contemporary copies appeared in Germany, if not elsewhere. The earliest type of the *Biblia Pauperum* block-book, only known in the impression at Heidelberg, is German, like most of the MS. versions, but the commoner type is Netherlandish in design. Apart from the Heidelberg *Biblia Pauperum*, only a few of the earliest block-books appear to be German, e.g. the *Symbolum Apostolicum*, and only one, the *Passion*, preserved in a unique copy at Berlin, can be assigned to Italy.

The tradition that ascribes the discovery of book-printing to Laurens Coster at Haarlem, might actually refer to the producer of some of the Netherlandish block-books. But whatever the truth in this obscure matter, the real development of printing from movable type undoubtedly took place in Germany, and at Mainz, about the middle of the xv century, under the leadership of Gutenberg, Fust, and Schoeffer.

Woodcut was soon adopted by the printers for the decoration of their books, as early as 1457 for the initials hitherto done by the rubricator's hand (in *Latin Psalters* printed by Fust and Schoeffer at Mainz), about 1460–61 for actual subject illustration (in certain rare books printed by Pfister at Bamberg); used little thereafter until 1467, when book-illustration begins in Italy, and until 1470 in Germany, a date which marks the beginning of the most fertile period of woodcut illustration, which continued unbroken until the latter part of the xvi century.

In the truest quality of book-illustration, i.e. in the perfect balance between woodcut illustration and the printed type in making a beautiful page, the best period in Germany was undoubtedly between 1470 and 1500. The woodcuts themselves may have become greater works of art in Dürer's hands, and achievements of greater accomplishment or interest as developed by Dürer's followers, but with the increase in the commerce of books the printers became careless of fine book-production, and even when care was given, the more complex art of the designer or cutter seldom made up for the simple vigour of the earlier cutters. Dürer himself might

[1] See pp. 84-89 for further notes and bibliography.

have been a great book-illustrator, but never was, most of his woodcut work being done for separate printing, though a considerable proportion was issued by himself in the form of series with text.

The outstanding exception to the decline in book-illustration in the xvi century was HANS HOLBEIN the younger, with his beautiful little series of illustrations to the *Old Testament* (fig. 16) and to the *Dance of Death* (cut in part at least by Hans Lützelburger; fig. 13), though even these were not given the full opportunity of a perfectly harmonious setting, such as they deserved.[1]

German woodcut at its best is notable for its single prints rather than for book-illustration. ALBRECHT DÜRER, who stands at the apex of its de-

Fig. 16. Hans Holbein II. Ruth and Boaz.

velopment in this respect, is perhaps the greatest figure in the whole history of woodcut design; while several of his German and Swiss contemporaries beside Holbein, notably HANS BALDUNG, HANS BURGKMAIR the elder, ALBRECHT ALTDORFER (fig. 17), HANS SEBALD BEHAM, and LUCAS CRANACH the elder, added lustre to the art.

In Italy, apart from isolated examples of great interest, comparatively little book-illustration was produced until 1490. Then the last decade of the century in Venice and Florence saw two phases of book-illustration, each unrivalled in their respective and characteristic qualities. Venetian illustration was the more prolific, and in its most perfect expression the more short-lived. For ten brief years it was characterised by purity of black

[1] See p. 8, note 2, for testimony that Holbein's cutters used boxwood, and for the possible influence of the supply of boxwood on the style of xvi-century Venetian woodcut illustration.

line, avoidance of all elaboration, and a perfect balance to a light Roman type. By the second decade of the XVI century its style was marred by a tendency to imitate the manner of line-engraving,[1] chiefly perhaps under the influence of JACOB OF STRASSBURG, an off-shoot of the illustrators of Grüninger's press.

Fig. 17. Albrecht Altdorfer. The Flight into Egypt.

Florentine illustration is remarkable for its use of the white line, landscape backgrounds in particular being generally worked out in this method. Though hardly as perfect in its balance on the page as Venetian illustration, it is yet full of charm, and reflects much of the Florentine virtue of linear draughtsmanship. The original and characteristic style of Florentine book-illustration lasted much longer than that of Venice; in fact persisted, though gradually weakening in quality and quantity, until the middle of the XVI century.

It is noteworthy that many of the Italian xv-century books so treasured to-day were the more popular works of the period, comparable to the chap-books of XVII-century England. Woodcut, in replacing the art of the illuminator, continued for some time to be despised as a cheap and popular alternative. The books regarded in their time as the finest productions, worthy of princely collectors, e.g. the best examples of Aldus at Venice and Miscomini at Florence, were for the most part without illustration.

In Italy during the xv century single cuts were far rarer than in the North, and it is only at the turn of the xv and xvi centuries that Italy begins to take an important place in the larger productions of woodcut, with the works of the Master ·I·B·̸ [2] and of JACOPO DE' BARBARI. Apart from these two artists the finest single cuts in Italy were produced after Titian's designs, or under his influence, by DOMENICO CAMPAGNOLA, NICCOLÒ BOLDRINI,

---

[1] A bad tendency noticeable at various periods in the history of woodcut and wood-engraving, e.g. in Robert Brandard, William Harvey, and Blasius Höfel. Abraham Bosse in the *Avant-propos* of his *Traicté des manières de graver* (1645) evinced a similarly perverted idea about the style of etching, declaring its best aim to be the imitation of the character of line-engraving.

[2] See p. 440 for a probable solution of his identity.

DOMENICO DELLE GRECHE, ANDREA ANDREANI and others, a large scale
being frequently chosen as one might expect from the Venetian love of

Fig. 18. Domenico Campagnola. St. John the Evangelist.

splendid pageantry. GIUSEPPE SCOLARI is noteworthy for his flamboyant
cuts in white line.

One of Domenico Campagnola's smaller woodcuts, the *St. John the Evangelist* (fig. 18), shows more evidence of original design, and a freedom of
handling which anticipates the work of Jan Lievens in the XVII century.

The Netherlands of the XV century, which took a leading part in the production of block-books, fell considerably behind Germany in book-illustration. In craftsmanship and decorative sense the Netherlandish woodcutters

were by no means equal to the Germans; but they possessed certain qualities of natural representation, particularly in the rendering of landscape, which gives them individual value and interest. Their greatest achievement was in the single prints of designers such as JACOB CORNELISZ and LUCAS VAN LEYDEN (fig. 19), while interesting work was done later in the XVI century after PIETER BRUEGHEL the elder.

The decorative sense, lacking in Netherlandish illustration, is the chief characteristic of Spanish work in the XV century. The Venetian style is clearly the inspiration, but the severer Venetian is varied and enriched in many borders of early Spanish and Portuguese books by elements of Moorish design. The earliest woodcuts in Spanish books are largely based on foreign designs, and it was only in the last decade of the century that there emerges anything like a national style.

French book-illustration of the XV and XVI centuries is also perhaps strongest on the decorative side, but apart from the unique and beautiful character of its decoration, which continued more clearly than elsewhere the traditions of the illuminators of manuscripts, it presents fine and subtle qualities in subject design. These qualities are seen at their best in works such as the *Danse Macabre* printed by G. Marchant at Paris in 1491/92.

The production of small Books of Hours decorated with woodcut borders began in France about 1488–89, and maintained its popularity well into the second quarter of the XVI century. Among the earliest of these books, those printed by Jean Dupré are more purely in the tradition of French illumination than most of the others; but the early works printed by Antoine Vérard are not far removed in tendency. Vérard's later *Horae*, and others printed by Pigouchet (for Vostre), by Thielmann Kerver, and by or for Gillet and Germain Hardouin, are more typical of the developed style of the school, in which black-line figures are frequently set on a black ground dotted with white, a type of work for which metal blocks were often used in place of wood.

The gradual assimilation of Renaissance ornament may be aptly studied in the history of these *Horae*, a development which reached its zenith in the purely classical work of GEOFFROY TORY.

Woodcut in England is of considerably less interest than work in France and the Netherlands during the XV century. But in spite of the generally inferior standard of craftsmanship, there are a few books with woodcuts of some quality in design and cutting. For attractive border designs, French in character, the rare *Primers* (i.e. Books of Hours) printed by Caxton,

Fig. 19. Lucas van Leyden. Samson and Delilah.

Wynkyn de Worde and William de Machlinia are noteworthy. For handsome decoration there is Pynson's fine *Morton Missal* of 1500, while Wynkyn de Worde's edition of Bartholomaeus, *All the Proprytees of Thynges*, 1495, shows a designer and cutter who adapted with considerable freedom and strength the Dutch and French originals.

Before leaving the xv century I would mention the *dotted prints* (prints in the *manière criblée*) and the white-line metal cuts, which form a group belonging chiefly to the last quarter of the xv century, and probably for the most part German in origin. *Paste-prints*, which form a smaller group, more uniform in technical character, may also come from one or two German workshops of the end of the xv century. Both these groups will be treated in separate historical sections.

In the course of the xvi century there is a growing deterioration in the quality of design in woodcut. The Gothic character which predominated in xv-century woodcut in the North, both in single cuts and in book-illustration, and which made so perfect a balance to the black-letter type, had gradually yielded to the renaissance of classical design and ornament. In Italian woodcut illustration the popular style was never a true Gothic, except that of the immigrant designers and cutters from the North, but there was a vernacular style, which contrasted even in the last decade of the xv century with the classic. The difference is clearly seen in comparing the two chief Venice editions of the Malermi Bible, that of 1490 showing the more naturalistic designer, and that of 1493 the more conventionalised classic. At first, classic design and ornament is for the most part restrained and tasteful in its character. Among the Teutons, Dürer, Burgkmair and Holbein all showed true sense of style in their adoption of its characteristic notation. In France, Geoffroy Tory was among the purest of stylists in his fine classical sense. But with all its dignity it was arid in comparison with the full-blooded youth of xv-century work. By the middle of the xvi century the aridity had degenerated into exuberance of fantastic ornament, which often merely served to cover emptiness of design.

This degeneration of style makes one regret the less the decay of the art of woodcut towards the end of the xvi century, and its gradual supersession in popularity by the process of line-engraving. The makers of books were no longer satisfied with woodcuts, but turned to the more effective tonality of intaglio work for the frontispieces and title-pages which formed such regular elements in xvii-century book-decoration. Nevertheless, though woodcut yielded chief place to the more meretricious attractions of line-engraving in book-illustration, the subsidiary elements in book-decoration (head- and tail-pieces and the like) still remained in the hands of the cutters.

Fig. 20. Jan Lievens. Portrait of an Ecclesiastic.

A vast number of liturgical books were issued with woodcut illustrations throughout the xvi century, the first centre of activity, that of Venice (notably in the publishing house of Lucantonio Giunta), yielding gradually in importance to that of Antwerp and the Plantin Press, which was at the height of its glory in the latter part of the century.[1]

The XVII century was a period in which naturalism was the outstanding spirit in art; and the painters most imbued with this spirit, such as Rembrandt, turned to etching rather than woodcut or line-engraving as the most immediate and vivid means of expressing and multiplying their ideas in prints. Woodcut in consequence lost its popular appeal, and it

Fig. 21. Dirk de Bray. February.

is only here and there that artists of eminence still used the process, CHRISTOFFEL JEGHER (at his best in designs by Rubens), JAN LIEVENS (in a few fine portraits), and DIRK DE BRAY, being perhaps the most notable.[2]

Woodcut in the earlier XVIII century lacked even the occasional distinction noted in the XVII century. JEAN MICHEL PAPILLON (1698–1776) was a most industrious woodcutter, exceedingly jealous for the reputation of his art, and the author of a valuable though discursive and historically unreliable book on the craft and history of woodcut. But the efforts of his pen did not avail to rehabilitate the art, for the simple reason that his quality as an artist was so far below that of contemporary painters and

---

[1] The Plantin-Moretus Museum, Antwerp, is a wonderful relic of the old printing establishment and its stock-in-trade.

[2] The unsigned cut reproduced under the name of Dirk de Bray (fig. 21) is one of a series of cuts of the *Months* (Blokhuyzen, No. 48, etc.), of which the *January* is signed by Jan de Bray. Only one of the series (*September*) has a signature B generally attributed to Dirk de Bray, while two others are signed by C. van Sichem. It is probable that they are after designs by Jan de Bray, and for the most part cut by Dirk de Bray. But their virtue is not dependent on the identity of the cutter.

draughtsmen who continued to express themselves in line-engraving, a medium which they may have rightly preferred as the better channel for the expression of the extraordinary refinement of their art. So for all his propaganda, Papillon, his family and followers plodded on their laborious way, doing such decorative pieces as the publisher required, and it fell to the lot of a truer artist, though in some ways a humbler craftsman, to infuse the art with new life.

Fig. 22. J. M. Papillon. His own trade-card.

THOMAS BEWICK (1753–1827) might have done much by the sheer faithfulness of his renderings of nature; but he achieved a really great influence by his realisation of the value of white line in wood-engraving. The use of the graver on sections of boxwood, in place of the knife on the plank, was known early in the XVIII century,[1] but Bewick was the first to practise the new art of wood-engraving to any considerable extent, and so to form a real turning-point in the history of the art.

Of his contemporaries who practised wood-engraving, WILLIAM BLAKE (1757–1827) was by far the greatest genius, but much of his work in wood-engraving and in allied methods of relief-etching on metal is so isolated and unique that it fits into no survey of the general development of the art. He is more nearly in the main stream of this development in the charming series of white-line wood-engravings he did to illustrate Thornton's *Pastorals of Virgil* (1821).

Fig. 23. Thomas Bewick. The Fowler.

A few prints by EDWARD CALVERT are almost unique as a reflection of Blake's spirit among the wood-engravings of Blake's own contemporaries. It remained for original engravers of the later XIX and early XX centuries, such as T. STURGE MOORE, to recapture something of the same inspiration.

Though most of Bewick's own engraving was original, yet his more

[1] See pp. 10-12.

immediate influence extended chiefly to reproductive engraving. For in the first place there were few original wood-engravers in the first three-quarters of the xix century; and in the second, the technical character of Bewick's white-line engraving, though naturally adapted for original work, actually helped even more towards the expression of tone, one of the chief requirements of reproductive work.

Fig. 24. William Blake. From Thornton's *Pastorals of Virgil*, London 1821.

It should be remembered that towards the end of his life, Bewick, at the time that he was engraving his *Waiting for Death* (a wonderful achievement in tone, not to speak of its qualities of pathos), was considering actual experiments in colour-woodcut which he never lived to realise.

I have already emphasised the distinction between *facsimile* and *interpretative* engraving. The distinction is particularly clear in the history of xix-century wood-engraving.[1] A very pure example of the facsimile style is seen in the series of illustrations engraved by LUKE CLENNELL after THOMAS STOTHARD, in Samuel Rogers' *Poems*, 1810. The wood-engravings of the 'Sixties' in England (taking the DALZIEL brothers as typical engravers, and SIR JOHN MILLAIS as the leading designer in the school) are partially, at least, interpretative. The draughtsman would generally provide the engraver with a drawing in pen or pencil and wash, which the engraver would translate with more or less freedom into the convention of his craft. More completely interpretative in character, as having no lines to follow, are such prints as those of the American engraver TIMOTHY COLE, reproducing pictures which carry the tonal capabilities of mixed black- and white-line work to its extreme limits.

Many attractive designs by Millais, Rossetti, Sandys and others were engraved for books and magazines between about 1855 and 1870, but the books themselves were no better than the average production of the earlier xix century. The movement was essentially a popular one, and occurred at a time hardly distinguished for artistic taste, when little thought was expended on the making of a beautiful book.

[1] Among contemporary artists Bangemann of Berlin may be noted for the skill with which he makes facsimiles of pen drawings (e.g. by Liebermann and Slevogt) in wood-engraving.

Work of a similar character had been done a few years earlier in Germany, chiefly after ADOLF VON MENZEL (1815–1905), by UNZELMANN and other engravers; while GUSTAVE DORÉ (1832–1883) was the inspirer of an even more popular school of wood-engraved illustration in France, with A. F. PANNE-

Fig. 25. Dalziel after J. E. Millais. Illustration to Coleridge's *Love*.

MAKER as its chief engraver. *L'Amateur d'Estampes*, a wood-engraving by A. A. PRUNAIRE after Daumier, might be cited as a most skilful example of this French group of reproductive engravers.

The tendency of most of the wood-engravers of these groups was to render the looser qualities of a pen-drawing without sufficient thought for the more formal conventions more naturally suited to wood-engraving.

From this there was only a short step to the reproduction of drawings by photo-mechanical processes, which did in fact by 1870–80 almost entirely superannuate the wood-engraver.

Here then was the time for a real revival of the craft of wood-engraving

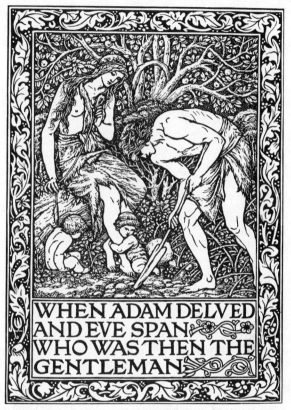

Fig. 26. W. H. Hooper after Burne-Jones. Frontispice to the *Dream of John Ball*.

in conjunction with an attempt at producing fine books, and WILLIAM MORRIS will always be remembered as an artist, apart from his poetry and prose romances, for his making of beautiful books. As designer for wood he turned back to the facsimile art of the older masters, for both he and BURNE-JONES, his chief collaborator in design, drew their designs for the most part in the linear convention of the engraver. The KELMSCOTT PRESS books, produced between 1891 and 1897, were the starting-point for numerous later ventures in the production of beautiful illustrated books, of which the most notable in England before the end of the XIX century were the VALE PRESS (with woodcuts designed by CHARLES RICKETTS and others), and the ERAGNY PRESS (conducted by LUCIEN PISSARRO) remarkable for its many woodcut decorations in colour. The XX century has seen more private presses with similar aims, and though it is outside our scope to name them here, it can at least be said that both France and England have shown something of a renaissance in the production of fine books, illustrated or decorated with woodcut.

In the wake of the revival of the best traditions of woodcut and wood-engraving in book-illustration, came a renewed regard for the art by collectors of separate prints. This has perhaps gained ground slowly as it has had to contend against an interest in etching which had grown almost to a passion with collectors during the last quarter of the XIX and the first quarter of the XX century. Moreover, if prints are considered as wall-decoration, intaglio-prints have an advantage in strength of effect over woodcuts. To attain this strength of effect in a woodcut the engraver may turn to an increased use of the black surface, but he thereby runs the risk of sacrificing in his art more than he gains as a decorator. On the whole recent wood-engravers have been right in following for the most part a style governed by the limitations of book-illustration.

Nevertheless, as prints for the portfolio, if not for the walls, wood-engravings are steadily regaining the public esteem, and the field is still comparatively free from the third-rate craftsmen to whom etching, during its inordinate popularity, had offered success.

For more purely decorative ends colour-woodcut in the Japanese manner is undoubtedly peculiarly adapted, and during the last few decades many European artists have adopted the process, J. D. BATTEN and FRANK MORLEY FLETCHER[1] having been among the pioneers in England. Its flat surfaces of colour are perfectly adapted to wall-decoration, and avoid the dangers of the over-emphasis noted in white-line woodcut, where large surfaces of black are left untouched.

I would here retrace my survey and refer to the development of *colour-woodcut* and *chiaroscuro-woodcut* from the XV century to the present day.

Woodcut may have developed in part in the illuminators' workshops as

---

[1] *Eve and the Serpent*, cut by Frank Morley Fletcher after a design by J. D. Batten, proved in 1895 and published 1896, is among the earliest English prints in the Japanese method.

a more expeditious mode of repeating designs intended to be finished in colour. It is natural then to find a large proportion of the single cuts, block-books and book-illustrations, from the beginning of the art and throughout the xv century, coloured by hand.[1]

The next stage was for the illuminator to save himself labour and insure regularity by the use of stencils for the colour. Their chief use in the xv and xvi centuries was in the colouring of playing-cards, and in the xvi century for popular broadsides. Only occasional examples of ordinary cuts in the xv century have been noted as coloured in this way, and in several of these cases the colour may actually have been printed from blocks and not from stencils.[2]

The third stage was for the cutter or printer to save labour still further, or to regularise the multiplication of the same colours, by cutting blocks for the colours as well as for the black outline. From the time of the bi-chrome initials of Fust and Schoeffer's *Latin Psalters* (printed in various editions from 1457), there are fairly frequent examples of colour-printing, heraldic cuts, initials and printers' marks being most commonly treated in this way. In Italy before 1486, and later at Augsburg, Erhard Ratdolt was the printer most addicted to the process, but other examples can be cited in the xv century, e.g. in Ketham's *Fascicolo di Medicina* (Venice, J. and G. de Gregoriis, 1493), and in the heraldic cuts of the *Book of St. Albans*, 1486. In the xvi century the practice continues fairly frequently in heraldic cuts and title-pages, and occasionally occurs in single cuts, the most notable example being Altdorfer's *Beautiful Virgin of Regensburg* (of about 1520).

The branch of colour-woodcut which was chiefly in use in the xvi century was that of *chiaroscuro*,[3] which may be described as colour-woodcut in which the scheme is limited to the various tones of a single colour or of nearly related colours.

The earliest certain date to which chiaroscuro-woodcuts can be assigned is 1508, the year of the *Emperor Maximilian I. on Horseback* (B. 32), cut by JOST DE NEGKER after HANS BURGKMAIR. It had probably been inspired by LUCAS CRANACH's *St. George* (B. 65), which is recorded in 1508 as having

---

[1] See pp. 114, 123, and 125.   [2] Cf. p. 171.

[3] For general works on chiaroscuro-woodcut see Adam Bartsch, *Le Peintre Graveur*, vol. xii., Vienna 1811; G. K. W. Seibt, *Helldunkel* (iii.): *Chiaroscuro (Camaieu). Studien zur Kunst und Kunstgeschichte*, Frankfurt 1891; Anton Reichel, *Die Clair-obscur-Schnitte des XVI, XVII und XVIII Jahrhunderts*, Zurich, Leipzig, Vienna 1926; Luigi Servolini, *La Xilografia a Chiaroscuro italiana nei secoli XVI, XVII e XVIII*, Lecco 1930. See also Vasari, *Le Vite*, 2nd. ed. 1568, p. 659, under *Marcantonio*.

Fig. 27. Johann Wechtlin. Orpheus.

been printed in silver and gold. An impression in the British Museum shows the ordinary black line printed on paper tinted dark blue by hand, with a printing in gold (or rather in paste to which powdered gold would adhere) from a second block.[1] Burgkmair's *Maximilian* is sometimes printed in gold in similar manner, as well as in the ordinary chiaroscuro.

To the next year, 1509, belong most of Cranach's chiaroscuro cuts proper, and in the succeeding years much similar work was designed by HANS BURGKMAIR, HANS BALDUNG and JOHANN WECHTLIN.

The first of the Italian chiaroscuro-woodcutters, UGO DA CARPI (about 1455–1523), was considerably senior to any of the German masters of the process, but nothing definite is known of his work in this manner before 1516, when he obtained a *privilegium* for his process from the Signoria at Venice, and none of his chiaroscuro-cuts is dated before 1518.

The few Italian woodcutters of the XVI century who devoted themselves to chiaroscuro (UGO DA CARPI, ANTONIO FANTUZZI DA TRENTO, GIUSEPPE NICCOLÒ VICENTINO and ANDREA ANDREANI), produced far more numerous prints of the kind than their German contemporaries. The painter Parmigiano (Francesco Mazzuoli) was the designer of by far the greatest number of the prints by the first three cutters named, and he was probably the immediate inspirer of their particular mode of expression, whereby a monochrome washed drawing heightened with white is reproduced with scarcely any abatement of its freedom of effect.[2]

It is this freedom of style in draughtsmanship which chiefly distinguishes the Italian from the German school of chiaroscuro-woodcut. The characteristics of the two schools no doubt depended in part on the respective styles of the two schools of draughtsmanship. The German craftsmen rendered the whole subject in complete outline, so that the line-block could be printed effectively by itself; and this outline was only supple-

[1] For notes on printing in gold see M. Geisberg, *Holzschnittbildnisse des Kaisers Maximilian*, Pr. Jahrbuch 1911, Heft 4, and C. Dodgson, *Catalogue of Early German and Flemish Woodcuts in the British Museum*, ii., 1911, p. 74. See also pp. 203 and 506.

[2] It has often been debated whether the painter made drawings to be rendered in facsimile by the chiaroscuro-woodcutter, or whether the woodcutter worked out the design independently within his own convention. Some of Parmigiano's original drawings, corresponding in design to these cuts, are known, e.g. the *Martyrdom of SS. Peter and Paul* (for the chiaroscuro, B. xii. 79, 28), so that we may assume, I think, that in certain cases the cutter intended something of a facsimile, either on his own account, or under the direction of the painter. On the other hand, series such as Andreani's *Triumph of Caesar* are more likely to have been worked out by the cutter in his own convention after Mantegna's paintings. Moreover, the fact that chiaroscuro-cuts of a single subject occur in a variety of tones shows that the cutter was playing his own variations on the original theme.

Fig. 28. Ugo da Carpi after Parmigiano. Pan.

mented and enhanced by the tones. The Italians, on the other hand, seldom approached any completeness with their line-block, and the tones were an essential addition to the presentation of the subject.

Good work was done in the Netherlands and in France at the end of the XVI century and in the earlier part of the XVII, e.g. by HENDRIK GOLTZIUS, ABRAHAM and FREDERIK BLOEMAERT and LOUIS BUSINCK, and the Italian tradition was continued, with less freedom and genius, by BARTOLOMMEO CORIOLANO in the XVII century, and revived more in the ancient style by ANTON MARIA ZANETTI in the XVIII.

Interesting prints were also produced in the XVIII century in France by NICOLAS and VINCENT LE SUEUR, and in England by ELISHA KIRKALL, J. B. JACKSON, ARTHUR POND, CHARLES KNAPTON and JOHN SKIPPE, the reproduction of Old Master drawings being one of their chief ends. J. B. Jackson also used his craft in the making of wall-papers.

In these later periods wood blocks were often combined with the etched line, or with mezzotint.

A similar combination of wood blocks with an intaglio metal plate is found in the middle of the XIX century in the colour prints of GEORGE BAXTER. His work is extremely accomplished in its rendering of a full colour scheme by the use of a large number of blocks, but it is entirely reproductive and possesses small artistic value on account of the poor quality of most of the originals reproduced.

Since the revival of wood-engraving as a vehicle for original expression towards the end of the XIX century, the most interesting work in colour has been done for book-illustration, and chiefly in France and England; the most distinguished production being that of LUCIEN PISSARRO in the books of his own Eragny Press.

In chiaroscuro, among the earliest examples of the revival at the turn of the XIX and the XX centuries were the *Roundels of the Months* by CHARLES SHANNON and the *Doings of Death* by WILLIAM STRANG (Essex House Press 1901). During the present century a considerable amount of good work has been done in England and France, but the process has potentialities which deserve to attract more exponents and greater recognition.

GENERAL BIBLIOGRAPHY

WALPOLE, Horace. Catalogue of Engravers who have been born or resided in England. Strawberry Hill 1763 (later editions 1765, 1782, 1786 and 1794; also incorporated in later editions of Walpole's Anecdotes of Painting in England. The first three editions were not given a volume number in relation to the 'Anecdotes' but from 'Directions to the Binder' were evidently regarded as belonging to the same work).

WALPOLE, Horace. Anecdotes of Painting in England. 4 vols. Strawberry Hill 1762–71 (2nd ed. 1765–71; 3rd ed., in 5 vols., the fifth being the 'Catalogue of Engravers', 1782; 4th ed. 1786; ed. J. Dallaway 1826–28; ed. J. Dallaway and R. Wornum 1849).

PAPILLON, J. B. M. Traité historique et pratique de la gravure en bois. 3 vols. Paris 1766.

HEINECKEN, C. H. von. Nachrichten von Künstlern und Kunstsachen. ii. Theil. Leipzig 1769 (pp. 87-314, on early woodcut and book-illustration, and notes on L. J. Coster). Nachrichten. Leipzig 1804 (pp. 134-275, on woodcut, book-illustration and playing-cards).

HEINECKEN, C. H. von. Idée générale d'une collection d'estampes. Leipzig and Vienna 1771.

GORI GANDELLINI, G. Notizie degli intagliatori. 3 vols. Siena 1771. 2nd ed. by L. de Angelis. 15 vols. Siena 1808–16 (see vol. iv. for bibliography and historical survey).

MURR, C. G. von. Journal zur Kunstgeschichte. 2te Theil. Nuremberg 1776 (pp. 75-179, Formschneiderkunst, with Sebastian Roland's copy of the 1423 'St. Christopher' at p. 104).

BREITKOPF, J. G. I. Versuch den Ursprung der Spielkarten, die Einführung des Linienpapieres, und den Anfang der Holzschneidekunst in Europa zu erforschen. Leipzig 1784, 1801.

ZANI, P. Materiali per servire alla storia dell' origine e de' progressi dell' incisione in rame e in legno. Parma 1802.

ZANI, P. Enciclopedia metodica delle belle arti. 28 vols. Parma 1817–24 (Part i. contains a very extensive dictionary of engravers' names with the briefest biographical details; Part ii. consists of a subject index, covering Old and New Testaments). Zani's MS. continuation of the *Enciclopedia* is in the Parma Library (MS. 3618).

BARTSCH, Adam. Le Peintre Graveur. 21 vols. Vienna 1803–21. Supplement, R. Weigel. Leipzig 1843; Zusätze, J. Heller. Nuremberg 1854. Reprint, 18 vols., Würzburg 1920.

DERSCHAU, H. A. von. Holzschnitte alter deutscher Meister in den Original-Platten gesammelt von H. A. von D. Als ein Beitrag zur Kunstgeschichte herausgegeben von R. Z. Becker. 3 Lieferungen. Gotha 1808, 1810, 1816. The Derschau Collection of 1852 original blocks (of which about half were printed in the above edition) are now in the Berlin Print Room: see M. J. Friedländer, Holzschnitte alter Meister: Sammlung Derschau. Einleitung und Verzeichniss der vierzig Tafeln. Leipzig 1922.

OTTLEY, W. Y. Inquiry into the Origin and Early History of Engraving. 2 vols. London 1816.

OTTLEY, W. Y. Inquiry concerning the Invention of Printing . . . including also notices of the early use of wood-engraving in Europe, the block-books, etc., with introduction by J. P. Berjeau. London 1863. (Ottley died 1836, but his work was not published till this edition.)

HELLER, Joseph. Geschichte der Holzschneidekunst . . . nebst zwei Beilagen enthaltend den Ursprung der Spielkarten und ein Verzeichniss der sämmtlicher xylographischen Werke. Bamberg 1823. (J. Heller, dealer, collector and connoisseur 1798–1849, left his collections to Bamberg.)

HAIN, Ludovicus. Repertorium Bibliographicum. 2 vols. Stuttgart and Liége 1826, 1831.

HAIN, Ludovicus. Supplements, indexes, etc., by Conrad Burger. Leipzig 1891, London 1902, Leipzig 1908; W. A. Copinger, London 1895, 1898; D. Reichling, Munich 1905–14.

NAGLER, G. K. Allgemeines Künstler-lexikon. 22 vols. Munich 1835–52 (the most extensive of all the dictionaries; of great value for its notices on the less generally known artists).

NAGLER, G. K. Die Monogrammisten. 5 vols. Munich 1858–79.

RUMOHR, C. F. von. Zur Geschichte und Theorie der Formschneidekunst. Leipzig 1837.

CHATTO, W. A., and JACKSON, John. A Treatise on Wood-engraving, historical and practical, with upwards of three hundred illustrations engraved on wood by J. J. [The historical part by W. A. C.] London 1839. 2nd ed., with a new chapter on the artists of the present day by Henry G. Bohn, and 145 additional wood-engravings. London (Bohn) 1861. Reprint of second edition by Chatto & Windus, London N.D.

CHATTO, W. A. Wood-engraving, its History and Practice. *Illustrated London News* 1844.

TIMPERLEY, C. H. Dictionary of Printers and Printing. London 1839.

BONNARDOT, A. Histoire de la gravure en France. Paris 1849.

MUCZKOWSKI, Józef. Recueil de gravures sur bois imprimées dans divers ouvrages polonais au XVIe et XVIIe siècles, dont les planches sont conservées à la Bibliothèque de l'Université de Jagellon. Cracow 1849 (2816 prints from original blocks, 10 pages text).

WEIGEL, Rudolph, Holzschnitte berühmter Meister. Eine Auswahl . . . in treuen Copien von bewährten Künstlern unserer Zeit. 12 Lieferungen. Leipzig 1851–54.

RENOUVIER, Jules. Des types et des manières des maîtres-graveurs. Montpellier 1853–56.

RENOUVIER, Jules. Histoire de l'origine et des progrès de la gravure dans les Pays-Bas et en Allemagne jusqu'à la fin du XVe siècle. Brussels 1860.

LE BLANC, C. Manuel de l'amateur d'estampes. 4 vols. Paris 1854–89.

TREVIRANUS, L. C. Die Anwendung des Holzschnittes zur bildlichen Darstellung von Pflanzen. Leipzig 1855.

EYE, A. von, and FALKE, Jacob von. Galerie der Meisterwerke altdeutscher Holzschneidekunst in Facsimile-Nachbildungen. Nuremberg 1858–61.

BRUNET, Jacques-Charles. Manuel du libraire. 6 vols. Paris 1860–65. Supplement (by P. Deschamps and G. Brunet). 2 vols. 1878, 1880.

PASSAVANT, J. D. Le Peintre-Graveur. 6 vols. Leipzig 1860–64. (Supplements Bartsch on XV- and XVI-century engravers).

DUPLESSIS, G. La Gravure en France. Paris 1861.

DUPLESSIS, G. Merveilles de la gravure. Paris 1869 (English transl., London 1871; Spanish, Paris 1873).

DUPLESSIS, G. Histoire de la gravure. Paris 1880.

[DODD, W. J.] Specimens of Early Wood-Engraving: being impressions of Woodcuts in the possession of the publisher. Newcastle 1863.

FIRMIN-DIDOT, A. Essai typographique et bibliographique sur l'histoire de la gravure sur bois. Paris 1863.

ANDRESEN, A. Der deutsche Peintre-graveur. 5 vols. Leipzig 1864–78.

BRUSSELS, Bibliothèque Royale. Documents iconographiques et typographiques. Ed. L. Alvin. Brussels 1864–77 (the separate parts quoted in footnotes or special bibliographies below).

WEIGEL, T. O., and ZESTERMANN, A. C. A. Die Anfänge der Druckerkunst in Bild und Schrift an deren frühesten Erzeugnissen in der Weigelschen Sammlung erläutert. 2 vols. Leipzig 1866.

HUMPHREYS, H. Noel. A History of the Art of Printing from its inception to the middle of the XVI century. London 1867.

ENSAYOS FOTOLITOGRAPHICOS. Madrid 1873 (a collection of reproductions of title-pages, pages of books with cuts, woodcut portraits, devices, etc. from Spanish books, XV-XVII centuries).

MEYER, Julius. Allgemeines Künstler-lexicon. 3 vols. Leipzig 1872–85 (incomplete, covering A-BEZ).

REDGRAVE, S. Dictionary of Artists of the English School. London 1874 (revised ed. 1878).

WILLSHIRE, W. H. Introduction to the Study and Collection of Ancient Prints. London 1874 (2nd ed. revised and enlarged 1877).

NUREMBERG, Germanisches Museum. A. Essenwein, Die Holzschnitte des xiv und xv Jahrhunderts. Nuremberg 1875.

SIEURIN, J. Manuel de l'amateur d'illustrations. Paris 1875.

HIRTH, Georg. Der Formenschatz der Renaissance. 2 vols. Leipzig 1877(–78): continued as Der Formenschatz. 33 vols. Leipzig 1879–1911.

HIRTH, G. Kulturgeschichtliches Bilderbuch aus drei Jahrhunderten. 6 vols. Leipzig and Munich [1881–1890]. French edition: Les Grands Illustrateurs. Trois siècles de vie sociale.

HIRTH, G., and MUTHER, R. Meister Holzschnitte aus vier Jahrhunderten. Munich and Leipzig. 1893.

LONDON, British Museum. W. H. Willshire, Descriptive Catalogue of Early Prints in the B.M. German and Flemish Schools. Vol. i. Woodcut and Dotted Prints. London 1879.

WESSELY, J. E. Anleitung zur Kenntniss und zum Sammeln der Werke der Kunstdrucker. Leipzig 1876.

BUTSCH, A. F. Die Bücher-Ornamentik der Renaissance. 2 vols. Leipzig 1878, 1881.

PORTALIS, R., and BERALDI, H. Les Graveurs du xviii siècle. Paris 1880–82.

DUTUIT, E. Manuel de l'amateur d'estampes. Paris 1881–88.

CHAVIGNERIE, E. B. de la, and AUVRAY, L. Dictionnaire général des artistes de l'école française. Paris 1882, 1885 (supplement 1897).

DELABORDE, H. La Gravure. Paris [1882] (English transl. 1886).

LINTON, W. J. History of Wood-Engraving in America. Boston (U.S.A.) and London 1882 (and in the *American Art Review*).

LINTON, W. J. The Masters of Wood-engraving. New Haven (U.S.A.) and London 1889.

BRIVOIS, J. Bibliographie des ouvrages illustrés du xixᵉ siècle. Paris 1883.

MUNICH, Graphische Sammlung. Wilhelm Schmidt, Die frühesten und seltensten Denkmäler des Holz- und Metallschnittes . . . im Kupferstichkabinett in München. Nuremberg [1883].

MUNICH, Graphische Sammlung. Interessante Formschnitte des xv Jahrhunderts aus dem Kupferstichkabinett zu München. Munich 1886.

WOODBERRY, George E. History of Wood-Engraving. New York and London. 1883.

BERALDI, H. Les Graveurs du xixᵉ siècle. 12 vols. Paris 1885–92.

BOUCHOT, H. Le Livre. Paris 1886 (English transl. by E. C. Bigmore, The Printed Book, London 1887, and enlarged edition, The Book, London 1890).

WEALE, W. H. J. Bibliographia Liturgica. Catalogus Missalium Ritus Latini. London 1886 (2nd ed. H. Bohatta 1928).

LIPPMANN, F. Kupferstiche und Holzschnitte alter Meister in Nachbildungen herausgegeben von der Direction der Reichsdruckerei unter Mitwirkung von F. L. Berlin 1889–1900 (English ed. 10 vols. Quaritch, London).

WARNECKE, F. Die deutschen Bücherzeichen. Berlin 1890.

SCHREIBER, W. L. Manuel de l'amateur de la gravure sur bois et sur métal au xvᵉ siècle. 8 vols. Berlin and Leipzig 1891–1910. 2nd ed. in German, Handbuch des Holz- und Metallschnittes des xv Jahrhunderts. 8 vols. Leipzig 1926–30.

    A remarkable catalogue, as nearly complete as possible, of all the single woodcuts and illustrated books of the xv century. Vols. i. and ii. of the 1st ed. include descriptions of 2047 woodcuts, the first subject being the only textile print (*Zeugdruck*) described, while the same field is covered by vols. i.-iv. of the 2nd ed., which with interpolated descriptions includes about 3400 woodcuts, the first nine subjects being textile prints.

Of the 1st ed. vol. iii. is devoted to dotted prints, white-line metal cuts and paste-prints, vol. iv. to block books, vol. v. (2 parts) to books illustrated with woodcuts (Germany, Switzerland, Austria-Hungary, and Scandinavia); vols. vi.-viii., folio, contain the plates, vi., single cuts, vii. and viii., block-books.

Of the 2nd ed. (which only covers the field of vols. i.-iii. of the 1st ed. in its revision), vols. i.-iv. (1926–27), misc. single cuts, Nos. 1-2047 (Nos. 2048-2171, 'Impostures', of the 1st ed., being omitted); vol. v. (1928), dotted prints Nos. 2171-2767; vol. vi. (1928), pasteprints (Nos. 2768-2863); white-line metal cuts (Nos. 2864-2879), supplementary Nos. 2880-2980, of vol. iii. of 1st ed., now referred to their proper place in the catalogue; woodcuts texts without pictures, Nos. 2981-2998; forgeries, Nos. 2048-2170 r; general index of monograms and names, list of passe-partout borders, and attributes of saints; vol. vii. (1929), general historical survey, Iconology, and Calendar of Saints; vol. viii. (1930), addenda and notes on localities of prints which had changed hands.

SCHREIBER, W. L. Holzschnitte in der graphischen Sammlung zu München. Vol. i. Strassburg (Heitz, Einblattdrucke) 1912 (contains a general survey of the development of early woodcut).

SCHREIBER, W. L. Der Buchholzschnitt im xv Jahrhundert in Original-Beispielen. 55 Inkunabeln deutscher, schweizer, niederländischer, tchechischer und italienischer Pressen. Munich 1929 [issued in 100 copies, some with English text; each copy had different original leaves detached from Incunabula].

POLLARD, A. W. Early Illustrated Books. London 1893 (2nd ed. 1917).

POLLARD, A. W. Fine Books. London 1912.

BIBLIOGRAPHICA. Papers on books, their history and art. 3 vols. London 1895–97.

CUNDALL, Joseph. A Brief History of Wood-Engraving. London 1895.

MADAN, Falconer. Oxford Books. Vol. i. (1468–1640). Oxford 1895.

MÜLLER, H. A., and SINGER, H. W. Allgemeines Künstler-lexicon. Frankfurt-a-M. 1895–1901 (Nachträge 1906).

PELLECHET, Marie. Catalogue général des incunables des bibliothèques publiques de France. Vol. i. (1897), A–Biblia; ii. (1905), Biblia Pauperum–Commandements; iii. (1909), Compagnies–Gregorius Magnus. [Marie Pellechet died 1900, and the succeeding volumes were edited by M. L. Polain.]

CRAWFORD, James Ludovic, 26th Earl of. English Broadsides, 1505–1897. Aberdeen 1898.

DÜRER SOCIETY. Notes by Campbell Dodgson and S. Montagu Peartree. London 1898–1911.

LEWINE, J. Bibliography of xviii-century Art and Illustrated Books. London 1898.

PROCTOR, Robert. An Index to the early printed books in the British Museum. Part i. To the year 1500 (with notes of books in the Bodleian Library). London 1898. Supplements for 1899, 1900, 1901, 1902, and Registers to the four supplements by Konrad Burger. London 1906. Part ii. 1501-20. Section i. Germany. London 1903.

HEITZ, Paul. Einblattdrucke des fünfzehnten Jahrhunderts. Strassburg 1899, etc.:—

1. Heitz, P., Neujahrswünsche 1899 (3rd ed. 1909).
2. Schreiber, W. L., Pestblätter 1901.
3. Fäh, A., St. Gallen, 1906.
4. Lehrs, M., Zürich, Stadtbibliothek, 1906.
5. Schreiber, W. L., Tübingen, Universitätsbibliothek, 1906.

6. Schreiber, W. L., Stuttgart, Landesbibliothek, 1907.
7. Molsdorf, W. L., Breslau, Universitätsbibliothek, 1907.
8. Schreiber, W. L., Donaueschingen, Fürstenberg. Sammlung, 1907.
9. Sillib, R., Heidelberg, Universitätsbibliothek, 1907.
10. Leidinger, G., München, Hof- und Staatsbibliothek, part i., 1907 (for part ii. see No. 21).
11. Major, E., Basel, Öffentliche Kunstsammlung, 1908.
12. Molsdorf, W., Niederländische Holzschnitt-Passion Delbecq-Schreiber, 1908 (see also Nos. 29 and 77).
13. Schulz, F. T., and Bezold, G. von. Nuremberg, Nationalmuseum (Schrotblätter), 1908
14. Molsdorf, W., Sammlung W. L. Schreiber, 1908.
15. Leidinger, G., München, Hof- und Staatsbibliothek (Schrotblätter), 1908.
16. Koegler, H., Basel, Universitätsbibliothek, 1909.
17. Clauss, J. M. B., Colmar, und Schlettstadt, Stadtbibliotheken, 1909.
18. Schmidbauer, R., Augsburg, Staats-Bibliothek, 1909.
19. Pfeiffer, M., Bamberg, Bibliothek, part i., 1909 (for part ii. see No. 24).
20. Weis-Liebersdorf, J. E., Eichstätt, Bibliotheken, 1910.
21. Leidinger, G., München, Hof- und Staatsbibliothek, part ii., 1910.
22. Geisberg, M., Dresden, Kupferstichkabinett, 1911.
23. Major, E., Freiburg i. Schw., Barfüsserkloster; Luzern, Kapuzinerkloster, 1911
24. Pfeiffer, M., Bamberg, Biblothek, part ii., 1911.
25. Benziger, C., Bern, Stadtbibliothek, 1911.
26. Röttinger, H., Wien, Albertina, 1911.
27. Vischer, E., Karlsruhe, Landesbibliothek, 1912.
28. Gugenbauer, G., Linz, Studienbibliothek, 1912 (see also No. 63).
29. Gugenbauer, G., Linz, Studienbibliothek. Die niederländische Holzschnitt-Passion Delbecq-Schreiber, 11 Teil, 1912.
30-32. Schreiber, W. L., München, Graphische Sammlung. 3 parts, 1912.
33. Sarnow, E., and Schreiber, W. L., Frankfurt-a.-M., Stadtbibliothek, 1912.
34. Zucker, M., Erlangen, Universitätsbibliothek, 1913.
35. Gugenbauer, G., Ober-Österreich und Salzburg, Klosterbibliotheken, 1913.
36. Schreiber, W. L., Berlin, Bibliothek, 1913.
37. Stengel, W., Nuremberg, Kupferstichkabinett, 1913.
38. Schreiber, W. L., Amberg, Colmar, Darmstadt, Dillingen, Hamburg, Mainz, Metten, München, Schlettstadt, Schwabach, Strassburg, Wiesbaden—Öffentliche und private Bibliotheken und Sammlungen, 1913.
39. Schreiber, W. L., Stuttgart, Bibliothek, 1913.
40. Baumeister, E., Maihingen, Öttingen-Wallerstein Sammlung, part i., 1913 (for part ii. see No. 52).
41. Schreiber, W. L., Meisterwerke der Metallschneidekunst, part i., Danzig, Pelplin, Riga, 1914 (for parts ii. and iii. see Nos. 43 and 62).
42. Eichler, F., Graz, Universitätsbibliothek, 1914.
43. Schreiber, W. L., Meisterwerke der Metallschneidekunst, part ii., Berlin, Darmstadt, Erfurt, Halle, Leipzig, London, Münster, Oxford, Strassburg, Ulm, Wittenberg, Würzburg, Zürich, 1914.
44. Zaretzky, O., Köln, Sammlungen, 1914.
45. Escherich, M., Ermlitz, Sammlung Apel, 1916.

46. Escherich, M., Hannover, Kestner-Museum, 1916.
47. Escherich, M., Darmstadt, Landesmuseum, part i., 1916 (for part ii. see No. 56).
48. Escherich, M., Dresden, Prinzl. Sekundogenitur-Bibliothek, 1916.
49. Henkel, M. D., Holländische Sammlungen: Amsterdam, Haag, Haarlem, 1918.
50. Major, E., Aarau, Basel, Romont, St. Gallen, Zürich—öffentliche und private Sammlungen, 1918.
51. Baumeister, E., München, Universitäts-bibliothek, 1920.
52. Baumeister, E., Maihingen, Öttingen-Wallerstein Sammlung, part ii., 1920.
53. Escherich, M., Frankfurt-a.-M., Städelsches Kunstinstitut, 1923.
54. Schreiber, W. L., Stuttgart, Kupferstichkabinett, and Kloster Odilienberg, 1923.
55. Schreiber, W. L., Bibliotheken Nord-deutschlands: Braunschweig, Halle, Königsberg, Leipzig, Magdeburg, Michelstadt, 1923.
56. Escherich, M., Darmstadt, Landesmuseum, Part ii., Schrotblätter, 1923.
57. Schreiber, W. L., St. Petersburg, Öffentliche Bibliothek, 1925.
58. Schreiber, W. L., Wolfenbüttel, Landesbibliothek, 1925.
59. Schreiber, W. L., Weimar, 1925.
60. Schreiber, W. L., Sammlung P. Heitz, Strassburg, 1925.
61. Schreiber, W. L., Strassburg, Landesbibliothek, Universitätsbibliothek, Bezirksarchiv; Trier, Stadtbibliothek, 1926.
62. Schreiber, W. L., Meisterwerke der Metallschneidekunst, part iii., Berlin, Breslau, Budapest, Cambridge, London, München, Paris, Wien, Würzburg, 1926.
63. Schreiber, W. L., Linz, Studienbibliothek; Innsbruck, Universitätsbibliothek; Stift Schlierbach; Salzburg, Studienbibliothek, 1927.
64. Schreiber, W. L., Gotha und Veste Coburg, 1928.
65. Schreiber, W. L., New York, James C. McGuire Collection, part i., 1928 (for part ii. see No. 72).
66. Schreiber, W. L., Hamburg, Kunsthalle and Museum für Kunst und Gewerbe; Lübeck, Stadtbibliothek, 1928.
67. Schreiber, W. L., Zürich, 1928.
68. Schreiber, W. L., Ravenna, Biblioteca Classense, 1929.
69. Ameisenowa, Zofja, Polen, (see also No. 74), 1929.
70. Schreiber, W. L., Gotha, Landesmuseum (Schrotblätter), 1929.
71. Schreiber, W. L., New York, Pierpont Morgan Library, 1929.
72. Schreiber, W. L., New York, James C. McGuire, part ii., 1930.
73. Schreiber, W. L., Minneapolis, Herschel V. Jones Collections, 1930.
74. Sawicka, Stanislawa, Polen, 1931.
75. Schreiber, W. L., Die Legende von S. Catharina von Alexandria. Holztafeldruck von Michel Schorpp, auf Schloss Hohen Liechtenstein bei Vaduz, 1931.
76. Schreiber, W. L., Kassetten-Holzschnitte, 1931.
77. Heitz, Paul, Vervollständigte Holzschnittfolge der Passion Delbecq-Schreiber nach dem ersten Antwerpener Drucke des Adriaen van Berghen von 1500, 1932.
78. Mabbott, T. O., Mabbott Collection, New York, 1933.
79. Heitz, P., Italienische Einblattdrucke, part i., Bassano und Berlin, 1933.
80. Heitz, P., Italienische Einblattdrucke, part ii., Bremen, Düsseldorf, Hamburg, London, Modena, 1933.
81. Heitz, P., Italienische Einblattdrucke, part iii., Modena, Oxford, Paris, Pavia, Prag, Prato, 1934.

82. Heitz, P., Italienische Einblattdrucke, part iv., Ravenna, Rome, Salzburg, Venice, Vienna, 1934.
83. Heitz, P., Italienische Einblattdrucke, part v., Berlin, Braunschweig, Cambridge (Mass.), Cortona, Innsbruck, London, Maihingen, New York, St. Leonhart bei Tamsweg, Wien, 1935.
84. Cohn, W., Holz- und Metallschnitte einer Süd-deutschen Sammlung, 1934.
85. Cohn, W., Holz- und Mettallschnitte in Aachen, Bamberg, Berlin, Breslau, Darmstadt, Dresden, Göttingen, Gotha, 1935.

HEITZ, Paul. Primitive Holzschnitte. Einzelbilder des xv Jahrhunderts mit 75 Abbildungen. Strassburg 1913. This and the following are chiefly selected plates from Heitz's series of *Einblattdrucke*, with short introductions.

HEITZ, Paul. Hundertfünfzig Einzelbilder des xv Jahrhunderts. Strassburg 1918.

WHITMAN, Alfred. Print-Collector's Handbook. London 1901 (6th ed., M. C. Salaman, 1912).

BOUCHOT, H., Un Ancêtre de la gravure sur bois. Paris 1902.

BAER, Leo. Die illustirten Historienbücher des xv Jahrhunderts. Strassburg 1903.

LONDON, British Museum. Campbell Dodgson, Catalogue of Early German and Flemish Woodcuts preserved in the Department of Prints and Drawings, B.M. London.

Vol. i. (1903). Part 1. xv century: single cuts and other prints; block-books; woodcuts from books. Part 2. First half of the xvi century: Div. A.—School of Nuremberg.

Vol. ii. (1911). First half of the xvi century (*continued*).

Div. B.—School of Augsburg.

Div. C.—Schools of Swabia, Bavaria, Austria, and Poland.

Div. D.—School of Saxony.

Index to the above, and a concordance with Schreiber's *Manuel*, by A. Lauter. Munich 1925.

LONDON, British Museum. Campbell Dodgson, Woodcuts and Metal Cuts of the xv Century (illustrated edition of an exhibition guide). London 1914.

LONDON, British Museum. Campbell Dodgson, Woodcuts of the xv Century in the Department of Prints and Drawings. 2 vols. London 1934–35.

PARIS, Bibliothèque Nationale. H. Bouchot, Les deux cents incunables xylographiques du Département des Estampes. Paris 1903.

HAEBLER, Conrad. Typen-Repertorium der Wiegendrucke.

i., Deutschland, etc. Halle 1905.

ii., Italien, Niederlande, Frankreich, Spanien, Portugal, England. Leipzig and New York 1908.

iii., Tabellen. Leipzig 1909–22.

HAEBLER, Conrad. Die deutschen Buchdrucker des xv Jahrhunderts im Auslande. Munich 1924.

KRISTELLER, Paul. Kupferstich und Holzschnitt in vier Jahrhunderten. Berlin 1905 (4th ed. 1922).

GRAPHISCHE GESELLSCHAFT. Berlin 1906–22. Several volumes on woodcuts, to which reference is made in the various sections of this book.

WURZBACH, A. von. Niederländisches Künstler-lexikon. Vienna and Leipzig 1906–11.

LACOMBE, P. Livres d'heures imprimés au xvᵉ et au xviᵉ siècles conservés dans les bibliothèques publiques de Paris. Catalogue. Paris 1907.

THIEME, U., and BECKER, F., Allgemeines Lexikon der bildenden Künstler. Leipzig 1907, etc. (in progress).

NEW YORK, Pierpont Morgan Library. Catalogue of Manuscripts and Early Printed Books With preface by A. W. Pollard. Early Printed Books. 3 vols. London 1907

Vol. i., Xylographica, Germany and Switzerland.

Vol. ii., Italy and France.

Vol. iii., France (*continued*), Netherlands, Spain, England.

BERLIN, Kupferstichkabinett. M. Lehrs, Holzschnitte der ersten Hälfte des xv Jahrhunderts. *Graphische Gesellschaft*, vii. Berlin 1908.

BERLIN, Kupferstichkabinett. P. Kristeller, Holzschnitte im Kupferstichkabinett zu Berlin. Zweite Reihe. *Graphische Gesellschaft*. Berlin 1915.

JENNINGS, Oscar. Early Woodcut Initials. London 1908.

LONDON, British Museum. Catalogue of Books printed in the xv Century. London 1908, etc. (in progress).

i. (1908), Xylographica; Books, Germany: Mainz, Strassburg, Bamberg, Cologne.

ii. (1912), Germany (*continued*): Eltvil-Trier.

iii. (1913), Germany (*concluded*): Leipzig-Pforzheim; German-speaking Switzerland; Austria-Hungary.

iv. (1916), Italy: Subiaco and Rome.

v. (1924), Italy (*continued*): Venice.

vi. (1930), Italy (*continued*): Foligno, Ferrara, Florence, Milan, Bologna, Naples, Perugia, Treviso.

vii. (1935), Italy (*concluded*).

DIEDERICHS, Eugen. Deutsches Leben der Vergangenheit in Bildern. Ein Atlas mit 1760 Nachbildungen alter Kupfer- und Holzschnitte aus den xv-xviii Jahrhunderten. 3 vols. Jena 1908, 1909.

ROSENTHAL, L. La Gravure. Paris 1908.

WEITENKAMPF, Frank. How to appreciate Prints. New York 1908 (London 1909).

MURRAY, C. Fairfax. Hugh W. Davies, Catalogue of a Collection of Early French Books in the Library of C. F. M. London (privately printed) 1910.

WIGGISHOFF, J. C. Les Graveurs et les livres illustrés des origines à Louis XIV. Paris 1910.

NUREMBERG, Germanisches Museum. W. Stengel, Holzschnitte im Kupferstichkabinett zu N. *Graphische Gesellschaft*, iii. Berlin 1913.

BOHATTA, H. Bibliographie des livres d'heures. Vienna 1909 (2nd ed. 1924).

BOHATTA, H. Liturgische Bibliographie des xv Jahrhunderts. Vienna 1911 (excludes *Horae*).

BOHATTA, H. Katalog der liturgischen Drucke des xv und xvi Jahrhunderts in der herzogl. Parma'schen Bibliothek in Schwarzau am Steinfeld. Vienna 1909.

BOHATTA, H. Livres de liturgie imprimés aux xvᵉ et xv1ᵉ siècles faisant partie de la Bibliothèque du Duc Robert de Parme. Ed. Seymour de Ricci. Sale, Paris (L. Giraud-Badin) 1932.

LONDON, Guildhall Library. C. Dodgson, Holzschnitte der Guildhall-Bibliothek zu London. *Graphische Gesellschaft*, xx. Berlin 1914.

RICHTER, Emil H. Prints. Their Technique and History. Boston (U.S.A.) 1914.

SINGER, H. W. Die moderne Graphik. Leipzig 1914 (2nd ed. 1920).

MANCHESTER, John Rylands Library. C. Dodgson, Woodcuts of the xv Century. Manchester 1915.

PLOMER, H. R. Short History of English Printing, 1476–1900. London 1915.

FRIEDLÄNDER, Max J. Der Holzschnitt. Berlin 1916 (2nd ed. 1921, 3rd ed. 1926).

GUSMAN, Pierre. La Gravure sur bois et d'épargne sur métal du xivᵉ au xxᵉ siècle. Paris 1916.

GUSMAN, Pierre. L'Art de la gravure. Gravure sur bois et taille d'épargne. Historique et technique. Paris 1933.

VIENNA, Hofbibliothek. Die Einblattdrucke des xv Jahrhunderts in der Hofbibliothek zu Wien. i. F. M. Haberditzl, Die Holzschnitte. ii. A. Stix, Die Schrotschnitte. Vienna 1920.

WEITENKAMPF, F. Illustrated Books of the past four centuries. A record of the exhibition held in the Print Gallery of the New York Public Library in 1919. New York 1920.

BYBLIS. Miroir des arts du livre et de l'estampe. Vols. i.-x. Paris 1921–31 (contains numerous articles on woodcuts by P. Gusman and others).

MANTEUFFEL, K. Zoege von. Der deutsche Holzschnitt. Seine Aufstiege im xv Jahrhundert und seine grosse Blüte in der ersten Hälfte des xvi Jahrhunderts. Munich [1921].

SULLIVAN, Edmund J. The Art of Illustration. London 1921.

WESTHEIM, Paul. Das Holzschnittbuch. Potsdam 1921.

BOCK, E. Die deutsche Graphik. Munich 1922.

PFISTER, Kurt. Die primitiven Holzschnitte. Munich 1922.

GERLACH, Martin. Das alte Buch und seine Ausstattung vom xv bis zum xix Jahrhundert. Mit einem Vorwort von H. Röttinger. Die Quelle, Mappe xiii. Vienna, Leipzig [1915].

COURBÖIN, F. Histoire illustrée de la gravure en France. Paris 1923, 1929.

COURBOIN, F. La Gravure française des origines jusqu'à 1900. Paris 1923.

COURBOIN, F., and ROUX, N. La Gravure française. Essai de bibliographie. 3 vols. Paris 1928–29.

GEISBERG, Max. Der Deutsche Einblatt-Holzchnitt in der ersten Hälfte des xvi Jahrhunderts. 43 portfolios of facsimiles, with Gesamtverzeichnisse, and Bilder-Katalog (1600 verkleinerte Wiedergaben). Munich (Hugo Schmidt) 1923–30.

OSLER, Sir William. Incunabula Medica (1467–80), Bibliographical Society, Illustrated Monograph xix. London 1923.

DELEN, A. J. J. Histoire de la gravure dans les anciens Pays-Bas des origines jusq'à la fin du xviii Siècle. 1re Partie. Des origines jusqu'en 1500. Paris and Brussels 1924. 2de Partie. Le xvie Siècle. Paris, 1934.

MARTIN, Henry (and others). Le Livre français illustré des origines à la fin du Second Empire. Paris 1924.

SCHLOSSER, Julius. Die Kunstliteratur. Ein Handbuch zur Quellenkunde der neueren Kuntsgeschichte. Vienna 1924.

AUDIN, Marius. Essai sur les graveurs de bois en France au xviiie siècle. Paris 1925.

AUDIN, Marius. Le Livre. Son illustration, sa décoration. Paris 1926.

AUDIN, Marius. Le Livre français. Paris 1930.

AUDIN, Marius. Étapes de la gravure sur bois. Paris 1933.

GESAMTKATALOG DER WIEGENDRUCKE. Leipzig 1925, etc. (in progress).

    Vol. i. (1925), Abano—Alexius.

    Vol. ii. (1926), Alfarabius—Arznei.

    Vol. iii. (1928), Ascher—Bernardus Claravallensis.

    Vol. iv. (1930), Bernardus de Cracovia—Brentius.

    Vol. v. (1932), Bréviaire—Byenbroeck.

    Vol. vi. (1934), Caballus—Confessione.

FUNCK, M. Le Livre belge à gravures. Guide de l'amateur de livres illustrés imprimés en Belgique avant le xviiie siècle. Paris and Brussels 1925.

KLEBS, A. C., and DROZ, Eugénie. Remèdes contre la Peste. Facsimilés, notes et listes bibliographiques des incunables sur la Peste. Paris 1925.

KLEBS, A. C. Die ersten gedruckten Pestschriften. Munich 1926.

NUREMBERG, Germanisches Museum und Stadtbibliothek. Martin Weinberger, Die Formschnitte des Katherinenklosters zu N. Munich 1925.

OLSCHKI, Leo S. Le Livre illustré au xve siècle. Florence 1926.

SUGDEN, A. V., and EDMONDSON, J. L. History of English Wall-paper, 1509–1914. London 1926.

KLEMPERER, Victor von. Frühdrucke aus der Bücherei V. von K. Dresden 1927 (introduction by Conrad Haebler).

PARIS, Bibliothèque Nationale. P. A. Lemoisne, Les Xylographies du XIVe et du XVe siècles au Cabinet des Estampes. 2 vols. Paris and Brussels 1927, 1930.

BLISS, Douglas Percy. A History of Wood-Engraving. London 1928.

BLISS, Douglas Percy. The Last Ten Years of Wood-Engraving. *Print Collector's Quarterly*, xxi. (1934), 251.

CZECHOSLOVAKIA. Zdeněk v. Tobolka, Die Einblattdrucke des XV Jahrhunderts im Gebiete der Cechoslovakischen Republik. Prague 1928–1930.

AZZI VITELLESCHI, Giustiniano degli. Über eine unbekannte Verwertung des Italienischen Holzschnittes im XVI und XVII Jahrhundert. *Mitteil. der Gesellsch. für vervielfält Kunst*, 1929, p. 37.

LONDON, Victoria and Albert Museum. C. C. Oman, Catalogue of Wall-Papers. London 1929.

OXFORD, Ashmolean Museum. C. Dodgson, Woodcuts of the XV Century, in the Ashmolean Museum. Oxford 1929.

JOHNSON, A. F. Decorative Initial Letters. London 1931.

POLAIN, M. L. Catalogue des livres imprimés au XV siècle des bibliothèques de Belgique. 4 vols. Brussels 1932.

SLEIGH, Bernard. Wood-engraving since eighteen-ninety. London 1932.

COHN, W. Untersuchungen zur Geschichte des deutschen Einblattholzschnitts im 2. Drittel des XV Jahrhunderts. Strassburg 1934.

KIRCHNER, Joachim, LÖFFLER, Karl, and OLBRICH, Wilhelm, Lexicon des gesamten Buchwesens. Leipzig, 1934 (in progress).

DONATI, Lamberto. Di alcune ignote zilografie del secolo XV nella Biblioteca Vaticana. *Gutenberg-Jahrbuch*, 1934, p. 73.

DAVIES, H. W. Devices of the Early Printers 1457–1560. London 1935.

Fig. 29. Albrecht Dürer. Tail-piece from his *Underweysung der Messung*, 1528.

CHAPTER III

THE ORIGIN OF WOODCUT WITH A SURVEY OF SINGLE CUTS BEFORE THE PERIOD OF BOOK-ILLUSTRATION (CHIEFLY IN THE FIRST HALF OF THE XV CENTURY)

THE present work is concerned with the Art of Woodcut only in so far as it aims at producing impressions on paper, or on allied material such as vellum. It is also limited in its scope to European practice and tradition.

It is impossible, however, to embark on the subject without a short review of the origin of the art in the East, and some reference to the use of wood blocks for various other purposes during the Middle Ages in Europe.

In principle, the impression of seals and the stamping of bricks, metal and other substances are crafts allied to that of the printing of wood blocks on paper: and these crafts were practised in early periods in Ancient Egypt, and well before the Christian era in China. But there is no trace of blocks having been used in Egypt before the Christian era to multiply characters or any details of decorative design, in black or colour, on papyrus documents, mummy cases or in any surface impression.

The first use to which wood blocks appear to have been applied in Egypt was in the printing of textiles, and the earliest examples at present known date from about the VI or VII centuries A.D.

It was about the same period that block-printing, whether on textiles or paper, appears to have been introduced in China,[1] and it is here that the earliest impressions on paper are known. The Chinese official record dates the invention of paper in the year A.D. 105. But the great impetus towards multiplication by printing does not seem to have arisen until the introduction of Tantric Buddhism into China in the VI century, with its devotion to Sanskrit formulae and charms. Printing in its most elementary form was certainly practised by the Chinese at an earlier date (perhaps before the end of the II century A.D.) if we regard as such their rubbings from inscriptions incised in stone.[2] But, so far as concerns wooden blocks, the earliest manifestations are the stamps of Buddha figures occurring

---

[1] See in particular T. F. Carter, *The Invention of Printing in China and its Spread Westward*, New York, 1925; L. Binyon, *Catalogue of Chinese and Japanese Woodcuts in the British Museum*, London, 1926; A. Waley, *Note on the Invention of Woodcuts*, New China Review, 1919.

[2] Later it was a practice to record the design of paintings by outlines incised on stone.

frequently in MS. rolls. Actual examples of the stamps themselves in handles (which show how they were used) have been found in Eastern Turkestan, and there seems good reason to date them before A.D. 800. As larger figures came to be required, the idea of making a print by rubbing instead of stamping would naturally occur, and lead to the development of actual block-printing.

The first authenticated prints rubbed from wood blocks (though here not from pictures but only from text) are the Buddhist charms printed in Japan and distributed between A.D. 764 and 770 in accordance with an edict of the Empress Shōtoku in A.D. 764, of which there are examples in the British Museum in addition to many remaining in Japanese temples.[1]

The earliest picture printed from a wood block to which a certain date can be assigned occurs in a roll of the *Diamond Sutra* printed by Wang Chieh in 868.[2] It belongs to the great collections acquired for the British Museum by Sir Aurel Stein from the Cave of the Thousand Buddhas near Tun-huang in Eastern Turkestan in 1907, a cave which had been discovered and reopened by a Taoist priest in 1900. But to judge from the accomplishment of its art there is little doubt that it must have had its predecessors. Many stamped or printed textiles also occur in the same collections. Colour-printing from wood blocks also dates from about the same period, for several examples of colour borders, printed from more than one block, occur in the Stein series.

In comparison with developments in Europe it is of interest to note that in China block-books (i.e. books in which both type and pictures were printed from blocks) preceded books printed from movable type by several centuries. The first record of the use of movable type goes back to about 1041–49,[3] but these early types, first made of earthenware, and a few

---

[1] Since Dr. Carter's work several prints of a single series have been found bearing the date A.D. 607. They are each about 12½ inches square, with a drawing of some Divinity with attendants above the inscription, which appears to be partly printed from a block, and partly perhaps (in the variable portion of the inscription) from stamps. Two impressions in the collection of Mr. Matsuda at Tokio were reproduced in the *Kokka*, July 1925, No. 416. Two others were exhibited at Yamanaka's, London, December 1927 (*Exhibition of Early Chinese Ceramic Art*, etc., Catalogue No. 49). They are reported to have come from the Cave of the Thousand Buddhas at Tun-huang in Chinese Turkestan, the site of Sir Aurel Stein's discoveries. Dr. H. A. Giles considers the script of a character later than the date of the inscription, and in consequence questions their authenticity.

[2] See L. Binyon, *Catalogue of Japanese and Chinese Woodcuts in the British Museum*, 1916, p. 576.

[3] But cf. p. 66, note 1.

decades later of tin, were never largely used. More success was achieved with wooden type which was in use about 1300; improvements were introduced by Wang Cheng about 1314 making accurate type-setting possible, and about 1390 the casting of metal types was introduced in Korea. But though the introduction of movable type in China preceded the practice in Europe, it did not continue the same uninterrupted development, and gradually fell out of use in favour of the old block-printing, until the XIX century brought European methods to the East.

And it must always be remembered that Chinese movable type is a very different problem from movable type in a Western language. The Chinese type, representing as it does a graph, is more like a little block in itself, which could be consistently cut in a convenient square shape, presenting none of the difficulties that minute characters offer to the Western type-founder.[1]

Apart from this distinction in the general character of Oriental type (even should it have been eventually cast in metal), the characteristic which most clearly separated the European from the Oriental development lay in the introduction of the printing-press, which contained the essence of progress and large production.

In Europe as in the East the use of small blocks for stamping probably preceded the practice of printing from wood blocks by the rubber or in the press. These stamps were used by royalties, notaries and other public officials for their sign-manuals. For royal signatures they are said to have been in use from the time of Charlemagne, if not before;[2] but the earliest royal signature to which I can refer with certainty as stamped is that of Henry VI. of England in 1436, and the practice only became common in the reign of Henry VIII. and Elizabeth.[3]

XVIII-century writers on Diplomatic have claimed certain notarial signatures of the XIII and XIV centuries as stamped,[4] but A. Giry in his *Manuel*

---

[1] The essential distinction between the Oriental and Western type is rightly emphasised by Victor Scholderer, *Wood and Metal in the Invention of Printing*, in the Woodcut (an annual), London 1929, p. 25. See also G. Mori, *Was hat Gutenberg erfunden. Ein Ruckblick auf die Frühtechnik des Schriftgusses*, Gutenberg Gesellschaft, Mainz 1921 (Beilage zum XIXten Jahresbericht, 1919–20).

[2] See Mabillon, *Diplomatique*, lib. ii. cap. 10.

[3] Sir Henry Maxwell Lyte, *Historical Notes on the Great Seal of England*, London 1926, pp. 82, 91, 92.

[4] D. E. Baringer, *Clavis Diplomatica*, Hanover 1754. For a recent study of the subject see Friedrich Leist, *Die Notariatssignete*, Leipzig [1897].

de Diplomatique (Paris 1894, p. 605) contests these earlier claims, and was unable to certify any before the XVII century.

Textile printing was common throughout the Middle Ages in Europe, and Dr. Forrer, who has published the most valuable works on the subject,[1] describes numerous examples from the VI century onwards. Cennino Cennini, to whose description of the process we have already referred,[2] begins his chapter by referring to two uses of the process, the decoration of children's fustian gowns (*guarnelli*), and for hangings for reading-desks in churches.[3]

Until about the XIV century the examples known are decorative patterns in which printing is repeated from one or more wood blocks. From about the second half of the XIV century there are occasional examples which correspond more nearly to the early woodcuts on paper in being, or including, pictured subjects. The most important of these is the *Sion Printed Textile* (fig. 30)[4] once in the collection of Mr. d'Odet, who acquired it at S. Maurice in the Valais (Switzerland), and now in the Historisches Museum at Basle. Opinion as to its origin is divided between assigning it to France (the region of Avignon), or to North Italy.[5] Another example of about 1400, once in Forrer's collection, a *Reading-desk Hanging* from Innichen (Tirol), shows two subjects printed from separate blocks set in a decorative border (reproduced Forrer, 1898, pl. xx).

A very attractive example is the *St. Anne, with the Virgin and Seraphim* [6]

---

[1] R. Forrer, *Die Zeugdrucke der byzantinischen, romanischen, gotischen und späteren Kunstepochen*, Strassburg 1894; *Die Kunst des Zeugdrucks vom Mittelalter bis zur Empirezeit*, Strassburg 1898; *Les Imprimeurs de tissus dans leur relations historiques et artistiques avec les corporations*, Strassburg 1898.

[2] See p. 4.

[3] *Perche all' arte del pennello ancora s' appartiene di certi lavori dipinti in panno lino che son buoni da guarnelli di putti o ver fanciulli, e per certi leggii di Chiese. . . .*

[4] First described by F. Keller, *Die Tapete von Sitten*, Mitteil. der Antiquar. Gesellschaft, Zürich 1857, p. 139. There is a fragment of the same textile in the Landesmuseum, Zürich.

[5] Bouchot and Kristeller favouring the former; Keller, followed by L. Venturi (*L'Arte*, vi. 265), the latter region.

[6] Reproduced by Forrer, 1894, pl. xxx, and 1898, fig. 7. A drawing which gives the same subject in reverse, and without the architectural setting, is in the Germanisches Nationalmuseum. It is probably an original study by the cutter, though it is possibly a few decades earlier, and its style adds support to the locality of origin (see Th. Hampe, *Der Zeugdruck mit der Heiligen Anna und einige altkölnische Handzeichnungen*. Mitteil. aus dem Germanischen Nationalmuseum, 1897, p. 91). It is also reproduced in R. Forrer, *Les Imprimeurs de tissus dans leurs relations historiques et artistiques avec les corporations*, Strassburg 1898, fig. 23; and in H. Sauermann,

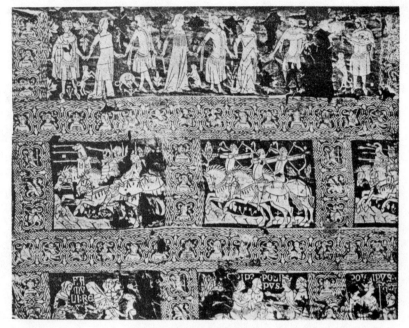

Fig. 30. The Sion printed textile (part).

(Germanisches Nationalmuseum, Nuremberg, from the Forrer Collection), which came from a church at Euskirchen, near Cologne, and is probably a local work of about 1440. A *Crucifixion* on a textile in the Oesterreichisches Museum für Kunst und Industrie, Vienna,[1] is flanked by two impressions of an ornament panel, and by borders.

Two other examples in the same Museum at Nuremberg, a *Death of the Virgin* and a *Resurrection*,[2] where embroidered work is partially worn away, show cuts printed on the linen as a basis or guide for the embroiderer. But this was probably an uncommon practice.

Deutsche Stylisten. Handzeichnungen altdeutscher Meister, Munich 1914, pl. 2. Dr. Kristeller has attributed the *St. Anne,* both drawing and print, to the North Italian School, but the character of the drawing in particular, in conjunction with the origin of the cut, seems to me against his view. Kristeller compared the character of the Gothic detail with that of the Venetian blockbook Passion.

[1] Reproduced, A. Weixlgärtner, *Ungedruckte Stiche,* Vienna Jahrbuch xxix. (1910/11), p. 280.

[2] Described by A. Essenwein, *Aelteste Druckerzeugnisse im Germanischen Museum,* Anzeiger für Kunde der deutschen Vorzeit, Neue Folge, Nuremberg 1872, p. 241.

Here and there textile prints, or fragments, occur in regular print collections, their preservation being sometimes due, in the case of ordinary woodcut, to their having been pasted inside bindings. This is the case with a *Christ on the Cross* (S. 1 b) in the Munich Library, from the binding of a MS. of 1444 from a convent at Ebersberg in Upper Bavaria (*Einbl.* x., Leidinger, pl. 1). A print of this character, and others such as the *Annunciation* and *Virgin and Child* in the Historisches Museum at Basle (*Einbl.* l., Emil Major, pls. 27 and 28), which formed part of an altar front in a church at Illgau in the Muotathal in Switzerland (Canton Schwyz), probably dating about 1450–75, show that most early woodcuts might serve, as far as their character and style is concerned, for printing either on textile or paper.[1] The Basle examples in particular, with their linear shading in addition to outline, seem more adapted to paper, and may in fact have been originally so intended. The empty banderole on the *Annunciation* would also be more fitted for a MS. addition on paper though it might also be argued that an inscription could be embroidered over the print on the linen.

The printers of textiles may also have sometimes pulled impressions on paper as patterns, and some of the earliest prints on paper (known for the most part only in single impressions) may have been made for this purpose. But unless a textile print is found to correspond, this can only be conjecture. Two ornamental designs in the British Museum printed on paper (each showing a *Griffin within a Wreath*, one in black outline, the other largely in black surfaces, S. 2004, fig. 31, and 2005), and a *Seated Gazelle* at Nuremberg (S. 1 h and 2003; Essenwein, 33; Forrer, *Die Zeugdrucke*, 1894, p. 29 and fig. 11), are all probably patterns of this sort, from wood blocks intended for textile or other decorative printing.

Another possible example of a pattern is the *Virgin and Child in a Glory* in the Stadtbibliothek at Nuremberg, from the old Convent of St. Catherine (S. 1048 b), which is printed in a white pigment on a green-tinted paper. But it is so well printed that it might on the other hand be intended in itself as a decorative subject for an altar in imitation of a textile.[2]

---

[1] Just as blocks and plates are known to have been used at later periods (e.g. XVIII century) for the various purposes of printing on paper, textile or pottery.

[2] A book of recipes for the preparation of colours for textile printers, now in the Stadtbibliothek, Nuremberg, came from the Nunnery of St. Catherine in the same city (edited by Hans Bosch, Mitteil. des Germanischen Museums, 1893, p. 7), a strong support for Forrer's suggestion that this convent was a busy centre in the production of textile printing. Cf. Martin Weinberger, *Die Formschnitte des Katherinenklosters zu Nürnberg*, Munich 1925.

Bouchot[1] suggested that the wood block in the collection of M. Jules Protat at Macon,[2] generally known as *le Bois Protat* (fig. 32), was intended for printing on textile rather than on paper. The block, which measures about $23\frac{1}{2} \times 9$ inches, and about 1 inch thick, contains on the obverse part of a *Crucifixion*, and, on the reverse, part of the angel's figure in an *Annunciation*. It was discovered in 1898 in the neighbourhood of the abbey

Fig. 31. Griffin within a Wreath. S. 2004.

of La Ferté-sur-Grosne (Saône-et-Loire), in the old Duchy of Burgundy, and from its costume and general style is probably localised rightly as work of this region, of a date round about the year 1400.

Bouchot's reasons for thinking that the block was intended for textile printing are as follows: (1) that at the early period to which he assigns it paper would be less available than textile;[3] (2) that the size of the whole composition (which he thought would require three more blocks of the same size to complete) would militate against the use of paper, several sheets being required for so large a subject; (3) that the block being cut on both sides favours the probability of its use for printing on stuff. Bouchot's contention is probably correct, but I doubt his reasons. There are existing blocks cut on both sides which were certainly intended for printing on paper, e.g. the *St. Sebastian* and the *Sacred Monogram* (S. 1678 and 1812;

---

[1] Bouchot, *Un Ancêtre de la gravure sur bois*, Paris 1902.

[2] The block is now in the possession of his son M. Émile Protat, to whom I owe my illustration. M. Jules Protat had one print pulled by hand from the original block. From this impression transfer was made to a lithographic stone, from which prints have been taken.

[3] See pp. 78, 79. Bouchot dated it conjecturally about 1370.

Fig. 32. Le Bois Protat. The original block and a modern impression.

C.D., A. 103 and 115) in the British Museum; the *Good Shepherd* (S. 839) and the *Holy Trinity* (S. 737) in Paris; another German block of about 1460–1470 with a *Crucifixion* and a *Pietà* once in the Figdor Collection, Vienna,[1]

[1] Modern impressions reproduced in Arpad Weixlgärtner, *Ungedruckte Stiche*, Vienna Jahrbuch xxix., 1910/11, figs. 47 and 48.

the *Twenty-Four Augsburg Saints* (S. 1766, C.D., A. 110) from the Dibdin Collection, and now in the John Rylands Library, Manchester, and a late xvi-century example in the John Rylands Library, Manchester, 14 × 11 in., with a *Virgin and Child and Saint Anne* on the obverse and a *Pietà* on the reverse. In regard to his second point I think that one further block might have been sufficient to complete the subject, and finally his conjectured date is possibly on the early side.

One of the finest examples of a xvi-century block probably intended for textile printing is the *Vine Pattern with Satyr Family*, once known under the name of Dürer (on whose engraving the figures are based), but now generally attributed to H. S. Beham. Only paper impressions are known, but Lippmann probably rightly interpreted its decorative purpose in reproducing the pattern in the style of a coloured textile on the cover of his edition of Dürer's drawings.[1]

Another design of the same period and style (*Pomegranate and Vase on a black ground*) bears in one state the address of Nicolaus Meldemann of Nuremberg (Geisberg, *Der Deutsche Einblatt-Holzschnitt*, 767; Wolfenbüttel, Erlangen, and fragments of the same or similar woodcut designs at Brussels, S. ii. 64173 and 64174, and Paris, *Réserve* 951).

The practice of using blocks for *stamping patterns on leather*, most commonly for *book-bindings*, is of course analogous to textile printing. In general, metal relief-blocks are stamped blind, and two examples might be cited in the British Museum, a *Scholar at a Desk* on the cover of Rainerus de Pisis, *Pantheologia* (Basle 1475), and *Augustus and the Sibyl*, on the cover of Ovid, *Epistolae* (Lyon 1528).

Occasional examples occur of blocks (either wood or metal) printed in black line on a leather book-binding, e.g. a *St. Benedict* (S. 1268 a; Berlin, Staatl. Bibl., *Einbl.* xxxvi., pl. 13), on the binding of a Basle book of 1484, a block which might have been cut some time earlier at the Convent of Reinhausen, near Göttingen; and a *Pilgrim receiving the Eucharist with two other figures*, of the earlier part of the xv century, on a binding in the Royal Archives at Brussels.[2]

Three fragments of decorative designs once in the Benedictine Convent

---

[1] See Dürer Society, vi., 1903, xxvii; Pauli, *Beham*, 1342, 1342a; Geisberg, *Der Deutsche Einblatt-Holzschnitt*, 769.

[2] See A. Delstanche, *Un Incunable de la xylographie imprimé sur une reliure*, Brussels 1905 (Extr. de la Revue des Bibliothèques et Archives de Belgique, tome iii. fasc. 3). It should be added that the plates of dotted prints are also used for stamping on bindings. See J. Theele, *Schrotdruckplatten auf Kölner Einbänden*. Gutenberg Jahrbuch, Mainz 1927, p. 256. Cf. p. 176.

of Melk (on the Danube, between Linz and Vienna) printed from wood blocks have also been described as on leather. So at least stated Albert Camesina, who orginally published and reproduced them in 1864.[1] They were then preserved on the binding of certain xv-century manuscripts, though in Camesina's opinion perhaps originally used to cover choir seats. But Lippmann referred to them as on vellum.[2] I failed to find them on a visit to the convent in 1928; the librarian, Dr. Wilhelm Schier, had no memory of them, nor are they mentioned in Hans Tietze's *Die Denkmale des politischen Bezirkes Melk* (Vienna 1909), so I was unable to verify Camesina's statement as to material.

But whatever the truth about the Melk example, prints on vellum were no doubt used on occasion for covering bindings of manuscripts. The vellum *Crucifixion* reproduced by Weigel[3] was probably intended for this purpose, only in this case it is very questionable whether any of the lines, as Weigel claims, were actually printed. Parchment or paper impressions may perhaps have been used as patterns by the textile makers.

Vellum is also occasionally used for impressions of ordinary woodcuts in the xv century and later,[4] just as Rembrandt used it in numerous impressions of his etching of the *Three Crosses*.

In continuation of the subject of the decorative uses to which wood blocks have been applied,[5] I would here for a few paragraphs anticipate the history of the later xv and the xvi century.

A few examples are known of ordinary woodcuts intended for the paper covers of book-bindings, chiefly Italian about 1490–1500. A fine example was first described by Kristeller (*Bibliographica*, i., 1895, p. 249), the front showing a *Circle with the Sacred Monogram*, the back *St. George and the Dragon* (S. 1815 a). An impression of this occurred pasted on the boards of a Milan book of 1496, Baptista Fulgosius, *Anteros* (H. 7393), once in

[1] *Drei Tapetenmuster aus dem Anfange des xvten Jahrhunderts*. Mitteil. der kk. Central Commission zur Erforschung und Erhaltung zur Baudenkmale, ix. 95, Vienna 1864.

[2] *Repertorium*, i. 216.   [3] Weigel and Zestermann, *Anfänge der Druckerkunst*, 1866, i. p. 25, No. 11 (now in the Edmond de Rothschild collection, Paris).

[4] E.g. *Christ on the Cross* at Linz (*Einbl.*, G. Gugenbauer, 1912, No. 14) from a MS. of about 1435–40 from the convent of Garsten, Upper Austria.

[5] See especially Max Lehrs, *Die dekorative Verwendung von Holzschnitten im xv und xvi Jahrhundert*. Pr. Jahrbuch xxix., 1908, 183; A. Weixlgärtner, *Ungedruckte Stiche*, Vienna Jahrbuch xxix., 1910/11, 268 (*Drucke als Appliken*); P. Kristeller, Bollettino d' Arte, iii., 1909, 429; P. Kristeller, *Gedruckte Kunst*, Die Graphischen Künste, xxxvii., 1914, 73. For examples of woodcuts used in the xvi and xvii centuries as trade account-book covers and trade-marks, see G. degli Azzi Vitelleschi, *Über eine unbekannte Verwertung des Italienischen Holzschnittes im xvi und xvii Jahrhundert*. Mitteil. der Gesellsch. für Vervielfält. Kunst, 1923, p. 37.

the Cernuschi Collection, Paris, and a damaged impression is at Berlin, while the same subject occurs in another version, which is probably the copy, at Vienna (S. 1815, Haberditzl 131). The *St. George* is a reversed and slightly modified copy of a woodcut in the *Leggenda de Sancto Maurelio*, printed by Laurentius de Rubeis (Rosso) at Ferrara, in 1489 (H. 10918),[1] and for this and general reasons of style Kristeller concluded that the cover was the work of the woodcutter or designer who worked for this Ferrarese printer. Another cover of similar design, with *St. Maurelius* on the front and *St. George* on the back, occurs on a copy of Phalaris, *Epistolae*, printed by Franciscus Ricardus de Luere at Cremona, 1505, in the collection of Mr. Dyson Perrins (Catalogue, by A. W. Pollard, No. 170; S. 1453 m; fig. 33). In each of these covers the subject is in outline, and the decorative design on a black ground, in the latter case varied with white line. In general decorative design both covers are Florentine in inspiration, comparable with the title-cut of the *Epistole e Evangelii*, published for Pacini, 1495.[2] A third example, in which each side of the cover shows five roundels, one with the *Expulsion from Paradise* and four *Patriarchs of the Early Church*, the other with *Christ driving the Moneychangers from the Temple* and four *Saints*, is known in impressions at Berlin and in the British Museum. The British Museum impression came from the cover of an Italian MS. (*The Picture of Cebes*),[3] dedicated by Niccolò Maria Estense, Bishop of Adria (1487–1507), to Ercole I., Duke of Ferrara (who died in 1505). The writer stated at the end of another copy (preserved at Venice) that he made the translation at Ferrara in 1498, and the time and place of the British Museum MS. is no doubt within a year or so of this date. But in this example the groundwork of the design is white, and subjects are not in outline, but cut with parallel shading in the manner of Venetian work of the early XVI century. Two Venetian examples of the early XVI century (signed z·a· and z·b) are described and reproduced by Essling (*Livres à figures vénitiens*, i. No. 444, and pp. 394-97).[4]

The designs for both covers and for the spine of the book were printed from a single block in the examples noted.

---

[1] Reproduced, Gruyer, Gazette des Beaux-Arts, 2e pér. xxxviii., 1888, p. 13. See p. 508.

[2] See p. 538 and fig. 298.   [3] B.M. Add. MS. 22331, from the Costabili Sale, 1858, Lot 194.

[4] For the most recent accounts of impressions of woodcuts used on bindings see L. Baer, *Mit Holzschnitten verzierte Buchumschläge*, Frankfurt 1923, and E. P. Goldschmidt, *Gothic and Renaissance Book-bindings*, London 1928, i. p. 163, No. 36. Goldschmidt agrees with Kristeller in placing the earliest and most important examples at Ferrara, others slightly later at Venice and a few in Germany: altogether not much over a dozen being known. See also a copy of J. Sannazaro, *Arcadia*, Venice 1502 (B.M.), and Heitz, *Einblattdrucke*, vols. 82 and 83.

Fig. 33. St. George. Woodcut on a book-cover. S. 1453 m.

Then woodcuts are frequently found pasted inside deed and travelling boxes. These boxes have been generally described as alms-boxes, but as they have no slit in the lid, it seems more probable that they were chiefly used by lawyers and merchants for their documents or accounts, or by priests to carry their breviaries and other requisites on their journeys. And most of such boxes with woodcuts which have been preserved are of French origin between about 1490 and 1520. One of the finest examples of these French woodcuts is the *Virgin and Child in a Glory with the Signs of the Evangelists* (Historisches Museum, Basle, fig. 441), and among the few German, Netherlandish and Italian examples may be mentioned a *Pietà* in the Museum für Kunst und Gewerbe, Hamburg (a German cut of about 1440, S. 972 b), and a xv-century Italian cut, *St. Albert of Sicily*, at Berlin (S. 1184 a).[1]

There are about eleven boxes in the Bibliothèque Nationale, Paris, containing cuts of the early xvi century (including another impression of the *Virgin in a Glory* as at Basle). Travellers probably pasted such cuts in their boxes, as they used to sew them in their clothes, as amulets for personal safety. There is another good specimen in the Metropolitan Museum, New York, a box-lid containing a French woodcut of about 1500, a *Nativity*.[2]

Many of these *decorative uses of woodcut* offered economical alternatives to paintings. Thus little altar-pieces were no doubt made by pasting on panel woodcuts, such as the *Triptych of St. Bridget and Saints*, a German cut of about 1480–90 (S. 1283), known in states, i. with the arms of Bavaria, Wittelsbach and Oettingen (Maihingen, Berlin, and Nat. Museum, Munich), ii. with the arms of the Palatinate and Bavaria (Munich, and B.M. from Maihingen, 1934). The woodcut must have been intended for Brigittine convents, and the heraldic changes were probably made to render its use more appropriate in other regions.

Another use for woodcuts in church furnishing is noted by Dr. Kristeller[3] in a series of cuts of the *Passion* by Jacob of Strassburg, which are pasted on the backs of the choir stalls in St. Damiano, near Assisi.

Two Italian woodcuts of the *Virgin and Child*, both belonging to the middle of the xv century (British Museum, S. 1158, fig. 72, and the other in the Victoria and Albert Museum, S. 1058 n, fig. 73), are known to have been

---

[1] For the whole subject, and reproductions of nearly all the prints found in such boxes, see W. L. Schreiber, *Kassetten-Holzschnitte*, Einblattdrucke 76, Strassburg 1931. See pp. 700–703.

[2] See Bulletin of the Metropolitan Museum, January 1929.

[3] Bollettino d' Arte, iii., 1909, 430.

pasted on doors, the latter example being still on its original wood. Both of these might have been originally attached to altar-pieces and transferred later to their more domestic uses. Moreover, a series of woodcuts (many in fragmentary condition) preserved at Berlin had been originally used in house decoration at Bassano (see p. 430).

There is also an interesting series of cuts (Northern Italian, possibly Lombard, about 1500) on a large cassone preserved in the Berlin Print Room. On the front are several woodcut panels (an oblong in the centre with a Samson and a lion (?) before a town, with various cup-like designs in the sky, flanked by two panels of geometrical patterns, and by two others representing the interior of a room with a lute, of varying design, pasted over the floor of each) within a border of crossed bars, and with a narrow strip along the foot of the cassone containing a design composed of a series of chairs; and on the top (though now very obscure) are five square panels of geometrical patterns, within a border of interlaced twine like Leonardo's knots.[1]

And a series of Venetian cuts of about 1487 (copied from the Italian block-book of the *Passion* at Berlin), belonging to the town of Nuremberg, was formerly pasted with other xv-century cuts on an altar-piece of several wings in the Church of St. Catherine in the same town.[2]

Sometimes decorative prints were used in ceiling decoration, examples being preserved at Berlin,[3] and in the Landesmuseum at Zürich, all Swiss work of the xvi century. This is analogous to the use of wood blocks for wall-paper which is known to have been practised at the same period, and became a common practice in the xviii century.[4]

---

[1] See A. M. Hind, *Catalogue of Early Italian Engraving in the British Museum*, 1910, p. 404. Some of the geometric designs in the Berlin Cassone should also be compared with line-engravings by the Master ⚮ (see Julius Hofmann, Vienna 1911). There are also two Italian woodcut knots, similar to the Leonardo School line-engravings, at Budapest (1915–2 and 3), from the Codex Zichy (see L. Zambra, Bibliofilia, Florence, xvi., 1915, p. 5). The Codex Zichy, which contained a medley of verse, geometry, notes on passing events, and miscellaneous drawings and cuts, appears to have been the original work and collection of a certain Angelo del Cortino (*b.* 1462, *d.* 1536), a draughtsman who was attached to the Venetian Waterways Department.

[2] See P. Kristeller, *Eine Folge venezianischer Holzschnitte*. Graph. Gesellschaft, ix., 1909, Berlin. Cf. p. 419.

[3] Reproduced by Lehrs, Pr. Jahrbuch xxix. pp. 189, 190, Abb. 4, 5, 6.

[4] See J. B. Jackson, *An Essay on the Invention of Engraving and Printing in Chiaroscuro . . . and the Application of it to the Making of Paper Hangings*, London [1754]; J. B. M. Papillon, *Traité historique et pratique de la gravure en bois*. 3 vols. Paris 1766; A. V. Sugden and J. L. Edmonson, *History of English Wall-Papers*, 1509–1914, London 1926; C. C. Oman, *Catalogue of Wall-Papers*, Victoria and Albert Museum, London 1929.

M. René van Bastelaer has noted some very early examples on certain Flemish tombs of the early xv century near Bruges, where the cuts had apparently been pasted on before the plaster was dry, i.e. at the time of the original construction.[1]

We will now return from this diversion on various decorative uses of woodcuts to consider the beginnings of printing woodcuts on paper. The practice of textile-printing shows that we need not regard these beginnings in the light of the discovery of a new method, but rather of a natural development rendered possible by the introduction of the use of paper.

It has been suggested that other examples anticipating ordinary woodcut are to be found in the stamping or printing of initial letters as a basis for the illuminator in certain MSS. of the xiii and xiv centuries. E. Fleury (*Les Manuscrits de la bibliothèque de Laon*, Laon 1863, 2e Partie, p. 3, No. 106) refers to a xiv-century MS. of Origen, *Commentaries on St. Paul*, which came from the Abbey of Vauclerc in Picardy. He reproduces an O, a V and an S (repeated in Bouchot's *Ancêtre de la gravure sur bois*, 1902).[2]

But examination of a xii-century MS. in the British Museum (Bede, *Commentary on Ezra*, Royal MS. 3. A. xii.) inclines me to doubt these statements. This MS. shows several initials which have the appearance of being impressed from a block, showing strong indentation on the back, clearly shown in the case of an initial U in brownish-yellow pigment on f. 70; but an initial P on f. 35 b in blue and brown pigment shows indentation under the brown, but a convex form of the vellum under the blue; and the plummet line is also visible in places. This goes to prove that, at least in this MS., indentation, which looks as if caused by a block, is really caused by the action of the damp pigment on the vellum, and I think it possible that the other examples cited by palaeographers may be of the same category.

The *importation of Oriental paper into Europe* is first found in Spain about the year 950, but it was not until two centuries later that any European manufactory was established, the first known being at Xativa, near Valencia, in Spain. France followed before the end of the xii century, and Italy, which founded its earliest factory at Fabriano about 1276, remained the most important source of supply in Europe throughout the xiv century. The manufacture was introduced in Germany in the last decade of the

---

[1] See footnote 2 on p. 17 of P. A. Lemoisne, *Les Xylographies du xiv*e *et du xv*e *siècle à la Bibliothèque Nationale*, Paris and Brussels, i., 1927, according to which M. van Bastelaer intends to publish something on these wall-paper cuts.

[2] See also A. Lecoy de la Marche, *Les Manuscrits et la miniature*, Paris [1884], pp. 317-18.

xiv century, in England at the end of the xv, but in the Netherlands apparently not before the xvi century.

During the xv century Germany as well as France gradually became self-supporting in paper; South Austria would turn more to Italy for supplies; England would receive her supplies from France and from Italy by sea, and the Netherlands would be supplied chiefly from France and from Germany.

Water-marks [1] may be a great aid to the student, but the transport of paper during the early period will show that the local origin of woodcuts cannot be determined thereby with confidence. Moreover, the uncertain period during which stocks of paper might be kept adds a further limitation in regard to the conjectured dating of woodcuts on the same basis.

It seems unlikely that any large supplies of paper were available before the latter part of the xiv century,[2] and this was probably an important factor in determining the period at which the printing of pictures was introduced. Judged from the style of their design, the woodcuts which appear to be the earliest printed on paper should be dated about 1400, hardly later, and hardly more than ten or twenty years earlier.

Before approaching the study of these works, I would first note the *earliest documentary records of woodcutters and block-printing in Europe*, drawing such conclusions as are possible from their often ambiguous terms.

One of the most definite of the early references to a woodcutter doing work probably intended for printing is a record of payment in 1393 (in the accounts for works in the Chartreuse of Dijon) to a certain '*Jehan Baudet, charpentier, pour avoir fait et taillié des moles et tables pour la chappelle de mon seigneur audit Champmol dicte la chappelle des Angles, à la devise de Beaumez*'.[3] This '*tailleur de molles (moles)*' (i.e. cutter of moulds or blocks)

---

[1] The great corpus of information is C. M. Briquet, *Dictionnaire des Filigranes*, 1907.

[2] Siméon Luce (*Histoire de Bertrand Duguesclin et de son époque*, Paris 1876, pp. 77 and 78) refers to the growing use of linen in clothing in the xiv century as contributing the linen-rag indispensable for the best paper.

[3] See Chrétien Dehaisnes, *Documents et extraits divers concernant l'histoire de l'Art dans la Flandre, l'Artois et le Hainaut*, Lille 1886, p. 711. There are various other references scattered throughout Dehaisnes, probably to textile blocks, several being quoted by Delen (*Histoire de la gravure dans les anciens Pays-Bas*, 1924, p. 15), e.g. Dehaisnes, p. 272 (anno 1327) to *tapis d'entailleure* by a certain Jehan Herenc of St. Omer, and p. 276 (anno 1328) to *deus dras ovrée de entailleure de brodures* by the same craftsman; p. 694 (anno 1391) payment at St. Omer to a Johannes Cruspondere *pro factura ymaginum lignearum*. There is ambiguity in certain documents quoted by Dehaisnes between sculpture and cuts for printing, but Delen notes the small fees

was probably cutting his blocks for printing textiles for altar hangings or similar work, after designs by the painter Jean de Beaumetz (if Bouchot's explanation of *à la devise de Beaumez* is correct).

The term *Formschneider* (i.e. cutter of the form or block, corresponding to the French term *tailleur de molles*, and essentially the same as wood-cutter) occurs in German documents as early as 1398,[1] but this record in its possible reference to the cutter of blocks for textile-printing (like the earliest French references) is no certain limit for the introduction of prints from woodcut on paper. The earliest places where it occurs are Ulm (1398), Nuremberg (1423) and Strassburg (1440). *Schreiner* (joiner or carpenter) and *Schnitzer* (wood-carver) also sometimes include the woodcutters (e.g. the HANS HURNING who collaborated with FRIEDRICH WALTHER of Nörd-lingen in the production of an edition of the *Biblia Pauperum* block-book is called a *Schreiner*, and the cutter of the map of the world in the Ulm Ptolemy of 1482 signs himself *Johannes Schnitzer de Armszheim*).

In some towns, e.g. at Augsburg, Nördlingen, Regensburg and Basle, the term *Formschneider* does not occur at all in the xv century, a fact which indicates that the block-cutters there had no special guild, but belonged to the larger class of carpenters.

The term *Kartenmaler* or *Kartenmacher* (painter or maker of playing-cards) occurs in German documents from 1402,[2] Ulm being again the earliest town in which the documents have been noted, and Nuremberg (1441) the second. Kristeller notes a certain Federico de Germania who sold *cartas figuratas et pictas ad imagines et figuras sanctorum* at Bologna in 1395, and a card-maker (*pittor di naibi*) of Florence, Antonio di Giovanni di Ser Francesco, who declares amongst his property in 1430 'wood blocks for playing-cards and saints'.[3] In France there are numerous records of *tailleurs de molles de cartes* at Lyon from the year 1444.

paid for some of these 'cuts' as evidence in favour of their being wood blocks. Other references might equally well refer to engravers on metal, e.g. Dehaisnes, p. 691 (anno 1391), payment to a certain *Jacobo le tailleur* at Cambrai, while an *Annunciacion entaillié* of the same year appears to be the work of a *Franchois l'orfèvre*, and therefore probably on metal.

[1] For the most complete list of the names, monograms and marks of cutters, see Schreiber, *Handbuch*, vi. p. 93, and see his Introduction to *Einbl.* xxx., Munich 1912, for the craft-terms under which they were known.

[2] Playing-cards are known to have been introduced into Germany by 1377 (see references in C. Dodgson, *B.M. Catalogue of Early German and Flemish Woodcuts*, vol. i. p. 6).

[3] *Kupferstich und Holzschnitt*, 1922, pp. 20 and 21. There is no proof that Federico de Germania printed his cards from blocks, but as the document in which he is mentioned is an accusation against him for coining false money, Kristeller thinks it highly probable that a die-cutter would have been equally conversant with block-cutting. It is worth noting in this relation a fact

Bologna appears to have been a hot-bed of gambling in the early xv century, and it needed St. Bernardino in his lenten sermons in this city in 1424 to persuade the players to burn their cards. Thereupon the story goes how a card-maker, coming to the saint complaining that he had lost his custom, was bidden to cut the Sacred Monogram (with which St. Bernardino was generally represented in pictures and prints) and so to recover his livelihood.[1]

Printers are noted as early as 1417 (Antwerp and Nördlingen). The Antwerp reference [2] is to a *Jan de printere*, who owed money to a maker of vellum, and had dealings with a certain Jan van Wezele, son of a Ghysbrecht van Wezele, who is known in records as a colourer (*verwere* and *tinctor*). Jan de printere, Jan van Wezele and a certain Jan Houbraken owed sums of money to certain manufacturers of Bruges and Audenarde, both of which towns were centres of the textile trade. It seems natural to infer that the work of Jan de printere may have consisted largely in supplying textile and vellum prints for decorative purposes. The Nördlingen record of 1417 is to a certain *Briefdrucker* Wilhelm Kegler, whose activity extended to 1453. Other printers are noted at Frankfurt-a-M. (1440), Antwerp (1442, belonging to the Guild of St. Luke), Bruges (1456), etc.

The term *Aufdrucker* also occurs (e.g. Regensburg, 1460–61; Nuremberg, 1461), and there is considerable ambiguity in its application, whether to the old manner of printing textiles (pressing on to the material), to the impressing of gold leaf on to illuminations or prints, or to bookprinting. It may have had different significations in different localities, and in some case may have come to be used almost synonymously with *Briefdrucker*.

Another term which in the latter half of the xv century has sometimes been regarded as almost synonymous with *Formschneider* is *Briefmaler*, i.e. strictly speaking, the painter, or illuminator of short documents, a lower class in the hierarchy of illuminators of MSS. Its meaning is distinct, and in the earliest reference known (Strassburg 1440) a certain Johann Meydenbach is referred to specifically under the two crafts of *Briefmaler* and *Formschneider*. In spite of this and other examples of men combining several of

emphasised by Bouchot (*Ancêtre de la gravure sur bois*, p. 22) that in France early woodcuts seem to have sometimes been regarded as *malefaçons* (contraband), a sort of false coin in the eyes of the guild of *Imagiers*.

[1] See P. Thureau-Dangin, *Life of St. Bernardino of Siena*, transl. by Baroness von Hügel, London 1911, p. 76.

[2] First quoted in Léon de Burbure, *Sur l'ancienneté de l'art typographique de Belgique*, Bulletin de l'Académie Royale de Belgique, 2e sér., viii., 1859, p. 294.

Fig. 34. Jost Amman. Der Briefmaler.

these crafts,[1] it appears to me very unlikely that the term *Briefmaler* was ever loosely used to include cutter. Every indication leads me to regard the distinctions made in records as based on definite Guild divisions. There was probably less distinction between the *Briefmaler* and *Kartenmaler*, the latter being perhaps the lowest class of illuminator. Jost Amman's woodcut in Schopper's *Panoplia omnium artium* (1568) shows the *Briefmaler* in the stricter signification of 'colourer of prints' (fig. 34).

Heiligenmaler (i.e. painter of pictures of saints) also occurs, e.g. in reference to LIENHART YSENHUT, *Heiligenmaler*, *Briefmaler* and *Kartenmacher* at Basle in 1464.

The term *Reisser*, which frequently occurs in the xvi century, denotes the designer in relation to a print, strictly speaking the artist who draws with a pen on the block or on paper for transfer to a block.[2] The root is the same as *riss* (i.e. sketch) in such words as *Grundriss*. Jost Amman gives an illustration of the *Reisser* drawing on paper in Schopper's *Panoplia omnium artium* (1568), in which he probably represents himself (fig. 35). He may have added the sword against the wall on purpose to show the higher rank that the painter and designer would hold in relation to the more modest cutter. On many xvi-century German prints the *Reisser* is indicated by a pen, just as the woodcutter's name is followed by a knife.

Passing from the documents which merely yield a bare reference to names of craftsmen and the denomination of their crafts, I would cite three documents for the interest of their contents and their bearing on our history.

The first of these[3] records a request of the woodcutters and makers

[1] Another instance is that of a certain Wenczl, noted as *Maler* and *Aufdrucker* at Regensburg, 1461.

[2] E.g. Johann Neudörfer, in his Records of Nuremberg artists written in 1547 (edited G. W. K. Lochner, Vienna 1875), describes Wolgemut as *Maler und Reisser*.

[3] First transcribed in G. C. Bottari, *Raccolta di lettere sulla pittura, scultura, ed architectura*, Rome, 6 vols., 1754–58. Vol. v. p. 320 (letter 173) (*nella vecchia matricola di questi nostri pittori ... al capo xxxiii*) MCCCCXLI *a dì xi otubrio conciosa che l' arte, e mestier delle carte, e figure stampide,*

of playing-cards in Venice brought before the Council of the City in 1441 in which they ask for protection against the foreign import which they declared had ruined their trade. As a result, regulations were made forbidding the import of every kind of print, including textiles and cards.

The second document records a dispute brought before the Town Council of Louvain in 1452 [1] in which representatives of the wheel-wrights (*rademakers*), carpenters (*scrynmakers*), turners (*draeyers*) and coopers (*cuypers*) request the wood-cutter (*printsnydere*) JAN VAN DEN BERGHE to enter the guild of the carpenters. He demurs, stating that

Fig. 35. Jost Amman. Der Reisser.

his art was not among the regular crafts practised in the town, and that it concerned the clergy more than the corporation in question, his work being the cutting of letters and pictures (*letteren ende beeldeprynten*). But it was pointed out that other 'printers of letters and pictures' had been compelled to join the Carpenters' Guild, and he was officially ordered to take the same course. The same Jan van den Berghe appears in a document of 1457 as having a house at Louvain, and is referred to again in a document of 1480.

The third document,[2] to which reference has already been made, con-

che se fano in Venesia e vegnudo a total deffaction, e questo sia per la gran quantità de carte da zugar, e figure depente stampide, la qual vien fate de fuora de Venezia, ala qual cosa è da meter remedio, che i diti maestri, i quali sono assaii in fameja habiano più presto utilitade, che i forestieri. Sia ordenado, e statuido, come anchora i diti maestri ne ha supplicado, che da mo in avanti non possa vegnir over esser condutto in questa Terra alcun lavorerio dela predicta arte, che sia stampido, o depento in tella, o in carta, come sono anchone e carte da zugare, e cadaun altro lavorerio dela so arte facto a penello, e stampido, soto pena di perdere i lavori condutti, e liv. xxx e fol xii p. 6 dela qual pena pecunaria un terzo sia del Comun, un terzo di Signori Justitieri vechi, ai quali questo sia comesso, e un terzo sia del accusador. Cum questa tamen condition, che i maestri, i quali fanno de i predetti lavori in questa Terra, non possano vender i predetti suo lavori fuor delle sue botege sotto la pena preditta, salvo che de merchore a S. Polo, e da Sabado a S. Marco sotto la penna predetta. . . .

[1] See Edward van Even, *L'Ancienne École de Peinture de Louvain*, Brussels and Louvain 1870, pp. 100-101, for the original document. See also Lippmann, *Anfänge der Formschneidekunst*, Repertorium, i., 1876. [2] See Edward van Even, *op. cit.*, p. 104.

tains evidence of the existence of a press for printing wood blocks (*unum instrumentum ad imprimendas scripturas et ymagines*) in the inventory of a certain Jacoba van Loos-Hensberge who died in the Bethany Convent at Malines in 1465. The inventory also included 'nine wood blocks [?] for printing images, with fourteen other stone blocks' (*novem printe lignee ad imprimendas ymagines cum quatuordecim aliis lapideis printis* [1]).

The above documents lead naturally to certain general conclusions.

In the first place the production of *playing-cards* must have been a thriving industry, especially at Ulm,[2] at the end of the xiv and beginning of the xv century. In spite of the fact that no existing pack of cards can be dated with any certainty before about 1450, this does not rule out the probability of woodcuts having been used by about 1400, if not earlier, in their production.

It is curious that the earliest engraved cards preserved should be in the junior process of line-engraving (i.e. those of the MASTER OF THE PLAYING-CARDS, which are known to date before 1446), but this may only be an indication of the greater estimation in which line-engraving was held than woodcut.

Through the very nature of their use cards are the most unlikely things to be preserved. Some of the earliest packs existing are painted examples, but fine packs illuminated for the use of princes would naturally be kept with more care than the popular woodcut cards.

I do not propose to write at any length on the somewhat special subject of *playing-cards*,[3] but I will interpolate here some notes on the most important xv-century examples:

[1] Lippmann's suggested reading of *ligneis* for *lapideis* has recently been contested and, I think, disproved, by W. L. Schreiber (*Printae Lapideae*, Gutenberg-Jahrbuch, Mainz 1927, p. 43). He refers to a little stone block engraved with an alphabet described and reproduced by Andrew W. Tuer, *History of the Horn-Book*, London 1896, i. p. 117, the sort of small stamp which is the actual predecessor of the horn-book.

[2] See Felix Fabri, *Tractatus de Civitate Ulmensi*, herausgegeben von G. Veesenmeyer, Litterarisches Verein in Stuttgart 1889, pp. 145, 146.

[3] S. W. Singer, *Researches in the History of Playing-cards*, London 1816; *Jeux de cartes tarots et de cartes numérales du xive au xviie siècle*, Société des Bibliophiles Français, Paris 1844; W. A. Chatto, *Facts and Speculations on the Origin of Playing-cards*, London 1848; R. Merlin, *Origine des cartes à jouer*, Paris 1869; W. H. Willshire, *Descriptive Catalogue of Playing and other Cards in the British Museum*, London 1876; Norton T. Horton, *Bibliography*, Cleveland, U.S.A., 1892; Lady Charlotte Schreiber, *Playing-cards*, 3 vols., London 1892–95; F. M. O'Donoghue, *The Schreiber Collection of Playing-cards in the British Museum*, London 1901; H. R. D'Allemagne, *Les Cartes à jouer du xive au xxe siècle*, Paris 1906 (the most comprehensive

(1) An Austrian pack from the Ambras Collection, now in the Ferdinandeische Kupferstichsammlung, Hofmuseum, Vienna. Described and reproduced by E. Hartmann von Franzenshuld, *Ein höfisches Kartenspiel des xv Jahrhunderts*, Vienna Jahrbuch, i., 1883, 101, and ii. 96.

The coats-of-arms used for the four suits (Roman Empire, Bohemia, Hungary and France) appear to fit with the circumstances of Ladislaus Postumus, King of Hungary and Bohemia. The dates of his reign (1453–57) probably fix the limits of the production of the pack (see A. Weixlgärtner, *Ungedruckte Stiche*, Vienna Jahrbuch, xxix., p. 262), and the costume points to Austrian origin.

The quality of the line is in many of the cards obscured by the heavy colour, but it is comparatively clear in the attractive *Jungfrau* (vi. from the suit of France) which is reproduced on fig. 36, and in the interesting *Stable-boy* (iv. from the suit of France).

(2) Two roundels of *Emperor* (fig. 37) and *King* on horseback in Munich University (S. 1994, m and n). Possibly fragments of a pack of cards, rather than a mere series of the Ranks and Conditions of Men. German, about 1470. Their form has, however, suggested another use, i.e. that they might have been intended for pasting on box-lids.

(3) Twenty-two examples or fragments of an Italian pack of Tarocchi (see P. Kristeller, *Beiträge zur Geschichte des italienischen Holzschnittes*, Pr. Jahrbuch, xiii., 1892, 172). North Italian, showing the influence of Jacopo Bellini. Should be compared with the Ferrarese Tarocchi (line-engravings) in the Sola-Busca Collection, Milan (see A. M. Hind, *Catalogue of Early Italian Engravings in the British Museum*, 1910, E.II), and with a woodcut, *St. George and the Dragon*, heavily illuminated, at Bassano (S.1445, cf. p. 164 and fig. 75). Found inside the binding of volumes of 1466 and 1469 in the Staatsarchiv at Rome. The impressions probably of about this date, though the type may go back a good deal earlier.

of recent works); Mrs. John King van Rensselaer, *Prophetical, Educational and Playing-cards*, Philadelphia 1912; Catherine Perry Hargrave, *A History of Playing-cards and a Bibliography of Cards and Gaming, compiled and illustrated from the Old Cards and Books in the Collection of the United States Playing-card Company in Cincinnati* (John Omwake), Boston and New York 1930.

(4) Fragments of two packs in the Musée des Beaux-Arts, Budapest, both probably Venetian of about 1500, though the type of design might be as much as thirty years earlier. (*a*) Inv. 5044,

Fig. 36. Jungfrau. From a pack of Austrian playing-cards.

5045, 5046, and 5062/63. Three duplicate sheets from this pack were included in the Hofmann sale, Leipzig, 1922, one being reproduced (No. 35). (*b*) Inv. 5047-5059, 5064-5067. (Inv. 5060 and 5061 in the same collection are somewhat later, and early XVI century.)

(5) Certain French (possibly Lyon) cards signed *Jaque*, of which the original blocks (found in the Dauphiny) were once in the col-

lection of M. Vital Berthin. First noted and reproduced by
R. Merlin, *Origines des cartes à jouer*, Paris 1869 (p. 110 and
plates *G a, b, c*). The figures show contemporary Burgundian
costumes of about 1450–60. Natalis Rondot (*Les Gravures
sur bois et les imprimeurs à Lyon*) quotes a certain *Jaques,
tailleur de moules* at Lyon in 1472, who might have been the
cutter.

Fig. 37. Emperor on Horseback. S. 1994 m.

(6) Cards signed *J. de dale*, acquired by the Bibliothèque Nationale,
Paris, in 1902 (described and reproduced by H. Bouchot, *A newly
discovered pack of Lyonnese Playing-cards*, Burlington Magazine,
i., 1903, p. 296; see my fig. 38). JEAN DE DALE appears to have
been born at Bresse, and to have worked in Lyon in the second
half of the xv century. Natalis Rondot quotes records of him from
1477 onwards, but confuses him with the Master, I. D., an
unidentified cutter who worked for the publisher Trechsel at
Lyon in a style more influenced by Netherlandish woodcut.
Bouchot attributes to Jean de Dale the woodcut series of *Les
Neuf Preux* (S. 1945, see p. 157 and fig. 71).

Fig. 38. French playing-cards, signed *J. de Dale*.

(7) Cards signed by F. CLERC of Lyon (*fl.* 1485–96) in the Bibl. Nat., Paris, and others by JEAN PERSONNE (*fl.* 1493–97) in Dijon Museum.[1]

---

[1] Others signed *P. Gayon* (Pierre Gayon, woodcutter at Lyon, 1485–1515) were in 1932 in the possession of Maggs Bros., London (described as No. 16 in their Catalogue No. 533, *Incunabula, One Hundred Towns*, part i., n.d.).

Few cards besides those noted can be definitely dated as impressions of the xv century, and the recurrence of old designs at later periods renders even approximate dating often very difficult. A pack of which much has been written, generally called *Stukeley's Cards* (from their owner in 1763), are crude and archaic enough in their style, but they were probably printed rather after than before 1500 (now in the British Museum, see F. M. O'Donoghue, *The Schreiber Collection of Playing-cards*, 1901, p. 75, No. 1. Other impressions in the Guildhall Library).

Returning to our argument we may conclude in the second place from the documents quoted that alongside the makers of playing-cards, and more definitely allied to the later woodcutters, were the *cutters and printers of the blocks for textile printing*, called *Formschneider* or *Aufdrucker* in German, *Printers* in Dutch. These textile printers belonged to various guilds during the Middle Ages, sometimes being classed among dyers with other textile workers, sometimes with the painters,[1] and sometimes with the carpenters, and there is evidence to show that the art was also practised in the convents. The pattern-block cutters, whose craft included all kinds of block-cutting, such as butter patterns and other wooden utensils for kitchen use, no doubt turned in the early xv century to the new craft of cutting pictures for printing on paper; and they were probably the class from which originated many of the early printers of type. It is at least known that several printers of books carried on textile printing even in the early xvi century.

So these textile-block cutters may be regarded as the most direct ancestors of our woodcutters. But the case of JAN VAN DEN BERGHE seems to show that the wood blocks intended for printing on paper were being cut in some cases by craftsmen outside the regular guilds, though when this occurred the guilds attempted to compel the irregular craftsmen to join their proper guild. It does not seem to be proven (as is sometimes inferred) that such craftsmen were *Briefmaler*, though they may have been so in some cases, nor that the cutters of the new form of pictures originated from this class, but it certainly shows that the development of a new art inevitably drew in new craftsmen from various sources. A large amount of early work was no doubt produced in convents, whether by the monks themselves, by the old professional cutters or by the *Briefmaler*. Jan van den Berghe refers

---

[1] Painting itself was a 'free' art in that the painters were not always bound to join any corporation, guilds of painters only being formed in the large towns, while in Ulm the painters were enrolled in the guild of the goldsmiths.

to his art being of a clerical or ecclesiastical character, though he himself was certainly a lay worker. The popularity of pilgrimages in the xv century was the chief incentive to the making of popular pictures of saints for sale at their shrines. Many itinerant craftsmen who avoided joining the guilds by claiming no citizenship would also be engaged in such work, the cause perhaps of some of the difficulties experienced in localising the production of many woodcuts.

At the end of the xv century and during the xvi century *designer* and *cutter* are generally recognised to have been for the most part distinct. The painter designed and engraved on copper, but seldom cut his own blocks; the professional cutter no doubt belonged, as before, to the guild of the carpenters. Apart from the necessity of joining the special guild, it may have been derogatory to the painter to cut, for, unlike the goldsmith's craft, carpentry was not one of the Liberal Arts. It is natural to assume that this distinction of craft was the traditional practice, and not an innovation of the time of known painter-designers such as WOLGEMUT. The practice at the time of Wolgemut is clearly illustrated in records relating to an unpublished work of Peter Danhauser, the *Archetypus Triumphantis Romae*, for which the blocks were being prepared between 1493 and 1497, at the expense of Sebald Schreyer (who had been also in part responsible for the publication of Schedel's *Weltchronik*). About the actual blocks further notes will be given in a later section, but from the document, of which the pertinent items are given in the footnote,[1] it appears that the author had preliminary designs drawn on paper, that the painters then drew the selected designs on the blocks, and that the blocks were then cut by a certain SEBALD GALLENSDORFER.

---

[1] First published by Bernhard Hartmann, in his *Conrad Celtis in Nürnberg*, Mitteil. des Vereins für Geschichte der Stadt Nürnberg 1889, Heft 8, p. 58 (and quoted by E. Flechsig, *Dürer*, 1928, p. 122):

'*Item* auf solche vorgemelte vertrege und verschreibungen hat Sebolt Schreyer meister Peter Danhauser entricht, auch die exemplar lassen abschreiben, die figur entwerfen, auf pretter reissen und auch solche pretter schneiden lassen, deshalben auch für andern unkosten er vom 93. iar bis in das 97. iar ausgegeben hat, wie hernach.

'*Item* erstlich meyster Peter Danhauser, das er, der Schreyer, ime laut der zweier vertrag gegeben, auch ine bei einem virtel iar in seiner cost gehalten und sonst gecost hat, tut fl. 93.

'*Item* vom buch archetipus abzuschreiben etlichen schreibern in seiner cost gehalten und für ire belonung, so gecost hat 32 fl. 6 u. 18 d.

'*Item* für zwei riss pappirs so darzu gebraucht und vernutzt sind worden 2 fl. 1 u. 20 d.

'*Item* von dem merern teil der figuren erstlich auf pappir zu entwerfen, nemlich von 192

The chief ambiguity that remains is whether the drawings on the blocks were done by the same hands responsible for the preliminary designs on paper. As 'painters' are expressly mentioned as doing the drawings on the blocks, it would seem most reasonable to infer that there were no intermediary draughtsmen to translate the original designs on paper into the woodcutter's convention on the block, but that this was done by the original designer himself.[1]

The co-operation of FRIEDRICH WALTHER and HANS HURNING in the production of an edition of the *Biblia Pauperum* block-book at Nördlingen in 1470 is a definite example of the division of labour at an earlier date. For Walther is called painter (*Maler*) in the colophon, and Hurning is described in documents as a carpenter (*Schreiner*).

The experience of GÜNTHER ZAINER, the famous printer of Augsburg, is another example of the jealousy of corporations. On his arrival from Strassburg about 1468 he found some difficulty in getting permission to print at all, and at first was not allowed to illustrate his books with cuts. Later he obtained this licence on the understanding that he only used the woodcutters of the guilds.

It looks as if he may have been able to cut blocks himself, but was restrained by the members of the special corporations; and that the latter, having been chiefly engaged in the cutting of block-books, were suspicious of the growth of illustrations in printed books as a dangerous rival to their older trades.

Another printer of books, LIENHART YSENHUT of Basle, seems to have belonged professionally to many crafts as he is mentioned in documents with the various titles of *Maler, Briefmaler, Heiligenmaler, Briefdrucker, Heiligendrucker* and *Kartenmacher*.

figuren 8 gulden 2 u.; mer von 20 figuren 1 u. 2 d. und von 5 figuren 1 u. 20 d. Tut in summa 9 fl. 3 u. 4 d.

'*Item* für die pretter klein und gross, darauf die figur geschnitten sind worden, dem schreiner zalt 9 fl. 4 u. 8 d.

'*Item* von den figuren auf pretter zu reissen den malern zalt nemlich von 233 grossen und 83 kleinen pretlein gegeben 37 fl. 1 u. 16 d.

'*Item* von den figuren in die hulzen prettlein zu schneiden zalt Sebolten Gallensdorfer, nemlich von 233 grossen, ie von einem 4 u. 15 d., und 83 kleinen, ie von zweien 4 u. 15 d. tut 1235 u. 8 d., facit an geld, den gulden zu 8 u. 10 d. gerechnet, 148 fl. 1 u. 28 d.

'*Item* meister Sebolten, furmschneider, gegeben das er das spil verreht hat, 1 guldin, mer für ein mess eichen prennholz und davon zu hauen und zu tragen, 6 u. 28 d. facit 1 fl. 6 u. 28 d.

'*Summa Summarum*, dans das buch mitsambt den figuren und anderen wie oben gemelt, gecost hat 334 fl. 1 u. 2 d.'

[1] But cf. pp. 375-76.

To what extent were the earliest woodcutters their own designers? This question cannot be answered at all definitely. One school of criticism emphasises the probable identity of designers and cutters, basing its arguments on the simplicity of the style of the cutters' work, and its essential harmony with the medium.[1] Another view, which seems to me more reasonable, is that the known practice of the late xv and the xvi century, in which the designer (the painter) was distinct from the cutter, was equally that of the early xv century; in fact that the traditional practice remained essentially the same.[2] We have a certain number of names preserved in xv-century cuts before the time of Dürer; but we cannot always say whether the name refers to designer or cutter. A definite indication that the name which occurs on several prints is that of the cutter and not the designer would be afforded by marked divergence in style between the prints of one cutter, as is the case with the woodcuts signed *Casper*. The same variety of style in design in the case of unsigned works, evidently by a single cutter, may be noted in the *Calvary* (S. 471) and the *St. Anthony* (S. 1215), both in the Graphische Sammlung, Munich,[3] while a third woodcut at Munich, the *Virgin in Robe decorated with Ears of Corn (Madonna im Ährenkleid)* (S. 1000),[4] was based, according to its inscription, on a painting once in Milan Cathedral (no longer known), and though the difference in style is still more marked, it is probably by the same cutter as the *Calvary* and *St. Anthony*.

---

[1] The arguments on this side are most ably presented by Paul Kristeller in his edition of the *Apocalypse*, Berlin 1916. See also Kristeller, *Über die künstlerische Selbständigkeit der ältesten Holzschneider*, Kunstgeschichtliche Gesellschaft, Berlin, Sitzungsberichte, viii., 1905.

[2] Most recently upheld by Dr. E. Flechsig, *Dürer*, Berlin 1928 (cf. p. 378). For earlier discussions on the relations of designer and cutter see C. F. von Rumohr, *H. Holbein der jüngere in seinem Verhältniss zum deutschen Formschnittwesen*, Leipzig 1836; and *Zur Geschichte und Theorie der Formschneidekunst*, Leipzig 1837 (favouring the theory that the older painters sometimes cut their own designs); *Auf Veranlassung und in Erwiederung von Einwürfen einer Sachverständigen* (i.e. Sotzmann) *gegen die Schrift H. Holbein*, Leipzig 1836; J. D. F. Sotzmann, Kunstblatt, 1836 (opposing Rumohr's arguments); A. E. Umbreit, *Über die Eigenhändigkeit der Malerformschnitte*, 2 vols., Leipzig 1840, 1843.

[3] See p. 130.

[4] For this subject see K. Rathe, *Ein unbeschriebener Einbl. und das Thema der 'Ährenmadonna'*, Mitteil., 1922, p. 1; R. Berliner, *Zur Sinnesdeutung der Ährenmadonna*, Die Christliche Kunst, xxvi. (1929/30); A. Pigler, *La Vierge aux Épis*, Gazette des Beaux-Arts, 6e Pér. viii. (1932), 129. Pictures of the subject are most commonly found in Upper Germany and the region of Salzburg. Schreiber (*Handbuch*, vii. p. 115) speaks of the costume as the Virgin's wedding robe, but I do not find confirmation for any such tradition. The representation, which always shows the Virgin alone, is generally supposed to refer to the years immediately preceding her marriage, the ears of corn symbolising creation.

Other early cuts seem more directly inspired by sculpture in wood, e.g. the *Pietà* once at Maihingen and recently acquired by the Albertina, Vienna (S. 973), one of the most impressive of all the cuts of the early xv century (see p. 121 and fig. 53).[1]

Two other sources from which the simple outline style of the earlier woodcuts might have drawn some inspiration are offered by glass-paintings and by the engraved memorial brasses and other plaques of the xiv and xv centuries. Further research in both relations might offer interesting results.

While examples of the direct relation to works of sculpture, painting or drawing have been lacking or unrecognised,[2] it is perhaps natural that it has been frequently assumed that the designers of the early xv century cuts (if not the cutters themselves) were either original, or fairly independent in their interpretation of the works of others; but it is a dangerous inference on which one cannot place great reliance. Moreover, recent research is finding closer and more specific relations between early woodcuts and paintings, and the position of the painters as designers is being more generally recognised.[3]

It was certainly a constant habit of cutters to repeat a popular design (e.g. that of the Buxheim *Annunciation*, S. 28, now in the John Rylands Library),[4] and it is tempting to think that these popular designs in some cases preserved pictures venerated by the pilgrims at the shrines they visited.

Finally, considering the position of the textile-block cutters at the beginning of the xv century, and that of Dürer and other masters who used the process of woodcut but left the cutting to others at the end of the xv century, it is most probable that the majority of work throughout the

---

[1] See also J. Jahn, *Beiträge*, Strassburg 1927, p. 16.

[2] Among the few examples of drawings related to woodcuts is one of *St. Anne with the Virgin and Seraphim*, apparently the original study in reverse for the textile print already mentioned (see p. 67). Ernest Stahl (*Die Legende vom Heil. Christophorus*, Munich 1920) refers to certain early sketch-books (generally works of several hands to serve the various uses of an atelier) as the kind of source from which the woodcutters may have derived their subjects, e.g. the Brunswick sketch-book of the early xv century, edited by J. Neuwirth, Prague 1897, though no definite relations between such drawings and cuts have been established. Cf. also p. 286, footnote 1.

[3] See especially Otto Benesch, *Zur altösterreichischen Tafelmalerei*, Vienna Jahrbuch, Neue Folge, ii., 1928, p. 63; and Kurt Rathe, *Bild-Beziehungen früher Holzschnitte*, Mitteil. der Gesellsch. für Vervielfältig. Kunst, 1930, No. 4; and J. Jahn, *Beiträge zur Kenntnis der ältesten Einblattdrucke*, Strassburg 1927.

[4] The three other versions known are at Washington, Library of Congress (S. 26), Nuremberg (S. 27) and the Barfüsserkloster, Freiburg (S. 27 a).

xv century was done on the same principle, the cutter working after the drawing done by a painter on the block.

What has been said will have indicated the *principal subjects of the early woodcuts*,[1] i.e. scenes from the life of the Virgin and of Christ, and pictures of Saints, such popular images as would have a ready sale at the larger convents, and the shrines chiefly visited by pilgrims. The subject of *Christ on the Cross* (e.g. S. 932) would probably be used chiefly at shrines dedicated to the Holy Cross, such as that of Tegernsee. Other popular subjects were cuts with prayers against plague, so rife at this period, generally with an image of St. Sebastian, sometimes with that of St. Roch, and often showing a cross in the form of the Greek T (*Tau*), which also occurs as an emblem of St. Anthony, on his staff, or robe (see fig. 41);[2] New Year's greetings, generally accompanied with the emblem of the Christ Child with a bird, orb, or signs of the Passion (the bird either the cuckoo for its reputed prophetic powers, or the sparrow as a symbol of weakness); series of the Nine Famous Heroes (*Les Neuf Preux*); allegories on death and reminders of mortality (*memento mori*), and the Ages of Man.

After the introduction of movable type and the printing of books, knowledge must have spread rapidly, and the increasing interests of the people are reflected in the variety of subjects treated by the woodcutter towards the end of the xv century. Large sheets with pictures and printed text (broadsides) became common, Prayers to the Virgin, episcopal proclamations, relics of various shrines, politics, satire, genre and popular poems (such as those of Sebastian Brant on the scourge of syphilis, which first appeared in Europe at this time), being some of the numerous subjects found in this form.

The *study of the single woodcuts of the earlier part of the xv century* (i.e. the woodcuts printed as separate impressions, not in books) is full of obscurity. Most of the cuts are anonymous, and rare, if not unique; and being scattered throughout a diversity of collections, comparison is difficult. Few are dated, and other clues to date and place of origin only occur in isolated instances.

Schreiber's Catalogue, and numerous publications of reproductions (to

---

[1] For comprehensive notes on the subjects illustrated in xv-century woodcuts see W. L. Schreiber, *Handbuch*, vol. vii. pp. 93-165.

[2] For the subject of the *Tau* Cross see W. H. Willshire, *Catalogue of Early Prints in the British Museum*, vol. i. D. 47 and 93.

which Heitz's series of *Einblattdrucke* has contributed most largely [1]), have greatly facilitated comparative study, but even so, the obscurity is only lifted here and there, and the conclusions that students have been able to draw in the attempt to construct some historical sequence and relation are scanty. But it is wiser to accept the uncertainties of the situation, and to draw conclusions in broad outlines, rather than to trust overmuch to one's personal conjectures (even when seemingly based on a practised sense of style) in constructing probable situations and personalities which the next critic may find reason to demolish.

In describing particular prints I shall quote Schreiber's numbers, generally without adding reference to reproductions, as the student who wishes to go further can always find these in Schreiber's Catalogue. Where I quote other authors, the references will easily be identified from my bibliography, generally under the collection in question.

I use the word Netherlands to include the Northern and Southern Netherlands, i.e. embracing the present Holland and Belgium, never in the limited sense of north Netherlands, which is sometimes implied by *Niederländisch* in German. Whenever possible, I would distinguish between Dutch and Flemish, allowing Flemish to apply generally to the Southern Netherlands, rather than using it in strict reference to the province of Flanders.

The surest basis for comparative criticism is founded on book-illustration, where one is generally informed in regard to place and date of issue; but this evidence only begins about 1461 in Germany, about 1467 in Italy, about 1475 in the Netherlands, and about 1480 in France, England and Spain. Before this certain standards are offered by the block-books, but they contain almost as many problems of origin (locality and date) as the single cuts themselves, so that their study cannot offer similar clues in solving historical difficulties.

Comparison with line-engravings (after the introduction of this art about 1430) yields here and there definite points of contact, more particularly in copies in the one medium from the other (whether woodcut from line-engraving, or line-engraving from woodcut); but even here what should be a simple problem provides an occasional field for great divergence of opinion (e.g. the question of the *Ars Moriendi* block-book and the engravings by the Master E.S.).[2]

---

[1] Though with less accuracy in colour than such publications as those of the Graphische Gesellschaft (see P. Kristeller, *Über Reproduktion von Kunstwerken*, Repertorium, xxxi., 1908, 538).

[2] The following examples may be quoted [*See* footnote overleaf]:

Finally the study of contemporary painting, sculpture and illumination must offer indispensable side-lights in the development of general style of design, though any close correspondences of design are rarely found.

It seems probable that while the single cuts may have been sometimes based on panel paintings, book-illustration was more frequently inspired by illumination. In any case, scribes and illuminators appear in some cases to have turned to designing woodcuts, if not to block-cutting.[1]

The *earliest dates* found on woodcuts are 1418 on the *Madonna with Four Virgin Saints in a Garden* (S. 1160; fig. 46; Bibliothèque Royale, Brussels),[2] 1423 on the even more famous Buxheim *St. Christopher* from the Spencer Collection (now in the John Rylands Library, Manchester, S. 1349; fig. 44), and 1437 on a *Martyrdom of St. Sebastian* (S. 1684; fig. 41) at Vienna. Except for a MS. date, 1443, on a *Christ bearing the Cross with St. Dorothy and St. Alexis* (S. 930; fig. 60) at Nuremberg, these three cuts are the only known examples dated in the first half of the xv century; and it is not until after the middle of the century that dated cuts are fairly frequent.

These dated examples (if the dates are admitted to be authentic, a question to which we shall give considerable attention), together with other prints whose date is fixed with fair certainty by their provenance, inevitably offer

Adoration of the Magi (Dresden, *Einbl.*, Geisberg, 3). Cf. the Master of the Playing-cards (Lehrs, 8).

Entombment (Paris, S. 518, Bouchot, 52). Cf. an engraving described by Lehrs under the so-called Master of 1462 (Lehrs, 5).

St. Peter, and St. Paul holding Veronica Napkin (S. 1656, Berlin and Munich, dated 1473), after the Master E.S., B. 86 of 1467.

The Good Shepherd (S. 839, Dresden). Cf. the Master E.S. (Lehrs, 52).

The Good Shepherd (S. 838, Breslau, Stadtbibliothek). Cf. the Master of the Amsterdam Cabinet (Lehrs, 18).

The Twelve Apostles (British Museum, C.D., A. 146). Cf. Martin Schongauer (B. 34-45).

Man of Sorrows (British Museum, C.D., A. 147). Cf. Israhel van Meckenem (B. 1).

Pietà (Dresden, Prinz. Second. Genitur Bibl., *Einbl.*, pl. 11). Cf. Israhel van Meckenem (B. 138).

Most of such examples are generally regarded as woodcut copies of the line-engravings. But there is considerable controversy about the *Good Shepherd* (S. 838); Schreiber and Molsdorf regarding the engraving on the original, Kristeller the woodcut.

I would also note in this place the occasional influence of the line-engraver's style in xv-century woodcuts, e.g. in the fragment of a large *Crucifixion* in Lucerne, Kapucinerkloster (*Einbl.*, Freiburg and Luzern, pl. 7), in which the parallel curving lines of shading are reminiscent of the Master of the Playing-cards.

[1] See p. 598, and Index of Subjects under *Illumination*.

[2] There is a good early copy at Basle, from St. Gallen (S. 1161, reproduced *Einbl.* iii., pl. 5, and in the Catalogue of Auction xliv., Holstein and Puppel, Berlin 1930, No. 24).

the soundest basis for a proper realisation of the stages of development of early woodcut.[1] The woodcutter (if separate from the designer) is probably far less independent than the line-engraver of the period, so that we need not hope to recognise as many definite personalities as have been identified among the exponents of this other craft.

From the category of prints whose dates are fixed roughly by their provenance, I would cite the following as leading examples:

(1) The *Rest on the Flight into Egypt* (S.637, Vienna; fig. 39) and the *St. Jerome* (S.1536, Vienna),[2] both of which come from the

---

[1] Apart from provenance, and dates in MSS. in which the cuts occur, one might mention among other aids in dating early cuts:

(1) *Canonisation of Saints*, e.g. (*a*) the cuts in the first part of a Dominican Prayer Book (MS.) in the British Museum (C.D., A. 142) are certainly before the Canonisation of St. Catherine (1461); the second part of the book (without cuts) refers to her canonisation and the new festival; (*b*) cuts of *St. Nicholas of Tolentino* in or after 1446, of *St. Simon of Trent* in or after 1475.

(2) References to Popes, e.g. to Pope Sixtus IV. (1471–84) on the *Virgin and Child in the Rosary* (S. 1133; British Museum, C.D., A. 59); references to Nicolas V. (1447–55) and Callixtus III. (1455–58) on the *St. Gregory's Mass* (S. 1462) at Nuremberg. But conclusions of a date between 1447 and 1458 made by Holtrop and others in regard to the latter have been questioned by Kristeller (*Die Apocalypse*, Berlin 1916).

(3) *Costume*. There is considerable reason to suppose that the costume, even of Scriptural subjects, followed contemporary fashions. The various series of one subject (notably in the block-books) gives the best support to this assumption.

In the early xv century the dresses of both men and women are long, often trailing in folds on the ground; and the women's bodice is close-fitting. Gradually men's skirts became shorter, until about the middle of the century they reach the knees. This is only one example of many details which might be cited.

(4) *The nature of the folds of drapery*, from the round folds, with or without loops, of the early xv century, to the more angular folds of the second quarter and middle of the century.

I would also note as the chief aids in localisation, apart from places actually named on the print:

(1) *Text* (see W. Molsdorf, *Schrifteigentümlichkeiten auf älteren Holzschnitten als Hilfsmittel ihrer Gruppierung*, Strassburg 1914). Some of his conclusions, e.g. the distinction of certain types of Gothic *r* (ꝛ) as specifically French, and not in common use until after 1450 (on which he bases his theory of the French origin of edition iii. of the *Apocalypse* block-book), are questionable; (2) *MS.;* (3) *convents noted;* (4) *patron saints* (see p. 130, *St. Ulrich and St. Afra*, p. 181, *St. Ursula and St. Gereon*); (5) *costume;* (6) *character of cuts* (treatment of subjects); (7) *colour;* (8) *water-marks*. But very comprehensive study is necessary under many of these heads to be of decisive value.

[2] There is another contemporary version of the *St. Jerome* in Berlin (S.1535), which came from a MS. from the Convent of Oliva near Danzig. I am unable to adjudge priority to one or the other. Comparable also is a smaller *St. Jerome* in the British Museum (S.1546).

Fig. 39. Rest on the Flight into Egypt. S. 637.

binding of a MS. of which the earlier part, a German translation from the Fathers dealing with St. Jerome, was written in 1410, and dedicated by Johann VIII., Bishop of Olmütz in Bohemia, to the Margravine Elizabeth of Moravia; the latter portion a German *Ars Moriendi* written in 1434.

The prints are on the same paper as the whole volume (with a water-mark near Briquet 14745, bull's head with flower), and as there are many blank pages, it may be assumed that the volume was prepared as a blank book for MS. in or before 1410, and that the prints are no later.

(2) *St. Dorothy* (S. 1395, Munich; fig. 40) and the *Martyrdom of St. Sebastian* (S. 1677, Munich),[1] both from the binding of a MS. of 1410 from the Convent of St. Zeno, near Reichenhall, on the borders of Upper Bavaria, in the neighbourhood of Salzburg.

These four examples may be provisionally accepted as forerunners of the Brussels *Madonna* and the Buxheim *St. Christopher*, and a rough differentiation of their respective styles will serve to distinguish what is probably rightly regarded as the earliest phase in the production of woodcuts from the succeeding stage in their development.

In the *earliest phase* the outlines are broad, shading is absent, and both contours and inner lines are generally characterised by graceful curvature. The arrangement of folds of drapery frequently falls either into hairpin-like bends 0 or into loops 0, the latter offering a characteristic form too widespread to justify Bouchot's use of it to distinguish a single master (his so-called *Maître aux Boucles*). Bouchot's *point de départ* for his title was the *Agony in the Garden* in Paris (S. 185, Lemoisne v.; fig. 50).

The woodcuts noted as belonging to the earlier phase are in a thick black ink, and the mottled surface quality of parts and the clearer lines near the edges point to stamping as the method of impression; the *Madonna* of 1418 and the *St. Christopher* of 1423 are in a brownish ink of thinner consistency, and appear to have been printed by the rubber. The *Martyrdom of St. Sebastian* of 1437 (S. 1684; fig. 41)[2] is a later example in the blacker ink, but it is printed more clearly than one would expect if stamped, and is somewhat indented as if it were a rubbed impression. In general the distinction described roughly characterises the respective impressions of woodcuts of the first and second phases in the development of woodcut.

---

[1] See J. Jahn, *Beiträge*, Strassburg 1927, p. 35.   [2] The inscription illustrates the common use of pictures of St. Sebastian for prayer and protection against plague.

In breadth and curvature of lines the earlier cuts follow naturally in development on the *Bois Protat*, which has already been described and reproduced (fig. 32). It was only as the cutter became more accustomed

Fig. 40. St. Dorothy. S. 1395.

to paper and its possibilities that he turned to a thinner line nearer to that of a pen-drawing, and while in the earliest cuts the aim was outline to be filled in with colour by hand, the cutter gradually realised that by shading in line he could in some sense replace the need of colour. In the *Madonna* of 1418 the contours and inner lines are already much thinner, and are already characterised by angles rather than curves; while the folds end like pothooks Γ. The 'loops' and 'hairpins' gradually give way (though still found in the second quarter of the century) to various forms such as $\uparrow$ Γ Γ Γ $\not\!\!E$ beginning somewhat before the end of the first quarter of the century and continuing into the second half of the century. The last form illustrated (of a branching character) may be noted in the *Christ bearing the Cross with St. Dorothy and St. Alexis* (S. 930; fig. 60) with the MS. date 1443, already mentioned.

The *St. Christopher* still preserves the broader and more curving line, and in this respect seems earlier in its character than the Brussels *Madonna*,

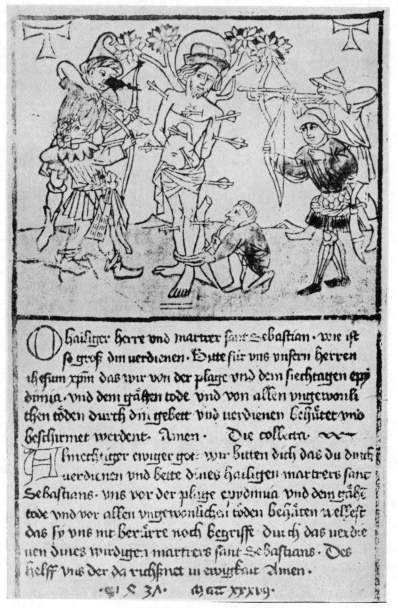

Fig. 41. The Martyrdom of St. Sebastian. S. 1684.

CARL A. RUDISILL LIBRARY
LENOIR RHYNE COLLEGE

but it shows the beginnings of linear shading. The *Martyrdom of St. Sebastian* of 1437 (fig. 41) is of necessity more delicate in line from the mere fact of its smaller scale, but other examples which can be approximately dated show that this is not only a matter of scale. Like many cuts of the middle of the xv century, it still preserves the simple outline manner, for the introduction of shading did not imply any general practice; in fact the full representation of tone by shading did not develop until the end of the century and the time of Dürer.

Fig. 42. St. Gertrude. S. 1454a.

As examples of the thinner line of the *second phase*, of which an approximate dating is fixed by their provenance, I would note the *St. Gertrude and St. Apollonia* in the University Library at Munich (S. 1454a and 1234x), two subjects on one block, of which the left half is reproduced in fig. 42), and a *Christ on the Cross between the Virgin and St. John* at Linz (Gugenbauer, *Einbl.* 14). The *St. Gertrude* comes from a MS. of Erasmus Schwab written in 1432 and 1435; the *Christ on the Cross*, which is printed on vellum,[1] from a MS. missal of the Convent of Garsten in Upper Austria, part of which is dated 1437.

The *St. Gertrude and St. Apollonia* is in many respects comparable in

[1] Cf. p. 73 for prints on vellum.

Fig. 43. St. Michael and the Virgin and Child. S. 1631.

details of style with the Buxheim *St. Christopher*, e.g. in the shading (chiefly in the angles of the folds), in the drawing of the hair, and the character of the plants; and a fine cut of *St. Anthony on a Gothic Canopied Throne* at Munich (S. 1218), with a water-mark of the bull's head, of a type which is largely found in Upper Germany,[1] has some of the same characteristics.

Among further examples of the thinner line another *St. Gertrude* (S. 1454, Berlin) may be mentioned, considerably damaged but otherwise even more attractive than its counterpart at Munich; and a *St. Michael and the Virgin and Child* (S. 1631, Berlin; fig. 43), already stiff, straight and angular, but dignified in design.

Similar in style to the Berlin *St. Gertrude* is a woodcut of *Peasants travelling*, at Wolfenbüttel (S. 1985 x), possibly suggested by some rendering of the Flight into Egypt. It is remarkable for the same vivid humanity as the *St. Gertrude*, and as one of the earliest-known cuts of a profane subject.

The development of woodcut in the middle of the century is perhaps best seen in the block-books which will be studied in the next chapter, and it will be found that what appear to be the earliest examples of such books show an outline manner roughly corresponding with what we have called the second phase of woodcut, while the later examples with the greater angularity and added shading correspond with the development seen in the book-illustrations of about 1470–80.

Before referring to further examples, I must recur to the question of the Buxheim *St. Christopher*[2] (fig. 44) and the Brussels *Madonna* in more detail: (1) in regard to their dates; (2) in regard to their local origin. Schreiber is unable to harmonise his view of the development of early woodcut with the date on the *St. Christopher*, which he conjecturally places in the period about 1440–60, regarding the date 1423 as having reference to some unexplained historical event. Now the print and its companion, the *Annunciation* (S. 28), coloured and no doubt cut by the same hand, are preserved in the binding of a MS., *Laus Virginis*, of 1417, which belonged originally to Jacobus Matzenberger, parish priest of Memmingen, and passed during the xv century into the neighbouring Carthusian monastery of Buxheim.

[1] But cf. p. 114 (re *Christ before Herod*).

[2] A woodcut copy was made by Sebastian Roland in 1775 and appeared as a folding plate in C. G. von Murr's *Journal zur Kunstgeschichte*, 2te Teil, Nuremberg 1776, at p. 104. Impressions of this copy have sometimes passed for late impressions from the original block. No impressions from the original block of any kind are known apart from the Manchester example. Roland's signature occurs beneath the border-line in lower right, so that it might be cut away leaving the print unimpaired.

Fig. 44. The Buxheim St. Christopher. S. 1349.

The volume was discovered there by Baron von Heinecken in 1769, passed later into the collection of Lord Spencer, from whose collection it came with other incunabula into the possession of Mrs. John Rylands, eventually to form part of her foundation, the John Rylands Library, Manchester, in 1899.

From the condition of the volume, there is every reason to think that the cuts were inserted within a short period of the completion of the manuscript, and present knowledge of Upper German painters of the earlier xv century (of whom Lukas Moser, Conrad Witz and Hans Multscher were the chief representatives) supports the natural acceptance of the date on the print as referring to its origin. Comparison with the paintings of this Swabian school also renders it unnecessary to look far from Memmingen for the production of the woodcut. Bouchot's suggestion of the region of Avignon, and his comparison of part of the background of the cut with a sketch of the fountain of Vaucluse by Petrarch in a MS. of the Bibliothèque Nationale, Paris,[1] are far beyond the mark. For landscape as well as for other features, Molsdorf[2] is right in comparing two woodcuts formerly at St. Gallen,[3] Switzerland, the *Nativity* (S. 84) and *Adoration of the Magi* (S. 98), which were both taken from MS. written by a St. Gallen monk, named Kemli, who was working in the Abbey there between 1428 and 1476. Another cut of the *Nativity* (S. 82, Berlin) is the same subject in reverse to the St. Gallen example, and is probably the earlier version.

The *Adoration of the Magi* shows the branching folds of drapery, which have been already noted in the *Christ bearing the Cross with St. Dorothy and St. Alexis* of 1443 (S. 930; fig. 60), a characteristic which is also seen in another print from St. Gallen, the *Virgin and Child and St. Anne* (S. 1194).

Bouchot was right in envisaging the possibility of an international trade in woodcuts in Europe (just as we know that Ulm sent its stores of playing-cards into far-distant regions);[4] and, carried away by his nationalist views in regarding as French most of the early woodcuts found in Germany or Austria, he finds his defence in the statement that the woodcutter would have no honour in his own country, and that the cuts most likely to be revered and preserved were those acquired from afar.

---

[1] Fonds Latin, No. 6802; for reproduction see Prince d'Essling and E. Müntz, *Pétrarque*, Paris 1902, p. 5.

[2] *Gruppierungsversuche im Bereiche des ältesten Kupferstiches*. Strassburg 1911.

[3] The St. Gallen prints were sold by Holstein and Puppel, Auction xliv., Berlin, 7th November 1930.

[4] An interesting woodcut record of pilgrims' roads in Europe (no doubt following trade routes in many places) is seen in a map of about 1480–90 of *Pilgrims' Roads to Rome from Germany and Austria*, preserved at Linz (Gugenbauer, *Einbl.*, 1912, pl. 25).

He pictured the travelling craftsman with his stock of prints with large margins ready for such inscriptions (added by hand or from a further block) as would be pertinent to the convents that purchased them; or plugging the original block with such lettering as was desired. On this assumption, and combined with his belief in Dijon and the region of the Burgundian court as the chief centre of the manufacture of the earliest woodcuts, the predominance of German or Austrian provenance for the majority of the earliest woodcuts, and of German inscriptions when any lettering occurs, were facts lightly swept aside.

In spite of these exaggerations Bouchot at least aroused further research into national origins, and I will return later to a consideration of what may be regarded as French among the earliest woodcuts.

How far the earliest xv-century work was produced by the monks themselves in their *convents* and how far merely supplied to the convents from the chief centres of art production (e.g. from places like Dijon and Avignon in France; Bruges in the Netherlands; Ulm in Swabia; Salzburg in Austria, etc.) may never perhaps be satisfactorily decided.

Throughout the Middle Ages the scribes were largely the monks, and the art of illumination developed as an essentially conventual occupation. So it is natural to suppose that the craft of printing images would be adopted by the monks on its earliest introduction as a more economical means of disseminating knowledge and interest in their faith among the laity. Several conventual societies are known to have taken especial advantage of art and the new learning for such ends, in particular the *Fratres Communis Vitae* (*Broeders van het gemeene Leven*) founded at the end of the xiv century in the Netherlands by Geerte de Groote of Deventer, whose efforts extended during the xv century from the main convent of Groenendael near Brussels to many other convents in the Netherlands and to Cologne in Germany; and later the *Rosenkranz* Brotherhood,[1] revived by Jacob Sprenger at Cologne, and the St. Ursula Fraternity founded by the Augustinians at Strassburg, both in the last quarter of the xv century.

It is noteworthy that even in the xvi century one of Luther's complaints against the Pope in his work *An den christlichen Adel deutscher Nation* was that he granted the revenues of a convent to some cardinal, who would leave a single monk in charge, one of whose chief duties was to sell pictures to pilgrims (*irgent einen apostaten vorlaufen munch hynein setzen der funff*

---

[1] See *Liber Fraternitatis Rosaceae Coronae*, Cologne (J. de Landen) *c.* 1498. Hain-Copinger 7356; Schreiber 4048.

*odder sechs gulden des jahres nympt, und sitzt des tages in der kirche vorkaufft
den pilgern zeychen und bildlin das widder singen noch leszen daselb mehr
geschicht* — ed. printed by Melchior Lotter, Wittenberg 1520, sig. D.
iv).

Here and there lay craftsmen of repute are known who from one reason
or another entered the convent cells as monks, or lay brothers, e.g. in
France the famous sculptor Claux Sluter was admitted in 1404 to a
convent at St. Etienne.

The monks were in one respect in a position of considerable advantage
in the early days of woodcutting, for in various places government regulations were issued (no doubt at the instance of the Guilds of Painters)
putting obstacles in the way of woodcutters who imitated pictures, regulations which could not touch the craftsmen within convent walls. Bouchot
speaks of the early coloured cuts as being regarded as a sort of 'fausse
monnaie graphique'.[1] The document quoted above, about Jan van den
Berghe of Louvain, shows the jealousy of the guilds in regard to extra-
mural workers who tried to keep free from trade regulations. And we have
already referred to analogous restrictions imposed on the illustration of
the new printed books, to some extent perhaps through the jealousy of
the block-book cutters.

One very definite early example of relation to a convent may be noted,
that of the *Christ on the Cross* (S. 932; fig. 45) with the arms of the convent of
Tegernsee in Upper Bavaria, of which impressions are known at Munich
and Nuremberg. The presence of the coat on both the impressions is strong
argument against Bouchot's theory that the arms was merely added as an
ex-libris; it is more probable that it indicates the place of origin.

Even admitting the possibilities of international commerce in prints, I
should in general be more inclined to accept original provenance as in some
near relation to the place of original production, as long as the style of the
print did not disagree with the general character of work produced in the
same region.[2] Therefore pending further evidence it seems reasonable to

---

[1] See above, p. 81.

[2] Among the convents from which a considerable number of the woodcuts of the first half of
the xv century are known to have come are:

St. Zeno, near Reichenhall, Upper Bavaria; Tegernsee, Upper Bavaria; Ebersberg, Upper
Bavaria; Buxheim, near Memmingen, Upper Swabia; Inzigkofen, near Sigmaringen, Upper
Swabia; Nuremberg, Nunnery of St. Catherine; Langenzenn, near Nuremberg, Franconia; Oliva,
near Danzig (many of the woodcuts at Berlin); Mondsee, near Salzburg (about a quarter of the
xv-century cuts in the Albertina, Vienna), and various Salzburg and other Austrian convents,
and St. Jacobskirchbibliothek, at Brünn in Moravia.

regard the Buxheim *St. Christopher* as a production of south Germany or German Switzerland. If not the work of a convent, it is more natural to look for its origin in one of the chief art centres of the region such as Ulm, where we have seen there had long been a large trade in playing-cards, or in Constance from the relations already noted to cuts preserved until lately since the xv century at St.Gallen, Switzerland.[1]

Fig. 45. Christ on the Cross. S. 932.

For all Bouchot's assertions to the contrary, a German inscription is certainly in favour of German production. For any satisfactory support of Bouchot's theory of local lettering on foreign blocks, it would be necessary to find examples of states of one cut with lettering in different languages — which so far have not been adduced. Inscriptions in two languages, e.g. Low German and Wallon French on the *Good Shepherd* (S. 838, Breslau), is a different matter and points to production in a bilingual region such as Liége.

The Brussels *Madonna* of 1418 (fig. 46) has on the whole aroused more

[1] See p. 106, footnote 3.

Fig. 46. The Brussels Madonna. S. 1160.

controversy than the *St. Christopher*.[1] In the style of its design, particularly in its angular treatment and in the square pot-hook ends to the lines showing the folds of drapery, it is closely allied to prints such as the *Virgin and Child in a Glory* (S. 1108, Berlin; fig. 47.), which has been dated by such authorities as Friedländer and Kristeller as late as 1460 to 1470. And for this conjectured dating considerable support is given by a comparison with the figures in the *Speculum Humanae Salvationis in the Form of a Hand* at Munich, a woodcut dated 1466 (S. 1859), which, though probably Swabian, seems from its style to be based on a Netherlandish original in the manner of the Berlin *Virgin and Child in a Glory* (S. 1108). There are two other versions known of the *Speculum Hand* (Nuremberg, S. 1860, and Berlin, S. 1859 a, dated 1476), both probably German, but hardly so good as the Munich example. On the other hand, it seems later than two other works with which it has much in common, i.e. the earliest of the Netherlandish block-books, the first edition of the *Exercitium super Pater Noster*, and the first and third editions of the *Apocalypse*, which are dated by the same writers about 1430.[2] In the Brussels *Madonna* the angular style seems to have reached a stiffer convention than in the *Apocalypse*, while the *Exercitium* has nearer relation in its more curving style than either *Apocalypse* or *Madonna* to the xiv-century traditions. But careful examination of the Brussels print leaves little room for suspecting that any later hand has tampered with the date. If it should be concluded that the date does not harmonise with the style,[3] it would be a more reasonable explanation that an early copyist had repeated the date of his original, just as the line-engraver, called the *Master of the Banderoles*, repeated the date on his copies of the *Woodcut Grotesque Alphabet* of 1464 (see below, p. 147). The existence of numerous versions of several early woodcuts,

---

[1] Apart from the general literature, see C. D. B. (C. de Brou), *Quelques mots sur la gravure . . . de 1418*, Brussels 1846; C. Ruelens, *La Vierge de 1418*, Documents Iconographiques et Typographiques de la Bibl. Roy. de Belgique, Brussels 1877; H. Hymans, *L'Estampe de 1418 et la validité de sa date*, Brussels 1903 (Bulletin de l'Académie Royale de Belgique, January 1903, No. 1); and J. Jahn, *Beiträge*, Strassburg 1927, p. 52. Two full-size reproductions are given by Ruelens, one showing the colour which obscures the lines considerably, the other in line only and no doubt partly made up. The reproduction given in my Fig. 46 is obscure, but at least faithful as far as it goes, having been made from a recent photograph from the woodcut. The dark shadow in the drapery is a dull red, the trees and grass are coloured a light green, and there is a yellowish-brown tint in various places (e.g. on the gate); the lines are strongly indented. The paper, which is torn and made up in pencil along the foot, is otherwise considerably damaged, foxed and worm-holed. It is impossible to judge the print apart from examination of the original.

[2] See p. 218.

[3] As Dr. Paul Kristeller has advanced.

Fig. 47. The Virgin and Child in a Glory. S. 1108.

e.g. three of the Buxheim *Annunciation*,[1] two of the Vienna *St. Jerome* (S. 1536)[2] and two of the Brussels *Madonna* itself,[3] makes us more inclined to consider this probability. It is at least difficult to think that the Brussels *Madonna*, in the version known to us, should precede the period when Van Eyck's influence became predominant, i.e. after the achievement of the Ghent altar-piece, about 1430–32.

Moreover the Brussels *Madonna* is considerably inferior in artistic qualities to such works as the *Apocalypse* on one side and the Berlin *Virgin and Child in a Glory* on the other, so that we may regret the less our uncertainties as to its actual position in the historical development of woodcut.

If the date is to be regarded as belonging authentically and originally to the Brussels *Madonna*, then we should be constrained to place the first editions of the *Exercitium* and the *Apocalypse*, like Bouchot, even earlier than our conjectured date of about 1430, but this position would perhaps be even less tenable. I shall return to this question in my study of the block-books in a later chapter. Here I have done little beyond presenting the difficulties that surround the problem of the Brussels *Madonna*, without presuming to solve them.

On one matter dogmatism seems justified, i.e. in reference to the Netherlandish origin of the Brussels *Madonna*. The comparison already made with the Berlin *Virgin and Child in a Glory*, which has a Dutch inscription, and its relation to another print with Dutch inscription, the *Mass of St. Gregory* (S. 1462, Nuremberg; fig. 62), which appears to belong to about the middle of the xv century, leaves little doubt on this score.

I would now retrace my steps after this discussion of certain documented examples and of the dated cuts of 1418 and 1423, neither of which can be regarded as the best representatives of their time, to give some account (or at least enumeration) of some of the more important examples of the earliest woodcuts, and to see if thereby any further light is shed on local origins.

Inferences from the dated and dateable cuts already discussed justify us in dating what we have described as the *first phase* as the first quarter of the fifteenth century; the *second phase*, the second quarter (corresponding with the earlier block-books); and if we continue to make such divisions in the second half of the century, the *third phase* may be regarded as covering the third quarter of the century (corresponding with the later block-books and earlier book-illustration), and the *fourth phase*, the last quarter, including the more developed book-illustration and the earlier works of the greatest German master of the century, Albrecht Dürer.

---

[1] See p. 93.   [2] See p. 97.   [3] See p. 96.

THE FIRST PHASE

The *Christ before Herod* (S. 265; fig. 48) is perhaps more nearly related in style of design to the *Bois Protat* than is any other early woodcut, a fact which might be regarded as favouring French origin of about 1400. The only two impressions known are in the British Museum, both originally pasted inside the cover of a copy of the *Vitas Sanctorum Patrum* printed by Koberger (Nuremberg, 1474), the one here reproduced having been transferred to the Print Room. They both have the water-mark of a bull's head with flower, which is fairly common to Italy, France and Germany at the period, most frequently found perhaps in Upper Germany, and occurring, it must be remembered, in the two early cuts at Vienna, the *Rest on the Flight into Egypt* (S. 637). and the *St. Jerome* (S. 1536), whose provenance points to Austrian, Bohemian or Upper German origin. Both impressions are in a thick oily black ink, showing here and there a mottled character in surface quality and stronger lines near the edges, indications of the method of stamping. They are uncoloured, a rare condition in early woodcuts, where the simple outline style was no doubt conditioned by the aim of the cutter, i.e. a coloured picture, in which the main structure of the design could be multiplied for the sake of economy in supplying a popular demand.

Almost equally early is a group of three prints preserved in the Graphische Sammlung, Munich, the *Annunciation and Nativity*, two subjects on one block, in upper and lower divisions as in the Apocalypse block-books (S. 51 and 65; fig. 49),[1] the *Death of the Virgin* (S. 709) and the *Coronation of the Virgin* (S. 729). Less monumental perhaps, they are gentler and more graceful in treatment (with less exaggeration in the lines of nose and brow, and in the length of the fingers), and reflect very closely the best spirit of XIV-century painting and illumination. Long forms with a tendency to graceful curves, close-fitting tunics and long mantles spreading wide on the ground about the feet, with folds frequently expressed in loops, all rendered in thick outline with no shading, characterise the group.

Nearly allied in general style, though not necessarily of the same school, is the *Agony in the Garden* (S. 185, Lemoisne v.; fig. 50; Paris), to which we have already referred.[2] The impression is a velvety black and the ink betrays its oily character by a brownish stain showing on the reverse.[3] In addition

---

[1] A fine impression of S. 65 was also more recently acquired for the Albertina, Vienna (1923 —971).

[2] See p. 99. See J. Jahn, *Beiträge*, Strassburg 1927, p. 29.

[3] See p. 5.

Fig. 48. Christ before Herod. S. 265.

Fig. 49. The Annunciation and Nativity. S. 51 and 65.

to the usual hand tinting (which here as in many of the cuts of the earliest phase is dull in tone, browns and yellows predominating), the background is painted a deep black, not an uncommon practice with the earliest wood-cutters.[1]

Comparable also is the large woodcut of *Christ bearing the Cross*, of which two impressions are known (Vienna, and Baron Edmond de Rothschild, Paris), and three smaller prints of different renderings of the same subject in the Bibliothèque Nationale belong to the same class (S. 342, 344 and 357). The Vienna impression came from the cover of one of the Imperial Registers of the Emperor Sigismund (1368–1437), a fact which carries some weight in favour of Austrian, Bohemian or Upper German origin.

Several versions of *Christ on the Cross* should be noted in the same relation: two at Munich, S. 387 (possibly by the same hand as the *Death and Coronation of the Virgin*, S. 709 and 729) and S. 389, and two at Berlin, S. 402 and S. 435 [2] (S. 402, very near in design to the large *Christ on the Cross* with the Tegernsee Arms, S. 932, already described and reproduced, fig. 45), and the *Four Saints* (*St. John Baptist*, *St. John Evangelist*, *St. Sebastian* and *St. Anthony*) at Munich (S. 1771), though somewhat stiffer in design,[2] belongs to the group.

The *Mass of St. Gregory* (S. 1461) and the *St. Barbara and St. Catherine* (S. 1264 m) at Berlin, and a pendant to the latter in the collection of Count Harrach at Vienna, *St. Dorothy and St. Margaret* (S. 1404 m) show differences in details of style and treatment, but all belong to the same phase.

Considerable controversy has centred round the large standing figure of *St. Erasmus* in Paris (S. 1315, Lemoisne ii.; fig. 51), one of most imposing prints of the same class. Martyrdom with the awls in the finger-tips had suggested the various titles of St. Cassian, Bishop of Imola, who was buried at Brixen (the original suggestion of Duchesne when it came to the Bibliothèque Nationale from M. Hennin in 1830), St. Benignus, Bishop of Dijon (Bouchot's identification), St. Erasmus (Schreiber) and finally St. Quentin (Delen). St. Quentin may, I think, be ruled out, as he was a Roman soldier but never a Bishop. Either St. Cassian or St. Benignus might fit, and of the latter Bouchot made good use in referring its origin

[1] E.g. the *Last Judgment* (Dresden, S. 2899); the *Annunciation* (Munich, S. 29); *Christ on the Cross* (Munich, S. 467).

[2] Contrast the stiffness of the *St. Augustine and St. Anthony* in the Munich Library (S. 1231 a), which still preserves elements of the first phase, but probably shows archaism of a later date. A *St. George and the Dragon*, Nuremberg (S. 1447), is another example where the broad and curving outline style of the early phase is mixed with branching folds in the drapery, more consonant with the middle of the xv century.

Fig. 50. The Agony in the Garden. S. 185.

to France, but his comparison with an episode in another early cut of martyrdoms which he called *Les Douze Martyrs* (Paris, B. 76, Lemoisne lxx.) was unhappy, as Schreiber is manifestly right in describing the latter cut as the *Twelve Tortures of St. Erasmus* (S. 1409 x).[1] Though the tortured finger-tips are seldom shown in the representations of St. Erasmus,[2] the other tortures shown leave no doubt as to the identification.

Now St. Erasmus, Bishop of Antioch, was especially venerated in Germany, and another woodcut of very similar style and date represents a Bishop of Regensburg, i.e. *St. Wolfgang* (Collection of Baron Edmond de Rothschild, Paris, S. 1734),

[1] See W. L. Schreiber, *Zeitschrift für christliche Kunst*, 1908, pp. 88-89.
[2] For another early example see S. 1412, Berlin.

Fig. 51. St. Erasmus. S. 1315.

a fact which certainly strengthens the case for Upper German origin in both instances.[1]

Not far distant in date, and analogous in manner though less powerful, are two woodcuts representing *St. Christopher*, S. 1355 (Nuremberg, and Baron Edmond de Rothschild Collection), and S. 1352 (Berlin).

More likely to be French is a crude woodcut of the *Flagellation* in Paris (S. 288, Lemoisne vi.). The large buttons on the doublets of the executioners are like those in the *Bois Protat*, and the colouring of the print (with its bright vermilion, green and rose) finds no counterpart in undoubted German work. But the *Martyrdom of St. Vitus* (Berlin, S. 1730 n) argues caution, for its style is similar, while its subject points rather to Bohemian origin.

There must have been very definite channels of influence between French and Bohemian art in the late xiv century, for the Emperor Charles IV. (1316–78) was in close relations with the papal court at Avignon, invited a French architect to build the Cathedral at Prague and may have employed French (as he certainly used Italian) artists in work at his castle at Karlstein.[2] So that we must not be tempted by similarities of style to be dogmatic on local origins. Resemblances of the sort to which I refer may be noted between the *Virgin and Child in a Gothic Niche* (Paris, S. 1069, Lemoisne iv.; fig. 52; commonly called *La Vierge de Lyon*, from its provenance in a MS. found at Lyon), and the *Virgin and Child on a Gothic Throne* in the St. Jacobskirchbibliothek at Brünn (S. 1114),[3] which came from an Olmütz missal acquired for the Church Library in 1435.

Two other important woodcuts at Brünn came from the same missal, i.e. a *St. Wolfgang* (S. 1733) and the *Holy Trinity* (S. 736), a cut of unusually large dimensions (about 17 × 11 inches),[3] neither being far removed in style from the *Rest on the Flight into Egypt* (S. 637) and the *St. Jerome* (S. 1536, and other versions) already described in reference to their Olmütz relation.[4]

---

[1] St. Wolfgang was also founder of the Abbey of Mondsee, near Salzburg.

[2] See in particular various studies by Joseph Neuwirth, issued by the Gesellschaft zur Förderung deutscher Wissenschaft, Kunst und Literatur in Böhmen, Prague 1896, 1897 and 1898, and Richard Ernst, *Beiträge zur Kenntnis der Tafelmalerei Böhmens im xiv und am Anfang der xv Jahrhunderts*, Prague 1912.

[3] Lithographs and notice of the three cuts by A. von Wolfskron, in *Quellen und Forschungen zur vaterländischen Geschichte, Literatur und Kunst*, Vienna 1849, pp. 139-162.

[4] See p. 97. Very close to the same group in style are the *Annunciation* and *Holy Trinity* preserved inside the binding of a MS. of about 1400 (Latin writings of St. Chrysostom and St. Augustine) in the University Library of Prague (Sign. MS. iii. A. 12), which originally

St. Wolfgang, Bishop of Regensburg has already been noted as founder of the great Abbey of Mondsee, near Salzburg,[1] and for this reason and from other comparisons the region of Salzburg has been suggested. The most immediate comparison referred to is with the *Pietà* (S. 972 a) in Stift-Lambach in Upper Austria, which came from a MS. of the Salzburg district written between 1430 and 1434.[2]

Another *Pietà* (Vienna, from Maihingen, S. 973; fig. 53), of the same period and style, to which we have already referred as an example which seems inspired by sculpture,[3] is even more beautiful, and shows Italian influence in the simple harmony of its design.

belonged to the Jesuit College at Prague (Z. V. Tobolka, *Einblattdrucke des XV Jahrhunderts im Gebiete der Čechoslovakischen Republik*, Prague 1928–29, Nos. 19 and 20.

[1] See p. 120, note 1.

[2] See Gugenbauer, Heitz, *Einbl.*, Bd. 34, 1913.

[3] Cf. p. 93. For these two *Pietà*, cf. J. Jahn, *Beiträge*, Strassburg 1927, p. 16.

Fig. 52. The Virgin and Child in a Gothic Niche. S. 1069.

I have confessed my inability to dogmatise about the respective claims
of France and Bohemia in regard to the origin of certain woodcuts, and
a fortiori I am less able to dogmatise as to the regions of Bohemia, Austria
or Upper Germany to which other early cuts may belong.

Somewhat isolated in its style among the very early woodcuts is a *Death
of the Virgin* at Nuremberg (S. 705). It has a water-mark of lily and star,

Fig. 53. Pietà. S. 973.

which is chiefly found in France at the end of the XIV century, a fact slightly
in favour of French origin, but the international traffic in paper renders
this an unreliable criterion. Perhaps its nearest relatives are an *Annunciation*,
a *Death of Mary* and a *Man of Sorrows*, which have only recently been discovered in a Codex of uncertain source in the Strahow Convent at Prague.[1]

A few other examples of the first phase may be cited, which are probably

[1] Published by Kurt Rathe, *Mitteilungen*, 1928, p. 41, and Z. V. Tobolka, *Einbl. des XV
Jahrhunderts im Gebiete der Čechoslovakischen Republik*, Prague 1928–29, Nos. 28, 27 and 29.

Upper German in origin: a *Martyrdom of St. Erasmus* in the British Museum (S. 1410 d), possibly by the same hand as the *Martyrdom of St. Sebastian* (S. 1677) from a Reichenhall MS. of 1410, already referred to,[1] a *Christ in the Wine-Press* at Nuremberg (S. 841), a *St. Dorothy* at Munich (S. 1394),[2] and an *Annunciation* (S. 34) of which the only two known impressions (Nuremberg and Dutuit Collection, Paris) came from a MS. of 1449 from the convent of Inzigkofen near Sigmaringen. The background of the *St. Dorothy* is painted with red stars like an *Annunciation* (S. 25)[3] at Munich, which is printed in brownish ink with the rubber, and has the general character of the second phase in the history of early woodcut (about 1425– 1450). Similarity in colouring cannot in fact be taken as a criterion of origin, for although the early woodcutters in general aimed at a coloured picture, yet they must frequently have supplied uncoloured impressions (no doubt at cheaper prices) for their customers to colour.

An interesting example of colour is the *Virgin and Child in a Glory* in the Stadtbibliothek at Nuremberg (S. 1048 b) which came from the nunnery of St. Catherine in the same city. This large cut, which is some- what in the style of the *St. Dorothy* (S. 1394), and hardly later than 1430, is printed in white pigment on green-tinted paper. It is almost impossible to be certain whether it is a pattern for textile printing,[4] or a print for decorative use on its own account in a manner imitating a textile print.

Two fragments of exceptionally large prints, which probably date about the end of the first phase or early in the second period, are the *Adoration of the Magi* at Dillingen (S. 97 a) and the *Last Judgment* at Dresden (S. 2899). If complete, the former would probably have measured about 11 × 16 inches (near the same size as the *Holy Trinity* at Brünn [5]), the latter still larger, and apparently about $16\frac{1}{2}$ × 22 inches. These very large cuts must have been definitely intended for wall or altar decoration in house or chapel, and though many such may have been cut, it is not astonishing that few prints are preserved,[6] the majority of existing impressions owing their preservation to their place within the binding of old MSS. or printed volumes.

[1] See p. 99.

[2] Kurt Rathe aptly compares with this *St. Dorothy*, a drawing of St. Mary Magdalene in the Louvre, dated 1410 (*Mitteil. der Gesellsch. für vervielf. Kunst*, 1932, p. 19).

[3] Water-mark, bunch of grapes, cf. Br. 13054-65, chiefly noted in Upper Germany and Switzerland. Another example of decoration of background with painted stars is the *St. Dorothy* at Berlin (S. 1397). See p. 134.   [4] See p. 69.   [5] See p. 120.

[6] One other large cut (about $10\frac{1}{2}$ × 16 inches), probably of the second quarter of the century, may be here mentioned, i.e. a *Flagellation*, of which a damaged impression is preserved at Vienna (S. 285, o); it came from the Convent of Langenzenn, near Nuremberg (see p. 130).

Fig. 54. St. Veronica. S. 1719.

It might be noted here that even smaller subjects were occasionally cut in groups on large blocks, the composite impression being afterwards cut up. Numerous series of the Passion and of Saints must have been done for economy in this way,[1] and such subjects as playing-cards, alphabets and the like. Another means of economy was the cutting of the block on both sides.[2]

Rather similar in style and type of face to the Dillingen *Adoration* (though cruder in treatment) is a smaller *Adoration of the Magi* once at Maihingen (S. 102) to which a print of the *Virgin and Child and Four Saints* from the same collection (S. 1172) forms a companion.[3]

Thinner in line, but in its flowing and rounded style still perhaps within the early phase, is a *St. Christopher* at Berlin (S. 1350 a), and the same may

[1] E.g. eight Passion subjects at Vienna (S. 22), the *St. Gertrude and St. Apollonia* in the University Library, Munich (S. 1454 a and 1234 x).

[2] E.g. the *Bois Protat* (see p. 70), and a block with a *St. Sebastian* (S.1678) and rev. *the Sacred Monogram* (S.1812) in the British Museum. See below, p. 322.

[3] S. 102 and 1172 were Nos. 1 and 2 in Auktion IX., Karl and Faber, Munich, 11 May 1934.

be said of a remarkable cut of *St. Veronica* (S. 1719; fig. 54) of which there are impressions at Berlin and Paris. The appearance of the line in the Paris impression of the *St. Veronica* (which is similar to that of a small *Christ on the Cross* in Paris, S. 459) inclined Bouchot[1] to suspect that it was printed from a metal plate, possibly etched in relief. But I have no doubt from the knowledge of both impressions that it is printed from wood.

Most of the prints hitherto described as belonging to the first phase are printed in the deep black ink of thick oily consistency which we have already described, and a considerable number have the appearance of having been stamped. For the convenience of technical comparison I would here note four other less important cuts in the British Museum which would appear to be stamped prints, i.e. the *Infant Christ with a Bird* (S. 786), *St. Barbara and St. Catherine* (S. 1265), the *Ecstasy of St. Mary Magdalene* (S. 1600) and the *St. Sebastian* (S. 1687), in addition to the two *Ornamental Designs* (S. 2004 and 2005) to which reference has already been made.[2] The ink presents a mottled appearance, and on larger blocks such as the *Christ before Herod* (S. 265) the impression would tend to be darker near the edges of the block.

In summing up the characteristics of the period I may be excused for some repetition. The earliest prints are for the most part cut in broad outlines, harmoniously curved and flowing in character, with no lines of shading. Nothing beyond outline was called for, for the artist intended the print to be the basis for colour: in fact an economical and popular substitute for a picture. The figures tend to length and to graceful and sinuous lines, which are emphasised by the long flowing robes which fall in full folds on the ground, covering the feet. These long robes or mantles were worn on state occasions by both men and women, and are the usual form in which Christ, the Virgin and Saints, and Biblical figures in general, were represented in the first quarter of the xv century. It is only the soldiers and serving men who regularly figure in the shorter garb. The painters and woodcutters of the period are generally found using contemporary costume in their illustrations, though no doubt partially modified by archaic flavour and fancy, and it is natural therefore to find the gradual shortening of men's skirts during the xv century reflected in the cuts of the second phase or period (about 1425–50), and continued until, towards the end of the century, they scarcely pass the hips. So women's dresses tend to become closer-

---

[1] Who referred in this relation to a record of payment to Jean Malouel for *une table de laiton* (brass) *pour tailler en icelle plusieurs estampes* (C. Dehaisnes, *Documents*, Lille 1887, p. 770).

[2] See p. 69.

fitting as the century progresses, ending in the fantastic exaggerations of the high waist and protuberant curves of the late xv and early xvi century.

In the first period folds of drapery are rendered in curving lines that follow the rhythm of the figures, ending in loops (*boucles*) or hairpin-bends. In the second period (about 1425–50) outline is generally thinner, a gradual tendency towards angularity appears (originating perhaps in the desire for vividness of expression), the loops and hairpins give way to the pot-hook forms, which we have already illustrated,[1] and shading is introduced.

In the first phase the figures alone were thought of, and they are designed against a blank ground, which is frequently painted black, to emphasise the design still further. In the second phase more thought is given to the setting, and landscape or other background begins to perform an important part in the design. The earliest cuts were enclosed in a single border-line; later, variety is sometimes introduced by the use of two or more border-lines, or a decorative border, whether on the block itself or cut on a separate block as a *passe-partout* to serve with various subjects.

With the growth of shading in line, colour became less essential; nevertheless until the end of the xv century it is more common in Germany and the North to find single cuts and book-illustrations coloured than uncoloured. The few Italian cuts of the middle of the xv century that are preserved are for the most part coloured, their aim, like so many of the Northern cuts, being the replacement of a picture; but except in its very beginning Italian xv-century book-illustration is more often left uncoloured than not, in spite of its tendency to pure outline style.

A final word in comparison of the cuts of the first phase in the North with the later developments. The finest examples, such as the *Rest on the Flight into Egypt* (S.637; fig. 39), the *Christ before Herod* (S.265; fig. 48), the *Annunciation and Nativity* (S.51 and 65; fig. 49) and the *Agony in the Garden* (S.185; fig. 50), show a dignity of style that is hardly matched in quality until Dürer, and for their particular virtues not overshadowed even by his greater individuality. The earliest woodcutters are less personal, more uniform in their reflection of the traditional style of the xiv-century painter, when individuality counted for so much less than the continuance of a noble tradition. And for that very reason, and for the simplicity of the style of cutting which they chose, they are often more convincing than were their immediate successors, who were struggling to develop on more individual

[1] See p. 100.

lines and essaying more complex technical problems in the representation of tone and plastic values in line.

In the second quarter of the century stamping appears to have largely given way to printing with the rubber, and the ink tends to lighter tones of brown or grey, though the brown tones may in some cases represent an original black oxidised in the course of time. In the third quarter of the century, with the introduction of book-printing, it gradually became the common practice to print single blocks in the printing press, and a blacker ink was again in common use (or an ink which has retained its original tone), but seldom of the deep carbon tones and thick consistency of the earliest prints.

THE SECOND PHASE

I would now pass from the general to the particular, and refer to various prints of the second phase (about 1425–50) supplementary to those already cited as *criteria*, continuing somewhat beyond this limit into the second half of the century, but chiefly dealing with woodcuts which preceded the introduction of book-illustration in their respective countries. Single cuts contemporary with book-illustration will be more appropriately treated alongside the illustrations of similar style, or of the same master.

Some of the single cuts of the second phase which are more directly related to the block-books may for similar reasons be discussed in the chapter on the block-books.

Characteristics of the earliest phase would be more likely to persist longest in the more popular subjects which would be frequently repeated, or in works of local craftsmen outside the main current of progress. As an example of the first category might be cited the series of the *Passion* in Berlin (S. 151 a, etc.; Lehrs 13-24), probably Upper German work of about 1430–50, where the early traditions of round folds and pure outline are still followed. To the second category may perhaps be assigned the *St. Francis and St. Louis of Toulouse* at Graz (S. 1432 p), where long curving figures, thick outlines and folds with loops reflect the manner of the earliest cuts, though its production may be within the limits of the second period. It came from the binding of a MS. written in Upper Styria in 1440, and is very probably a production of that region of Austria.

To the Austrian[1] or Bohemian school may belong two companion wood-

---

[1] See Otto Benesch, *Zur altösterreichischen Tafelmalerei*, Jahrbuch der Kunsthistorischen Sammlungen in Wien, Neue Folge ii., 1928, p. 69. Dr. Benesch seems justified in attributing

cuts of very marked style, preserved at Vienna, an *Annunciation* (S. 25 b) and a *Visitation* (S. 52 b), which were taken from the binding of an Olmütz MS. The MS. belongs to the late xv century, but to judge from the breadth of style, curving folds and slight use of shading, the cuts probably date from the second quarter of the century. Not unlike in manner is a *Virgin and Child with St. Anne* in the British Museum (S. 1190).[1]

One of the earliest documents of localisation and identification is provided by the cut of the *Vision of St. Bernard* (S. 1271, Vienna, fig. 55) which is signed *Jerg Haspel ze Bibrach*. I see no reason to follow Bouchot in suspecting the signature to be a later addition, particularly as the style fits in perfectly with other cuts which can be localised in the same region about the same date. Bibrach (or Biberach) is near Ulm in Swabia; the arms which appear on the print are referred by Haberditzl to the Cistercian Abbey of Ebrach (between Würzburg and Bamberg), but they probably apply to the Cistercian order in general. They appear on several other prints, e.g. on a later woodcut of the same subject (differently rendered) at Basle (S. 1273).[2]

In design the cut still retains the loops and the rounded folds of drapery, but the line is thinner than is usual in the earliest phase, and the work may reasonably be dated in the second quarter of the century. Nagler states that Jerg Haspel died about 1430–40, but I cannot find on what authority.

The only other signed woodcut which might just fall within the first half of the century (though it is more probably in the second) is the *Mass of St. Gregory* at Nuremberg (S. 1471) signed *Bastion Ulmer* (i.e. Bastion or Sebastian of Ulm).

Two other prints at Vienna have been attributed by Schreiber to Jerg Haspel or his workshop, i.e. the *Pietà* (S. 983) and the *Holy Face* (S. 761), but the marked resemblance is in the colouring, which points to the same illuminator, but not necessarily to the same cutter. Somewhat nearer in the matter of linear style is a *St. Nicholas of Tolentino* (S. 1635, Vienna and British Museum), which probably dates within ten or fifteen years after

---

the design of these two woodcuts to the Master of the Linz Crucifixion, a painter whose works are preserved in Styria, Upper and Lower Austria. He places his work about 1420–30, and suggests that the style derives from art at the Burgundian Court, typified in Broederlam's Dijon altar-piece.

[1] Comparable, though less monumental and possibly later, is another *Virgin and Child with St. Anne* (S. 1194, formerly St. Gallen, *Einbl.* iii. pl. 4).

[2] See J. Meder, *Mitteilungen der Gesellschaft für vervielfältigende Kunst*, 1909, p. 45.

Fig. 55. Jerg Haspel. The Vision of St. Bernard. S.1271.

1446, the year of the Canonisation of the Saint. Dr. Kristeller compares
the last-named print with the *Last Supper* (S. 169) and the *St. Martin*
(S. 1619) at Ravenna, regarding them with other prints such as the *Death
of the Virgin* in the British Museum (S. 710), and the *St. Christopher* at
Weimar (S. 1348), as Swabian, and probably Ulm, work early in the second
half of the century.[1] The prints cited show shading which does not occur on
the *St. Nicholas*, and are more angular in character. They are very possibly
a slightly later development of the same school. The large *St. Christopher*
seems by a different hand from the rest, but it is a characteristic example of
the large whole-length figures of saints common in Upper German woodcuts of about 1470–80.

Not far removed in style from the work of Jerg Haspel is the woodcut
of *St. Ulrich and St. Afra* at Munich (S. 1706), and Augsburg is very
probably the locality of origin as they were Augsburg's patron saints.
Two versions of *Christ on the Cross*, one at Berlin (S. 400), the other at
Munich (S. 398), may be quoted as near relations in style, and perhaps in
locality.

A large cut of the *Agony in the Garden* at Paris (S. 184) is a good example
of the second period (probably about 1440) to compare with the *Agony in
the Garden* of the first phase (S. 185). Apart from the scheme of colour
(which is a much brighter one, in which lake and bright green are the
most striking), the differences in character are chiefly in the thinner line,
the tendency to angularity, a more natural proportion in the drawing of the
figures and greater emphasis on the background and its recession. The
impression is backed, but a water-mark of the bull's head with star appears
to be in the original paper, and the style in general would point to Upper
Germany. It is not unlike the large *Flagellation* at Vienna (S. 285, o), to
which reference has already been made,[2] though the latter is somewhat
cruder in its drawing.

Three large cuts at Munich may be mentioned together, though they
do not immediately strike one by their similarity, i.e. a *St. Anthony* (S. 1215),
the *Calvary* (S. 471; fig. 56), and the *Virgin in a Robe decorated with ears
of corn* (S. 1000).[3] But they are all on the same paper, with the water-
mark of a bell, and it is very possible that the differences of style, as we

---

[1] See P. Kristeller, *Holzschnitte des Meisters des Abendmahls in Ravenna*, Festschrift für Max
Friedlander, Leipzig 1927. Cf. W. Cohn, *Untersuchungen zur Geschichte des deutschen
Einblattholzschnitts*, Strassburg, 1934, p. 29.

[2] See p. 123, note 6.

[3] Cf. p. 92.

Fig. 56. Calvary. S. 471.

suggested above,[1] may indicate a woodcutter basing his work on the designs of different artists.

Perhaps the somewhat colossal dignity of the figure of St. Anthony obscures the really close relation between the smaller figures in this woodcut and in the *Calvary*. The *Calvary* has the appearance of being related to some more monumental work, probably some Upper German altar-piece of about 1440–50,[2] and is of great interest besides in its representation of a great variety of costume. The water-mark does not help in the localisation, as it is found in France and Italy as well as Germany, but the general character of all three designs points to Upper German origin about 1450.

One of the most decorative of the woodcuts of this period, and probably also of Upper German origin, is the half-length *Virgin and Child* of which impressions are known at Paris and Munich (S. 1023, Lemoisne xxvii.; fig. 57).[3] It is a design of great simplicity, and with the bright colouring of the Paris impression, in which light rose and green predominate, it has the value of a little painted altar-piece.

A woodcut of very marked individuality of style is the *Last Judgment and the Twelve Apostles* at Paris (S. 604, Lemoisne li.), with its emphasis on rounded forms, and it finds its nearest analogy in the Munich edition (S., ed. iii.) of the *Symbolum Apostolicum* block-book, which is probably Upper Bavarian or Austrian work of about 1450.

In his edition of the *Symbolum Apostolicum* (Graphische Gesellschaft 1917) Kristeller has rightly noted the relation to this block-book of a considerable group of woodcuts, including the *Last Judgment*. Belonging to the series are the *Christ before Herod* at Vienna (S. 266), the *Entry into Jerusalem* (S. 149 m) and the *Last Supper* (S. 166 a) at Graz (the last two coming from a MS. from Neuburg in Upper Styria); and among others analogous in style are a *St. Sebastian* at Berlin (S. 1683) and the *Fourteen Auxiliary Saints* at Munich (S. 1763).

A very considerable number of the cuts of the second period are surrounded with *passe-partout* borders. The *passe-partout* border (i.e. a border cut on a separate block for general use) was particularly common, as we shall see, in the printing of dotted prints of the xv century.

---

[1] See p. 92.

[2] For comparison with Upper German paintings of this period, see F. Bassermann-Jordan, *Unveröffentlichte Gemälde alter Meister aus dem Besitze des Bayerischen Staates, III. Schleiszheim,* Leipzig 1910.

[3] There is another version in reverse in the University Library, Breslau (S. 1023 a), and other variants are in the British Museum (S. 1024), and at Basle (S. 1022, from St. Gallen).

Fig. 57. The Virgin and Child. S. 1023.

One example which we reproduce, the *St. Dorothy* at Berlin (S. 1397; fig. 58), has a border which contains the arms of Bavaria, the Palatinate and Austria. The border is found with four other cuts (i.e. S. 700, 962a, 1466 and 1681) all of which come from MSS. belonging to the Convent of Tegernsee. Here the loops and round folds of the earliest phase persist in conjunction with the finer linear character of the second period. The background is painted with red stars, a feature already noted in other cuts.

Another characteristic woodcut within a border, a *St. Catherine* at Bamberg (S. 1321 a) is somewhat similar in style to the *St. Ulrich and St. Afra* (S. 1706) mentioned above,[1] and is noteworthy for its background of arabesque scrollwork in the manner of the early *St. Dorothy* (S. 1395).[2] It is probably nearly contemporary with the Nuremberg MS. (completed in 1451) from which it came.[3]

Borders of very striking rosette and arabesque design, analogous in style to the bichrome initials in Fust and Schoeffer's *Latin Psalters* (Mainz 1457 and 1459), may be noted in the *St. Catherine* (S. 1321 b) in the Stadtbibliothek, Nuremberg (from the nunnery of St. Catherine in the same town), in a *Martyrdom of St. John* (S. 1524) in the Germanic Museum at Nuremberg, and in a *St. Mary Magdalene* (S. 1595) at Darmstadt.

I would also mention here for its attractive border a *St. Dorothy* in the Guildhall Library (S. 1401a; fig. 59). At first sight the border with its isolated flowers is reminiscent of Dutch illuminations and prints (e.g. the cuts of the *Visitation*, S. 55, and the *Presentation of the Virgin*, S. 630, at Amsterdam). But the subject of St. Dorothy is more like Upper German than Netherlandish work, and the little hunting scene at the foot of the border, as well as a certain crudeness in the design of the flowers, points rather to German than Netherlandish origin,[4] and I think Schreiber's suspicions in this respect are justified.

I would mention another print within a *passe-partout* border, the *Christ on the Cross* at Nuremberg (S. 961), as something of a criterion in regard to locality and date, as it came from a MS. of 1441 from the Convent of Inzigkofen, near Sigmaringen. The MS. passes over the border of the cut, a fact which definitely fixes the date of the cut as not later than 1441, and comparison with other Upper German prints of the period already cited renders it almost certain that its production belongs to the same district.

---

[1] See p. 130.   [2] See p. 99.

[3] For evidence of Nuremberg work of this period, see Martin Weinberger, *Die Formschnitte des Katharinenklosters zu Nürnberg*, Munich 1925. Cf. p. 69, note 2.

[4] I should add that Mr. Campbell Dodgson regards the border as later than the subject enclosed.

Fig. 58. St. Dorothy. S. 1397.

A somewhat similar border (also a white design on a black ground) surrounds a woodcut of the *Adoration of the Magi* at Tübingen (S. 101 a), of which another version without border exists at Dresden (S. 101 b).

Fig. 59. St. Dorothy. S. 1401 a.

This subject is based on a line-engraving of the Master of the Playing-cards, so that it can hardly date before about 1445.

The influence of the Master of the Playing-cards, whose activity is now generally placed in the region of Basle on the Upper Rhine, may be re-marked in various other woodcuts, e.g. a *Christ before Pilate* at Dresden (S. 273 m), and an *Ecce Homo* at Paris (S. 327, Lemoisne xxxix.).

Comparable in costume and date is an interesting cut of the *Three Living and Three Dead Kings* at Berlin (S. 1899), but in this case Kristeller sus-pected a Netherlandish basis for the design.

Fig. 60. Christ bearing the Cross with St. Dorothy and St. Alexis. S.930.

Similar in tradition, but probably well into the second half of the xv century and comparable with the engraved work of the Master E.S. in its treatment of figures and background, is the *Beheading of John the Baptist* (S. 1516), of which there are impressions at Berlin and in the British Museum.

The woodcut of *Christ bearing the Cross with St. Dorothy and St. Alexis* (S. 930; fig. 60), with MS. date 1443, has already been mentioned[1] and reference made to the style of its drapery. Similar branching folds may be noted in certain woodcuts which reflect the influence of Schongauer, and are probably of Alsatian origin about 1460, i.e. a *Madonna with a Rose* at Colmar (S. 1060 a) and a *St. Mary Magdalene* at Darmstadt (S. 1595), the former taken from the cover of a German Prayer Book of the xv century, the latter from a French MS.

These two examples, though probably as late as 1460, show a suaver treatment of form than is usual in the second half of the century, when curvilinear design gradually yielded to angularity.[2] The beginning of this tendency to angular treatment is found in the second quarter of the century (e.g. a *Crucifixion*, S. 468, and a *Pietà*, S. 983, at Vienna, in both of which round folds still persist, the angularity being chiefly marked in the drawing of nose and brow).

A large cut of *St. Anthony* at Berlin (S. 2926 = 1217 a), may be noted in this relation. In its broad outline and simplicity of treatment it still bears marks of the early period, but its angularity verges on the grotesque in the sharply pointed fingers, and the very crudeness of its cutting suggests that it is the work of an amateur, possibly some brother in the convent at Altenmünster (Mainz), from one of whose MSS. it came. A third-rate craftsman of about 1450 might easily preserve some of the characteristics of the infancy of the art.

An example of exaggerated angularity which shows how this characteristic may be used to intensify expression is the *Christ bearing the Cross* at Vienna (S. 337; fig. 61), a composition of dramatic power though crudely forced in its emphasis.[3]

When this angularity of manner is kept within limits (as in the best of the Ulm and Augsburg illustrations of about 1470–80) it possesses great potentialities for vivid illustration.

A series of twenty-eight small cuts of the *Passion* in the British Museum

---

[1] See pp. 96, 100. Cf. also notes to the *Adoration of the Magi* once at St. Gallen (S. 98), p. 106.

[2] See p. 130.

[3] Otto Benesch attributes this woodcut to the painter of the Organ Wings at Salzburg (see his article already quoted in the Vienna Jahrbuch, Neue Folge ii., 1928, p. 69).

Fig. 61. Christ bearing the Cross. S. 337.

(C.D., A. 7; S. 127, etc.) in thin outline, somewhat angular in treatment and with little shading, may be taken as typical work of the middle of the century, one of the subjects, the *Last Supper*, being dated 1457. Another series very closely related in style and design, which occurs at the end of a MS. containing the dates 1433 and 1435, and probably belonging to the same time, or at the most a few years later, was formerly at Salzburg (Stift Nonnberg).[1] Both the British Museum and the Salzburg series are printed direct on the vellum page of their respective MSS., so that they form definite indications of the beginning of the idea of the illustrated book.[2]

LOCALISATION

Most of the woodcuts of the first half of the xv century which we have accepted as certainly or probably German have been conjecturally placed in Bavaria and Swabia and the neighbouring regions of Upper Germany. This accords with the evidence in regard to provenance,[3] with kindred style seen in works of other kinds, and is at one with the early repute of Ulm as the most active centre in the production of playing-cards throughout Europe. But the fact that we have been less able to localise any of the earliest cuts in other parts of Germany does not mean that among the unassigned cuts there might not be many from other regions such as Franconia (with Nuremberg [4] and Bamberg as the chief centres), and from important centres of activity on the middle and lower Rhine such as Mainz and Cologne. Cologne had been long famous for its goldsmiths, and our next section will show that one special class of relief-prints (that of the *manière criblée*) was probably practised here as early as in any other centre, and probably by 1450, if not earlier.

The towns where woodcut illustration was used earliest in books should be some indication of earliest activity, and in this respect, apart from the initial letters of Mainz, Bamberg was in the van with Pfister's cuts of about 1461–62. But these cuts were rather isolated in character and found no immediate successors in the same place, and it was at Augsburg, and Ulm, from 1470 onwards, that the most important of the early illustrations were

---

[1] See G. Gugenbauer, *Einbl.*, 35; *Klosterbibliotheken Oberösterreichs und Salzburgs*, 1913, Nos. 9-27. The MS., a *Beichtbüchl. Auslegung des Paternosters*, is described by H. Tietze, *Die illuminierten Handschriften in Salzburg*, Leipzig 1905 (p. 85, No. 112). It is now in the Huntington Library, San Marino, California.   [2] See Vol. I. p. 280.

[3] See pp. 107-109 for notes on convents.

[4] Note especially M. Weinberger, *Die Formschnitte des Katharinenklosters zu Nürnberg* (Munich 1925), for valuable notes on the early Nuremberg School.

issued. But Franconia and bordering regions certainly had their book-illustrators in 1470–71 (e.g. Hans Spörer, with his *Biblia Pauperum* of 1471, probably printed at Nuremberg,[1] and Walther and Hurning, with their edition of the same work issued at Nördlingen in 1470). The early illustrated books at Cologne (e.g. the Bible of about 1478–79) and at Lübeck (e.g. the *Rudimentum Noviciorum* of 1475) are strongly under the influence of Netherlandish work, an influence which is shown even more clearly at Lübeck, later in the century, in the Bible of 1494.

THE NETHERLANDS

So in leaving Austrian and German territory and looking for other cuts of the earlier half of the xv century, we naturally turn to the Netherlands, which was the centre of so much original activity in painting both in illuminated MSS. and in works on panel.

We have already quoted documents referring to work which may have been cut after Jean de Beaumetz, a painter of Netherlandish origin attached to the court of Philip the Bold of Burgundy at Dijon in the last quarter of the xiv century, and other documents of the same period naming other craftsmen of the borderland of the Netherlands and France who may have been cutters of wood blocks,[2] but we have been unable to refer to any existing woodcuts which can be placed within this period and region of influence, unless it be the few cuts already noted as possibly French of the early xv century.[3]

The distinction between Netherlandish and French work at this period is obscured, or at least complicated, by the development of political groups. In referring to the Netherlands we naturally think in terms of the present boundary between France and the Low Countries, fixed by the Congress of Vienna in 1815, which roughly followed the boundary that existed after the wars of Louis XIV. with Spain and the Treaties of 1713–15. This boundary leaves France with several of the ancient counties of the Low Countries (e.g. Artois, with its chief town of Arras) and considerable portions of others (e.g. Flanders, including Lille, and Hainault with Valenciennes). Moreover, between 1384 and 1477 (from the time of Philip the Bold to the death of Charles the Bold) the whole of Artois and Flanders

---

[1] Neither Hans Spörer's *Biblia Pauperum* 1471, nor his *Ars Moriendi* block-book of 1473 give place of printing, but it is probable (as Schreiber suggests) that he is the Hans briefftruck who printed at Nuremberg in 1475–76, particularly as a Hans Spörer occurs in a Nuremberg document in 1479. Between 1487 and 1494 he printed at Bamberg; from 1494 to 1500 at Erfurt.

[2] See pp. 79-84.   [3] See pp. 99, 114-120.

(from Arras to Bruges) was fief to the Dukes of Burgundy, whose court was centred at Dijon. After 1477 most of the Burgundian suzerainty passed to Louis XI. of France, but in 1529 Flanders and Artois became fiefs of the Emperor Charles V., who by 1543 was at least the nominal sovereign of practically the whole of the Northern and Southern Netherlands.

But political boundaries have actually meant less than geographical divisions in the distinction of the peoples concerned, and the characteristics which have divided France (including Burgundy) from the Netherlands, or rather the French-speaking countries from the Flemish, certainly persisted without regard to the changes in the political situation. The division, on the other hand, between the Northern and Southern Netherlands must have gradually grown with the Reformation, and with the difference of feeling that the Protestant republic (formed with such heroic and repeated struggles from the end of the xvi to the middle of the xvii century) brought in its train. In spite of the partial union of the Northern and Southern Netherlands during the xviii and early xix centuries (though at one time under Austrian and at another under French sovereignty), the division of the two sections culminated in the foundation of the Belgian Kingdom in 1831, and in the present partition between Belgium and Holland. Though the popular language of the two countries has remained the same (for Dutch is practically identical with Flemish), the division has gradually become more marked through the penetration of the French language among the higher classes of the Southern Netherlands.

I have given this short account of the political condition of the Netherlands to clarify or qualify the rough distinctions that must often serve in my historical survey.

Among woodcuts of definitely Netherlandish character nothing can be dated even conjecturally before 1418, the date on the Brussels *Madonna*, which has already been discussed at length.[1] The conclusion to which we inclined in regard to this woodcut was to regard it as a copy of about 1450, which preserved the date of an earlier original, for its angular style and its square pot-hook folds corresponded with a phase of woodcut later than other early Netherlandish work (the two block-books, *Exercitium super Pater Noster*, first edition, and the first edition, S.I-II, of the *Apocalypse*) which can hardly be placed earlier than about 1425–40.[2]

The phase of development to which the *Apocalypse* belongs already shows the influence of Jan van Eyck, and though his style (if not his work) is seen in the illuminations of the *Hours of Turin* and *Milan* (done between

[1] See pp. 109-113.   [2] See p. 218.

about 1412 and 1417),[1] its expressive power and angularity of manner contrasting with the more placid sentiment, the sinuous forms and long curving draperies of Beauneveu and his illuminations in such late xiv-century works as *Les Belles Heures du Duc de Berri* at Brussels,[2] yet his influence could hardly have prevailed until about the beginning of the second quarter of the century, and the period of the Ghent Altar-piece (about 1425–32).

We have already reproduced the Berlin *Virgin and Child in a Glory* (S. 1108; fig. 47), with its Dutch inscription, as a typical example of Netherlandish work of about 1460, and here add a reproduction of the *Mass of St. Gregory* at Nuremberg (S. 1462; fig. 62), which also bears a Dutch inscription, and is probably earlier, as it is nearer the *Apocalypse* in style. The inscription refers to indulgences granted by Pope Gregory (i.e. Gregory XII., regn. 1406–17) and two other popes (who from other evidence should be Nicholas V., regn. 1447–55, and Calixtus III., regn. 1455–58). As the next pope who added to the indulgences was Sixtus IV. (regn. 1471–84), all that might reasonably be inferred is that the print dates between 1455 and 1471.[3] But Kristeller has shown reason to doubt the reliability of such evidence, and would date the print rather before than after 1455.

Assuming the earliest editions of the Netherlandish block-books where regular shading is added to outline (the *Ars Moriendi* and *Biblia Pauperum*) to be about 1460, a date supported by their relation to the later book-illustration, Kristeller argued that the *Mass of St. Gregory* with its simple outline style, nearer to the earliest editions of the *Apocalypse* block-book, could hardly date after 1450.

Another version of the *Mass of St. Gregory* (S. 1463, British Museum) is probably an Upper German copy of the Netherlandish original. It is noteworthy that a considerable number of German cuts, probably of Swabian origin, show Netherlandish characteristics somewhat crudely translated (e.g. often with a dull regularity of straight parallel shading).[4]

Not far removed from the *Mass of St. Gregory* (S. 1462) in style are two interesting cuts at Cologne, the *Last Judgment* (S. 607; fig. 63) and the *Virgin and Child with Six Saints under a Vine Trellis* (S. 1168). If produced in the region of Cologne and not in the Low Countries, they would

---

[1] See Paul Durrieu, *Heures de Turin*, 1902; G. Hulin de Loo, *Heures de Milan*, 1911. I refer above to Jan van Eyck alone, leaving the vexed question of Hubert van Eyck on one side.

[2] See Pol de Mont, *Le Musée des Enlumineurs*, Haarlem, Fasc. i., 1905.

[3] See J. W. Holtrop, *Monuments typographiques des Pays-Bas au xve siècle*, The Hague, 1868, p. 13; and P. Kristeller, *Die Apocalypse*, Berlin 1916, p. 23.

[4] See p. 111, re *Speculum Humanae Salvationis in Form of a Hand*, and Erwin Rosenthal, *Die Anfänge des Holzschnitt-Illustration in Ulm*, Munich 1912.

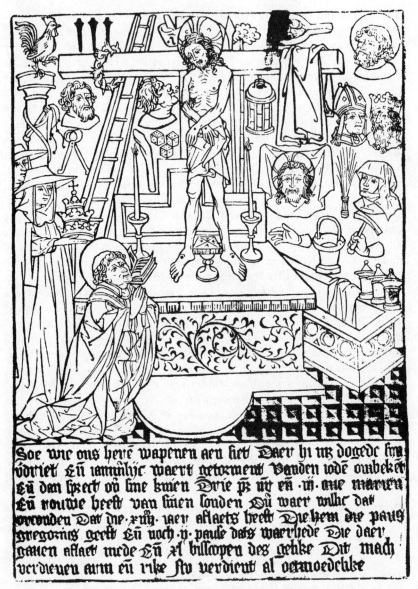

Soe wie ons here wapenen aen siet Daer hi mr dogede sm
vdriet Ēn iammliic waert getormeut Vanden iode oubeker
Ēn dan sprect ou sine kuien Drie pr uy eñ · iii · one nauwē
Ēn rouwe heest van suen souden Dū waer wilhe dat
orcouden Dat die xlix iaer aflaets heest Die hem die paus
gregorius geeft Ēn noch · ii · paule das waerhede Die daer
gauen aflaet mede Ēn xl bisscopen des gehke Dit mach
verdieuen aum eñ rike sto verdieut al oetmoedclike

Fig. 62. The Mass of St. Gregory. S. 1462.

only exemplify the pervasion of Netherlandish influence up the Lower Rhine into the neighbouring parts of Germany; but they are more probably actually Netherlandish work of about 1450.

I would mention here, though very different in character, the *Man of Sorrows* in the British Museum (S. 864; fig. 64), which has been located by Schreiber on the Lower Rhine, but is more probably Netherlandish. It possesses a noble simplicity of expression, in type reminiscent rather of the Master of Flémalle (Robert Campin)[1] than of Rogier van der Weyden, and can hardly be later than 1450.

In its severely conventionalised manner of pot-hook folds a *St. Jerome* at Paris (S. 1549, Lemoisne xix.) is near in development to the Berlin *Virgin and Child in a Glory* (S. 1108), and probably Netherlandish of about 1460. A variant of the same subject without the background, in which looped folds occur together with the pot-hooks, is preserved at Vienna (S. 1548) and may be somewhat earlier.[2]

Cruder, though not necessarily earlier, for it already shows regular parallel shading, is the *St. John Baptist and St. Christopher* at Berlin (S. 1518). It anticipates the stage of development represented in the *Good Shepherd* in the Stadtbibliothek, Breslau (S. 838), which is described and reproduced in my second volume (p. 595, fig. 347).

Similar parallel shading, used rather ornamentally than plastically, is also seen in a *Virgin in Robe decorated with Ears of Corn* at Copenhagen (S. 999 x),[3] which is more nearly related to the Berlin *Virgin and Child in a Glory* than any of the last three prints mentioned.

Somewhat isolated in character, but probably Netherlandish work of about 1450–60, is a large woodcut of *Prophet and Sibyl* in the Ashmolean Museum, Oxford (S. 2008; fig. 65).[4] It has hitherto been usually described as a 'Turk and his Wife', but the pointing finger of the woman strongly supports the title given, which was suggested to me by Dr. Kristeller. Moreover, the Turkish costume might easily have been used for such a subject. It is cut in thin outline, printed in brownish ink, with some light grey shading

[1] Mr. A. E. Popham suggests a comparison with the Christ in the *Mass of St. Gregory* by Robert Campin (or a follower) once in the Weber Collection, Hamburg (reproduced, No. 6 in the Weber Auction Catalogue, Berlin 1912).

[2] Comparable in subject is another print which appeared in a sale of Gilhofer and Ranschburg, Lucerne, 19th-20th May 1925, No. 9. But this is probably somewhat earlier (1440–50), and German rather than Netherlandish.

[3] First described by Kurt Rathe, *Mitteil.*, 1922, p. 1. Cf. pp. 92, 130, 324, 325.

[4] C. Dodgson, *Woodcuts of the XV Century in the Ashmolean Museum, Oxford*, Oxford 1929, No. 7 (pl. v.).

Fig. 63. The Last Judgment. S. 607.

which has the appearance of being printed, and local colour in yellow, red and green which might also be printed in part from blocks. The thin and strongly indented line has inclined Mr. Dodgson to regard it as a metal-cut, but in spite of its thin line (comparable to the *St. Veronica*, S. 1719, which has also been regarded as on metal),[1] I think it is more likely to be on wood.

Fig. 64. The Man of Sorrows. S. 864.

The most considerable woodcut work done in the Netherlands apart from the block-books is the *Grotesque Alphabet* of 1464 (S. 1998), a most attractive series of designs, excellent in cutting, and full of humour. It is complete in the collection of Mr. Dyson Perrins, at Malvern, and represented in the British Museum in a series, lacking the letter S and fragmentary in A, B, T and

[1] See p. 125.

Fig. 65. Prophet and Sibyl. S. 2008 f.

V, though clearer in some respects than the Perrins set.[1] The letter A is dated on its cross-bar (cut away on the British Museum impression), and the figures look like minclxxiii, but from the Basle woodcut copy, in which a similarly obscure date is corrected in an early hand to MCCCCLXIIII, and from the same date occurring in the engraved copy by the Master of the Banderoles, it would appear likely that MCCCCLXIIII was the figure written by the designer, and wrongly cut by an illiterate engraver.

The position of water-mark in the British Museum impression enabled Sotheby[2] to reconstruct the three original sheets from which the letters were cut, and the margins of the separate letters support this reconstruction. Two of the three blocks were cut with eight letters in two rows, the third block having an ornamental foliage design in place of the eighth letter. The blocks were spaced as follows:

A	B	C	D
N	O	P	Q

I (to the left of the first block)

E	F	G	H
R	S	T	V

II (to the left of the second block)

I	K	L	M
X	Y	Z	orna-ment

III (to the left of the third block)

showing twenty-three letters, or the English Alphabet with the omission of J, U and W.

[1] Described and reproduced by C. Dodgson, London 1899; in his British Museum Catalogue of German and Flemish Woodcuts, i., 1903, A. 131. An article by the same writer, *Two Woodcut Alphabets of the XV Century*, Burlington Magazine, xvii., 1910, 362, describes the more recently found series in the collection of Mr. Dyson Perrins, in addition to another alphabet in twisted scrolls (like strap-work) in the same collection (see p. 152).

[2] *Principia Typographica*, i. 122.

There are two early series of copies:

(1) The woodcut series at Basle, which has frequently been regarded as another series of impressions of the original blocks.[1]

(2) The engraved series by the 'Master of the Banderoles', which,

Fig. 66. The Letter L from the Grotesque Alphabet of 1464.

from the mere repetition of the date 1464 of the woodcut series, gave him the unjustified title of the 'Master of 1464'.

There are also early XVIII century copies on wood and in pen and ink in two volumes of John Bagford's Collectanea in the British Museum (Harl. 5934 and 5966). Bagford projected but never achieved a History of Printing, and these copies were no doubt intended for this work. Bagford

[1] Reproduced in Jaro Springer, *Gothic Alphabets*, International Chalcographical Society, Berlin 1897.

also included copies of the *Alphabet in twisted Scrolls* now in the Dyson Perrins Collection.

That the British Museum series of the Grotesque Alphabet was in England at an early period is proved by the English MS. inscriptions, on some of the letters, and on the reverse of the ornamental subject, which probably belong to the first half of the xvi century. On the letter L (see fig. 66) the inscription on the sword is clearly *London*; that on the reclining figure

Fig. 67. The Letter H from the Basle Copies of the Grotesque Alphabet.

has been read as *Bethemsted* (whatever that implies), though it is tempting to think that it might be *Westminster*. But this is even less evidence of English origin than the French *rebus* on K (*mon ♥ aues*) is necessarily evidence of French or Burgundian rather than English or Flemish origin.

Personally I have little hesitation in attributing the cutting of the original *Grotesque Alphabet* to the woodcutter of the first edition of the *Ars Moriendi* block-book.[1] Not only is it near in general style (discounting the different

---

[1] It should be noted in relation to the French motto on the Alphabet, that there is an issue of the first edition of the *Ars Moriendi* with French text.

character of the subjects, and possibly, though not certainly, a different designer), and closely allied in the peculiar strength and precision of its cutting; it also corresponds in the use of similar borders (the framework being given depth by shading on two of the four sides).

The copies at Basle, which must be nearly contemporary with the originals (see fig. 67), are inferior in strength and precision of cutting, and I think that they may very well have been cut by the craftsman (or one of the craftsmen) engaged on the first edition of the *Biblia Pauperum* block-book (S. I).

The *Woodcut Alphabet in twisted Scrolls* (like strap-work) in the Dyson Perrins Collection, which is printed on six sheets each containing four letters (two forms of S being given), is also no doubt a contemporary Netherlandish work, but hardly by the same strong cutter as the original *Grotesque Alphabet*. In its line and shading it is nearer the quality of the set of copies at Basle.[1]

The most remarkable of Netherlandish woodcuts of this period, and one of the most beautiful cuts of the xv century, is the *Virgin and Child* of the Diocesan Museum, Breslau (S. 1039 b; fig. 68). It shows very directly the influence of Rogier van der Weyden, and a close relationship, as Dr. Rathe[2] has suggested, with the Salting *Madonna* in the National Gallery (No. 2595). A similar type recurs in a *Madonna in Glory* (S. 2913, Berlin) and in several dotted prints, including one signed *Bernhardinus Milnet*, which will be discussed later.[3]

With all its stiff and angular character, there is real distinction and sensitive feeling in the precise drawing of the Breslau *Madonna*, and it stands nearer to the inspiration of the great art of its period than any contemporary German woodcut.

In mass of production of woodcut, Germany was far in advance of the Netherlands in the middle and second half of the xv century, but the bulk of Netherlandish work of the period is contained in the block-books, which will be treated in a separate chapter. And in this field the Netherlands were undoubtedly the inspiring force.

Before leaving the Netherlands I would refer to four small cuts of Saints at Paris: *St. Bartholomew* (S. 1267 b), *St. Matthew* (or *St. James the Greater?*) (S. 1624 a), *St. Lambert* (S. 1581 m) and *St. Leonard* (?) (S. 1589 m), the first two of which bear the coat-of-arms of Liége. They have a kind of

[1] See p. 149, footnote 1.
[2] See K. Rathe, *Mitteil. der Gesellsch. für vervielfältig. Kunst*, 1922, pp. 28 ff.
[3] See p. 183.

Fig. 68. The Virgin and Child. S. 1039 b.

crudity which inclines one to suspect forgery, but if they are genuine they are merely bungler's work of the latter half of the xv century, and certainly no criterion for early Netherlandish woodcut.

If the bungling of an amateur, perhaps of convent manufacture, they might be compared on that score with such cuts as the *St. Anthony* at Berlin (S. 2926), to which we have already alluded,[1] a *St. Altho* (S. 1185),[2] possibly cut in the Convent of Altomünster, near Augsburg (if indeed it is genuine), and the *Adoration of the Reliquary of St. Claude* (S. 1380 m) and the *Holy Trinity* (S. 736 b) at Paris.[3]

And I would also add a word of warning in regard to the series of seven little portrait cuts representing, or pretending to represent, *Laurens Coster, Volckert Claesz, Jan Mandyn, Hugo Jacobsz van Leyden* (the father of Lucas), *Jan van Hemessen, Albert van Ouwater* and *Israhel van Meckenem* (S. 2164–2170, Amsterdam, Haarlem, British Museum). There is definite evidence to show that they were forgeries done to deceive (or merely mystify) a Haarlem collector, Jacob Marius, by another Haarlem amateur CORNELIS VAN DEN BERG (1699–1774).

FRANCE

We have already referred to documentary evidence of French woodcuts before the middle of the xv century, and discussed the possible participation of French artists in the earliest phase of the history of woodcut. But in spite of evidence of activity, we have had to confess to little conviction in the attempt to establish definite achievement.[4] Apart from the examples discussed, of which the *Vierge de Lyon* was the most probably French, the most primitive in appearance of the early cuts which are certainly French is the *Passion* series in the Metropolitan Museum, New York, from the McGuire collection (S. 21 c; see fig. 69).[5] Each block included three series under arches; above, in Latin, are Christ's words from the Cross, below each subject four lines of lettering in French. One section of the series is practically complete; in addition, fragments of two other sheets are preserved, each with part of two subjects. The architectural construction is similar to the

---

[1] See p. 138.

[2] Coll. G. . . ., Brussels, Sale, F. Muller, Amsterdam, 1922, No. 21 (reproduction in catalogue).

[3] See below, p. 156.

[4] See pp. 99, 114-120. See also chapter on Block-books, pp. 210, 211, 218, 219.

[5] From the Boerner Sale, May 1929, No. 32.

three central panels of the Netherlandish *Biblia Pauperum*, and I incline to

Fig. 69. The Kiss of Judas, from a series of the Passion. S. 21 c.

regard the prints as later than their crude and primitive appearance would at first suggest, i.e. nearer 1450 than 1430.

Another woodcut of still cruder character for which French origin is claimed is the sheet in Paris with the two subjects of the *Adoration of the Reliquary of St. Claude* (S. 1380 m; Lemoisne xvii.) and the *Holy Trinity* (S. 736 b; Lemoisne xvii. *bis*). Bouchot was probably justified in regarding the *Reliquary* as that ordered by Louis XI. when visiting the Convent of St. Claude (Franche-Comté) in 1456, an incident which provides a limit

Fig. 70. St. John, St. Thomas and St. James the Less. From a series of the Twelve Apostles. S. 1759.

of date. The style of drapery in the *Holy Trinity* is of an earlier period, but I see no reason on that account to place it earlier than the other subject. They are both the rough work of some amateur, probably a monk of the Convent of St. Claude, and this is enough to explain the archaistic tendency.

Of much better quality and of about the same period (1450–60) are the *Twelve Apostles* (S. 1759; Lemoisne lix.-lxii.; fig. 70). They were cut on a single block, but the only impression known (Paris) is divided into four pieces. The inscriptions are in French, and according to Bouchot in the dialect of Picardy, but the style is entirely in the Netherlandish tradition (i.e. if the first and third editions of the block-book of the *Apocalypse* are, as we believe, Netherlandish), and might even be based on lost Netherlandish originals.

Somewhat more independent, but still under the influence of Flemish work, is the series of *Les Neuf Preux* in Paris (S. 1945; Lemoisne, pl. lxxiv.-lxxvi.; fig. 71) with French inscriptions. The 'Nine Worthies' or Heroes of Antiquity, Jewry and Christendom [1] are represented under arches on horseback, with little artistic virtue beyond a certain stolid simplicity. The impressions (from three blocks) came from a MS. written, according to Bouchot, in the dialect of the Île de France (i.e. the old province of which Paris was the capital) by Gilles le Bouvier (King-at-Arms of Charles VII.) who died in 1458. The paper, with water-mark of an anchor, is different from that of the MS., but the impressions are probably of the same period, and hardly later than about 1460.[2] Bouchot suggested that *Les Neuf Preux* were cut by Jean de Dale, who signed certain *playing-cards* now in the Bibliothèque Nationale;[3] a possible, but by no means certain attribution.

Mention should also be made of a woodcut acquired by the Bibliothèque Nationale since Bouchot's publication, a *Virgin and Child in the form of a Flower flanked by Roundels representing the Four Elements* (Acq. 6914), with French inscription, and probably dating about 1470.

Other French woodcuts of the second half of the xv century, which demand our attention, already belong to the period of book-illustration, and will be discussed in a later chapter.

---

[1] Hector of Troy, Alexander and Julius Caesar; Joshua, David and Judas Maccabaeus; King Arthur, Charlemagne and Godefroi de Bouillon.

[2] Three other woodcut examples of the subject of *Les Neuf Preux* (which appears to have originated in France) may be mentioned:

(1) Fragments of three standing figures at Metz (S. 1947) with French text, probably about 1460–70 (see F. van der Straeten-Ponthoz, *Les Neuf Preux*, Pau 1864, for the suggestion of a much earlier date).

(2) Complete series of nine standing figures at Berne (S. 1947 m). From a MS. Austrian chronicle written at Königsfelden (Canton Aargau) in 1479. Probably Basle or Upper German work of about 1470–80.

(3) Six figures of the series at Hamburg (S. 1948). Netherlandish, about 1490. (See Volume II. p. 594.)

(4) Fragment of four figures, at Brussels, with Dutch text (S. 1949). Netherlandish, probably about 1500 (see E. Fétis, *Les Neuf Preux*, Documents iconographiques et typographiques de la Bibl. Roy. de Belgique, Brussels 1877).

[3] See pp. 87, 88.

Fig. 71. Joshua, David and Judas Maccabaeus. From a series of *Les Neuf Preux*. S. 1945.

ENGLAND

England seems to have produced little or nothing in single woodcuts before Caxton's introduction of book-illustration about 1481 (not to mention his blocks for initial letters already used in his *Indulgences* of 1480), so that the few single cuts of the xv century produced in England will be chiefly discussed later in conjunction with contemporary book-illustration.[1] Most of these single cuts are so-called *Images of Pity*, or *Piety* (figures representing the Man of Sorrows, with or without the signs of the Passion), with inscriptions referring to Indulgences, for which the subject of the *Mass of St. Gregory* was in use abroad.

A *Man of Sorrows* in the Bodleian Library, Oxford (inserted in MS. Bodl. 939, s.c. 27691), and another version in the British Museum (S. 869) are among the earliest of the type, but even so they can hardly be earlier than 1480, and might be some years later. Whether these and similar cuts with English inscriptions were done by English craftsmen or supplied from the Netherlands is impossible to say. But they are sufficiently crude to render it probable that they were done by unpractised native hands. There is certainly no reason to regard the British Museum example (as Schreiber suggested in the first edition of his *Manuel*)[2] as by the same hand as the *Grotesque Alphabet* of 1464; it is far inferior, and indeed shows little relation at all. The only woodcut certainly anterior to 1480 which has been even tentatively assigned to England is the *St. George on Horseback* in the British Museum (S. 1448), but there is little evidence in favour of its English origin except the subject. It is related in style to the *Grotesque Alphabet* of 1464, but though the cutter's hand seems less skilful, it is an attractive and vigorous subject, probably cut by a Fleming between 1460 and 1470. The impression is in a very pale brown, and the lines considerably obscured by the hand colouring in vermilion and green, so that a reproduction has not been attempted.

ITALY

Little profit comes from discussions as to whether Germany, the Netherlands, France or Italy led in the field of woodcut. If it seem probable that the earliest impressions on paper are Northern, it might be contended, on the other hand, that woodcut for printing textiles had been practised

---

[1] See p. 737, where bibliographical references will also be found.

[2] The suggestion is omitted in the 2nd edition.

earlier in the south, and that the distinction between the two kinds of work is a matter of application rather than essential character.

In any case, the Venetian document of 1441, already quoted,[1] referring to an indigenous trade in printed playing-cards ruined by importation from abroad, must presuppose a considerable history in the art of woodcut. A second document, first quoted by Kristeller,[2] refers to a certain Federico di Germania at Bologna in 1395, who made cards and figures of saints which may well have been printed from blocks; and a third document[3] definitely proves the existence of 'wood-blocks for playing-cards and saints' in the possession of a certain card-maker (*pittor di naibi*), Antonio de Giovanni di Ser Francesco, at Florence in 1430.

The fact that no existing woodcut Italian playing-cards can be dated before the second half of the xv century in no way invalidates such documentary evidence, for popular cards are the last thing likely to be preserved with care.[4] But the great rarity of Italian woodcuts of religious or other subjects whose style corresponds with the painting or sculpture of the first half of the xv century, certainly confirms the view that Germany and neighbouring regions, with their far more numerous examples of the same period, were the more active early centres of the art. And the documents themselves, generally and personally (in the case of Federico di Germania), imply a flow of influence from the north, an influence which is also borne out by the character of one or two of the few Italian woodcuts which can be reasonably dated before the introduction of book-illustration in Italy (1467).

Among the most important of these early Italian cuts are two large representations of the *Madonna* preserved in the Victoria and Albert Museum and the British Museum (S. 1058 n and 1158), each of which, if complete, would have measured about two feet by one and a half (figs. 72 and 73). Both were originally pasted on panel, and the British Museum example is known to have come from the door of a house in Bassano, possibly the same to which originally belonged numerous fragments of woodcuts of about 1500 now at Berlin, to which fuller reference will be made in a later chapter.[5] The South Kensington example still remains on its original panel, though this has been planed down on the back to a somewhat dangerous thinness. Both belong almost certainly to North Italy, and possibly to the region of Verona, whose position rendered it most accessible to German influence. The South Kensington subject, in which the Virgin and Child are represented alone within a glory of rays, shows perhaps the more definite traces of Northern influence. The impression, which, to judge from its indentation,

[1] See p. 82.   [2] See p. 80.   [3] See p. 80.   [4] See p. 84.   [5] See p. 430.

Fig. 72. The Virgin and Child. S. 1058 n.

was probably rubbed, is in a brownish ink, with only slight traces remaining of its original hand-colouring. It is for the most part in strong outline, but the parallel shading seen on parts of the drapery would hardly favour a date earlier than 1450, though the type of the Virgin, as far as it reflects painted work, might easily be two or three decades earlier. A traditional style or type is more likely to persist longer in a subordinate craft such as woodcut, and this fact, in conjunction with the crude archaisms of certain of the Berlin cuts from the Bassano house, might lend some credence even to a considerably later date than 1450.

The British Museum *Madonna* is of similar type, but somewhat gentler in character than the South Kensington cut; the opaque blue and red colouring of the Virgin's mantle hides the lines of this part of the drapery, but elsewhere, at least, the cut is in pure outline and without shading. The figures of the flanking saints are comparable in their straight parallel lines with the saints in the side compartments of another early woodcut, the so-called *Madonna del Fuoco*, preserved in the Cathedral at Forlì (fig. 74).[1] According to the local tradition, which gives this Madonna its name, this woodcut was miraculously saved from fire in 1428, and there is nothing impossible from its style in so early an origin, though were it not for the story I should have been more inclined to place it nearer the middle of the century in the company of the two London Madonnas.

A fragment of another *Madonna* which, if not Italian, shows strong Italian influence is pasted on the back of a diptych in the Pilgrimage Chapel of St. Leonhard, near Tamsweg, Province of Salzburg (S. 1148 m), but though as archaic as the South Kensington example, it may already date well into the second half of the century. A considerable number of Northern cuts of the late xv century might be cited, either copied from lost Italian originals, or under Italian influence, but few before the last quarter of the century. Possibly the *St. Jerome in a Rocky Landscape*, of which there are several versions, may be one of these (e.g. S. 1538, 1539, 1540 and 1540 a, at Berlin, the British Museum, Munich and Tübingen), and the *Assumption of the Virgin* at Erlangen, dated 1500 (S. 724), has the appearance of being based on an Italian composition, while the details of the singing and playing angels are definitely borrowed from an early Florentine engraving in the Uffizi.[2]

---

[1] See L. Venturi, *Sulle origini della xylografia*, L' Arte, vi., 1903, 267. For its miraculous history see Giuliano Bezzi, *Il fuoco trionfante*, Forlì 1637.

[2] Reproduced by Lehrs as by the 'Master of the Berlin Passion' in the Pr. Jahrbuch, xxi., 1899, 145. The large Florentine Broad Manner engraving of the same subject should also be compared (B xiii. 86, 4).

Fig. 73. The Virgin and Child. S. 1158.

We have actual documentary evidence of Florentine woodcuts in 1430, but no existing print can be assigned to Florence before about 1450–60. And even then a comparatively poor specimen, an *Agony in the Garden* (S. 159 m), preserved among the drawings of the Library of Christ Church, Oxford, is almost the most important example to which I can refer.[1] The cut is an outline, without shading, printed in brownish ink, and coloured by hand (chiefly in red and blue on Christ's tunic and cloak, in grey on the trees, and with traces of gold on the angels' hair). Its style only reflects Florentine painting of the earlier xv century at a considerable remove, such as might originate in the hands of a poor though individual craftsman, in the wake of Fra Angelico and Lorenzo Monaco.

Among the few other cuts that might be assigned to Florence are certain fragments of decorative designs (roundels with figures, animals, etc.) discovered by Dr. Kristeller in the inside paper of original bindings of volumes of the years 1466 and 1469 in the Archivio di Stato, Rome.[2] They suggest comparison in character of subject with the Florentine line-engravings of about 1465–70, called the 'Otto Prints',[3] but there is hardly enough material for any certainty of localisation. The other fragments found in the same place, of Tarocchi Cards, are probably North Italian, and comparable with the engraved Tarocchi, of Ferrarese origin, in the Sola-Busca collection, Milan.[4] They have already been mentioned as the earliest known Italian printed cards.

A *St. George and the Dragon* at Bassano (S. 1445; fig. 75) is not unlike a playing-card in its present form, but it may have been cut down from a larger subject. Under its heavy illumination, with tooled gold characteristic of Venetian painting and coloured cards, the woodcut lines are almost hidden. But as far as can be judged the woodcut is in outline only, and in a style which cannot be much later than 1450.

I would note in passing four large designs of *Angels holding Candlesticks*, at Berlin, which have sometimes been regarded as woodcuts. Careful comparison of the two similar pairs[5] of supporting angels has convinced me that there is no basis of woodcut, though the outlines brushed in a strong black are done by a craftsman who must have been familiar with the making of pattern-blocks. They are brightly coloured, and the background decorated

---

[1] See A. M. Hind, Burlington Magazine, May 1928.

[2] See P. Kristeller, *Beitrag zur Geschichte der ältesten Holzschnittes*, Pr. Jahrbuch, xiii., 1892, 172.

[3] See A. M. Hind, *Catalogue of Early Italian Engravings in the British Museum*, 1910, p. 62.

[4] *Ibidem*, p. 257.

[5] Arrangements are being made for the acquisition of one pair by the British Museum by means of exchange.

Fig. 74. The Madonna del Fuoco.

by stencil with a damask pattern, the whole in the style of a secondary craftsman of the following of Filippo Lippi about 1460–70. They were

probably intended as furniture or wall-decoration, ends to which both woodcut and line-engraving had been occasionally put in the late xv and early xvi centuries.[1]

Perhaps the most important of early Italian woodcuts is the large *Calvary* (S.470 k, measuring about 22 × 16 inches) in the Museo Civico at Prato.[2] But this and numerous woodcuts preserved at Ravenna show so definite a relation to the earliest Italian book-illustration, though they are in part hardly later than some of the cuts already described, that their discussion is reserved for a later section.[3]

Rather isolated among the Ravenna series for its archaic character is the fragment of a large *Holy Trinity and Saints* (S. 603), but it is probably already well into the second half of the xv century, and by the hand of a crude craftsman working on old traditions rather than a work of the earliest period.

Even more definitely archaistic is a *St. George and the Dragon* in the Museo Civico at Pavia,[4] probably done to-

Fig. 75. St. George and the Dragon. S. 1445.

wards the end of the xv century or in the early xvi century, and based on some East-European original preserving the Byzantine tradition. A

---

[1] Cf. pp. 34, 77, 160, 430.   [2] P. Kristeller, Le gallerie nazionali italiane, ii., 1896, 184.
[3] Vol. II. pp. 423-26.   [4] Malaspina Catalogue, 1824, ii. p. 23.

painting in the Jarves Collection at Yale University, New Haven,[1] is so near in design that it might have been the original used. It is probably a work of the xv century. Comparison should also be made with a Russian painting of the xvi century, from the Guslitski Monastery, which figured in the Exhibition of Russian Icons at the Victoria and Albert Museum, 1929 (Catalogue No. 95).

GENERAL NOTES ON COLOUR

The study of the hand-colouring of xv-century woodcuts has not been developed as much as it deserves. A systematic record of the various colours used on the book-illustrations of various towns and printers would probably be of considerable value in helping to localise isolated cuts. But this is still to seek, and I can offer here little more than a brief summary of the general characteristics of certain countries, regions and towns of Germany, the Netherlands and France, chiefly based on Schreiber,[2] and the earlier notes of Weigel,[3] followed by a table of the various colours in use in the xv century,[4] with reference from the colours to their local occurrence.

In Germany the Swabian, Bavarian and Franconian schools[5] all show the common use of reds (both rose-madder lake and vermilion), yellows and greens, and less regular use of browns, blacks (greys) and blues. A few distinctions may be noted.

[1] Osvald Sirén, *Descriptive Catalogue of the Pictures in the Jarves Collection, New Haven*, 1916, No. 108. A similar type is seen in a panel belonging to Prof. D. Talbot Rice (reproduced Burlington Magazine, February 1933).

[2] In his introduction to Einblattdrucke, *Graphische Sammlung München*, 1912, and in his *Handbuch des Holz- und Metallschnittes*, vii., 1929, p. 55.

[3] Weigel and Zestermann, *Die Anfänge der Druckerkunst in Bild und Schrift*, Leipzig 1866, i. pp. xix-xxi.

[4] Based largely on Professor A. P. Laurie's works (e.g. *Materials of the Painter's Craft*, Edinburgh 1910; and *Pigments and Mediums of the Old Masters*, London 1914).

[5] Some confusion is caused by the rather indefinite and changing implications of these local divisions. Ulm and Augsburg may rightly be regarded as the chief centres of Swabia at this period, though Augsburg was later incorporated in Bavaria. Nuremberg is the most important town of Franconia as far as concerns the history of woodcut, and Nördlingen has more definite relations to the Franconian group, though actually within the old Swabian circle. Within the limits of Bavaria, Weigel cited Freising, and the Convents of Tegernsee, and Mondsee. Munich and Landshut, however, were perhaps even more important centres. St. Zeno at Reichenhall, and Altomünster, might be added to the Bavarian convents, while Mondsee is more strictly defined as outside Bavaria, and within the neighbouring archiepiscopal domain of Salzburg. In the early xii century the domain of the Dukes of Bavaria extended over Austria, but by the end of this century Austria and Styria were made into duchies, and important territories were in the hands of the Archbishop of Salzburg.

The brightest colours, especially in reds and greens, are characteristic of Ulm. Blue was apparently little used in that centre, and backgrounds were generally left uncoloured. Ulm borders were frequently coloured yellow in contrast with the red borders of Augsburg prints. At Augsburg blue was used for the sky; backgrounds in the earliest cuts were generally of brown, sometimes with a tapestry pattern; in the later cuts dark blue or gold backgrounds occur, and gold was commonly used for the *nimbus*; walls were sometimes coloured to imitate marble.

Blue appears to have been regarded in Swabia as the colour proper to the fool's dress; it was more general in its use at Nuremberg and throughout Franconia. At Nuremberg light blue is more common, and the use of silver is specially characteristic. The skies in Nuremberg cuts of the later xv century were more often grey or grey-brown than blue.

Colours used at Nördlingen, to judge from the *Biblia Pauperum* of Walther and Hurning (1470), were almost as bright as those of Ulm.

The colours used by the schools of the Lower Rhine and the Netherlands were certainly paler. I would also note a dull scheme of colour tones (yellow, brown, green and rose) on several of the earliest woodcuts of uncertain locality, i.e. the *Agony in the Garden* (S. 185), the *Vierge de Lyon* (S. 1069), the *St. Erasmus* (S. 1315), the *Christ on the Cross* (S. 435) and the *Christ bearing the Cross* (S. 344), all preserved at Paris. I mention this without venturing to relate its bearing on French, Austrian or Bohemian origin. There is at least a clear distinction from Upper German characteristics.

Among the colours most characteristic of France, the Netherlands, and the Lower and Upper Rhine, is violet. In France it is sometimes used even for skies.

Colour	Notes on Local Use
RED	
Red-ochre. Mineral earth. Light red and Indian red are varieties. *Red-lead*. Peroxide of lead. The term *minium* (*mennig* in German) is used both for red-lead and native cinnabar. *Cinnabar*. Native sulphide of mercury. *Vermilion*. Sulphide of mercury. Artificial cinnabar.	The bright reds, of vermilion and scarlet tones, are commonest at Ulm and Augsburg. Red borders at Augsburg.

Colour	Notes on Local Use
Rose (and other red) madders. Vegetable reds. *Lake (lac)* is added to this red when used in conjunction with various forms of gum (e.g. from ivy twigs), which renders the red shiny and transparent like a varnish.	Rose-madder lakes are commonest at Ulm, but in general use in Upper Germany.
YELLOW *Yellow-ochre.* Mineral earth. *Massicot.* Oxide of lead: a dull orange-yellow. *Orpiment.* Sulphide of arsenic and auripigmentum, i.e. golden yellow. *Naples yellow.* Oxide of antimony. *Vegetable yellows.* Various.	Yellow tones characteristic of Ulm, and frequently used there (and in W. Upper Germany) for borders. Yellow backgrounds chiefly at Regensburg.
GREEN *Malachite.* Carbonate of copper. *Verdigris.* An acetate of copper, prepared by subjecting the metal to the action of vegetable acid, e.g. that of fermenting grape-skins. *Terre-verte.* *Vegetable greens.* Various.	Bright green commonest at Ulm. Dark and light greens also characteristic of Augsburg.
BLUE *Indigo.* A vegetable blue from an East India plant. *Woad.* A vegetable blue comparable with indigo (used, e.g., by ancient Britons for staining their bodies). *Egyptian blue.* Silicate of copper. It is doubtful whether this was used after the VII century. *Azure* or *Azurite.* Natural carbonate of copper. *Ultramarine. Lapis Lazuli.* Made from ground and calcined lazulite. First mentioned in the XIII century.	Light blue commonest at Nuremberg. Blue strokes used for sky, and dark blue for backgrounds most commonly at Augsburg.

Colour	Notes on Local Use
PURPLE	
Tyrian purple. From the *murex*, shell-fish. *Vegetable purples*, e.g. purple-madder.	Purple or violet tones are commonest in France, the Netherlands, and the Lower and Upper Rhine. Violet is sometimes used for the sky in France.
BROWN	
Umber. An ochreous earth, first found in Umbria. *Brown earths.* Miscellaneous. *Bistre. Fuligo.* From burnt wood. *Asphaltum. Bitumen.* Pitch.	Common at Augsburg in dark and light tones; often used for backgrounds. The lighter browns (and generally paler tones of other colours) characteristic of the Lower Rhine and the Netherlands. The nimbus is frequently brown in the Netherlands. The ground is shown frequently in brown (instead of green) in region of the Upper Rhine.
BLACK	
Chalk. *Charcoal.* *Lamp-black.* *Bone-black.*	Grey or grey-brown is frequently used for the sky at Nuremberg.
WHITE	
Chalk. *Gypsum.* *White lead.*	
GOLD	
Gold-leaf.	Used considerably at Augsburg for aureoles and backgrounds.
SILVER	
Silver-leaf.	Used chiefly at Nuremberg.

STENCIL

Among the earliest uses to which stencil was put was probably the colouring of wall-hangings and playing-cards. Stencilled wall-hangings are recorded in the Netherlands during the xiv century, and playing-cards may have been so coloured at an early period. For the colouring of woodcuts in general it did not become common until its application to broadsides in the later xvi century, particularly in Germany. One of the earliest instances to which I can refer is the large *Calvary* at Prato (S. 470 k),[1] and it was used by the printer Johann Schoensperger at Augsburg in the botanical illustrations of his editions of his *Herbarius* (based on Schoeffer's *Gart der Gesuntheit*) from 1485 onwards (e.g. those of 22nd August 1485 and 15th December 1488 in the British Museum).

A somewhat later example is the *Virgin and Child with St. Anne* acquired by the British Museum in 1926 (S. 1195 a), probably a French work of about 1500. It should be compared with another print in the British Museum, a *Virgin and Child with St. Barbara and St. Catherine* (S. 1151 a), though the use of stencil is not so clear in this case.

The earliest examples of actual printing in colour will be noted in dealing with xv-century book-illustration (under Ratdolt, at Venice and Augsburg).

TINSEL-PRINTS

I would also mention here the occasional use of tinsel (i.e. small fragments of thin and sparkling metal), and an incrustation of small quartz crystals in addition to colour on certain xv-century woodcuts. The tinsel or incrustation would be applied on to a basis of paste or gum on the impression.

Two early examples are an *Annunciation* at Munich (S. 29) and a *St. Francis* at Dresden (S. 1425), which probably date in the second quarter of the xv century; another, somewhat later, is a *St. Dorothy*, in the British Museum (S. 1398);[2] all three showing gold tinsel and incrustation on part of the costume, and the *St. Dorothy* similar embellishment of a tree.

Other examples show only quartz incrustation, i.e. a *St. Catherine* at

---

[1] See p. 426 and fig. 202.

[2] Possibly by the same hand as a smaller *St. Dorothy* in the British Museum (S. 1402) from the Huth Collection. This little *St. Dorothy* is a charming example of bright colouring (madder lake, bright green, yellow, blue and vermilion), and the aureoles are embellished in gold-leaf like the *St. Dorothy*, S. 1398.

Munich (S. 1341) with the border so treated, and a *St. Mary Magdalene* at Darmstadt (S. 1595).

Gold tinsel without incrustation may be noted on *Christ bearing the Cross* at Cologne (S.922), on a *Christ Child* at Munich (S.810) and a *Man of Sorrows* at Hanover (S. 868), in the last two cases the gold being used to embellish a black background, on the *Man of Sorrows* in the form of stars.

The few prints noted in this manner (and these are practically all whose locality is known) all seem to date between about 1430 and 1460.

FLOCK-PRINTS

Flock-prints offer a method analogous to tinsel-prints in that paste is used and the printing done in relief from ordinary wood blocks. In spite of the use of paste, they are more appropriately dealt with here than in the section on *Paste-prints*, as the latter term has been limited to a special process. Altogether only six flock-prints are known:

(1) *St. George on Horseback* (S. 2844), Nuremberg. Reproduced by Weigel and Zestermann, ii. 401.

(2) *St. Barbara* (S. 2833, and vol. vi. pl. 34), Würzburg.

(3) *The Christ Child with Angels and Signs of the Passion* (S. 2812), Würzburg.

Both the Würzburg examples pasted inside the binding of a contemporary volume.

(4) *St. Catherine* (S. 2833 x), Munich, Staatsbibliothek (from the Provinzialbibliothek, Neuburg), and Erlangen, Univ. Library.

The Munich impression (reproduced by Leidinger, Münchner Jahrbuch ii. (1907), ii. 24) is pasted inside the cover of a volume which dates about 1475.

(5) *Christ on the Cross between the Virgin and St. John* (S. 2789 x), Oxford (Ashmolean Museum). Reproduced by C. Dodgson, *Woodcuts of the XV Century in the Ashmolean Museum, Oxford*, 1929, No. I. and frontispiece.

(6) *Allegorical Device, with Castle, Hind and Panther* (S. 2862 m). Pasted inside the binding of a book (*Formularium Instrumentorum ad usum curiae Romanae*) which probably dates about 1479. (See G. Leidinger, *Ein Sammt-Teigdruck*, Archiv für Buchgewerbe und Gebrauchsgraphik, lxiv., 1927, Heft 3.)

Passavant, who only knew (1),[1] entitled it *Empreinte veloutée* (i.e. velvet-print); Leidinger and Schreiber describe them as *Sammt-Teigdrucke*, i.e. *velvet-paste-prints*.

They are all mock-textile prints, imitating a patterned velvet (all red, except perhaps the *St. Barbara*).

The process may be described as follows:

(*a*) The surface of the paper first prepared to look like textile web either by the impression of an actual textile on to the paper covered with a thin glutinous substance (which seems to be the case with the *St. Barbara* and the *Christ on the Cross*), or by some other means.

(*b*) The wood block covered on the surface with a brownish paste or glue, which is impressed on the paper treated as in (*a*) and already dry.

(*c*) Powdered wool (or other stuff) sprayed over the impression while the paste is wet, and hand pressure probably applied to fix the *flock*; the flock shaken off the other parts of the impression.

The method of producing the effect of a textile ground or web was produced differently in other prints, e.g. in the *St. Catherine* by regular short flicks made with a point on the surface of the coloured paper.

An entirely analogous process used in the making of flock paperhangings for wall-papers is described by T. R. Spence in his paper on *Wall-Papers and Stencilling* in the Journal of the Society of Arts, xli. (1893), at p. 367. 'Flock paper-hangings are printed in the details of the design in size. The flock—which is composed of the cuttings of woollen cloth, cut up in a mill to the necessary degree of fineness, and dyed—is then sprinkled over the paper, adhering to the part charged with size. To get a higher surface the sizing and sprinkling is repeated.'

If the xv-century subjects had been purely decorative designs, one would have been tempted to suspect that they were patterns for wall-papers. But as they are all subjects that would hardly bear multiplication in a large series, and as they were preserved in bindings, it is more likely that they were chance experiments of one or more craftsmen in imitation of the character of textile.

They are all probably Upper German work of about 1450–75, the device of the *Castle, Hind and Panther* possibly borrowed from an Italian source, and containing some political allegory. Leidinger may be right in

---

[1] A second print described by Passavant (*Le Peintre-Graveur*, i. p. 102) as *Empreinte à guise de broderie* is one of the tinsel-prints mentioned above (*St. Francis*, S. 1425).

referring its origin to Regensburg, an active centre of the craft of weaving, where the influence of Italian weavers was strongly felt.

BIBLIOGRAPHY

(See also General Bibliography, especially under *Collections*)

WEIGEL, T. O., and ZESTERMANN, A. Die Anfänge der Druckerkunst in Bild und Schrift an deren frühesten Erzeugnissen in der Weigelschen Sammlung erläutert. 2 vols. Leipzig 1866. (The earliest important series of reproduction of early woodcuts, including dotted prints and examples from block-books.)

LIPPMANN, F. Über die Anfänge des Formschneidekunst und des Bilddruckes. *Repertorium*, i. (1876), 215.

LIPPMANN, F. Der italienische Holzschnitt im xv Jahrhundert. Berlin 1885 (originally issued in the Pr. Jahrbuch, v., 1884; English edition with extensive corrections and additions. London 1888).

DELABORDE, Henri. La Gravure en Italie avant Marcantoine. Paris 1883.

SCHREIBER, W. L. Manuel de l'amateur. Berlin and Leipzig 1891–1910. Vols. i. and ii., and vol. vi. (plates). See General Bibliography for further details of this and the following entry.

SCHREIBER, W. L. Handbuch des Holz- und Metallschnittes des xv Jahrhunderts. Leipzig. Vols. i.-iv. (1926–27), vi. (1928), vii. (1929), viii. (1930).

SCHREIBER, W. L. Holzschnitte in der graphischen Sammlung zu München. Vol. i. Heitz, *Einbl.* Strassburg 1912. (Contains a general survey of the development of early woodcut.)

HEITZ, Paul. Einblattdrucke des fünfzehnten Jahrhunderts, Herausgegeben von Paul Heitz. Strassburg 1899, etc. (see General Bibliography for complete list).

BOUCHOT, Henri. Un Ancêtre de la gravure sur bois. Paris 1902.

BOUCHOT, Henri. Les Deux Cents Incunables xylographiques du Département des Estampes. Paris 1903 [the introduction develops the critical study opened in the publication of 1902].

DODGSON, Campbell. Catalogue of Early German and Flemish Woodcuts preserved in the Department of Prints and Drawings in the British Museum. Vol. i. London 1903 (the introduction is one of the soundest and most comprehensive studies of the general subject of the origins and early history of woodcut). The catalogue includes single cuts, dotted prints, paste-prints, and block-books.

    Index, and Concordance with Schreiber, by A. Lauter. Munich 1925.

DODGSON, Campbell. The Invention of Wood-engraving: a French claim considered (Review of Bouchot, 1902). *Burlington Magazine*, iii. (1903), 205.

DODGSON, Campbell. Woodcuts of the xv Century in the Department of Prints and Drawings, British Museum. 2 vols. London 1934–35.

KRISTELLER, Paul. (Review of Bouchot, 1902). *Mitteil.* (1903), p. 48.

SCHREIBER, W. L. M. Bouchots Ansichten über die Erstlinge der Holzschneidekunst. *Zeitschrift für christliche Kunst* (1908), pp. 50 and 83.

LEHRS, M. Geschichte und kritischer Katalog des deutschen, niederländischen und französischen Kupferstiches in 15. Jahrhundert. Vienna 1908. Vol. i. pp. 9, etc.

MOLSDORF, W. Gruppierungsversuche im Bereiche des ältesten Kupferstiches. Strassburg 1911.

MOLSDORF. W. Schrifteigentümlichkeiten auf älteren Holzschnitten als Hilfsmittel ihrer Gruppierung. Strassburg 1914.

Molsdorf, W. Über die Bedeutung des Typus bei den mittelalterlichen Bilddruckern. Beiträge zur Geschichte und Technik des ältesten Bilddrucks. Strassburg 1921, p. 89.

Goldschmidt, Victor. Farben in der Kunst. Heidelberg 1919 (1 vol. text, 3 vols. plates, including numerous early woodcuts reproduced in colour facsimile).

Pfister, Kurt. Die primitiven Holzschnitte. Munich 1922.

Delen, A. J. J. Histoire de la gravure dans les anciens Pays-Bas et dans les provinces belges des origines jusqu'à la fin du xviiie siècle. Ire Partie. Des origines à 1500. Paris and Brussels 1924. (For review see M. Lehrs, *Zeitschrift*, October 1925.)

Glaser, Curt. Gotische Holzschnitte. Berlin [1924]. (Short introduction to a series of 55 plates.)

Blum, André. Les Origines de la gravure en France. Les Estampes sur bois et sur métal. Les Incunables xylographiques. Paris and Brussels (Van Oest) 1927.

Jahn, Johannes. Beiträge zur Kenntnis der ältesten Einblattdrucke. Strassburg 1927.

Hind, A. M. A Note on the Printing of Early Woodcuts. *Print Collector's Quarterly*, xv. p. 131 (April 1928).

Lemoisne, P. A. Les Xylographies du xive et du xve siècle au cabinet des estampes de la Bibliothèque Nationale. 2 vols. Paris and Brussels 1927, 1930.

Cohn, W. Untersuchungen zur Geschichte des deutschen Einblattholzschnitts in 2 Drittel des xv Jahrhunderts. Strassburg 1934.

Playing-cards: see footnote, p. 84.

Dotted Prints and White-line Metal-cuts

The special class of *Dotted Prints*, whose process was described summarily in the technical introduction,[1] consists chiefly of German work of the second half of the xv century. The outstanding characteristic of such prints is the use of white instead of black for the positive parts of the design, the general result being a darker effect than in most black line cuts. This sombre quality may, as Kristeller has suggested, account for the rarity of subjects of a lighter vein in this process, practically all dotted prints being of a religious character.

The process in its more complex forms is seldom completely satisfying, chiefly perhaps in the case where the use of two distinct methods of expression, the white and black line, introduce disturbing elements; for the internal shading is often in black line, when the main lines of the design are in white.

This is only one of the factors that lead to the probability that a considerable number of the plates were primarily intended for decoration in themselves, and not for printing on paper. In the copper plate, particularly if filled with some transparent enamel or varnish, the contrasts of light and dark would not be emphasised so crudely as in black ink on paper.

The very use of metal points to the origin of the method, like that of

[1] See p. 20.

line-engraving, as in the goldsmith's workshops. It might be argued on that account that the process were better described in conjunction with line-engraving. But dotted prints are printed in relief, and we have taken this factor, rather than the material of the block, as the more important distinction.

If the design of such plates were in white line throughout, i.e. as it would appear white on black in a relief impression, it would be practically identical in process with line-engraving, and the plate could be used decoratively by filling the furrows with niello. The *Angel of the Annunciation*, of which there are two impressions at Paris (Bouchot, *Les Deux Cents Incunables*, No. 56; Hirth and Muther, 27 and 28), was probably a plate of this order. The left arm being raised renders it certain that the impression is a reverse, and that the plate was not intended for printing. But dotted prints are never of this uniformity of white line and dot, and offer more difficult problems in relation to the purpose for which they were intended.

Several distinct masters can be recognised among the producers of these dotted prints, though in only one instance is a signature attached (that of BARTHOLMEUS), and in only one other an initial, i.e. ꝺ.

It is the MASTER ꝺ whose plates offer the most definite relation to goldsmith's work, and he is certainly among the earliest of the craftsmen who used the process. Two plates bear what appears to be the artist's signature, a gothic ꝺ within a heart, i.e. the large *Last Judgment* at Paris (S. 2407) and the *Resurrection* at Vienna (S. 2375). The other inscriptions on the *Resurrection* being in reverse render it almost certain that it is a ꝺ and not a ꝺ as has sometimes been assumed.[1] Bouchot's explanation of the ꝺ within the heart as indicating *Douai* lacks support, and the dialect of the inscription on the *Mass of St. Gregory* at Danzig (S. 2645), which from its style can be attributed to the same hand, seems to point to the region of the Lower Rhine on the borderland of the Netherlands. Molsdorf's suggestion that the town in the background of another large print attributed to the Master ꝺ, the *March to Calvary and the Crucifixion* at Paris (S. 2332 x), is Cologne has not found general acceptance, but from reasons of style Cologne

---

[1] In regard to this ꝺ which might be an atelier mark, it is worth while to note the existence of various figured stamps with ꝺ and ᐧiᐧꝺ on Cologne bindings of about 1510. See E. P. Goldschmidt, *Gothic and Renaissance Bookbindings*, London 1918, Nos. 57 and 72. For the actual use of dotted prints in stamping bindings, chiefly on Cologne books in the first decade of the XVI century, see J. Theele, *Schrotdruckplatten auf Kölner Einbänden*, Gutenberg Jahrbuch, Mainz 1927, p. 256. Bouchot also noted that the Master ꝺ's *Mystery of the Incarnation* (S. 2481) was copied in a stamp used for a book-binding of the atelier of Simon Vostre of the year 1495 (*Les Deux Cent Incunables*, No. 145).

is none the less probable as a localisation. Cologne was a great centre of goldsmiths, and the Cologne arms on a plate by another master of the process, the existence of a series of dotted prints in Cologne books, and the con-

Fig. 76. The Master D. The Mystery of the Incarnation. S. 2481.

siderable number of dotted prints preserved in North German collections (while woodcuts of the period figured more largely in Upper German Libraries) all point to such an origin.

The clearest indication that some of the plates by the Master D were intended for decoration in themselves rather than for printing is offered by the three plates of the *Apostles with the Creed* (*St. Simon and St. Matthias*, S. 2745, at Munich and Vienna; the *St. John and St. James the greater*, S. 2746, and the *St. James the less and St. Thomas*, S. 2747 at Dresden), where the inscriptions are, as in several other cases, in reverse. When, as here, such an inscription is of essential import, and not a mere appendage to a generally understood episode (e.g. *ecce agnus Dei* attached to St. John Baptist), it is far more likely that the subject was not intended for printing. There is actually a copper plate of exactly similar character in the Louvre, representing *St. John and St. Paul*,[1] with

---

[1] A modern impression (printed in relief) is reproduced by P. Gusman, *La Gravure sur bois*, 1916, fig. 18.

a date 1423 on the banderoles above. The date is, I think, a later addition, probably suggested by someone who knew the famous Buxheim *St. Christopher* with its date of 1423, for the work of the Master ꝟ can hardly be

much earlier than about 1450. The line work of the design is positive, i.e. chiefly black line in a relief impression from this plate, so that the original plate could not be treated as a niello. Its design would be effective without any filling, though some form of translucent enamel might have been used.[1] As St. John had already appeared with St. James the greater in S. 2746, it is difficult to regard the Paris plate of *St. John and St. Paul* as of the same series, but the different combination of Apostles may have originated in some special request.

Fig. 77. The Annunciation. S. 2865. Printed in relief.

Though certain of the master's plates such as the *Last Judgment* and the *Apostles with the Creed* were probably intended as ornamental plaques, others, whose inscriptions read in the right direction on paper, were with equal prob-

[1] I should add that M. Marquet de Vasselot, whose knowledge of goldsmith's work is so extensive, regarded the plate, in spite of the inscriptions, as more likely to have been intended for printing than for decoration in itself.

ability intended as prints. In the latter category falls the attractive little subject of the *Mystery of the Incarnation*, or *Hortus Conclusus* (S. 2481; British Museum and Paris; fig. 76), in which the Angel of the Annunciation with three hounds, entitled *veritas, humilitas* and *castitas*, are in pursuit of a unicorn (the emblem of purity) which has taken refuge at the Virgin's knees. The process shows a mixture of white and black line, and includes dots only in the hem of drapery, just as dotted work only occurs in the borders of other subjects by the same master.

We have accepted the term *dotted manner* (*manière criblée*) as the title most generally in use, though occasionally masters of the process use dots very sparingly, and others not at all. The German term *Schrotblätter*

Fig. 78. The Annunciation. S. 2865. Printed in intaglio.

(*geschrotene Arbeit*) may, from its origin, merely imply 'cut or engraved' plates, but it has somehow assumed the implication of the dotted work, which does in fact characterise the majority of the prints under review.

I would mention here two other original plates, an *Annunciation* in the Louvre from the collection of Victor Gay (S. 2865), and a little *Visitation* in the Museum für Kunst und Gewerbe at Hamburg.[1] Modern impressions from the *Annunciation* show the inscriptions *recto*, and there is no question that the plate was intended for printing. Comparisons of modern impres-

Fig. 79. Christ and the Woman of Samaria. S. 2215.

sions printed (*a*) in relief, (*b*) in intaglio (figs. 77 and 78), show quite clearly that relief printing was intended, as the intaglio gives a negative character to the design. The subject is closely related to the *Annunciation* by Stephan Lochner on wings of his Altarpiece in Cologne Cathedral, and this fact is considerable support to Cologne origin in this important dotted print.[2] A tablet on the wall to the right of the Virgin has an inscription which, if read recto, looks like *Miloni · l*, but nothing has been made of this, and it must be remembered that the use of fanciful, or cryptogram, let-

ters is not uncommon on illuminations of the late xv and early xvi century, particularly in Flemish work. If read in reverse it might be a dedication

[1] See M. Lehrs, *Über eine Schrotschnittplatte*, Mitteilungen des Gesellschaft für vervielfältigende Kunst, 1912, p. 1.

[2] Though, as Lehrs has noted, the dotted print may have borrowed from Stephan Lochner through the Master of the Banderoles (Lehrs, 10).

to the Virgin by the engraver under his initials, i.e. *Mar*[*iae*] *vo*[*vit*] *A·I.*

The *Visitation* is based on an engraving of the Master E.S., and one of several known variants from a series of little dotted prints with borders, which were issued with text in Cologne editions of Bertholdus, *Horologium Devotionis*, during the last decade of the xv century.

Allusion has already been made to the presence of the *Arms of the City of Cologne* on a dotted print. They occur on the *Christ and the Woman of Samaria* at Munich (S. 2215; fig. 79), and it is unthinkable that they should appear on the well in such a subject if the plate did not emanate from a Cologne workshop. The student may be referred to Schreiber's work *Die Meister des Metallschnittes* (1926) for a detailed attribution of prints to various masters and groups, and it will suffice here to state that a considerable number of plates can be ascribed to the same hand as this MASTER OF THE COLOGNE ARMS, and to such another Cologne group as has its chief representative in the Louvre *Annunciation*. Many of the plates are enclosed within *passe-partout* borders of several types, of which clouds and stars, and roundels with the signs of the Evangelists, and the Four Fathers of the Church, form the chief elements.

The signs of the Evangelists and the Four Fathers of the Church on the border which surrounds, among other prints, a *St. Christopher* and a *St. Jerome* at Munich (S. 2592 and 2672), a *St. Gregory* at Berlin (S. 2646), and an *Assumption* once in the Huth Collection (S. 2435), are based on these elements in the roundel design of *St. John the Baptist* by the Master E.S. (L. 149), a fact which supplies a *terminus a quo*, as E.S.'s plate is dated 1466. The Louvre *Annunciation* is possibly by the same hand as these plates.

Another plate which is probably Cologne work from its subject, *St. Ursula and St. Gereon*, the Patron Saints of the City (Paris, S. 2734 m), is simple in its technique, a combination of line in the figures with dotted work in the background, but many other plates of the school show a complex use of a great variety of stamps, e.g.:

○ ◉ ✧ ◈ ◇ ◇ ✡ ✿ ⊡ ✚ ⚜ ♣ ♚ ⚬ ⊶ ◠ ◡

One might expect punched work of this character to be done on soft metal, but the plates known are of copper, like the line-engravings of the period. Moreover, soft metal would hardly preserve any regularity of surface under the repeated impact of the punch. Nail holes frequently appear near the margin, which indicates that the plates have been fixed on wood.

This would probably be for the convenience of printing in the same

Fig. 80. Bernhardinus Milnet. The Virgin and Child. S. 2482, II.

press as type, which would necessitate mounting metal plates on wood. If the impression were obtained by rubbing, this would of course be unnecessary, and in some cases the nail holes may have been added to fix a plate to be used as a piece of decoration in itself.

Another technical matter to which I would refer is the possible use of casts rather than the original engraved plates or blocks. I find myself unable to express a decided opinion on this point, and will merely state that a printer of great experience, Gustav Mori,[1] is convinced that prints such as those from Bertholdus, *Horologium Devotionis* (Cologne, J. Landen), and Turrecremata, *Meditationes* (Mainz, J. Neumeister), show surface qualities which indicate a cast plate (e.g. occasional spottiness resulting from sand detached on to the metal: clearer printing near the margin, as the plates cool more quickly at the edges, which thus remain at a slightly higher level than the centre). He also states that if punches were used to any extent on metal, the surface would become irregular and pressed down, a condition which would need careful rectification with the burnisher. He thinks that this difficulty would not occur if the punches were used on wood, and the metal casts made from the wood.

I confess to considerable doubt as to this last contention, but give Mr. Mori's argument for the consideration of the more technical student.

To recur to further work comparable to that of the Master with the Cologne Arms, I would cite in the first instance the famous *Virgin and Child* within a border inscribed *bernhardinus milnet* (S. 2482; fig. 80). Much has been written about this print and its signature, but most of it based on the print in Paris, which is only a lithographic facsimile. The original, which was purchased by Mr. Nathan Hill, of Manchester, at Frankfurt in 1818, was acquired in 1914 by the British Museum.[2] It was Mr. Hill who

---

[1] See G. Mori, *Was hat Gutenberg erfunden? Ein Rückblick auf die Frühtechnik des Schriftgusses*, Gutenberg Gesellschaft, Mainz 1921 (Beilage zum 19ten Jahresbericht, 1919–20).

[2] See C. Dodgson, Burlington Magazine, xxv., 1914, 169, and *Catalogue of Early German and Flemish Woodcuts in the British Museum*, i. (1903), pp. 157 and 566. Mr. Hill gave the print to F. R. Atkinson in 1856, and it was acquired by the British Museum from the executors of his son, Mr. Henry Atkinson (†1901). Schreiber in his *Manuel* refers to impressions of the original at Althorp (Lord Spencer) and at Paris (Bibl. Nat.), but there appears to be no foundation for either reference. In his *Handbuch* Schreiber again erred in describing the Stuttgart print as an early state of the Milnet before the addition of the border, but it is clearly from another plate. Schreiber describes the Stuttgart print as if it were the impression described by Weigel and Zestermann 345, but Dr. Braune, the Director of the Stuttgart Gallery, informs me that their impression differs in various details of colour from the description in Weigel and Zestermann,

arranged, through Mr. van Praet of the Bibliothèque Royale, Paris, for the lithograph to be done, issuing forty impressions, of which six were coloured. It should be noted that the name is attached to the *passe-partout* border, and might even have been added later; but I incline to think that it is contemporary with the print. But I am not completely convinced that the print itself is contemporary xv-century work. It must be remembered that there are several engraved versions of this Madonna, and the present example is certainly not the best. The two *criblée* prints most nearly related are at Stuttgart (S. 2482, I; fig. 81) and at Nuremberg (S. 2482 a), the latter probably copied from the Stuttgart version, which is certainly the best of the three in quality. There is a fourth dotted print of similar subject at Königsberg (S. 2488), but this shows a variety in the pose, which relates it more nearly to the fine Netherlandish woodcut at Breslau, which has already been discussed and reproduced (S. 1039 b, and fig. 68).

Everything considered I would not lay much stress on the Milnet version, even if the signature should happen to be genuine; *Milnet* [1] sounds French, but the spelling of *bernhardinus* is Germanic, and the style of work (whether of the period, or a later imitation) ranges itself with the Cologne group.

The 'Milnet' *Madonna* has been sometimes [2] attributed to the same hand as a *St. Bernardino of Siena* in Paris (S. 2567; fig. 82). They are both within a border of the same design, clouds and stars with the signs of the Evangelists at the corners, [3] but there is little else to connect them in style. The *St. Bernardino* is distinctly more archaic in design, and less complex in its technical characteristics, the shading of dress and ground being entirely punched in white dots. It is an important landmark in the history of the art, for the date it bears, 1454, can hardly be long after the introduction of this particular manner of engraving. [4] Two versions of *St. Francis* (S. 2626,

so it can hardly be the same impression. Dodgson referred in 1903 to the Weigel impression having been sold by Ludwig Rosenthal of Munich, but I cannot now trace its locality. Schreiber also refers to an impression in the Lanna collection (H. W. Singer, 1895, No. 36), and of this also I have no present knowledge.

[1] I would note as nothing more than a possible coincidence the relation of *Milnet* to the *Miloni* (?) on the Louvre *Annunciation* (see figs. 77 and 78, and p. 180).

[2] Originally by Duchesne, *Essai sur les nielles*, 1826, p. 10. See also Delmotte, *Facsimile du Saint-Bernardin de 1454, et de la première estampe gravé sur bois avec nom de l'auteur*, Mons 1833 (only five copies said to have been printed). Mr. van Praet had a lithograph made of this print (and issued in 25 impressions), as well as of the Milnet.

[3] Not the same as those based on E.S. in the border noted above (see p. 181).

[4] The date has been sometimes read as 1474. But the forms of numerals used in the xv century is entirely in favour of 1454 (see G. F. Hill, *On the Early Use of Arabic Numerals in Europe*, Archaeologia, lxii., 14th April 1910).

Fig. 81. The Virgin and Child. S. 2482, I.

Fig. 82. St. Bernardino of Siena. S. 2567.

Oxford and Munich; S. 2627, Paris), a *St. Christopher* in Paris (S. 2598), a *St. George* once at St. Gallen (S. 2635), and a *St. Sebastian* at Nuremberg (S. 2725 b) are all closely related, and several of them in the same border, or a variant in reverse.

The *St. Bernardino* and other works of the same master or workshop are noteworthy as examples of a method corresponding to the goldsmiths'

Fig. 83. St. George and the Dragon. S.2633.

practice of *opus interrasile* (pierced work), in which the background of the design is cut away on the plate (such work being sometimes used to decorate bindings), in contrast with the *opus punctile* (punched work), where the background is decorated with punched and dotted work.[1]

Occasionally parts of a plate might be completely detached from the main design, but even if this were not the case, the plate with its silhouetted

---

[1] Methods described by Theophilus, *Diversarum artium schedula* (probably early xii century), ed. A. Ilg, Vienna 1874, cap. lxxi., *De opere interrasili*; cap. lxxii., *De opere punctili*.

design would require nailing to a wooden block for printing. Other interesting examples of this method, which like the *St. Bernardino* probably belong to the region of the Upper Rhine, are a *St. Christopher* and a *St. George* at Paris (S. 2590 and 2633; fig. 83). Comparable in style with the *St. George*, and *St. Christopher* (but not cut away round the figures in the same way), are two versions of another *St. George*, at Vienna (S. 2636 a) and Nuremberg (S. 2636; fig. 84). Both these plates are noteworthy for the manner in which outline is almost entirely omitted and everything achieved by dotted work. In the subtle variety of the dotting, the Nuremberg plate is perhaps the more remarkable.

Fig. 84. St. George and the Dragon. S. 2636.

The same, almost exclusive, use of dots in shading noted in the *St. Bernardino*, and a similar blank background behind the silhouetted design, may be remarked in the large *Calvary* (S. 2333, London, Berlin, Breslau, Riga), of which the British Museum impression was found pasted inside the binding of a copy of the so-called *Mazarin Bible* (Hain 3031; Mainz, about 1455).[1] Its provenance led to occasional reference to dotted prints as in the "manner of the Mazarin Crucifixion".

---

[1] Two other versions show that this was a popular subject (i.e. S. 2334, Edmond de Rothschild and Halle, and S. 2334 a, Dresden and Königsberg).

In comparison with a completely white background, it should be noted that sometimes a background, or other part of the design (drapery, etc.), shows black lines only partially printing. The intention, in such cases, may have been to clear spaces with the graver, and though the level of the plate had by this means been reduced, it was not always sufficient to prevent the paper being pressed below the surface, and taking a partial impression from the lines in the cavities (e.g. the *Raising of Lazarus* by Bartholmeus, reproduced in fig. 85, the *Ten Commandments and the Ten Plagues* in the British Museum, S. 2757, and the *St. Ursula and St. Gereon* at Paris, S. 2734 m).

One other group, probably belonging to the region of Cologne, should be mentioned, called from a mark on three or four prints the WORK-SHOP OF THE ANCHOR.

Fig. 85. Bartholmeus. The Raising of Lazarus. S. 2218.

The chief print on which the Anchor occurs is that representing the *Events of the Day of Resurrection* (S. 2382, British Museum), and it is accompanied by another mark which has been variously interpreted as two A's or two compasses. The mark of the Anchor is not so clearly shown on the *Christ in the House of Martha and Mary* (S. 2220, Berne), and the print is hardly equal in quality to the former. *A Virgin and Child with St. Anne* (S. 2527, Munich) also shows the anchor, and a *Circumcision* at Treves (S. 2197 k) a double anchor with the initials D A, which are probably those of the engraver. But these prints differ considerably among themselves in quality, and apart from the initials the marks are probably those of a workshop rather than a master. Schreiber has gone to considerable length in classing dotted prints under numerous 'masters' (e.g. from his S. 2220 he calls the present engraver the 'Master of Jesus in Bethany'); a method helpful to study, but questionable in the actual facts it claims to present.

It is noteworthy that a considerable number of the prints of the 'Workshop of the Anchor' were based on engravings by the Master of the Berlin Passion (Israhel van Meckenem the Elder), which again supports the neighbourhood of the lower Rhine. The same may be said of a large proportion of the series of *Forty Small Cuts illustrating the Life and Passion of Christ* originally in a Munich private collection, now in the British Museum (S. 2173 b, etc.), of which a few examples are known in other collections.[1]

Apart from the questionable *Milnet*, and there is at least one engraver of dotted prints whose name is known, i.e. BARTHOLMEUS of the *Raising of Lazarus* in the British Museum (S. 2218; fig. 85). The *Christ and the Woman of Samaria* (S. 2216) printed on the same sheet has an inscription which suggests the locality of the lower Rhine. Two further prints in the British Museum, the *Entry into Jerusalem* (S. 2221) and *Christ driving the Money-changers from the Temple* (S. 2228), are the only other subjects known from what may have been a longer series of the Life and Passion of Christ.

Another workshop mark which is found on several dotted prints is that of a *Coat of Arms with Crossed Clubs*, e.g. on the *Three Crosses* (S. 2341, Berlin, Munich Library, Dutuit, with its characteristic background of patterned tapestry), and on the *Duel between Husband and Wife* (S. 2763),[2] a rare example of a profane subject in this process, unfortunately only known in a fragmentary state in the British Museum.

As decorative in their quality as any other prints of this genre are certain examples of a master whose work is characterised by a background of a repeated pattern of four curves imitating a textile web (*fond maillé, Maschen-Hintergrund*). His work often shows a peculiarly decorative use of two flanking columns, twined round with branches which form an arch above. The *Virgin and Child* at Vienna here reproduced (S. 2483; fig. 86), a

---

[1] See Leidinger, *Vierzig Metallschnitte aus Münchner Privatbesitz*, Strassburg 1908. Similar subjects occur in other series, e.g. in Bertholdus, *Horologium Devotionis*, printed by Zel, Cologne, about 1490 (see p. 194).

[2] Illustrating the struggle between man and wife for the mastery of the house, symbolised by the 'breeches'. A remarkable variation on the same theme is seen in the 'Fight for the Hose' shown in two unique xv-century prints by the German Master of the Banderoles (Lehrs 89, Berlin) and by an anonymous Florentine engraver (Pr. Jahrbuch vii. p. 73, Munich).

Fig. 86. The Virgin and Child. S.2483.

St. Christina in the British Museum (S. 2589), and a *St. Michael* at Berlin show similar elements of decoration.

An interesting series of dotted prints of the earlier phase, in which the backgrounds are largely decorated either with arabesque foliage, or tapestry patterns, is the so-called *Stoeger Passion*,[1] of which the *Christ bearing the Cross* (S. 2302) from the British Museum is reproduced on fig. 87. The complete series of twenty subjects of the *Passion*, preceded by eight subjects relating to the Virgin (the *Virgin on a Crescent* and the *Seven Joys of Mary*), is only known in the Library at Munich, and being issued with text printed from movable type forms one of the earliest illustrated books. The plates average about 4×3 inches.

Fig. 87. Christ bearing the Cross. From the Stoeger Passion.
S. 2302.

Several of the plates (chiefly in the series of the *Seven Joys of Mary*, which is only known at Munich) appear at first sight to be more crudely cut than the rest (e.g. S. 2181, 2192, 2210, 2199, 2214 and 2400),[2] but I think this may depend on the condition of the plates and the fact that in the first five of those noted part of the background has been cleared away (though

---

[1] First edition by F. X. Stoeger, *Zwei der ältesten deutschen Druckdenkmäler*, Munich 1833. For Schreiber's notes see his No. 2500 and No. 4750 a. See Dodgson, B.M. Catalogue, vol. i. p. 171, B. 4. For recent research respecting the various editions see Konrad Haebler, *Die italienischen Fragmente vom Leiden Christi das älteste Druckwerk Italiens*, Munich (Rosenthal) 1927.

[2] Haebler may have been led by this appearance to describe the *Seven Joys of Mary* as woodcuts. They are *metal*, like the rest.

not always deeply enough cut to avoid some smudging of the white ground), and I see no reason to think that they are not all by the same hand, or at least from the same workshop.[1]

The other fragments of the *Passion* series show, from variations in the type and in the condition of the blocks, that there were several editions of the work. One series begins with a blank page with a cut on the reverse, followed by a succession of pages with *obv.* text, *rev.* cut, ending with a blank page. Another series begins, as before, with a blank page with a cut on the reverse, but continues with leaves containing alternately (*a*) text on both sides, (*b*) cuts on both sides.

Fragments in the British Museum (showing two editions) and at Dresden are in the former manner, the Munich edition and fragments in the Bodleian, Oxford, and at Braunau (Dr. F. Langer), and the recently discovered fragment of an Italian edition, are in the latter form.[2]

According to Dr. Haebler's minute researches in regard to the character of the type, the earliest issue appears to be that of the series of eight leaves in the British Museum, while the latest German edition is that of Munich, other fragments showing intermediate issues. The condition of the blocks as well as the form of the type places the Italian edition at the end.

The general character of the type used has been rightly compared with that of the 36-line Bible (Gutenberg?), later used by Pfister of Bamberg. Dr. Haebler goes further in his distinctions, and finds the closest analogy in the type of a Calendar of 1462 preserved at Donaueschingen, which comes nearest of all to the particular character of the Munich edition.

Another interesting point that Dr. Haebler makes is the presence of new nail holes in the plates of his latter issues.

For these various reasons he envisages a travelling printer, brought up in the printing shops of Mainz or Bamberg, who detaches his plates from the wood-blocks to which they are fixed for printing to lighten his load on travel, and attaches them again to new blocks at his new centre.

The earliest editions with text can hardly be long anterior to 1461–62, and the latest, i.e. the Italian edition, not much later, as the character of type is still considerably earlier in its development than that of Ulrich Han,

---

[1] One must be careful not to confuse the original Stoeger *Passion* with a series of copies, to which Schreiber refers, noting sixteen with printed text on the back, in a catalogue of Ludwig Rosenthal of Munich. They are free translations of the original subjects, executed with less dotted work and considerably inferior in quality. Fifteen of this series, with MS. on the reverse, were in the hands of Jacques Rosenthal of Munich, 1932 (and *L'Art Ancien*, Zurich 1933).

[2] This fragment is now in the collection of the Hon. Edward Alexander Parsons, at New Orleans.

who printed Turrecremata's *Meditationes* at Rome in 1467, which had hitherto been regarded as the earliest Italian book with woodcut illustrations.

The blocks appear to be in the best condition in some of the impressions without printed text, of which the largest number are at Vienna (eighteen subjects) and Berlin (fourteen subjects), isolated examples occurring at Paris, Nuremberg, in the Bodleian and Guildhall Libraries, and in the collection of Mr. J. E. Scripps at Detroit. They may have been engraved and printed independently some years before the wandering printer obtained possession, but hardly before the middle of the century. A rough *terminus a quo* may be provided by the fact that at least one of the series, the *Resurrection* (S. 2376) appears to be based on an engraving of the School of the Master of the Playing-cards (Lehrs 10), which can itself hardly date before 1440–50.

I would here add reference to the few other printed books of the period which are illustrated with dotted prints or white-line metal-cuts. A series of thirty-four small oblong cuts (about 87 × 110 mm.) appeared in Turrecremata, *Meditationes*, printed by J. Neumeister, Mainz, 1479 (S. 5395), and re-issued by the same printer at Albi in 1481.[1] They are adapted from the woodcuts in the Rome edition of Ulrich Han, 1467. They are chiefly engraved in black line, the use of white on black being reserved for the borders, in which each subject is framed.

Another series of somewhat smaller upright cuts within decorative borders (about 70 × 49 mm.), in which dotting is freely used, was issued in editions of Bertholdus, *Horologium Devotionis* at Cologne (e.g. in the British Museum copies, thirty-eight prints, of which fourteen are in the dotted manner, in the edition printed by Zel about 1490, S. 3444, and thirty-five, partly identical with the preceding, in the edition printed by J. Landen about 1498, S. 3446).[2]

One of the larger dotted prints generally assigned to the neighbourhood of Cologne, a *St. Jerome* (S. 2672), appeared much later in Spain, on the reverse of the title-page of *Epistolas del glorioso dotor sant Hieronymo*, Seville (Juan Varela 1532,[3] and Juan Cromberger 1537[4]).

---

[1] A few of the cuts also appeared in books at Lyon, where Neumeister printed between 1487 and 1498, but only, as far as I find, in books issued by other printers after Neumeister's retirement, e.g. Robert de Balsat, *La Nef des Princes*, printed by Balsarin, 1502 (Claudin, iii. p. 526), and Symphorien Champier, *Liber de quadruplici vita*, printed by Janot de Campis, 1507.

[2] See H. Bradshaw, *Collected Papers*, Cambridge 1889 (p. 241). Cf. p. 190 for another series of similar designs (S. 2173 b, etc.).   [3] E. P. Goldschmidt, Cat. vi. No. 75.

[4] J. P. R. Lyell, *Book-Illustration in Spain*, London 1926, p. 168. W. L. Schreiber has noted it in an earlier edition of the *Epistolas*, Valencia (Jofre) 1520, but I have not been able to verify this.

Of less importance than the Turrecremata or Bertholdus series are some sixty-nine metal-cuts (partly in dotted work) which appeared together with thirty woodcuts in the *Auslegung der Messe*, printed by G. Böttiger, Leipzig 1495 (S. 4645, Breslau).

Apart from such series there are isolated examples of dotted prints or white-line cuts in book-illustration or -decoration of the period, chiefly at Cologne (leaving out of count the illustrations in French *Horae*, which will be dealt with in another chapter), and an occasional metal-cut in black line such as the printer's mark of Nicolaus Gotz, e.g. in editions of W. Rolewinck, *Fasciculus Temporum*, Cologne (the earlier edition of about 1473-74 showing the mark with Gotz's name, which was later cut from the foot of the plate).[1]

Although the French developed a method of book-illustration on metal plates closely allied, it yet seems almost certain that nearly all the dotted prints proper belong to Germany or neighbouring parts of the Lower Rhine.

There are, however, a few exceptions which should be mentioned.

The Vienna impression of the little *View of a Town* (S. 2760) was taken from the back of a folio sheet containing a printed list of Aldus's Greek books, *Libri Graeci Impressi*, Venice 1498. A MS. note beneath the place where it was pasted gave it the title of *Padua* and referred to a certain page 129 (in *Sabellicus secundae decadis liber octavus*, Venice 1487). But the cut itself certainly does not represent Padua, and the windmill suggests a Northern origin, although the cut appeared at Venice.

A series of six *Standing Saints* at Vienna (S. 2522, 2560, 2611, 2715, 2721, 2372) may be assigned more confidently to an Italian hand, the style of figure and architectural setting being thoroughly Venetian of about 1500.[2] A few examples may also be noted in Italian books of the last decade of the xv century, especially at Milan, e.g. in the *Petrarch* printed by Antonius Zarotus at Milan in 1494.[3] And certain English illustrations and border-pieces of the early xvi century (e.g. in the *Golden Legend* of 1503/04, and the *Chronicles of England* of 1504, printed by Julian Notary) should be compared with dotted prints proper, though their nearest relationship is found in contemporary French illustration.[4]

A few instances are also known of single metal-cuts in which the black

---

[1] See H. Bradshaw, *Of the Engraved Device used by Nicolaus Gotz of Sletzstat, the Cologne Printer, in 1479, Collected Papers*, Cambridge 1889, p. 237.

[2] See A. Weixlgärtner, *Eine Folge venezianischer Metallschnitte*, Mitteil., 1907, p. 73.

[3] See p. 521.   [4] See pp. 734-736.

line is so much more essential than the white that they scarcely come within the present category, e.g. a *Man of Sorrows, with a Monk*, in the British Museum (S. 2464), a cut of uncertain origin of the end of the xv century, in which little except the modelling of the body is done in white line (where it is cross-hatched).

Design in pure white line on black (whether on wood or metal) is not known to me before the beginning of the xvi century, the earliest examples I can cite being the white-line woodcuts, *Frater Pelbart de Themesvar* in his *Pomerium de Sanctis* (and *Pomerium de Tempore*), Augsburg 1502 (S. 2876), and the *Virgin and Child Crowned by Angels* in the same author's *Stellarium Corone benedicte Marie*, Augsburg, Schoensperger for J. Otmar, 1502 (S. 2869).[1] They correspond in aim with the series of white-line cuts of the *Standard-bearers of Swiss Cantons* by Urs Graf.[2]

A curious forerunner of this pure white line is seen in a line-engraving by the Master E.S., *The Virgin and Child* (L.70), which is printed in white on black in the four known impressions (Basle, Darmstadt, Felix Warburg from Junius Morgan, and S. Maltzan at Militsch). But here the copper is actually printed in intaglio, in white pigment on blackened paper.[3]

BIBLIOGRAPHY

KOEHLER, S. R. Schrotblätter. *Chronik*, ii. (1889), 65.

KOEHLER, S. R. White-line Engraving for Relief-Printing in the xv and xvi Centuries. Washington 1892 (from the Report of National Museums, 1890).

SCHÖNBRUNNER, J. Über den Schrotschnitt und die Technik des älteren Holzschnittes. *Chronik*, ii. (1889), 90.

SCHREIBER, W. L. Manuel de l'amateur. Berlin and Leipzig, iii. (1893), Nos. 2171-2767. 2nd ed., Handbuch des Holz- und Metallschnittes; Leipzig, v. (1928).

SCHREIBER, W. L. Meisterwerke der Metallschneidekunst, Strassburg (Heitz), i. (1914), ii. (1916), iii. (1926).

SCHREIBER, W. L. Die Meister der Metallschneidekunst nebst einem nach Schulen geordneten Katalog ihrer Arbeiten. Strassburg 1926.

DODGSON, Campbell. Catalogue of Early German and Flemish Woodcuts in the British Museum. Vol. i.(1903), pp. 152-208.

DODGSON, Campbell. Prints in the Dotted Manner and other Metal-Cuts of the xv Century in the Department of Prints and Drawings, British Museum (in preparation).

---

[1] C. Dodgson, *Early German and Flemish Woodcuts in the British Museum*, ii. p. 202. See H. Hymans, *Documents iconographiques et typographiques de la Bibl. Roy. de Belgique*, i^e sér. 2e livr., 1877. Hymans refers to an impression of a *St. Dorothy* in white line which is merely a line-engraving printed, as an experiment, in relief.

[2] See p. 20 and fig. 12.

[3] A curious inversion of this method may be noted in Eric Gill's occasional printing of a wood-engraving in black-line intaglio.

Lewis, J. F. 'Schrotblätter' or Prints in the 'Manière Criblée'. Proceedings of the Numismatic and Antiquarian Society of Philadelphia, October 1, 1903. Philadelphia 1904 (p. 195).

Molsdorf, W. Die Bedeutung Kölns für den Metallschnitt des xv Jahrhunderts. Strassburg 1909.

Molsdorf, W. Negative Abdrucke geschnittener Metallplatten, ⎰ in his 'Beiträge zur Geschichte
Molsdorf, W. Der Formschneider mit dem Anker, ⎱ und Technik des ältesten Bilddrucks'. Strassburg 1921.

Gusman, P. La Gravure en taille d'épargne sur métal. Byblis, i. (1922), 118.

Gusman, P. Un Incunable et son histoire. Gazette, 4ᵉ pér. vii. (1912), 271. (Gusman here comes to the same conclusion as was reached by Molsdorf in his work of 1909 about the character of the plate of the *Annunciation* in the Louvre.)

Among the numerous works dealing with Collections (e.g. in Heitz's Einblattdrucke), including dotted prints, the most valuable for special study are:

Geisberg, M. Die Formschnitte des xv Jahrhunderts zu Dresden. Strassburg (Heitz) 1911.

Stix, A. Die Einblattdrucke des xv Jahrhunderts zu Wien. ii. Die Schrotschnitte. Vienna 1920.

Leidinger, G. Die Einzel-Metallschnitte (Schrotblätter) des xv Jahrhunderts in der Staatsbibl. München. Strassburg (Heitz) 1908.

Schulz, F. T., and Bezold, G. Die Schrotblätter des Germ. Nat. Museums zu Nürnberg. Strassburg (Heitz) 1908.

See also H. Hymans, Gravures criblées, in 'Documents iconographiques et typographiques de la Bibl. Royale de Belgique'. Brussels 1877.

Paste-prints

Paste-prints are impressions taken in a special method from white-line metal-cut or *criblée* plates. In several cases paste-prints are known based on the same plate as existing *criblée* impressions. That in all these cases the paste-print is in reverse to the *criblée* print is a problem we shall discuss later. For the most part the plates used for paste-prints show less use of dot than line in the shading, but the distinction is not sufficient to class one type of metal-cut as intended for paste and the other for *criblée*. But the deeper the cutting, the simpler the scheme of shading, the better will the plate be adapted for printing in paste.

Altogether little over one hundred and fifty plates are known, the majority of these in a single impression each, only some eighteen being known in either two or three impressions. Most of them are so badly preserved as to render their method of printing obscure, but a few good impressions help one to formulate certain conclusions, though even so without dissipating many obscurities as to method and intention.

One of the best preserved paste-prints is the *Calvary* in the Guildhall, and as this happens to be one of the examples corresponding with a plate printed as a *criblée*, i.e. with a print at Munich (S. 2344), it offers a double

Fig. 88. Calvary. Paste-print.

basis for a discussion of the subject in general, both as regards process and intention. Three reproductions are given, first that of the paste-print itself (fig. 88), then the *criblée* print at Munich (fig. 89), and finally a print showing how the *criblée* plate would appear if an impression were taken in intaglio in black ink (fig. 90).[1]

The substance in which the Guildhall *Calvary* is printed is a brownish paste, like the crocus 'paste' still used by goldsmiths for proving their plates, keeping a record, or for transferring to another plate of different and possibly more precious metal. Crocus or saffron originally implied a reddish yellow made from the stigmata of the autumnal crocus, but is more often referred by transference to yellows and brownish yellows of metallic composition. Such crocus, mixed with tallow or gum tragacanth to form the 'paste', is used by goldsmiths in preference to printer's ink as it can more easily be washed out of the lines of the plate with sponge and water. An original reddish tinge (seen in certain examples of paste-prints) might turn in time to a more brownish tone.

Comparison with the Munich *criblée*, which is printed in relief, shows that the *paste* lines of the Guildhall *Calvary* are the negative parts of the design, the positive parts being the lighter portions (e.g. outline of faces). It is also clear that the paste lines stand in such relief on the surface of the paper that they must be printed from the intaglio of the plate, which corresponds to the intaglio (showing white) on the *criblée* print. Moreover, although the paste-print and the *criblée* print are in reverse to each other, they tally so exactly in dimensions and detail (e.g. in such accidental detail as the relative position of the five dots on the forepart of the harness of the centurion's horse) that their relation must be mechanical, not that of original and copy. The effect of the paste is not so much that of the rounded relief of the ink on a direct intaglio-print, but somewhat flattened in appearance, a fact which leads one to accept the suggestion which has already been made that this paste-print is an offset from another paste-print. Why in all the cases of correspondence only such offsets remain, and not the original paste-print, I cannot explain, though it is possible that the original print might have been used to transfer to another plate (for the repetition of the subject on a different metal) and then destroyed, and the offset kept as a record of the original plate (like a sulphur cast of a niello) with which it would correspond in direction.

Such surmises assume that the original plate was done as a decorative

---

[1] I do not know of an intaglio impression of this plate, but have obtained the effect by a photographic reversing of black and white.

plaque, a fact which has been shown to be probable on account of reversed inscriptions, etc., in the case of certain of the white-line metal-cuts (e.g. by the Master **Ð**). The *criblée* print corresponding with the present example

shows the inscription in reverse, and also represents the bad thief, contrary to traditional practice, on the right side of Christ. This favours the assumption that the plate was intended as a decorative plaque.

To continue the examination of the appearance of the paste-print: certain parts represented by the relief (i.e. surface) of the original plate are in black, e.g. the background. This black is bitumen, and its brittle quality has been attested to me by Mr. John McKerrow, the print assistant and restorer in the Guildhall, who mounted the print, and has noticed that

Fig. 89. Calvary. S. 2344. Printed in Relief.

in the course of a few years (even with careful keeping and little handling) further pieces of the black have detached themselves. This clearly explains how in the course of a few centuries prints of this sort are mostly mere wrecks of their original appearance.

Originally this black bitumen almost certainly covered not only the background, but all the positive lines (relief on the plate) which now show light, forming a black design on brownish ground. That the black was added by

hand and not by printing is clear (1) from the fact that the black lines do not extend beyond the edge of the paste (which does not cover the whole plate) and (2) from the fact that in careless application it covers several lines of the paste in certain places.

The fact that the paste does not ex-tend to the edge of the plate also proves that in the original printing the paste was first laid on the paper over a space roughly calculated to be that of the plate, and that the unfilled plate was then pressed on to this paste to give the intaglio paste impression.

The above notes will have shown that I incline to believe that paste - prints are proofs of plates which were in-tended as decorative plaques. But if the colouring of the Guildhall paste-print were intended to

Fig. 90. Calvary. S. 2344. As it would appear if printed in Intaglio.

represent the effect of a niellated plate, it is curious that the black portion represents the surface of the plate and the furrows the lights, for in a niello the black is usually in the furrows.[1] Several plates are known of the

---

[1] An experienced goldsmith, Mr. H. de Koningh, to whom I once showed the Guildhall print, said there was no practical reason why the plate should not have been intended for enamel or niello, though he inclined to think it was more probably intended for printing. He said that it was a common fallacy (even of some goldsmiths) to think that enamel or niello would only

kind from which paste-prints are printed, e.g. a *Christ on the Cross between the Virgin and St. John* in the Bavarian National Museum at Munich (S. 2321), of which there are more or less modern intaglio impressions (giving a negative effect) at Dresden and in the collection of Professor Paul Sachs (Cambridge, Mass.), a relief impression in the Graphische Sammlung, Munich, and a paste-print in the reverse direction at Berlin (S. 2792), which has the common characteristic of plain background (showing white if printed in intaglio) and scroll border.[1] Moreover, plates such as the Louvre *St. John and St. Paul* by the Master ꝺ are of the simple kind of metal-cut which might well have been proved in paste,[2] and in fact any *criblée* plate, even more complex, such as the *Annunciation* in the Louvre (S. 2865, and figs. 77 and 78), might have been so treated.

Certain paste-prints (more particularly those such as the Guildhall example where the black is largely detached) give the appearance of stamped leather, and Mr. Dodgson had suggested that the plates were intended as book-binder's stamps.[3] The suggestion has at least some support in the more recent discovery of bindings actually stamped by *criblée* plates, to which allusion has already been made.[4] In any case the effect aimed at in paste-prints is of ridges standing in high relief as in stamped bindings.

That all the paste-prints known have been preserved, like most of the early woodcuts, within the cover of contemporary bindings, has inclined most writers to consider them as prints done on their own account, and the method as representing experiments in decorative printing. The fact that so many are unique does not militate against this view, as the same may be said of so many early woodcuts. A great number are in a uniform style, and there are several simple forms of scroll borders which are frequently repeated. It is not improbable, if this view is correct, that the experiments belong to one, or a very limited number of workshops. And every indication of style limits the period of production to thirty or forty years at most. Many examples are copies from line-engravings of about 1450–60 (e.g. the Guildhall print after the Master E.S.), and certainly not many years after the date of their originals.

hold on a rough surface; he stated that they would hold equally well without lines or under-cutting, as they fuse with the metal.

[1] See Geisberg, *Monatshefte*, v., 1912, 311.

[2] See pp. 177-178.

[3] *Catalogue of Early German and Flemish Woodcuts in the British Museum*, vol. i. p. 204.

[4] See p. 176. Comparison should be made with such bindings in the British Museum as those on *Postilla Thome de Aquino in Job*, Esslingen 1474; Ovid, *Epistolae*, Lyon 1528; and a New Testament in Croatian, Tübingen 1563.

On one example in the Munich Library (Leidinger 23) occurs the MS. date of 1487,[1] which must in any case be about the time when the method was chiefly practised. Little can safely be inferred from the further MS. note, 'bought for 10 kreuzer', as it is uncertain whether it refers to the print or the book.

I would refer to certain varieties in the methods of printing used, which have been discussed in considerable detail by Dr. Leidinger and Dr. Geisberg. Leidinger makes two classes according to whether the paper is, or is not, prepared with a ground tone. Personally I think the distinction is uncertain, as in many cases the ground tone is probably a stain from the paste which shows where the paste is pressed away. But it is possible that a thin glutinous foundation may have sometimes been laid to help the paste to adhere.

In several examples there are traces of gold, and Geisberg believes that gold may have originally existed on the majority, though it has now disappeared. The most perfectly preserved example in which gold has been used is the *St. John the Evangelist* at Munich (S. 2850). This print was probably made by first laying gold leaf over a thick paste on the paper,[2] then either printing in black (like a wood block in relief) on this, or (*a*) impressing the empty plate to give relief effect to the gold, and (*b*) drawing in black in the furrows between the relief of the paste and in the background (i.e. in the parts corresponding to the surface of the original plate); and finally touching the flesh in white (and possibly rose, though this colour no longer remains).

In other examples (e.g. the *St. Dorothy* in the British Museum, S. 2842) the paste shows in grey-black lines standing in relief on the paper over a reddish foundation, while the background is in a still deeper black (bitumen, like the background of the Guildhall print). It is possible that the grey-black paste (which corresponds with the intaglio of the plate impressed on the paste) may have changed from another colour,[3] and that the black, showing the positive of the design, drawn between the ridges or surfaces of paste lines or surfaces, may have been largely detached, except for the background, as in the Guildhall example.

There is considerable difference of opinion as to whether the plates were commonly, or only occasionally, filled with printer's ink before impressing

---

[1] *Ad 15 Decemb. anno [14]87 kaufft pro 10 k[reuzer]*.

[2] Cf. examples of printing in gold in the early XVI century. In some examples of paste-prints the gold may have been applied locally (with a brush?).

[3] In certain cases silver leaf might have oxidised.

on the paste,[1] and even so it is not always quite clear whether the plate was inked in intaglio or on the surface as in relief printing. Personally I favour the view that in general the plate was not filled with ink, and that in the black paste-prints the plate was impressed on to a prepared black paste; and in the other cases where black appears between the ridges of paste and in the background, that this black was more generally added by hand than in the printing.

The *Christ on the Cross between the Virgin and St. John* (S.2790, Heidelberg) seems, on the other hand, to be a clear example where a plate, inked like a woodcut in relief, was impressed on to the paste. The paste would thus stand out where the plate was in intaglio, and the positive black would be impressed in the spaces between the ridges of the paste.

It is difficult to dogmatise as to whether the plate was laid face upwards and the paste-covered paper laid on it and rubbed from the back, or whether the paste-covered paper was laid face upwards and the plate pressed downwards on to it as in early block-printing, but I incline to think the latter would be the more natural process. It is at least unlikely that a printing press was used.

The makers of paste-prints, as of *criblée* prints in general, were undoubtedly of the craft of goldsmiths and engravers, rather than of the woodcutters and carpenters. The large number of examples copied from line-engravings of the period emphasises this connection.

The justification for including dotted prints on metal in the history of woodcut rather than in that of line-engraving, is the method of printing. To be consistent, paste-prints should be considered with line-engraving, but as the plates often serve for printing in relief as well as in intaglio, we have here, for convenience, treated both *criblée* and paste-prints together. And actually it is the surface of the plate and not the intaglio which is the positive factor in the design of paste-prints.

Supplementary Note

Mr. T. O. Mabbott in the valuable studies cited in the following bibliography has brought into the circle of the normal paste-prints a variety of other methods, in one of which no paste is used. I have discussed some of these methods in other parts of this history, but add here, for convenience, a summary of Mabbott's classifications, a note of one or two of the prints he describes, which I have not mentioned elsewhere, and cross-references to my own text.

---

[1] Geisberg holding the former view, Schreiber the latter.

I. WOODCUTS WITH PASTE DECORATION
Chiefly referring to tinsel-prints (see pp. 22 and 171).

II, A. SEAL PASTE-PRINTS
Imitating the appearance of a seal or wood-carving. Obtained by impressing an intaglio plate, or a matrix, on to a thick layer of paste on paper.
   (1) *The Virgin and Child* (S. 2824 b). Mabbott Collection.
   (2) *The Virgin and Child and Saints* (S. 2828 m). Metropolitan Museum, New York.

II, B. SEAL-PRINT
A blind embossed impression on paper (cf. p. 24).
   (1) *The Coronation of the Virgin* (S. 2863 m). The surface covered with a thin brown coating (of paste?). New York Public Library.
   (2) *St. Denis, St. Emmeram and St. Wolfgang (patron saints of Regensburg)* (S. 2863 x). Metropolitan Museum, New York.

III. PASTE-PRINTS WITH FLAT PASTE. FLOCK-PRINTS.

III, A. FLOCK-PRINTS ON LINEN
   No specimens known, but method described in the receipt book of the Convent of St. Catherine, Nuremberg (quoted by Forrer, and by Leidinger; cf. p. 69). See my notes on textile prints, p. 67 ff., and bibliography of Paste-prints.

III, B. FLOCK-PRINTS ON PAPER
   See my notes above, pp. 172-174.

III, C. WOODCUT PASTE-PRINTS WITHOUT WOOL
   St. Catherine (S. 2833 y). General Theological Seminary, New York. Pasted in a volume of Bonaventura, *Quaestiones super IV Libros Sententiarum P. Lombardi*, printed by Koberger, Nuremberg, about 1491.
   The paper has been prepared with a paste ground, to which a canvas-like grain has been given (probably by the impress of canvas). A woodcut is printed over this, and the subject then coloured by hand.

III, D. FLOCK-PRINT WITHOUT PASTE
   This refers to the *Allegorical Device, with Castle, Hind, and Panther* (S. 2862 m), which I have noted under Flock-prints (p. 173).

III, E. SILVER-PRINT ON LINEN
   The *Madonna of Loreto* (S. 1). Formerly in the W. L. Schreiber Collection. Neither Mabbott nor I have seen the original. The basis may be linen covered with silver-leaf, with a woodcut subject printed on this base, and touched by hand.

IV. NORMAL PASTE-PRINTS
IV, A. DOTTED PRINTS ON THICK PASTE WITH A GLUE BASE
   E.g. *Crucifixion* (S. 2790). Heidelberg.
   St. Veronica (S. 2859). Heidelberg.

IV, B. NORMAL PASTE-PRINTS WITH MODERATELY THICK PASTE

IV, C. PASTE-PRINT INKED THIN, WITHOUT A GLUE BASE
    St. Elizabeth (S. 2842 m). Vienna (from W. L. Schreiber).

IV, D. NORMAL PASTE-PRINTS WITHOUT A GLUE BASE
    E.g. St. Margaret (S. 2854 b). Metropolitan Museum, New York.

BIBLIOGRAPHY

PASSAVANT, J. D. Le Peintre-Graveur. Leipzig 1860 (vol. i. p. 102).

SCHREIBER, W. L. Manuel de l'amateur. Berlin and Leipzig, iii. (1893), Nos. 2768–2863. 2nd ed., Handbuch des Holz- und Metallschnittes, Leipzig, vi. (1928).

DODGSON, C. Catalogue of Early German and Flemish Woodcuts in the British Museum, vol. i. (1903), p. 203.

LEWIS, J. F. Teigdrucke, Prints in Paste. Proceedings of the Numismatic and Antiquarian Society of Philadelphia. October 1, 1903. Philadelphia 1904, p. 189.

LEIDINGER, G. Die Teigdrucke des xv^{ten} Jahrhunderts in München. Munich (1908).

LEIDINGER, G. Teigdrucke in Salzburger Bibliotheken. Munich 1913.

GERSBERG, M. Holzschnittbildnisse des Kaisers Max. Pr. Jahrbuch 1911, Heft 4.

GERSBERG, M. Teigdruck und Metallschnitt. Monatshefte, v. (1912), 311.

MOLSDORF, W. Zur Technik des Teigdrucks, in his Beiträge zur Geschichte und Technik des ältesten Bilddrucks. Strassburg 1921, p. 79.

DUDLEY, Laura. Three Paste-Prints. Fogg Art Museum, Harvard University. Notes, vol. ii. No. 2 (June 1926). [Containing a list of paste-prints not described by Schreiber.]

MABBOTT, T. O. Seal-prints and a Seal Paste-print. Bulletin of the New York Public Library, August 1928.

MABBOTT, T. O. Paste-Prints and Seal-prints. Metropolitan Museum Studies, vol. iv. part i. (February 1932).

MABBOTT, T. O. Woodcuts and Paste-prints of the Mabbott Collection, New York. Einbl. 78. Strassburg 1933.

CHAPTER IV

BLOCK-BOOKS

A BLOCK-BOOK is a book whose pages (whether text only, or text and pictures combined) are printed entirely from wood blocks, the text being cut on the block and not printed separately from movable type.

A considerable number of the single woodcuts of the first half of the xv century contain text, as well as picture, cut on the block, and from this it is no far cry to the idea of producing a series of blocks with pictures and text (or with text alone) to be issued in the form of a book, i.e. the block-book as defined above.

Block-cutting for printing pictures being at least half a century older than the printing of books from movable type (which may be dated roughly within a few years of 1450), one would naturally expect the block-book to have been the earlier form in which book-making was conceived. And this conclusion is supported, I think, not only by the style of several of the existing block-books, but by one of the earliest authoritative references to the discovery of printing, which occurs in the Cologne Chronicle of 1499.

On the other hand, the conclusion drawn by Dr. W. L. Schreiber from the wealth of his erudition in early woodcuts was that none of the existing block-books could be dated before about 1455-60, and that therefore the influence of block-books in the development of printing from movable type should be discounted.[1]

This is the position of the controversy which I will now describe in sufficient detail to explain, if not justify, my own conclusions.

The Cologne Chronicle[2] owed its passage on the early development of

[1] See also Victor Scholderer, *Wood and Metal in the Invention of Printing*, in the Woodcut (an Annual), London 1929, p. 25, for the view that emphasises the essential difference between type cut on wood and type cast on metal. Cf. Chapter III. (p. 66), for further references.

[2] *Die Cronicavan der hilliger Stat van Coellen*, Cologne (J. Koelhoff) 1499, f. 311, verso, *Van de boyckdruckerkunst* (under the year 1450): *Item dese hoichwyrdige kůst vurss is vonden aller eyrst in Duytschland tzo Mentz am Rijne. . . . Ind dat is geschiet by den iairen uns heren, anno dñi 1440 und vā der zijt an bis men schreve 1450 wart undersoicht die kunst ind wat dair zo gehoirt. Ind in den iairē . . . 1450 do was eyn gulden iair, do began men tzo drucken ind was dat eyrste boich dat men druckde die Bybel zo latijn, ind ward gedruckt mit eynre grouer schrifft. as is die schrifft dae men nu Mysseboicher mit druckt. Item wie wail die kunst is vonden tzo Mentz, als vurss up die wijse, als dan nu gemeinlich gebruicht wirt, so is doch die eyrste vurbyldung vonden in Hollant*

printing to Ulrich Zel, who had been printing at Cologne since 1466 and was still working at his craft, and its evidence consequently carries great weight. It states, in effect, that the art of printing was first discovered at Mainz in 1440, and that experiments were being made from that year until 1450, when the first printed book, a Latin Bible, was issued; but that the 'first prefigurement' of the art occurred in the grammars of Donatus printed before that time in Holland.

Leaving on one side the minute technicalities of the controversy about the earliest actual sheets of printing from movable type,[1] I would run somewhat counter to purist bibliographers who generally contend that an experienced printer like Zel could only have been referring to some half-developed form of type-printing in his 'prefigurement'. But some recent philologists dispute the traditional translation of *vurbyldung*, and think it implies no more than 'precursor'. In any case, it seems to me at least probable that either 'prefigurement' or 'precursor' (whichever is the correct translation) may have included the printing of block-books,[2] and though Zel's direct reference to the existence of Dutch *Donatuses* before the introduction of printing at Mainz has not been verified, there is considerable reason to regard certain picture block-books produced in the Netherlands as anterior to 1440. Such an interpretation

vyss den Donaten, die daeselffst vur der tzijt gedruckt syn. Ind vā ind uyss den is genōmen dat begynne der vurss kunst ind is vill meysterlicher und subtilicher vonden dan die selve manier was, und ye lenger ye mere kunstlicher wurden. . . . Item idt syn ouch eyndeill vurwitziger man. und die sagen. men have ouch vurmails boicher gedruckt, mer dat is niet wair. want men vynt in geynen landen der boicher die tzo den selven tzijden gedruckt syn.

[1] For the bibliography and documentation of this subject the student should refer to A. van der Linde's *Gutenberg* (Stuttgart 1878), and to the article by J. H. Hessels on *Typography* in the Encyclopædia Britannica, even though he may not agree with its championship of Coster as against Gutenberg as the discoverer of printing. An illuminating survey of the development of early printing is Mr. A. W. Pollard's introduction to Part III. of the British Museum Catalogue of xv-Century Printed Books (1913); more recent studies in favour of Coster are G. Zedler, *Der holländische Frühdruck und die Erfindung des Buchdrucks* (Leipzig 1921), and the same author's *Die neuere Gutenberg-Forschung und die Lösung der Coster-Frage* (Frankfurt 1923), while a good résumé of the position by an upholder of Gutenberg's claim appears in the introduction of Conrad Haebler, *Die deutschen Buchdrucker des xv Jahrhunderts im Auslande* (Munich 1924). See also Adolf Tronnier, *Ein 'Costerfund' in Mainz, zugleich ein Beitrag zur Gutenberg-Coster Frage*, Gutenberg Gesellschaft Jahrbuch (Mainz), 1926, p. 144.

[2] As early as about 1530 the 'Dutch manner' of the passage in the Cologne Chronicle was interpreted as *woodcut* (see van der Linde, *Gutenberg*, p. 270).

Another reference which has been frequently quoted to support the theory that the block-books were regarded in the xv century as a stage in the development of printing from type is contained in a set of colophon verses supposed to have appeared in one of the books printed at

might help in the rehabilitation of the traditional place held by LAURENS JANSZOON COSTER of Haarlem in the discovery of printing, if block-book printing could be regarded as leading towards the discovery of movable type, and if a sufficiently strong link should be found between the style of the earliest block-books and the earliest illustrations in Haarlem printed books.

A connection with Dutch printers is circumstantial in the *Speculum Humanae Salvationis*, the *Canticum Canticorum*, and the *Biblia Pauperum* (S. Ed. I), but these block-books probably all date after 1460, while the earlier block-books, the *Exercitium super Pater Noster* (S. Ed. I), and the *Apocalypse* (S. Ed. I-III), seem more nearly related to the art of the Southern Netherlands, so that the solution of the Coster controversy is not thereby appreciably advanced.

Moreover, even if it should be proved that any of the early fragments of printing from movable type were due to Coster, it is still necessary to remember that analogous experiments, prefigurements of the use of movable type in its full development, were probably being made in other countries about the same period.

For example, the notices preserved of a Bohemian goldsmith, PROCOPE

Lyon by Johannes Trechsel, who came to France from Mainz in 1487, of which the pertinent passage runs as follows:

> *Sic prima in buxo concisa elementa premendi*
> *Parva quidem scribae damna tulere bono*
> *At ubi divisas Germania fudit in aere*
> *Inciditque notas iisque ter usa fuit,*
> *Extemplo inventis cesserunt artibus omnes.*

(Which might be paraphrased: 'The beginning of printing, when the letters were cut in boxwood, caused little injury to the good scribe's activities; but when Germany cut and cast movable type, and made frequent use of it, the scribes in a body lost their old employment through the new methods').

The verses were first quoted by Johann Wetter as appearing at the end of a quarto edition of *Expositio Georgii super Summulis Petri Hispani* (J. Wetter, *Kritische Geschichte der Erfindung der Buchdruckerkunst durch J. Gutenberg*, Mainz 1836, p. 189), and have been repeated by many bibliographers since (e.g. A. Van der Linde, *The Haarlem Legend*, London 1871, p. 77; C. Zedler, *Der holländische Frühdruck*, Leipzig 1921; C. Haebler, *Die deutschen Buchdrucker des XV Jahrhunderts im Auslande*, Munich 1924; A. Börner, Zentralblatt für Bibliothekswesen, xliii., 1926, p. 69). I have shown the verses to Mr. Stephen Gaselee, one of the best authorities on medieval latinity, and he sees no internal reason for doubting their authenticity. On the other hand, neither Claudin (*Histoire de l'imprimerie en France*, vol. iv., 1914, p. 51), nor Dr. M. J. Husung, the secretary of the 'Kommission für den Gesamtkatalog des Wiegendrucke', has been able to find any copy of either Hain 7602 or Reichling 922, or any other Trechsel book, with the verses in question.

For the reference to boxwood see Chapter I. (p. 8).

WALDFOGHEL, working at Avignon in 1444, point to experiments in printing letters from metal. These experiments may not have progressed beyond the stamping of letters from dies cut by the goldsmith, but they are more likely to have been related to the search for movable type than to printing from engraved plates or blocks.[1] On the other hand, the records in Italy of a certain Bolognese illuminator (*miniator*) ZUANE DE BIAXIO in 1446 at Venice using *forme da stampar donadi e salterj*,[2] probably refer to little grammars and psalters printed from wood or metal blocks.

Two Netherlandish records also seem to refer to something in the nature of block-books. The earlier of these is contained in the diary of Jean Le Robert, Abbot of Saint-Aubert at Cambrai,[3] who in 1445 sends to Bruges for two copies of a *doctrinal gette en molle*, and in 1451 sent to Arras for another doctrinal similarly described as *jettez en molle*. The natural interpretation of *jetté en moule* would be *cast (in a mould)*, which might well refer to block or type printing.[4] And it appears that an old French term for a printed book which survived in Cambrai till the later XIX century was a *livre jetté en molle, livre mollé* or *moulé*, and in Belgium *moulé* was also sometimes provincially used for 'printed'.

These extracts, then, can hardly have reference to any of the block-books with pictures which are our study, for these all appear to have been cut in wood, but it is by no means improbable that some of the small grammar books, or sheets, were, as these extracts imply, printed from metal casts.

The further claim made by Gilliodts van Severen that the doctrinal referred to was the undated Johannes Gerson, *Instruction et doctrine de tous chrétiens*, printed by JOHANNES BRITO CIVIS BRUGENSIS (original in the Bibliothèque Nationale, Paris; Campbell, p. 220, No. 807), and that Brito was a forerunner of Gutenberg, does not find support among scholars to-day, who place the work nearer 1470–80. In fact the first extract seems to refer, in

---

[1] See the Abbé H. Requin, *L'Imprimerie à Avignon en 1444*, Paris 1890; *Origines de l'imprimerie en France (Avignon 1444)*, in Journal Général de l'Imprimerie et de la Librairie, 28th February 1891; and L. Duhamel, *Les Origines de l'imprimerie à Avignon: Notes sur les documents découverts par M. l'Abbé R.*, Avignon 1890.

[2] See Cecchetti, *Archivio Veneto*, xxix. p. 88.

[3] The original MS. at Cambrai, first published by the Abbé Ghesquière in 1779. See L. Gilliodts van Severen, *L'Œuvre de Jean Brito*, Annales de la Société d'Émulation de Bruges, sér. v. tome x. (1897).

[4] The objection brought against this interpretation by A. Tronnier in his article in the Gutenberg Jahrbuch of 1926 already referred to, that *jetté en molle* was commonly used for any worthless thing at this period, seems to me an unnecessary attack on a strong point in his opponent's argument.

'Sandrius', to the doctrinal of Alexander (the regular children's grammar book of the time), though this also has been contested.[1]

It should be remembered that some of the simplest early 'doctrinals' were merely metal tablets with letters of the alphabet, such as one reproduced by Andrew Tuer in his *History of the Horn Book*, 1896 (i. p. 117), though the reference to paper in the second extract of 1452 would render this explanation unlikely in the instances quoted from the Cambrai document.

Another still earlier reference, a note in the will of Eustache Lefebvre, Vicar-general of Cambrai in 1377, describing *II livres de papiers de legende de sains et de expositions d'evangilles*, was supposed by Bouchot to refer to block-books, but it is far too vague for any specific interpretation relating to anything printed.[2]

On the other hand, the document of 1452 already quoted almost certainly refers to the making of regular block-books.[3] The representatives of various guilds in Louvain had lodged a request with the Town Council that Jan van den Berghe should join the Guild of Carpenters like other printers of 'letters and pictures' (*letteren ende beeldeprynten*). He was officially ordered to comply in spite of his contention that his art was not among the regular crafts, and concerned the clergy rather than the guilds. It can therefore be inferred with certainty that he was engaged on the cutting of some book of a religious kind, like the existing block-books, but no indication has been found to show for which of these he was responsible. He is known to have been working at Louvain until 1480.

Another episode touching the jealousy of the guilds for their rights has been quoted[4] in which Günther Zainer the book-printer found difficulty at Augsburg about 1468 in being allowed to illustrate his books with cuts, and in the end only obtained the licence on the understanding that he used the woodcutters of the guilds. This appears to have been a case where the block-book cutters may have been jealous of the natural progress of the illustrated book, which was the doom of their primitive method, and, failing to stem the tide, at least did their best to retain for their own guild the monopoly of cutting illustrations for the new printed books.

---

[1] See Tronnier, *op. cit.* For notes as to text of the other chief doctrinal, Donatus's grammar, see P. Schwenke, *Die Donat- und Kalender-Type*, Veröffentlichungen der Gutenberg Gesellschaft, No. 2 (1903).

[2] Quoted by Chrétien Dehaisnes, *Documents et extraits divers concernant l'histoire de l'art dans la Flandre, l'Artois et le Hainaut*, Lille 1886, p. 551.

[3] See pp. 83 and 89. [4] See p. 91.

Apart from Jan van den Berghe, whose actual work is not identified, the only known authors of block-books belong to the last generation of their class, i.e. from about 1470. An edition of the *Biblia Pauperum* is described in its colophon as done by *Friderich walthern mauler zu Nördlingen* and *Hans Hurning*. HANS HURNING is known in a Nördlingen document as a carpenter (*Schreiner*), therefore it may be inferred that he cut the blocks after the drawings of FRIEDRICH WALTHER. This shows a division of labour which was commonly authenticated by signatures of both designer and cutter in the XVI century, and which was probably generally the case, through the restrictions imposed by the guilds, throughout the XV century as well.

Friedrich Walther's name is also found on the first edition of Franciscus de Retza's *Defensorium Virginitatis Mariae* of 1470, of which a second edition was issued by Johannes Eysenhut, probably at Regensburg, in 1471. *Salve Regina*, of about the same period, appeared under the name of *lienhart czu regenspurck*, who was possibly a certain LIENHART WOLFF, recorded as a *priefdrucker* at Regensburg in and after 1463.

Another name is that of HANS SPÖRER, the printer of a *Biblia Pauperum* of 1471, an *Antichrist* of 1472 and an *Ars Moriendi* of 1473 (S. VIII). The division of labour is not made clear in these examples, but he is probably the cutter as well as the printer. And in the case of copies from earlier editions a professional designer could certainly have been dispensed with. In the colophon of the *Ars Moriendi* he calls himself *Priefmaler*. A Hans Spörer occurs in a Nuremberg document of 1479, so that he is probably also the *Hans briefftruck* who published Calendars of Johann Müller (Regiomontanus) at Nuremberg about 1474 and 1476,[1] and later printed books at Bamberg and Erfurt.

Another edition of the *Ars Moriendi* (S. VII A) is signed LUDWIG ZU ULM. Schreiber mentions Ludwig Kuch, and Ludwig Friess, who are known in Ulm documents about 1475, as more probable identifications than Ludwig Hohenwang, who worked at Augsburg.

A further name, that of JORG SCHAPFF ZU AUGSBURG (who is known in records from 1478), is found in two of the editions of Johann Hartlieb, *Die Kunst Chiromantia*.

The latest name to be found on any block-book is that of HANS WURM of Landshut on the xylographic edition of the *Art of Wrestling*, which is only known in the Print Room at Berlin, and probably belongs to the early years of the XVI century.

Apart from these isolated examples of dated works, we are largely

[1] British Museum Library, IA. 26 and IA. 7.

reduced to conjecture in estimating the probable date of the block-books. For the other date which appears in a block-book, that of 1440 in the MS. of the *Pomerium Spirituale*, may refer to the original composition of the text, but certainly not to the date of the cutting of the blocks, which must be nearer 1470.

In respect of locality there is a little more evidence with regard to the *Biblia Pauperum* (S.I), the *Canticum Canticorum* (S.I), and the *Speculum Humanae Salvationis*, for fragments of some of the blocks were used in Dutch books, i.e. fragments from the *Biblia Pauperum* in the *Epistelen en Evangelien* printed by PIETER VAN OS at Zwolle, 1487 (and in later books by the same printer until 1500); the upper half of the first block of the *Canticum Canticorum* in the *Rosetum Exercitiorum Spiritualium*, Zwolle (Pieter van Os) 1494; and fragments of the *Speculum* in the *Epistelen en Evangelien* printed by JAN VELDENER at Utrecht in 1481, in the *Speculum* (*Speghel onser Behoudenisse*) and *Kruidboeck* printed by Jan Veldener at Culenborg in the years 1483 and 1484 respectively. There is no absolute evidence of locality in such reappearance of the blocks, as printers frequently borrowed blocks from other printers or towns. But the correspondence of style between these later block-books and certain Dutch illustrations (a subject to which we shall recur) at least reduces the problem to narrower limits.

Before proceeding with a more detailed survey of the block-books, there are a few other general questions on the origin and production of block-books which demand attention.

The defence made by Jan van den Berghe of Louvain that his work concerned the clergy rather than the guilds reminds one of the religious order called the *Fratres Communis Vitae*, founded in the XIV century by Geerte de Groote of Deventer, and Florent Radewijn, which carried on considerable educational propaganda through literary and artistic channels. Its chief centre was the Abbey of Groenendael, near Brussels, and though most of its convents were in Holland (e.g. at Deventer, Louvain, Alost, Gouda, Utrecht, Zwolle and Bois-le-Duc), its field extended to Cologne and several other parts of Germany.[1] It is highly probable that members of such a community used, or even made, some of the block-books in the course of their activities.

The simplest form of religious propaganda among the unlearned would

[1] E.g. printing-presses were conducted by Brothers of the Order (sometimes called the *Michaelisbrüder*) at Marienthal (about 1474–84), Brussels (about 1476–87) and Rostock (about 1476) until the early XVI century. The Brussels press may have started at Cologne, 1475, and moved soon after to Brussels.

have been by pictures alone, so that it is natural to expect woodcut representations of the Virgin, saints and miscellaneous Biblical subjects without text to have preceded blocks on which lettering was also added, and *a fortiori* to have preceded the block-books or collection of such lettered prints.

The idea of issuing series of prints in book form was not confined to woodcut; it may also be noted in works of the early line-engravers such as the Master E.S., whose early Passion series is found in book form with MS. text. Sometimes the dividing line between a series of woodcuts probably intended for issue in book form, and what is strictly defined as a block-book, is somewhat uncertain. Moreover, several early Passion series with woodcut text, kept together in the form of broadsides, may have been intended to be divided and bound up as books (e.g. Schreiber, *Manuel*, iv. p. 330, Paris, Bouchot 170).

But the block-book proper, in its most regular form, was made up of a series of leaves, in folio, printed on one side only. The block would cover either one page, or the whole space opening of two pages.[1] This leaf being folded would leave a blank page one, pages two and three with cuts, and a blank page four. This would be followed by another folio similarly arranged, and so on, so that after the initial blank page two pictured pages would be followed in regular rotation by two blank pages, and the latter were sometimes (perhaps usually) pasted together to preserve an uninterrupted continuity of picture and text. Even where the blank pages are now open there are often traces of the gum or paste that had formerly held them together.

In some examples the book is made up in a single gathering of folios (in which case the blocks of the first and last pages would be printed together and so on), e.g. the 1470 and 1471 editions of the *Biblia Pauperum*. In occasional instances a book might be made up in several gatherings of folios (e.g. *Ars Moriendi*, S. XIII).

The blank reverses were advisable, if not necessary, in the early block-books as the printing was done by the rubber, for this method of hand-printing causes too much indentation for satisfactory double-sided printing.

Many of the later block-books which appeared in the second half of the century were printed on both sides of the page in the ordinary book-printer's press. We shall do no more than refer to the ugly terms by which these two kinds of block-books are sometimes defined: *opisthographic* for

[1] The latter certainly in the case of several editions of the *Biblia Pauperum*. A split in the block which crosses two pages (e.g. in the British Museum Grenville copy of S. IX at page signatures ·c· and ·d·) would be a definite indication. Cf. p. 234 and fig. 100.

those printed on both sides, *anopisthographic* for those printed on one side only.

Like the corresponding single prints, the earlier block-books printed with the rubber are generally found in lighter brown or grey ink; the later examples printed in the press in the usual black ink of the printer. In describing the block-books and their various editions it may be assumed that the printing is on one side only, unless the contrary is definitely stated.

Classed with the block-books are certain early examples in the same form, in which, however, the text is not cut, but only in manuscript (and therefore called *chiro-xylographic*).[1] In certain cases they might have been proofs for blocks with cut lettering which were never carried out.

With regard to the form of their letters the cutters of the early block-books were of course inspired by the writers of Gothic script, but the use of the knife in cutting inevitably led them into conventional forms which must have helped in the development of the conventions that ruled later in movable type. The only block-book which reflects very closely the manner of a scribe is one of the later examples, the *Mirabilia Romae* (of about 1475).

The woodcuts of block-books, as of book-illustration in general, would be treated most appropriately in direct relation to the single woodcuts of the same period; for the same workshops would no doubt be responsible for work done for the varying purposes. Comparisons will of course be made, but the convenience of certain subject classifications in such a history as the present inevitably implies some compromise in method. Moreover their study in a separate section is convenient as the same series of designs, notably those of the *Biblia Pauperum*, occur in block-books of various nationalities.

The chief centre of the production of the most important block-books was undoubtedly the Netherlands. Germany follows with an almost equal number of block-books, but many of little importance and a considerable number based on Netherlandish originals. France scarcely enters the field except in so far as there remains uncertainty in localising the *Apocalpyse* and *Ars Moriendi*, and in relation to certain Breton Almanacs of the early xvi century. And Italy only produced one important early block-book, the *Passion* (which will be treated in a later chapter in its relation to Venetian book-illustration), the interesting little guide for German visitors in Rome (*Wie Rom gebauet ward* or the *Mirabilia Romae*) and an early xvi-century imitation of the *Biblia Pauperum*, entitled the *Opera Nova Contemplativa*.

[1] Schreiber, *Manuel de l'Amateur*, vol. iv. p. 90, writes *xylo-chirographic* in error.

SURVEY OF THE PRINCIPAL BLOCK-BOOKS

We will now make a survey, roughly chronological, of the more important Netherlandish and German block-books, beginning with the Netherlands. The earliest, or one of the earliest, is the first and chiro-xylographic edition of the *Exercitium super Pater Noster*,[1] only known in a defective impression, with MS. text in Flemish, at Paris (see fig. 91). Judging from later editions the work should contain ten plates, Nos. 1 and 9 being missing.

The second edition of the *Exercitium*, from a new set of blocks, freely copied from the first, with Flemish and Latin woodcut text (Mons and Paris) is very similar in style to the *Pomerium Spirituale*,[2] a series of twelve blocks with manuscript text (in praise of twelve attributes of the Deity), which is only known in the impression at Brussels. The *Pomerium Spirituale* cannot be strictly classed as a block-book, for the cuts are merely pasted into a MS., and there is no evidence that this was intended as basis for a woodcut text; nevertheless, it is generally described in connection with its near relations among the block-books. The text of the *Pomerium* was written by Henri van den Bogaerde (*Latine*, Henricus ex Pomerio, *b.* 1382, *d.* 1469), a brother of the Order of the Common Life at the Convent of Groenendael, near Brussels (of which he was Prior in 1431). The date 1440 which occurs at the end of the MS. doubtless refers to the original composition,[3] not to the actual MS. or blocks, which, with their angular style and regular parallel shading, can hardly be earlier than about 1470. Lists of Bogaerde's writings include works on the Lord's Prayer, so that common authorship of the text of the two related books is very probable. And it is a natural inference that the first edition of the *Exercitium* also belonged to the same region of the Southern Netherlands.

There was also a German edition of the *Exercitium*, of which only the first page is preserved (at Kremsmünster). It offers a good example of the characteristic differences between Netherlandish and German work of about 1470, the Dutch being more sensitive but less decided in line, the German harder in quality, more clearly cut and well printed (see Schreiber, vol. vi. plates lxxxviii and lxvii).

[1] Paul Kristeller, Graphische Gesellschaft, vi., Berlin 1908.

[2] MS. 12070, reproduced and described by L. Alvin, Documents iconographiques et typographiques de la Bibl. Royale de Belgique, 1ʳᵉ sér., 1 livr., Brussels 1864.

[3] This is proved by the existence of another MS. of the *Pomerium* (without cuts) in Brussels (No. 2769) which also bears the date 1440 (see Auguste Vincent, Revue belge de Philologie et d'Histoire, ii. No. 2, 1923). M. Vincent's researches show that the cuts are independent of either version.

Fig. 91. Exercitium super Pater Noster. First edition. The eighth plate.

In style the first edition of the *Exercitium* is related to the work of the Master of Flémalle (Robert Campin of Tournai), and the earlier work of Rogier van der Weyden, who appears to have been Campin's pupil about 1426, working later at Brussels till his death in 1464.[1] It is less decided and angular, and more rounded in line than either the *Apocalypse* block-book (S. I-III) or the Brussels *Madonna* (dated 1418, though perhaps only a later and more conventionalised version, about 1450, of a lost original of 1418).[2] The costume is that of the Burgundian court in the second quarter of the xv century, and this evidence combined with the characteristics of the design and cutting would favour a date of about 1430, or hardly later than 1440.

The *Apocalypse* block-books are a far more important series than the *Exercitium*, and the first two series of blocks (S. I-III; see figs. 92 and 93) probably belong to about the same period.[3] In subject the series includes certain illustrations of the apocryphal life of St. John as introduction to scenes from the *Apocalypse*.

Kristeller has rightly estimated the general development of woodcutting seen in the editions I-III as corresponding to the second phase in Germany and Austria, i.e. after the supersession of the more flowing style by a more angular manner, and to the development shown in the illuminations of the Books of Hours attributed to Van Eyck (about 1412-17)[4] from the *Très Riches Heures du Duc de Berry*, completed by the Limbourgs in 1410 (Chantilly).

The *Apocalypse* cannot be related at all closely to the work of Van Eyck or other well-known Flemish painters, but its general position in the chain of development to later block-books more indisputably Netherlandish (i.e. the *Ars Moriendi, Biblia Pauperum, Canticum Canticorum,* and *Speculum Humanae Salvationis*) renders it far more likely to be Flemish than French,[5] in spite

[1] See E. Rosenthal, *Die kunstgeschichtliche Stellung der chiro-xylographische Exercitium,* Mitteil., 1916, p. 19; and F. Winkler, *Der Meister vom Flémalle und R. van der Weyden,* Strassburg 1913.

[2] See pp. 109-113.

[3] See P. Kristeller, *Die Apocalypse,* Berlin 1916 (which reproduces the impression of S. ii. in the Munich Library. Cf. Walter Cohn, *Ein Gemälde aus den Umkreis der niederländischen Blochbuch Apocalypse.* Mitteil. der Ges. für vervielfältig. Kunst, 1933, p. 24.

[4] Paul Durrieu, *Heures de Turin,* 1902; G. Hulin de Loo, *Heures de Milan,* 1911.

[5] Molsdorf's argument that the form of the *r* in edition S. iii. is specifically French (W. Molsdorf, *Schrifteigentümlichkeiten auf älteren Holzschnitten,* Strassburg 1914) is not supported by a comparison of examples of MSS. reproduced by the Paleographical Society. Kristeller described the Apocalypse block-books as French in the first edition of his *Kupferstich und Holzschnitt,* but in the 4th ed. of 1922 he incorporates the conclusions of his larger work of 1916, calling them Netherlandish.

Fig. 92. From the *Apocalypse*. S. 1

of the fact that most of the related manuscripts of the subject are Northern French or English in origin.

In the subject of its illustrations the *Apocalypse* block-books have immediate forebears in various illuminated manuscripts, nearest among them being several of the so-called 'first family',[1] i.e. Paris (B.N. 403), Bodleian,[2] Pierpont Morgan (from Blin de Bourdon Collection), and Manchester (John Rylands Library, from Crawford Collection), of Northern French or English origin. The Manchester manuscript, which belongs to the latter half of the xiv century, is particularly close in some of its pages to the block-books.[3] But though the general disposition of the designs is similar, the character of the figures and style of drawing are very different in the block-books.

Students of illumination are inclined to place the block-books on a much lower artistic plane than the best of the miniatures. This arises partly from a lack of comprehension of the particular qualities required in a designer for woodcut, for the stern and simple conventions of the art are not a sign of poverty of genius or crudity of execution, but of a just estimate of the medium. The very simplicity of these outline cuts gives them much of their noble and expressive character.

Whether the designer was also the cutter will no doubt remain an unsolved problem, a problem which touches most other cuts of the century.[4]

If the early block-books and cuts were the work of artists in convents not belonging to the regular guilds, as Jan van den Berghe wished to remain,[5] there is more likelihood of the cutter being his own designer (or adapting another's designs freely into his own conventions) than in the outside world where the laws of the guilds with regard to the division of labour held good.

Before further discussion of the *Apocalypse*, it will be advisable to tabulate the various editions, according to Schreiber (S.) and Sotheby, with reference to the locality of the principal impressions. Most of the earlier block-books are coloured by hand, and the exceptions are noted. All the editions are printed on one side of the paper only.

[1] See L. Delisle and P. Meyer, *L'Apocalypse en Français*, Paris 1891.
[2] Ed. H. O. Coxe, Roxburgh Club 1876.
[3] Comparison should also be made with the tapestries of the Cathedral of Angers, done in 1380 by Nicolas Bataille after designs by Jean Bandol of Bruges.
[4] See Index of Subjects, under *designer and cutter*.   [5] See pp. 83, 89, 211.

Fig. 93. From the *Apocalypse*. S. III.

THE APOCALYPSE: TABLE OF EDITIONS

S.	SOTHEBY	NOTES
{ I	I	48 leaves. Netherlandish. Even if the paper used should be proved to be French or German, this is no evidence of similar locality for the cutting, as no paper factories appear to have been established in the Netherlands until the XVI century. Manchester (water-mark: Gothic **p**).
{ II	II	The same blocks as I with page signatures added. Oxford (from Inglis and Douce; water-mark: ox's head). Munich (Univ. and Staatsbibl.). Earl of Pembroke.
III	III	50 leaves. Netherlandish. Abbreviations in text are lengthened (i.e. p and ū now read *per* and *um*). It is far more probable that this and later editions go back to S. I(II), either directly or indirectly (e.g. V through IV), than that they should derive independently from a lost MS. B.M. (uncoloured). Paris. Chantilly. Pierpont Morgan (33 leaves).
IV	IV	48 leaves. Probably German, about 1465. Kristeller compares with the *Salve Regina* issued by Lienhart Wolff at Regensburg (see p. 257). Manchester (bound with *Biblia Pauperum*, S. III, in binding signed by Johannes Richenbach de Gyslingen 1467). [Gyslingen is near Ath between Brussels and Tournai]. Oxford (Auct. M. iii. 15, with German MS. intercalated). B.M. (with German MS. intercalated). Berlin. Cologne. Heidelberg. Paris (uncoloured). Haarlem. New York Public Library (lacking ff. 14 and 18). Pierpont Morgan (12 leaves). Holford (formerly). Huth (formerly).

S.	Sotheby	Notes
V	VI	48 leaves. Probably German, about 1470. On the whole better cut and slightly less crude and angular than IV, but far inferior to I-III. Kristeller compares with the *Historia Davidis* (or *Liber Regum*) q.v., p. 248 Oxford (M. iii. 4). Vienna (with German MS. intercalated). Berlin. Munich (Univ. and Staatsbibl.). Paris. Manchester. Heidelberg (uncoloured), New York Public Library. Pierpont Morgan.
VI	V	48 leaves, probably German, about 1470. B.M. New York Public Library.

There is also a wood block of f. 2, from an unknown edition, preserved at Manchester (from the Ames Collection; modern impression in Sotheby, vol. ii. p. 50 a).

All the above editions are separate series of blocks except S. I and II, which are the same blocks in two states. Editions S. I (II) and S. III are far superior to the rest in quality. Each of these early sets of blocks has distinctive character, and Kristeller regards S. III as a close copy of S. I (II). That the text in S. III is the more correct is in favour of its being the revised copy, but I cannot agree with Kristeller's further qualification of the copy as 'mechanical and crude'. To me it appears more vigorous in expression and humour, in contrast with the gentler and perhaps subtler characteristics of the drawing in S. I (II). The fingers, sharper in S. I (II), are somewhat exaggerated in length and roundness in S. III. There is rather more naturalism in S. I (II), a tendency to more definite conventions in S. III (e.g. in the more systematised formula for the mouth). The pot-hooks of the folds in the two editions are sometimes formed with a single angle, and at others with round or square ends. The rounded ends in S. I (II) become squarer in S. III, those of S. I (II) being more like the *Mass of St. Gregory* at Nuremberg (S. 1462),[1] which with its Dutch text provides some evidence of Netherlandish origin, and the *Last Judgment* at Cologne (S. 607), while S. III is nearer to the Brussels *Madonna* (dated 1418) and the *Virgin and Child in a Glory*, at Berlin (S. 1108).[2]

In comparing the general characteristics of S. I (II) and S. III it must also

[1] See pp. 113, 143, and fig. 62.　　　　[2] Cf. pp. 111, 113, and fig. 47.

be noted that there is more variety in the quality of the various subjects in S. I (II) (so much indeed that Kristeller recognised three hands), while S. III is more uniform in quality.

On technical grounds I incline to date S. III about 1450, and S. I (II) somewhat earlier and nearer 1440 than 1425.

Artistically I would rank it first among the block-books and as holding a most honourable place in the great achievements of art.

Second only to the *Apocalypse* in aesthetic quality among the block-books comes *Ars Moriendi* in its first edition. With its regular panelled shading it already belongs to a later stage of development, and in its angular and forcible character the influence of Van Eyck is more definitely present. With the addition of shading, hand-colouring is no longer so common as in the *Apocalypse* series.

For convenience and the avoidance of vague reference I would again tabulate the editions but omit a special column for Sotheby as his descriptions of the *Ars Moriendi* are very incomplete. He describes the Pembroke and Haarlem impressions as his Ed. I, confusing the careful copy S. II A with the original.

THE ARS MORIENDI: TABLE OF EDITIONS

S.	NOTES
I A	Latin text. Netherlandish.
	B.M. (from Weigel, 1872) (reproduced, T. O. Weigel, Leipzig 1869, and L. Cust, *the Master E.S. and the Ars Moriendi*, Oxford 1898).
	Earl of Pembroke (incomplete). Sotheby refers to the Pembroke copy but confuses it with S. II A (Haarlem).
I B	French text. The same picture blocks.
	Comte de Wazières.
II A	Careful copy of S. I, similar in character of cutting, but not nearly so good or subtle. Probably Netherlandish. Haarlem (incomplete).
II B-D	Varieties of the same edition in which several of the blocks are replaced by cruder copies. Berlin. Frankfurt. Heidelberg. In D the woodcut text has been replaced by movable type. (With text in single column, S. 3370, British Museum. With text in double column, S. 3371, Dresden, Paris, etc.).
III	Vigorous, but cruder in cutting than II, from which it is probably copied. Netherlandish or German. Berlin.

S.	NOTES
IV A-D	Probably copied from I A. Even broader in line than III. and somewhat more angular. Near in quality to VII. Vigorous. Probably German.
IV A	Three border-lines round most of the subjects. Early impressions printed on one side only. Later impressions printed on both sides in the ordinary press. Heidelberg. Munich (Univ. and Staatsbibl.). New York Public Library. Paris. B.M. (printed on both sides).
IV B-D	The outer border-line cut away. Printed on both sides in the press.
IV B	Breslau. Bamberg. Pierpont Morgan.
IV c	With two additional subjects: The *Creation and the Fall* and *Christ interceding with the Father*. Dresden. Munich (Staatsbibl. and Graph. Samml.). Manchester. New York Public Library.
IV D	With two further cuts: *St. Michael with the Scales* and the '*Cours du Monde*'. Munich. Paris. Wolfenbüttel.
V	Copy of IV, and hardly so good. Probably German. Hanover.
VI	Very bad condition, and difficult to estimate. Vienna.
VII A	Copy of IV. Signed *Ludwig ze Ulm* on pl. 23. Inscription on banderoles in German, and with German text. Fair. Very angular. German, about 1470–75 (see pp. 212 and 321). Munich. Paris.
VII B	Same picture blocks as VII A. Pages of text in Latin. Wolfenbüttel.
VIII	Crude copy of VII A. Outline only. Signed *Hans Sporer* 1473 on last block. German. Zwickau.
XIII	Very angular. Banderoles as in I A, but details (e.g. erroneous perspective) follow the Master E.S. Costume considerably altered. Low German. Probably about 1470. Paris.
IX	Smaller edition in quarto. Frame about 136 × 98 mm. Latin text. Printed on both sides. The cutter probably knew both block-book and the engravings of the Master E.S. B.M. Manchester. Paris.
X, XI, XII	Editions in octavo. German text. Printed on both sides.
X	Without banderoles. The cutter probably knew both block-books and the engravings of the Master E.S. Formerly in the Schreiber Collection.
XI	Exact copy of X. Basle.
XII	Copy of X, with omission of the hatchings. Border-line 97 × 77 mm. B.M. Donaueschingen.

The signed later editions VII A and VIII give the only definite clues to date, but they are evidently several decades later than the original edition.

There is now general agreement that the edition described by Schreiber as I (in its two issues, with Latin and French text respectively) is the original, for it easily leads in quality, and apart from the short notes tabulated above we shall limit our discussion (unless otherwise noted) to this edition. This is the more justified as practically all the other woodcut editions derive directly or indirectly from this version.

The subject of the book was very popular at this period,[1] and probably intended as a guide to the clergy and others in giving comfort or counsel to the dying, but the actual author of the text of the block-book (all the editions except S. X-XII being practically the same) is unknown. It represents a series of ten scenes, in pairs showing alternately the Temptation of the Devil, and the Comfort of an Angel, on Faith, Despair, Impatience, Vainglory, and Avarice, and a final eleventh scene of the Triumph over all temptations in the Hour of Death.[2]

We must now approach the difficult problems of the locality and date of the block-book, and its relation to the line-engravings of the Master E.S.

I have already stated my opinion that the *Grotesque Alphabet* of 1464

[1] Jean Charles de Gerson (1363–1429) and Johannes Geiler von Kaiserberg (1445–1510) being the most famous writers who handled the theme. The popularity of the subject is shown by the number of editions printed from movable type during the xv century in which the cuts are copied from the block-book. Apart from S.IID (in which some of the blocks are from a block-book), the following may be mentioned:

LEIPZIG, printed by Kacheloven, from 1493 onwards (*Ein Büchlein von dem Sterben*, S.3376-3378), containing 13 cuts, Nos. 2-12 being copies from the block-book series, No. 1 being a new subject of *Extreme Unction* and No. 13, *St. Michael weighing Souls*.

LEIPZIG, Kacheloven, Latin editions, between about 1497 and 1500 (S.3372-3375), with 14 cuts, 13 as in the German edition, and an additional cut of a Confession from the *Beichte*, printed by Kacheloven about 1494 (S.3423).

LYON, two series about 1485-90 (see p. 615).

PARIS (*L'Art de bien mourir*) 1492 (see p. 660).

DELFT and ZWOLLE, two series, about 1488–91 (see pp. 573 and 582).

VENICE, end of xv century (see Essling, *Livre à figures vénitiens*, i. (1), 1907, No. 271). In the early years of the xvi century:

VENICE, J. B. Sessa, about 1503 (Essling, No. 272).

PARIS, Vérard, 1503, *Art of good lyvyng and good deyng* (see p. 662).

LONDON, Wynkyn de Worde, 1505, *Arte or Crafte to lyve well and to dye well* (see p. 663).

[2] Cust's reproductions are numbered I a and b, II a and b, to V a and b, with a final VI instead of simply numbering the plates I-XI.

might be by the same cutter as the first edition of the *Ars Moriendi*, from similarity in the character of the line and system of shading and in type of border used. In any case the date of 1464 that attaches to work so near in style, even if not by the same hand, will hardly allow any considerably earlier date for the *Ars Moriendi*. I would incline to place it about 1450, and not much later, because of the still strong influence of the school of Van Eyck. This influence seems to locate it in the Southern Netherlands, and its appearance in a French as well as a Latin edition would perhaps favour this presumption rather than the possibility of Dutch origin. It is perhaps not without significance that Jan van den Berghe was making block-books at Louvain in 1452, though the link with any definite book is still wanting.

The relation of the block-books to the series of small engravings by the Master E.S. has caused much controversy. Max Lehrs, the most learned authority on German and Netherlandish line-engraving, was the first to recognise the importance of the series, which is only known complete at Oxford, as authentic early work by the Master E.S. He also contended that the designs, which closely correspond with the block-book cuts, are the originals on which the cuts were based, not copies from the block-book.[1]

On the aesthetic side the woodcuts appear to be decidedly the greater works of art, and I would be inclined, instinctively, on that account to regard them as the originals. There is of course the further alternative that both block-book and E.S. derive from some lost series of original designs. But against this, as well as the strongest argument against the block-book being the original, is the fact that the types of face and figure in both engravings and block-book are essentially those which E.S. used throughout his life. So that if we are to presuppose an original designer he would, as Lehrs contests, be practically identical with the engraver E.S. himself. How far E.S. was an original designer, and how far he depended on others, can never perhaps be decided with certainty. But the consistent character of his style certainly points to the probability that he, like his natural successors in line-engraving,

---

[1] Lehrs, Repertorium, xi., 1888, p. 51, under No. 5; *Der Künstler der Ars Moriendi und die wahre erste Ausgabe derselben*, Pr. Jahrbuch, xi., 1890, 161. See also Lionel Cust, *The Master E.S. and the 'Ars Moriendi'*, Oxford 1898 (with complete reproduction of the block-book, and the series by E.S.); A. Schmarsow, Berichte der philologisch-historisch. Classe der kgl. Sächsischen Gesellschaft der Wissenschaften zu Leipzig, 4th February 1899; L. Kaemmerer, Zeitschrift für Bücherfreunde, iii., 1899, 225; M. Lehrs, Repert., xxii., 1899, 458; H. Thode, Repert., xxii. 364; A. Schmarsow, Repert., xxiii., 1900, 123; Sitzungsberichte der kunstgeschichtlichen Gesellschaft, Berlin, 25th January 1901; M. Geisberg, *Der Meister E.S.*, Leipzig 1924, and Berlin 1924.

Fig. 94. *Ars Moriendi*. S. I A. The Fifth plate: Impatience.

Schongauer and Dürer, was largely independent. And on the whole it seems to me less likely that the wood-cutters of the period should have been as independent, for they either belonged to a lower craft (ranking with carpenters in the guilds), or to a less professional order if they happened to be brothers in a convent.

Fig. 95. *Ars Moriendi.* Impatience. Line-engraving by the Master E.S.

The secondary matters of comparison which favour the conclusion that the woodcutter copied E.S. are—

(1) Several pieces of poor perspective in the line-engravings are correctly drawn in the woodcuts, especially in the drawing of the head of the bed.

(2) Plate 1. A functionless row of buttons on a man's coat is made to function in buttonholes in the woodcuts.

(3) Plate 4. An impossibly placed cock in E.S. is given a comfortable position in the cuts.

Other matters of comparison, such as the windows in plate 10, the reversal of the subject in plate 11, and the absence of banderoles in the engravings, might be cited by pleaders on either side, but it seems more

Fig. 96. From the *Ars Moriendi.* S. I A.

improbable that E.S. should have introduced errors such as those cited above in copying the block-book, than that the woodcutter copyist should have corrected palpable errors. Lehrs is also right in emphasising the fact that line-engravings were probably more precious things than woodcuts at this period, collected by the well-to-do to paste in their MS. prayer-books, while the woodcuts would more often find their public among the poorer clergy and laity. The size of works means nothing in respect of their artistic credit (I will not say merit), and on this score it should be noted that many of the engravings of E.S. and Schongauer were well known and copied by engravers in Italy within a few years of their production.

The probable date of either series does not help in solving the problem, for the early works of E.S. may be considerably anterior to 1450,[1] and the block-book is as likely to be slightly after, as before, 1450.

In spite of my estimate of the artistic superiority of the block-book to the line-engravings, constant recurrence to the problem over a number of years fails to remove what I still regard as the convincing arguments of Lehrs.

We must now consider the *Biblia Pauperum*, which from the number of its editions, both Netherlandish and German, must have had a popularity equal to that of the *Ars Moriendi*, if not even more extended. The general scheme of this devotional treatise, the comparison of Old and New Testament subjects, was repeated in numerous MSS. during the xiv and xv centuries, but the title by which it is now known, though attached in the xv century to kindred works, e.g. Bonaventura's *Biblia Pauperum*, does not appear to have been in general use until adopted by Heinecken in the xviii century.[2] More than one of the MSS. bears the title of *Speculum Humanae Salvationis* in later hand, but this title would confuse it with another series of block-books.

It was a sort of compendium and harmony of scripture intended probably for the poor (or lesser) clergy rather than for the poor layman (or the unlearned). Each subject of the Life and Passion of Christ is provided with two parallels from Old Testament History, and a witness from the Prophets.

---

[1] Both Lehrs and Geisberg now date the early work of the Master E.S. about 1440, or even earlier.

[2] See C. H. von Heinecken, *Idée générale d'une collection d'estampes*, 1771, p. 292. Heinecken describes the block-book under the title *Historia veteris et novi Testamenti* (and refers to analogous titles used by other iconographers, i.e. *Figurae typicae veteris atque antitypicae novi testamenti, seu Historiae Jesu Christi in figuris*, and *Vaticinia veteris testamenti de Christo*), but states that the title current in Germany, and the one that he preferred, was *Biblia Pauperum*. French xvi-century printed editions are entitled *Regard des deux testaments*.

Fig. 97. *Biblia Pauperum*. The Incredulity of St. Thomas, from the chiro-xylographic edition.

Fig. 98. *Biblia Pauperum*. S. I. The Incredulity of St. Thomas.

Fig. 99. *Biblia Pauperum*. S. III. The Incredulity of Thomas.

Most of the MSS. known, of which a large number is preserved in the Munich Library, are probably Upper German or Austrian in origin.[1]

I will again tabulate the various editions, keeping to Schreiber's order for convenience of reference, adding short notes on the quality of the cuts, possible date and locality, and indication of a few important impressions. Discussion of the subject is constantly marred by vague references to the *Biblia Pauperum* without the essential qualification of edition, and even if no progress can be made, it is at least some gain to classify the channels along which research should proceed.

The interrelations of edd. I-VII are complex, certain blocks continuing through several editions, other subjects being recut at various intervals.

As aids in finding to what edition (among I-X) any copy or stray leaves may belong, Schreiber gives a series of sketches of the varieties in the drawing and shading of the architectural details (columns and mouldings) of each subject in the various editions. Varieties in the banderoles and grass, etc., are further indications.

The German chiro-xylographic edition (S. p. 90) has only thirty-four leaves (the same number of subjects as in many of the MSS.); most of the editions are of forty leaves, while one edition (S. p. 100) has fifty leaves, the ten extra subjects being partly borrowed from the *Speculum Humanae Salvationis*.

Most of the editions are printed on one side of the leaf only, so placed that an opening of two figured pages is followed by a blank opening. In some editions a single block may have covered the two adjoining pages. A split across two pages (as in the British Museum Grenville copy of S. IX sigg. ·c· and ·d·) is among the proofs that can be cited in support of this. The inner margins are often so narrow that the inner border-lines are almost in the binding. The separate impression from two pages in the British Museum Print Room, i.e. sigg. *a* and *b* of S. III (C. D., C. 2; fig. 100), shows this relation very clearly.

---

[1] For studies of the MSS. see Hans von der Gabelentz, *Die Biblia Pauperum und Apokalypse der grossherzogl. Bibl. zu Weimar*, Strassburg 1912; and Henrik Cornell, *Biblia Pauperum*, Stockholm 1925. See also Campbell Dodgson, *The Weigel-Felix Biblia Pauperum* (MS.), London [1906] (description of a MS. now in America, with general introduction); cf. A. Schmarsow, *Konrad Witz und die Biblia Pauperum*, Repert. xxviii., 1905, 340; and *Conradi Sapientis de Basilea Biblia Pauperum cod. pergam. Weigel-Felix*, Zeitschrift für christliche Kunst, Dusseldorf 1907 (attributing the drawings to Conrad Witz); C. Dodgson, *Die B. P. und nicht Konrad Witz*, Repert. xxx., 1907, 169. Most of the MSS. are outlines in pen and ink, only a few like B. M. King's 5 being fully illuminated. For a list of the MSS. and a general study of the *Biblia Pauperum* see the introduction to Heitz and Schreiber's edition and reproduction of the Paris *Biblia Pauperum* in 50 leaves (Strassburg 1903).

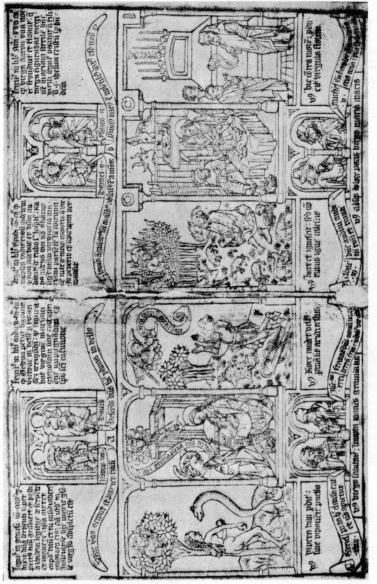

Fig. 100. *Biblia Pauperum*. S. III. The first opening, with the Annunciation and the Nativity.

The second series of page signatures in edd. I-X are made by the same letters with dots on both sides, i.e. ·a·.

Another method of making up the book, i.e. by means of a single gathering, is seen in the German editions of 1470 and 1471, in which the subjects in the first half of the book come on the left-hand page, and in the second half on the right.

The Biblia Pauperum: Table of Editions

S.	Sotheby	Notes
1st Group I-III		
I	V	Netherlandish, probably Dutch. B.M., Print Room (C. D., C. 1, uncoloured) (reproduced, J. P. Berjeau, London 1859, unreliable lithographs based on tracings). Brussels. Chantilly. St. Gallen. Zurich. Dresden. Edmond de Rothschild (Paris). Forty-four pieces cut from the blocks were used in *Epistelen en Evangelien*, Zwolle (Pieter van Os), 1487, and some of these in various other books printed by Pieter van Os at Zwolle, between 1487 and 1500.
II	··	A composite copy made up of 32 impressions from I, and 8 impressions from III (i.e. sigg. *e f g h p q ·e· ·f·*). Berlin. Direct comparison with the B.M. impression of I, and the Berlin and Cambridge impressions of III, proves that it is later than any of these.
III	IV	Probably Netherlandish. A different series of blocks, stronger in character of line than I, though less naturalistic in drawing. In its sterner convention and dignity of style it is nearer to the tradition of the *Apocalypse*, S. I-III, and the *Ars Moriendi*, S. I, than to the *Biblia Pauperum*, S. I. On purely stylistic grounds S. III would seem earlier than S. I, but details, such as the omission of the trees in sig. *o* in III, favour the priority of S. I.

S.	Sotheby	Notes
2nd Group IV-VII		Manchester (Spencer B; complete, uncoloured; in binding by Johannes Richenbach de Gyslingen 1467, including the *Apocalypse*, S. IV; Ghislenghen is near Ath, on the road from Brussels to Tournai). Corpus Christi College, Cambridge. Paris. B.M., Print Room, sigg. *a b c* only (C. D., C. 2). Oxford (Douce 248; 20 leaves only).
IV	I	Netherlandish or German. Strong outline and clear cutting as in S. III and similar in general character of style, but on the whole poorer in details of drawing. In some respects the details are more fully developed, and follow S. I rather than S. III, but the cutter of S. IV probably had both editions before him. Manchester (R. 4588, from Borghese Library, Rome; complete, uncoloured). Paris. Modena. B.M., Print Room, sigg. *·n· ·o· ·p·* only (C. D., C. 4).
V	II	Netherlandish or German. The same blocks as IV, except two which are new, i.e. sigg. *c* and *d*, B.M. (King's Library; uncoloured, good impression).
VI	II	Twenty-four blocks from S. IV. Sixteen new blocks, i.e. *a b c d i k l m p q ·c· ·d· ·l· ·m· ·t· ·v·* The latter very inferior in quality of cutting to S. I-V; the outline not much stronger than the shading. Netherlandish or German. B.M. (Sotheby's 'Lucca' copy, with the last three leaves from S. I). Manchester (Spencer A, 17238 cc, uncoloured). Darmstadt. The Hague. Munich. Hanover. Gottweig. Vienna (ed. and reprod., A. Einsle and J. Schönbrunner, Vienna, 1890).
VII		Same blocks as VI with page signatures erased. Vienna. W. L. Schreiber sale (1909).

S.	Sotheby	Notes
3rd Group VIII; IX ⎧VIII		Powerful but crude cutting, angular, regular shading. Probably German, about 1470. Paris. Chatsworth. Cologne. Gotha. Weimar. B.M. Print Room (C. D., C. 3, fragments of *d k* and *l*). Rome. Wolfenbüttel.
⎩IX	III	Thirty-six blocks from S. VIII. Four new blocks (i.e. sigg. *r s t v*). B.M. (Grenville). Basle.
X		Crude and angular cutting, little shading. Black shoes as in Spörer's edition. (Note that relation of S. X to S. VIII in shading is like that of Spörer's ed. to Walther's.) Probably German about 1470. Oxford (Auct. M. iii. 13). Paris. Berlin, Leipzig. Vienna. Darmstadt. Munich. Wolfenbüttel.
p. 90		Chiro-xylographic. A few names only cut on the blocks. Each page printed from four blocks for the main scheme, and three separate blocks for the three subjects from the Old and New Testament. German MS. text. German, probably about 1450. Heidelberg (unique; ed. and repr. P. Kristeller, Graph. Gesellschaft 1906). Thirty-four subjects only (like many of the MSS.). See W. Molsdorf, in *Beiträge zur Geschichte und Technik des ältesten Bildruckes*, Strassburg 1921, p. 27.
p. 93, I	Vol. ii. p. 58	With German text. Page signatures in middle of page below. Regular shading. Inscribed at end *Friderich Walthern Mauler zu Nördlingen und Hans Hurning habent dis buch mitt einander gemacht*, 1470. Freely adapted from one of the earlier Latin

S.	Sotheby	Notes
		editions (S. I-X), with some suggestions from the Heidelberg edition. B.M., Munich, etc.
p. 95, II	Vol. ii. p. 60	With German text. Signed by *Hans Spoerer* 1471; probably done at Nuremberg. Page signatures in lower middle of the folios below (and thus hidden in the binding). In general, a close copy of the preceding edition, but stronger in outline; little shading, and in some elements of style nearer to the Heidelberg chiro-xylographic edition. B.M. (uncoloured and unbound). Wolfenbüttel (Ed. and reprod. R. Ehwald, Weimar, 1906).
p. 100	ii. p. 55	Fifty leaves. Corresponds to S. I-X in both subjects and style, with ten additional subjects partly borrowed from the *Speculum Humanae Salvationis.* Netherlands, or Lower Rhine. Black shoes, as in Spörer's edition of 1471 and S. X, and probably about the same date. Paris (from Wolfenbüttel, unique, uncoloured). Watermark: Gothic ꝑ as in books printed at Cologne 1470–80, and in the 2nd Latin ed. of the *Speculum Humanae Salvationis.* Ed. and reprod., Paul Heitz and Schreiber, Strassburg, 1903.
p. 105		*Opera nova contemplativa.* G. A. Vavassore, Venice (not before 1510), 8vo. *Opera di Giovanni Andrea Vavassore ditto Vadagnino stampata novamente nella inclita citta di Vinegia.* Essling, *Livres à figures vénitiens,* part i (1907), No. 206, and Part iii (1914), p. 112. B.M., Oxford. Paris. Florence. Venice, etc. Printed on both sides of the paper in the

S.	SOTHEBY	NOTES
		ordinary press. Each of the 120 subjects is now given a separate page (instead of three on the page). Text in Italian printed from a separate block below, which also contains King and Prophet beneath arches. The work is only distantly related to the Netherlandish block-books in general scheme, and in the rendering of certain subjects. The cutter borrowed from Dürer's *Little Woodcut Passion* as source for various subjects, so that the work could not have been printed before 1510.[1] There is signed work by Giovanni (or Zoan) Andrea Vavassore, detto Guadagnino, printer, publisher, bookseller, cartographer and woodcutter, between 1522 and 1572. Prince d'Essling attributes the cutting to Florio Vavassore, brother of Giovanni Andrea.

Though the majority of the editions are probably Netherlandish, the earliest edition known, and one that stands apart from the rest in its style and scheme of design, is almost certainly the chiro-xylographic edition (with German MS. text) preserved at Heidelberg.[2] In number of plates (thirty-four) it followed many of the MSS., and the same number occurs in the earliest type-printed *Biblia Pauperum* (that of Pfister at Bamberg).[3]

The chief difference in its scheme on the page from S. I-X is that the half-figures of Kings and Prophets are given at the four corners instead of in pairs under arches in the centre above and below. Moreover, the three subjects from the Old and New Testaments are cut on separate blocks,

[1] I find no evidence for the date 1516 given by Lippmann (*Wood-engraving in Italy*, 1888, p. 109).

[2] P. Kristeller, *Biblia Pauperum. Unikum der Heidelberger Universitäts-Bibliothek*, Graphische Gesellschaft, ii., 1906, Berlin.

[3] Later type-printed editions: Augsburg (A. Sorg, 1476), with the usual 40 and 6 additional subjects; Lyon (M. Reinhard, 1489; *Book of Hours*), with 50 marginal illustrations based on the 50-leaf editions; Paris (Vérard, 1503, *Regard des deux testaments*, with 40 illustrations as in S. Ed. I-X); Antwerp (J. van Doesborch, 1517, *Der vorspronck onser salicheyt*), with adaptations from the *Biblia Pauperum*.

and printed separately on to the leaf on which the main scheme had already been printed. Considerable economy was effected by this method, as only four variant blocks were used for the border setting.

In its simple outline style, and round and branching folds the cuts correspond with German work of about 1450, and the preceding decade. It is not far removed from the first and third editions of the *Symbolum Apostolicum* block-book (see p. 249), and a group of woodcuts to which reference has been made in the preceding chapter.[1]

Most of the other editions are Netherlandish in character of design, whatever the nationality of the original source from which they derived. S. I-X (all with Latin text) form one large group in their general scheme of design, and number of plates, and I would without hesitation regard S. I (II), III and IV (V) as far better than the others. S. I (II) is perhaps the most sensitive in quality, but it is hardly as strong in its line and cutting as S. III, which in these respects stands nearer to the *Apocalypse*, S. III. They are so near in detail that one is almost certainly based on the other, but I cannot be dogmatic as to which is the original. In the tabulated notes above I have shown some reason to regard S. I as the earlier, in spite of the fact that in general dignity and convention of style S. III seems to belong to an earlier tradition. Perhaps S. III, from its affinity to Apocalypse III, might be regarded as of the Southern Netherlands, and S. I as Dutch, which is the more likely from the appearance of portions of the blocks of the latter in the *Epistelen en Evangelien*, Zwolle (Pieter van Os) 1487, and in later books of the same printer. The further suggestion that this probably Dutch edition of the *Biblia Pauperum* is Haarlem work of Laurens Janszoon Coster is a reasonable conjecture, but entirely lacking in documentary evidence. Nor is one justified in inferring a Zwolle origin for the *Biblia Pauperum* (S. I) from its use in a later state by a Zwolle printer, for the printers of the period frequently borrowed blocks, and sometimes outside their own country. Pieter van Os himself is known to have borrowed blocks from Bellaert of Haarlem, from Leeuw of Gouda, and from Snellaert of Delft.

S. IV (V) is, like S. III, clear and strong in line and cutting, but poorer in details of drawing. The other editions, S. VI (VII), VIII (IX) and X are much poorer in quality, some certainly being German copies.

The Latin edition in fifty leaves (Paris) is spirited in expression, better in quality than S. VI-X, but looser and less precise in draughtsmanship than the Latin forty-leaf editions, S. I (II), III or IV (V). It is no doubt copied from one of the former group in forty subjects (which it occasionally reverses

[1] See p. 132.

in part), adding other subjects made up from such sources as the *Speculum Humanae Salvationis* which renders a date anterior to 1470 improbable. The chief differences from the forty-leaf editions are added banderoles with inscriptions in most of the subjects (which had occurred in the former editions only in the *Annunciation*, in *Gideon* and in the picture of the *Bride seeking the Bridegroom*), frequent additions of architectural backgrounds (exterior or interior) and a tendency to orientalise in the costume.

From the relation of the cuts in S. I to Dutch book-illustrations, especially to those in books printed by Bellaert at Haarlem, 1484–85, I should be inclined to date the first Netherlandish edition of the *Biblia Pauperum* about 1460, or slightly later, certainly not before 1460.

The two German editions of 1470 and 1471 appear to be based on a knowledge of both the Heidelberg edition and the Latin editions (S. I-X). In the arrangement of the greater part of the text in two columns at the foot of the page they follow the scheme shown in the MS. of the Heidelberg edition, and the letters themselves are nearly allied to the same style of script. On the other hand, they follow the Latin editions more nearly in the treatment of the subjects represented, and also in uniting kings and prophets in couples in the centre of the page.

The *Life of Saint Servatius*, which is only known in the impression of the Royal Library at Brussels,[1] is loosely related in style to certain of the Netherlandish editions of the *Biblia Pauperum* and to the early Haarlem book-illustrations. In its somewhat sketchy manner, with little or no shading, it is in some ways a later continuation of the style of the first edition of the *Exercitium super Pater Noster*. As observed by Kristeller, it looks as if the cutter were skilfully reproducing rapid pen studies. Compared with the *Biblia Pauperum* it is nearest in character to S. VI (VII) and the fifty-leaf edition, but is still looser in quality of draughtsmanship.

It is small quarto in size, six sheets in a single gathering, lightly printed on both sides of the paper, each opening (i.e. two pages) being printed from a single block, tinted in bright colours (vermilion, yellow and green) and accompanied by MS. text. The subject connects it with the Church of St. Servatius at Maestricht, and it was probably done to sell to pilgrims at one of the occasional exhibitions of the relics of the Saint. Ruelens found

---

[1] C. Ruelens, *La Légende de Saint-Servais*, Documents iconographiques et typographiques de la Bibl. Roy. de Belgique, 1ᵉ sér. 6 livr., Brussels 1877; H. Hymans, *Die Servatius-Legende,* Graphische Gesellschaft, xv., Berlin 1911.

a note of the order of their exhibition in 1458, which corresponds to the last four cuts, and there were later exhibitions in 1461 and 1468. These later dates would fit well with the style of the woodcuts.

The *Canticum Canticorum* (Song of Songs), another block-book of Netherlandish origin, is known in two editions, each printed from sixteen blocks arranged in pairs at alternate openings, on one side of the paper only. There are thirty-two subjects, each page being divided horizontally into two oblong compositions. Of the first edition there are two issues, the earlier being before the title, which was added in the later issue at the top of the first subject, viz. *Dit is die voersienicheit vā mariē der mod' godes en is gehetē in laty cantice.*

There are impressions of the first issue at Manchester, Paris, Rome and Munich, the last named being coloured (a practice which becomes less frequent in these later block-books). Of the second issue there is a good impression in the British Museum.[1]

The upper part of the first block of the first edition was used on the front page of the *Rosetum Exercitiorum Spiritualium* printed at Zwolle, 1494, by Pieter van Os, the same printer who was using parts of the *Biblia Pauperum* blocks.

The blocks of the second edition are so decidedly inferior in quality to the first, that there has never been any doubt as to the order of issue. One material difference is the double border-line to the banderoles on the first two pages instead of the single line in the first edition.

Most impressions of the first edition are printed by hand-rubbing in brownish ink; many of the second edition are in blacker ink. Impressions of the second edition may be cited in the British Museum, and at Oxford, Berlin, Munich and Paris.

In style of design and cutting the first edition of the *Canticum Canticorum* is nearly related to the *Biblia Pauperum* S. I-V. Rocks, trees and grass are of the same character, but there are several varieties of plants which do not occur in the *Biblia Pauperum*. If there is any marked difference in general design it is in an added elegance, a certain sinuous grace in the tall figures. Whether this is due to another draughtsman, or merely to the inspiration.of the subject matter, is difficult to say. In cutting it is even more precise than the *Biblia Pauperum* S. I (II), and in its strong and clear outline comparable rather to S. III and IV (V). The shading is in general more closely laid than in the *Biblia Pauperum*. But the cutter may well

---

[1] Reproduced J. P. Berjeau, London 1860 (unreliable; lithographs after tracings); Marées Gesellschaft, 1922 (very fine facsimile in colours of the Munich Library copy).

Fig. 101. *Canticum Canticorum*. S. I. The Seventh Plate.

have been identical with one of the cutters of *Biblia Pauperum* S. I-V, and the date of work equally about 1460–70, though probably nearer to 1470.

The second edition of the *Canticum* shows a thinner outline (not much stronger than the shading), the noses sharply drawn, the design in general less precise. In the first and last of these differences it has some relation to the *Biblia Pauperum* S. VI (VII), and to the fifty-leaf edition, but it is less expressive than the latter.

It should be noted that in the Bodleian impression the second edition of the *Canticum Canticorum* is coloured in similar tints to the *Biblia Pauperum* S. X, and they were certainly both illuminated in one workshop. But this does not imply that the blocks were of similar origin, for I incline to regard the *Biblia Pauperum* S. X as German, and the second edition of the *Canticum* as Netherlandish.

The *Speculum Humanae Salvationis (Speghel onser Behoudenisse)* approaches ordinary book-illustration more nearly than the other block-books, for it is largely printed with typographic text, only certain pages of one edition being from blocks which include both pictures and text. But it still carries on the tradition of the block-book throughout in being printed only on one side of the paper. Like the *Biblia Pauperum* the work was a Harmony of Old and New Testaments, and intended (as is explicitly stated in the preface) as an aid to the poor clergy *(pauperes praedicatores)* in their teaching.[1] Twenty-six scenes from the New Testament (from the *Annunciation* to the *Resurrection*) each with three parallels from the Old Testament (fifty-two blocks), preceded by four blocks with eight scenes from the Old Testament (the *Fall of Lucifer* and the *Creation* to *Noah*), and concluded by two blocks of the *Last Judgment* and its parallels,[2] i.e. fifty-eight blocks in all, form the total illustrations.

[1] See J. M. Guichard, *Notice sur le Speculum Humanae Salvationis*, Paris 1840. For a lithographic reproduction of the British Museum Grenville impression, made from tracings, see J. P. Berjeau, London 1861; another facsimile, ed. Ernst Kloss, published by Piper & Co., Munich; for a study of the MSS. see J. Lutz and P. Perdrizet, *S.H.S. texte critique, Traduction inédite de Jean Mielot* (1448). *Les Sources et l'influence iconographique sur l'art alsatien du XIVᵉ siècle. Avec la reproduction en 140 planches du manuscrit de Sélestat, de la série complète des vitraux de Mulhouse, de vitraux de Colmar, etc.*, Mulhouse 1907, 1909. The block-book version is a considerably shorter form of the text than the numerous type-printed versions of the xv century.

[2] It is worth noting that Sotheby (vol. i. p. 178) thought that the printer might have intended to represent himself in the last subject of *Daniel interpreting the writing on the wall*. He cites Dibdin (*Bibliographical Decameron*, pp. 285-96) for a reference to Jacobus de Breda, printer at Deventer, using a copy of the Daniel figure in one case to represent himself, and in another to represent his author (see Conway, *Woodcutters of the Netherlands*, p. 159).

Each block contains two scenes under adjoining arches, and is printed at the top of each page of double-columned text; the blocks are printed by hand with the rubber, and consequently only on one side of the leaf; two leaves are printed together with subjects arranged in such a way that the book might be made up in three gatherings of fourteen leaves, and one of sixteen leaves. An introductory text on four or six leaves (the latter including a blank leaf), according to the edition, precedes the illustrated section.

Fig. 102. *Speculum Humanae Salvationis*. The Nativity and the Dream of Pharaoh's Butler.

The text beneath the illustrations is printed separately from movable type in the ordinary press, except for twenty pages of one issue which were printed from blocks.

It had once been conjectured that the mixture of block- and type-printing for the text showed the printer (to wit, Coster) inventing movable type in the course of his work, but this theory has long since been abandoned, for the type cannot be before about 1471 (as Bradshaw proved),[1] and the blocks in the edition with xylographic text are more worn than in two of those printed entirely from movable type. The reason for the partial replacement of movable type by block lettering must go back to some accidental occurrence which we can no longer hope to explain.

There are two Latin editions (with six-leaf introduction) and two Dutch

[1] *Lists of the Founts and Type and Woodcut Devices used by the Printers of Holland in the xv Century*, Henry Bradshaw, *Collected Papers*, 1899, p. 258. He locates the printer of the *Speculum*, like Veldener, who used the blocks later, at Utrecht. But there is no certainty in the location.

editions (with four-leaf introduction), and judging from the condition of the blocks (which are the same throughout) the order of issue was—

I. *The First Latin Edition.* E.g. Munich, New York Public Library, Vienna (H.B.), Florence.

II. *The First Dutch Edition.* E.g. Manchester (John Rylands Library from Spencer), The Hague, Earl of Crawford (Haigh Hall).

III. *The Second Latin Edition.* E.g. B.M. (Grenville), Berlin, Oxford, Paris, The Hague, Manchester (John Rylands Library from Spencer). This is the only edition with xylographic text, and of this only twenty pages. The text and subject above look as if printed from a single block, but as the condition of the upper part is later in III than II, the blocks for the text portion must have been added, and placed carefully alongside the subject blocks.

IV. *The Second Dutch Edition.* E.g. Haarlem, Lille, Earl of Pembroke.

The quality of the blocks varies considerably, those at the end of the work tending to be poorer in cutting than the earlier subjects. The best of the blocks are probably by the same hand as the first edition of the *Canticum Canticorum*; there is the same strong, clear outline, the same precise cutting, the same regularly broken lines of parallel shading and a close correspondence throughout in details of design, in rocks, trees and plants. For the relations to the *Biblia Pauperum* S. I–V reference may be made to the description of the *Canticum Canticorum*.

The later blocks, apparently cut by some weaker craftsman, are more nearly related to the looser work seen in the *Biblia Pauperum* S. VI (VII).

The blocks were later cut each into their two portions and used as book-illustrations by Jan Veldener at Utrecht and Culenborg between 1481 and 1484 (i.e. all the blocks and twelve added subjects in the same style in *Speghel onser Behoudenisse*, Culenborg 1483; and some in *Epistelen en Evangelien*, Utrecht 1481, and the *Kruidboeck*, Culenborg 1484).

This fact in conjunction with the relation in style to the *Biblia Pauperum*, and to the illustrations in books printed by Bellaert at Haarlem 1484–85, inclines one to place the *Speculum* in Holland, about 1470–75.

Apart from the important Netherlandish block-books which we have described, there is a small octavo with Dutch text, the *Septem Vitia Mortalia* (only known at Haarlem), and three others which demand a passing mention in this place as Netherlandish in origin, though the copies that exist are probably German, i.e. the *Historia Davidis* (or the *Liber Regum*), the *Oracula Sibyllina* and the *Historia Sanctae Crucis* (*Boec van den Houte*, History of the Holy Cross).[1] But further notes on other German block-books[2] will show that these are not the only German works which appear to be based on Dutch or Flemish originals.

The *Historia Davidis*[3] is only known in one edition, with Latin text, in twenty leaves, each with two upright subjects and two columns of text beneath, printed on one side of the paper (Chantilly, Innsbruck, Vienna). The outline is hard and regular, and apart from its shading in regular parallels (which places it somewhat later) it has something of the character of the *Apocalypse*, S. V. It is probably German work of about 1470.

The *Oracula Sibyllina* (Prophecies of Christ in the mouth of the Twelve Sibyls),[4] of which the only known copy is at St. Gallen, consists of twenty-four leaves, printed with the rubber on one side only, one cut of a Sibyl always facing another cut with a scene from the life of Christ in the upper half, and a subject with a prophet or evangelist in the lower. The original was probably near in style to the *Biblia Pauperum* or *Speculum Humanae Salvationis*, but the St. Gallen edition, with strong outline and regular parallel shading, is probably German of about 1470–75.

The *Historia Sanctae Crucis*, based on a legend in the *Oracula Sibyllina*, is known in a fragment with Latin text at Nuremberg (a sheet of about 15 × 10 inches printed on one side with part of six subjects in two rows).[5] It is possible that this German edition was never, properly speaking, a block-book, but sheets intended for cutting up into its various subjects to be mounted in a manuscript like the *Pomerium Spirituale*. It is dull work with regular parallel shading, and probably of about 1470–75.

There was almost certainly an original Netherlandish block-book of the subject, but the only relics are the dismembered pieces of larger blocks in the *Boec van den Houte*, Culenborg (J. Veldener), 6th March 1483. It is probable they once formed a block-book like the *Speculum*.

I would also mention here a series of thirty-eight cuts illustrating the *Life and Passion of Christ* which are only known in modern impressions, one of these editions being published in 1877 in London under the title

[1] Cf. p. 562 for fragments of the last-named block-book, issued by Veldener.

[2] See p. 252 (*Planets*), p. 257 (*Defensorium*).

[3] See R. Hochegger, *Liber Regum, nach dem in der Universitätsbibliothek zu Innsbruck befindlichen Exemplare*, Leipzig 1892. The subjects cover the two Books of Samuel, and the first two chapters of the Book of Kings.

[4] P. Heitz and W. L. Schreiber, *Oracula Sibyllina*, Strassburg 1903.

[5] Weigel and Zestermann, 255.

A New Biblia Pauperum.[1] They appear to be from worn-out xv-century blocks, rather near in style to the cuts in Ludolphus de Saxonia, *Leven ons Heeren* (Antwerp, G. Leeuw, 1487), and though there is no ground for thinking that they were ever a block-book, the title under which they have been published is my excuse for referring to them here.

An impression in the British Museum acquired in 1839 has English text in red below each subject, printed in the early xix century in imitation of Caxton's English, possibly with intent to deceive. From notes in this copy, and in another at Oxford (Douce Collection), it would appear that the blocks were found at Nuremberg in the last decade of the xviii century. An edition without text was published by Boosey and Sons in 1818 as a 'Collection of thirty-eight old woodcuts . . . from the original blocks in the possession of the publishers' (New York Public Library). The original blocks were recently acquired by Mr. Elmer Adler in New York, and have been partially distributed among other collections.

The earliest and most important German block-book has already been described among the other editions of the *Biblia Pauperum*, as have also numerous other German copies of Netherlandish originals.

There are no other German block-books of interest comparable with the Netherlandish examples, nevertheless they are sufficiently numerous, and several merit something more than a passing allusion.

The nearest in date to the Heidelberg *Biblia Pauperum* is the *Symbolum Apostolicum*, consisting of twelve subjects based on the Apostles' Creed,[2] which occurs in three editions, each from a different series of blocks, S. I, Vienna,[3] S. II, Heidelberg,[4] S. III, Munich.[5]

S. I has spaces left for text, which is supplied in Latin MS.; in S. II the names of the Apostles, in Latin, are cut on the block and spaces left for further text; in S. III the whole text is cut on the block, the names of prophets and apostles in Latin, the rest of the text in German.

In the main elements of the design S. II follows S. I, but differs in introducing below half-figures of prophets in addition to the half-figures of apostles, which alone appear in S. I; in this detail S. III is related to S. II,

[1] See Schreiber, *Handbuch*, vol. vi. p. 87. Schreiber regards them as modern fabrications.

[2] Entirely different representation of the same subject may be seen in a series of drawings by a Netherlandish master of the late xv century (at Hamburg, Berlin, Coburg, Paris and Chantilly).

[3] Ottokar Smital, Munich 1924 (and Paris 1927).

[4] Paul Kristeller, Graphische Gesellschaft, iv., Berlin 1907 (with the *Decalogus* and *Septimia Poenalis*).

[5] Paul Kristeller, Graphische Gesellschaft, xxiii., Berlin 1917.

but is largely independent in treatment of the subject, though not far removed from S. I in style. Both S. I and III, in their simple curving linear style with no shading, are related to a group of cuts, probably of Upper German or Austrian origin, which have been described in the preceding chapter,[1] a relation which is strengthened by the provenance of the Munich copy (S. III) from the Convent of Weyarn (near Miesbach, in Upper Bavaria) and the agreement of its dialect with this region. Moreover a single leaf of an issue closely related to the Vienna edition (S. I), once in the Wessner Collection at St. Gallen,[2] bore a MS. inscription which fixes its provenance, i.e. Unzkofen, a nunnery on Lake Constance which had relations with Augsburg.[3] This Wessner leaf has its text cut in German, but I have been unable to make the necessary comparison to decide whether it is of a different state of the Vienna block, or from a different block.

The date of all three editions can hardly be far removed from 1450. The style of the Heidelberg edition (S. II) is comparable with the cuts in the books printed by Pfister at Bamberg about 1461.

It is the second edition of the *Symbolum Apostolicum* which stands in nearest relation to the Heidelberg *Biblia Pauperum*, and three other block-books preserved with it in the University Library at Heidelberg belong to the same group, i.e. the *Decalogus*, the *Septimia Poenalis*[4] and a *Dance of Death*.[5] Branching folds, occasional rounded pot-hooks and long fingers characterise all but the *Septimia Poenalis*, which is somewhat cruder and more angular in execution and in fact more nearly allied to the cuts in Pfister's books.

The *Decalogus* is a block-book of ten leaves, each subject with one of the Ten Commandments in Latin, a German rhymed translation and the Devil's reply in German. The *Septimia Poenalis* should contain seven subjects (meditations for the days of the week), but it is only known in the Heidelberg fragment of five leaves.

The Heidelberg *Dance of Death* is a block-book of twenty-seven leaves,

---

[1] See p. 132.

[2] Reproduced, E. Major, *Einbl.* (Aarau, etc.), L., 1918, pl. 4. I was informed by Prof. Smital that this leaf had been acquired by the Staatsbibliothek, Munich, though I failed to find it there in 1928.

[3] This identification was discovered by Prof. Smital after his edition of 1924, where he referred to an Unzkofen near Augsburg.

[4] P. Kristeller, *Drei Blockbücher der Heidelberger Universitätsbibliothek*, Graph. Gesellschaft, Berlin, iv., 1907. See also W. Molsdorf, *Spuren eines verlorenen niederländischen Blockbuches der Biblia Pauperum*, in *Beiträge zur Geschichte und Technik der ältesten Bilddruckes*, Strassburg 1921, p. 38.

[5] W. L. Schreiber, *Der Totentanz*, Leipzig 1900.

Das ortil yst also gegeben .
Das ir lenger nicht sullet leben .
Her iurist das tut des todts crafft .
Mogt ir zo beweist ewr meisterschaft

Keyn appelliren zu desir zeit
hilft voe todts harten streytt
Her obir wint myt seynem geslecht
Das geystliche vnd das werdliche recht

Fig. 103. The Dance of Death. The Lawyer. S. IV, p. 438, No. 13.

printed in black on one side of the paper, with German text, four lines above (Death's bidding) and four below (the victim's reply). It is slightly more angular in style and clumsy in design than the *Decalogus*, but is not lacking in vigour and expression. There is another block-book of the same subject at Munich of twenty-six leaves of smaller oblong subjects (within a double border-line), which came from the same convent of Weyarn as the Munich *Symbolum Apostolicum* (S. III) and was coloured by the same hand. Neither of these block-books equal in vigour and expressive power the woodcut series first printed about 1489 without indication of place or date (S. 5372; see Vol. I. p. 343, and fig. 155).

Another block-book at Heidelberg, the *Fable of the Sick Lion* (twenty pages, including nine subjects, with some inscriptions cut in the blocks and the remaining text in German MS.), is near to the *Septimia Poenalis* in style, and is in some sort a skit on the *Ars Moriendi*.

There is still another block-book at Heidelberg which Schreiber relates to the *Decalogus* and *Septimia Poenalis*, regarding them all as deriving from some similar Swiss or Upper German source, i.e. an edition of the *Planets*, with the arms of Basle on its tenth block (fig. 104).[1] It consists of fourteen subjects, the defective Heidelberg copy being printed on one side of the leaf only, two subjects, embracing one Planet, facing each other. A complete impression in the library of Prince d'Essling, from which an illustration is reproduced, is printed on both sides. There are two other block-books of similar scheme, one, distinctly poorer in quality, represented in imperfect copies at Vienna and in the British Museum (S. II), the other, somewhat more precisely cut, at Graz (S. III). They both probably date about 1470–75.

Among other series of *Planets* allied to the block-books, if not strictly so classed, is one at Berlin, in which the cuts (with only a few inscriptions on the blocks) are pasted in a volume with MS. text similar to the Heidelberg-Prince d'Essling *Planets*.[2] Though in its present form it is not actually a block-book, it was evidently intended as such. It is probably a German copy (of about 1470) of some lost Netherlandish original,[3] and the same may be said of another set of which only two subjects are preserved in the Zürich library.[4] The xv century was a period much given to astrological lore, and the influence of the Planets on humanity was a fertile field for entertaining

---

[1] See W. L. Schreiber, *Basels Bedeutung für die Blockbücher*, 1909.

[2] For reproduction of this and other series of the same subject see F. Lippmann, *The Planets*, Internat. Chalcographical Society, 1895.   [3] See p. 265, additions and corrections.

[4] M. Lehrs, *Einbl.* iv., 1906, Nos. 5 and 10; Heitz, *Primitive Holzschnitte*, 1913, pls. 45 and 46.

Fig. 104. The Planets. The Influences of Venus (with the arms of Basle). S. IV, p. 420, No. 10.

illustration. The subject reproduced from the Berlin series, which shows the lively character of their illustration, is interesting in relation to the various arts and crafts over which *Mercury* was held to preside (fig. 105).

One of the most attractive of the German block-books is the *Ars Memorandi*, an aid to the less learned clergy and laity in memorising the Gospels. In each of the three editions known (which are all from different blocks, with unimportant differences in detail)[1] it consists of thirty leaves, fifteen subjects alternating with pages of block-cut text, printed on one side of the paper. The centre of each subject is the symbol of an Evangelist, and round about it are a variety of other mnemonic symbols. All three editions show strongly cut outline, angular design and regular parallel shading, in the style of Upper German work of about 1470. The first and second editions are somewhat better than the third, and about equal in quality. The type is particularly well cut and shows fine initial letters, and the decorative motives, e.g. lizards (as in the *Ars Moriendi*, S. I, and the *Septima Poenalis*), are especially attractive.

We now come to several block-books, to which we have already alluded, issued by known printers, the most important being the editions of Franciscus de Retza's *Defensorium Virginitatis Mariae*,[2] the first printed by FRIEDRICH WALTHER (Nördlingen) in 1470, the second by JOHANNES EYSENHUT, probably at Regensburg, in 1471. Copies of both are in the British Museum, the first being coloured, the second uncoloured. The first edition (a work of little quality) is of sixteen leaves printed on one side, facing in pairs, in which most of the pages show four subjects, each with Latin text below. The second is a book of twenty-seven leaves, printed on one side, most of the pages like the example reproduced (fig. 107), containing two subjects on one block. This second edition is far more interesting in design, well cut (with regular parallel shading), expressive in figure drawing, and remarkable for

---

[1] S. I. Including three issues in which the page corresponding to that reproduced in fig. 106 shows in: (*a*) no large initial. Gotha, Vienna; (*b*) the place of the initial taken by a square of black. Munich; (*c*) initial U with a fruit like a raspberry or strawberry and a mark (of engraver?) in the centre. Leipzig, Munich, Vienna. S. II. British Museum (uncoloured), Bamberg, Munich. S. III. The initial U is closed at the top. Manchester (Spencer), Dresden, Munich, Paris, New York Public Library, British Museum (from the Huth Collection).

[2] An illustrated book of the same subject, printed with ordinary type, but put together in the manner of a block-book (i.e. alternate pairs of facing pages (*a*) woodcut and text, (*b*) blank pages), was printed by Hurus at Saragossa in Spain (between 1485 and 1499). See W. L. Schreiber, *Defensorium* . . . Weimar (Gesellschaft der Bibliophilen), 1910 (reproducing the copy in the Bibl. Nationale, Paris).

Fig. 105. The Planets. Mercury. S. IV, p. 419, No. 6.

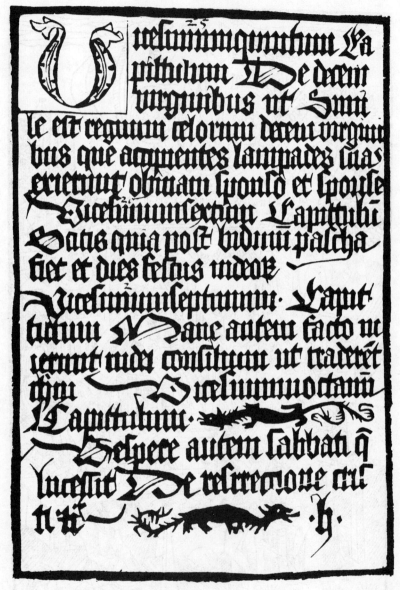

Fig. 106. From the *Ars Memorandi*. S. II.

landscapes of an excellent decorative convention. Dr. M. J. Friedländer suggests that both these editions may derive from some lost Netherlandish original.[1]

Salve Regina, a Hymn in honour of the Virgin in German, a block-book of sixteen leaves, printed on one side, only known in the British Museum impression, is signed on the fifteenth block *lienhart czu regenspurck*. A LIENHART WOLFF *priefdrucker*, with whom he is probably identical, is known in records at Regensburg from 1463 onwards, but the book is hardly likely from its style to have been produced before about 1470-75. It is crude work, strong in outline, angular in design, with regular parallel shading, and of little artistic merit.

Johann Hartlieb's *Die Kunst Chiromantia*, known in four editions, the third and fourth of which bear on the last page the name of *Jorg Schapff zu Augsburg* (the third having the same name spelt *Irog Scapff*), is even less interesting in its illustration, except to experts in palmistry. It is quite uncertain whether JORG SCHAPFF, who is known in Augsburg records from 1478, is the cutter or only the printer of the blocks, which are the same throughout the various issues. The title-page, which is dated 1448 (no doubt the date the book was written), has a woodcut of the author presenting his book to Anna, Duchess of Bavaria. Apart from two pages of introduction, the book consists of forty-four pages of hands and their meaning. All except the first edition are printed on both sides of the page; the first is only known in the Deutsches Buchmuseum, Leipzig, the second is preserved at Augsburg and Munich, the third is at Manchester (John Rylands Library), the fourth at Munich, Paris, and (incomplete) in the British Museum.

Antichrist and the Fifteen Tokens of Judgment is another crude block-book which bears in two of its issues the name of a craftsman who is probably to be identified with HANS SPÖRER. Most of the blocks show two subjects, one above the other, with German text beneath each. Apart from the chiro-xylographic edition, which is probably the earliest issue (complete copy until recently at Maihingen,[2] and fragments at Paris and Vienna), there are two sets of blocks with xylographic text, i.e.

I. Outline and shading. Munich (complete); British Museum (fragments).

II. Outline only, and probably copied from I.

(*a*) Signed *De Jung Hanns prieffmaler hat das puch zu nurenberg A 1°4°7°2 ff*. Gotha.

---

[1] *Der Holzschnitt*, 2te Auflage, 1921.

[2] Auktion xi, 7 May 1935, No. 21, Karl & Faber, Munich.

(*b*) Signed *Der . . . Hanns prieffmaler hat das puch 1°4°7° . . .* The blocks cut in half, and part of the artist's signature removed; printed on both sides of page. Munich.

Three other unimportant block-books may be mentioned, both printed in the ordinary press on both sides of the page, i.e. a *Confessionale*,[1] possibly Nuremberg work of about 1475 (The Hague), the *Vita Sancti Meinradi* (Einsiedeln and Munich),[2] probably done in Upper Germany or Switzerland late in the xv century, in the neighbourhood of the pilgrimage chapel of Einsiedeln, which was built on the site of St. Meinrad's hermitage, and the *Ars et Modus Contemplativae Vitae*, Nuremberg (F. Creussner) 1473, for its two xylographic pages forming part of an ordinary printed book (Munich).

Far more attractive is the block-book Donatus, *De Octo Partibus orationis*, printed by DINCKMUT at Ulm (Deutsches Buchmuseum, Leipzig), with border and figured initial D, showing a master and his pupils in the style of the ordinary type-printed book decoration at Ulm about 1475–1480 (fig. 108).[3] Dinckmut's first type-printed book is an Almanack for the year 1478, so that his block-book probably preceded this, though hardly by a long interval. The earliest record found of Dinckmut as a printer belongs to the year 1476.

The most popular guide-book of the period, of which various MSS. exist from the xiii century onwards, also appeared in its first printed edition as a block-book, i.e. the *Mirabilia Romae* (*Wie Rom gebauet ward*). Over thirty editions in movable type were printed between 1484 and 1500. The block-book (of which there is a complete copy in the British Museum, another lacking the first leaf at Gotha)[4] contains the arms of Pope Sixtus IV. (the *Oak Tree* device of the Della-Rovere family), so that it must date between 1471 and 1484, and was probably done for the Jubilee year of 1475. It is small octavo, but one of the most lengthy of the block-books, containing ninety-two leaves, printed on both sides. It contains three figure subjects, i.e. *Rhea Silvia and Romulus and Remus*, a *Priest showing a portrait of Christ from a pulpit*, and *Angels holding the St. Veronica Napkin*, coats-of-arms, and a couple of initial letters with scroll decoration (of which the S is reproduced

---

[1] Reprod., ed. J. W. Holtrop, The Hague 1861.

[2] Reprod., ed. P. Gall-Morel, Einsiedeln 1861. For type-printed versions see Vol. I. p. 327.

[3] Schramm refers to a copy in the British Museum. This is a misreading of Proctor's Index, where the obelus means Bodleian Library, and not B.M. Unfortunately the fragment in the Bodleian is without initial or border.

[4] The Gotha impression reproduced by R. Ehwald, Berlin (1905) (Gesellschaft der Bibliophilen, Weimar). The British Museum copy, reproduced by J. P. Berjeau, London 1864.

Iupiter genoziden falſi ſub ymagine thauri Si
luſetat cur herilem · v · n · g · Ouidius in ·
methamorphoſius

Si tile in vitroze ſemp maneze valet · Cur deuoi
pudoriſ floze · v · n · g · Augꝯ · xxiꝰ · ἀ ciui · dei · ca
pitulo · mꝯ idul ſꝉo

Fig. 107. From the *Defensorium Virginitatis Mariae*. S. II.

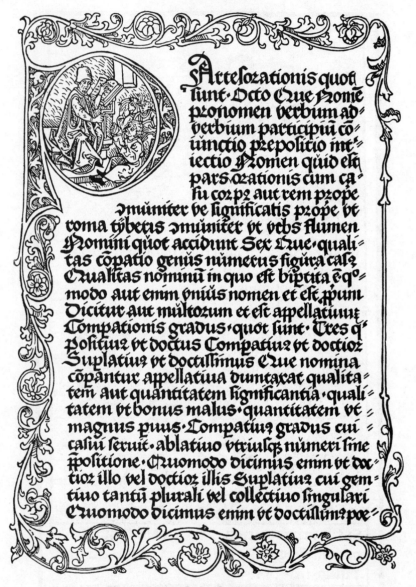

Fig. 108. Donatus, *De Octo Partibus Orationis*. Ulm.

in fig. 109), but its real interest is in its German text, with its descriptions of relics and indulgences, and a variety of entertaining stories about historic characters.

It was undoubtedly issued by a German printer at Rome, but his identity has not yet been discovered. All the figures and orna-mental parts of the block-book, except the capital letters and scroll decora-tion, were used later, with the Della-Rovere device removed from its shield, in a type-printed edition issued at Rome (B.M. Catalogue of xv-Century Printed Books, part iv. p. 144, unknown printer, not before 1485).[1] This edition had been formerly attri-buted to Planck, and the suggestion had in conse-quence been made that the block-book might have been printed by Ulric Han, whose stock descended to Planck. The type corre-sponds to that used at Gaeta, in 1487, by Andreas Freitag, who printed later at Rome (1492–94).

Fig. 109. Initial S from the *Mirabilia Romae*. Rome, about 1475.

The latest of the German block-books is the *Art of Wrestling*, which was probably printed during the first decade of the xvi century, and is only known in an impression at Berlin.[2] It consists of twelve leaves, each, except the first and last, containing a picture of two men wrestling, with explanatory text, the last leaf inscribed *gedruckt zu landshut Hanns Wurm*, and bearing

---

[1] The blocks are still in good condition in the British Museum copy, and printed better and more delicately than in the British Museum impression of the block-book. It must not be con-fused with Planck's edition of 20th November 1489 (with copies of the block-book cuts), of which a facsimile is issued by the Wiegendruckgesellschaft, Berlin 1925.

[2] There are ordinary editions from movable type printed by Hans Sittich, Augsburg, about 1511 (S. 5097), and by M. Hupfuff, Strassburg, about 1512 (S. 5098); they contain cruder woodcuts.

the arms of Landshut. The only other signed work of Hans Wurm is a wood-cut reproducing the same design as a line-engraving by Mair of Landshut, *The Reception at the Door of a Gothic House* (P. II. 157, 13; Lehrs, 17).[1] The block-book cuts are also entirely in the manner of Mair, who may actually have been the designer.

Apart from the books already described there is a variety of small editions of the *Passion*,[2] some block-books in the proper sense, others more in the nature of series of cuts, sometimes many on one block, with text attached to each subject, which may either have been issued as broadsides, or cut up and bound in octavo form.

Likewise in the border-land are various *Calendars* (whether for single years, or for a cycle of years) printed from wood blocks, some intended as broadsides or wall-calendars, others for issue in book form, or to be folded in a pocket-cover or rolled, according to convenience. Several editions are known of a calendar of Johann Müller (Regiomontanus), printed at Nuremberg about 1474–76 by a HANNS BRIEFFTRUCK (e.g. in the British Museum), who was probably the Hans Spörer of the *Biblia Pauperum* of 1471, and of the *Ars Moriendi* of 1473, and the *Hanns prieff-maler* of the *Antichrist* of 1472, and of another Nuremberg calendar in 1478, S. 1904 c; Gotha). The illustrative cuts of this calendar in book form are of practically no artistic interest. More attractive are those in a calendar compiled by Johann Nider de Gamundia and in another issued by CONRAD KACHELOFEN. The wood blocks of one edition of Nider's calendar (about 1470?) are preserved in the Berlin Print Room (from the Derschau Collection), and late impressions are not very rare (e.g. British Museum). The calendar was evidently intended as a broadside, though the only old impression known, from an edition of about the same date, is cut into six pieces (Berlin).

The calendar bearing the name of *Cunradt Kacheloven* (who printed at Leipzig between 1485 and 1509) forms an attractive little book, in which each of the pages of the months contains a row of little half-figures of saints above an illustration of the month, while another calendar printed at Mainz (inscribed *Mentz* in Schoeffer's type, and with the initials G. N. in reverse) is somewhat more crudely cut after the same designs. Examples of both of these calendars calculated for the years 1493–1450, and probably printed about 1493, are in the British Museum.

---

[1] British Museum. See C. Dodgson, *Catalogue of Early German and Flemish Woodcuts in the British Museum*, ii., 1911, p. 263. See also pp. 389-391.

[2] The most important block-book of the *Passion* (Berlin) will be described in a later chapter (see pp. 416-421).

Related in form to the Mainz and Kacheloven calendars in the rows of half-figures of saints, are various *Bas-Breton Almanacks* and an English calendar of the earlier part of the XVI century. They are all printed on long and narrow sheets of vellum, and generally folded lengthwise once, and then cross-wise in concertina form to close like a map into a small pocket form of about $2\frac{1}{2} \times 1\frac{1}{2}$ inches. There are three impressions of the English calendar, inscribed with the initials M S, in the British Museum,[1] originally printed between 1500 and 1521, one of them being in its original leather pocket-case. The last named is dated in manuscript 1537, the others 1538 and 1542 respectively, and other copies known bear dates between 1521 or 1522 and 1554. In addition to the figures of saints (some specifically English) and miscellaneous calendar material, it includes a series of occupations of the months.

The *Bas-Breton Almanacks*, which were printed for the Breton fisher-folk, are in all essentials of the same form as the English calendar of M S (though cruder in execution), and printed either in Latin, French, or Bas-Breton. An example in the British Museum [2] is signed *G. Brouscon du Conquet*,[3] and is folded in pocket form, like the English calendar, and bears a manuscript date 1551. A fragment in the British Museum from a similar almanack shows maps of England and Ireland. Another similar calendar is signed *I. Trodec*, of which an impression is preserved in the John Rylands Library, Manchester (from the Spencer Collection). No manuscript date earlier than 1529 has been quoted as on such Bas-Breton Almanacks (for the XV century dates in the margin of the Spencer example are false additions), and they were evidently printed until the second half of the XVI century.

From similarity of form it is possible that the English calendar, inscribed M S, might also have been chiefly intended for the use of sailors.

The Breton examples are hardly noteworthy except as provincial survivals of an earlier genre of book production long after the establishment of printing with movable type.

Of block-books in the broader signification, i.e. books in which both illustrations and lettering are printed entirely from blocks, there are of course various later examples, the most notable being the books of William Blake.

---

[1] See E. F. Bosanquet, *English printed Almanacks to 1600*, London (Bibliographical Society, Illustrated Monographs No. 17) 1917, Bibliography No. II.

[2] Once Sloane MS. 966, now in the library, C. 36. aa. 4. Another by G. Brouscon is at Chantilly.

[3] Le Conquet is a small port near Brest.

BIBLIOGRAPHY

HEINECKEN, C. H. von. Nachrichten von Künstlern und Kunstsachen. II. Theil. Leipzig 1769 (pp. 87-240 largely concerned with block-books).

HEINECKEN, C. H. von. Idée générale d'une collection d'estampes. Leipzig and Vienna 1771 (pp. 292-482 largely concerned with block-books; similar material to that in the preceding volume in German).

GUICHARD, J. M. Recherches sur les livres xylographiques. Paris (*Bulletin du Bibliophile*) 1840.

SOTHEBY, Samuel Leigh. Principia Typographica. London, 3 vols., 1858. (Vol. i., Holland and the Low Countries; vol. ii., Germany; vol. iii., paper-marks.)

DUTUIT, Eugène. Manuel de l'amateur d'estampes. Vol. i. Paris 1884. A compilation of no particular value.

HOCHEGGER, Rudolf. Über die Entstehung und Bedeutung der Blockbücher. Leipzig 1891.

SCHREIBER, W. L. Darf der Holzschnitt als Vorläufer der Buchdruckerkunst betrachtet werden? *Centralblatt für Bibliothekswesen.* Leipzig 1895.

SCHREIBER, W. L. Manuel de l'amateur de la gravure sur bois. Vol. iv. (1902), and various reproductions in vols. vii.-viii., 1895 and 1900 fol. An invaluable corpus of information.

SCHREIBER, W. L. Basels Bedeutung für die Geschichte der Blockbücher. Strassburg (Studien zur deutschen Kunstgeschichte) 1909.

DODGSON, C. Catalogue of Early German and Flemish Woodcuts in the British Museum. Vol. i. (1903), pp. 16-20 and 209-12.

See also p. 54, General Bibliography (General Histories) and bibliographies of the various sections on book-illustration, especially the Netherlands.

Collections, see especially—

BRITISH MUSEUM, Catalogue of Books printed in the xv Century. Part i., Xylographica, etc. London 1908.

PIERPONT MORGAN COLLECTION. Catalogue of Early Printed Books. Vol. i. London 1907.

THE HOLFORD COLLECTION. Burlington Fine Arts Club. Catalogue of Pictures, etc. London 1921-22 (pp. 32, etc.).

Reproductions—

Most series have been cited above under the various block-books. Only the more recent of these, done by photographic methods direct from the print (and not through the medium of tracings), can be trusted in any comparison of the style and quality of the various editions. The same charge of unreliability applies also to the series (not cited above): *Monuments de la xylographie* reproduits par Ad. Pilinski, ed. G. Pawlowski. Paris 1882–83. (i. *Apocalypse*, S. V; ii. *Biblia Pauperum*, S. VIII; iii. *Ars Memorandi*, probably S. III; iv. *Ars Moriendi*, S. IVB; v. *Exercitium super Pater Noster* (Latin edition); vi. *Cantica Canticorum*, S. I A.)

They succeeded in vols. i. and vi. in obtaining the effect of the original block-books, of the paper being indented from a relief-block, as in the originals, but exact linear truth was not always preserved here or in the other volumes.

The plates in Dutuit's *Manuel de l'amateur* were also done by A. Pilinski.

Schreiber, *Manuel*, vols. vii. and viii. (1895 and 1900), gives photographic facsimiles from most block-books.

ADDITIONS AND CORRECTIONS
TO VOLS. I. AND II.

P. 252, footnote 3. Since this passage was written I note Dr. M. J. Schretlen has found the larger part of what he regards as the original edition in the Copenhagen Print Room. To judge from reproductions, the *Jupiter* seems to be from the same block as the Berlin set, but the others appear to be from different and better blocks (*Kunstmuseets Aarskrift*, Copenhagen 1929–31, p. 1).

P. 518. *Antiquarie prospetiche Romane.* In the Tammaro de Marinis Catalogue (Milan 1925) this book is attributed to the printer Johann Besicken at Rome, about 1499–1500, on the basis of the type, an ascription which is probably correct. Apart from this identification of the type, one might have been tempted to explain the initials PM as referring to the Milanese printer Petrus de Mantegatiis.

P. 522. *Specchio dell' Anima* and *Tesauro Spirituale.* The woodcuts were for the most part reprinted in *Opera nuova historiata della Divinita et Humanita di Christo*, Milan (Vicenzo Girardin) 1563. (E. P. Goldschmidt & Co., Catalogue xxxviii., 1935, No. 1.) It includes 68 prints from the original *Specchio* blocks, and 7 copies from the same series; also prints from the 5 *Tesauro* blocks. Mr. Goldschmidt appears to be the first to have noticed a remarkable passage in G. P. Ferraro's dedicatory epistle to Lodovico Sforza, in which it is stated that he found the originals, from which he had the woodcuts made, in Spain. If the original *Specchio* designs are Spanish, the unique character of the woodcuts in contemporary Italian work is explained.

P. 330. Add to footnote 1: *Le Livre du Chevalier Geoffroy de La Tour Landry pour l'enseignement de ses filles*, written in the latter half of the xiv Century, was first printed by Caxton in his own translation (the *Knyght of the Toure*) 1484. Furter's German issue of 1493 (translated by Marquart vom Stein) was the first illustrated edition (Berlin, Vienna, etc.; no copy recorded in England). The earliest French edition, with cuts of different design, was printed at Paris in 1514. For the original work and its various editions see A. de Montaiglon, Paris 1854.

REFERENCES TO THE LOCALITY OF BOOKS

In respect to German books reference is seldom given to locality as these are recorded in Schreiber's *Manuel*. The locality of books of other countries is only given if there is no copy in the British Museum, and then only to one or more of the most easily available copies.

THE DATING OF BOOKS

Variety in the styles of calendar in the xv century presents difficulties, as the year began at various dates in relation to the present style beginning 1st January, i.e.

(*a*) 25th March, preceding (the Pisan style in Italy).

(*b*) 1st September, preceding (the Byzantine style).

(*c*) 25th December, preceding (common in Germany and Austria; occasional in France).

(*d*) 1st January (infrequent, but occasional at Paris).

(*e*) 1st March, succeeding (the Venetian style in Italy).

(*f*) 25th March, succeeding (the Florentine style in Italy; the usual style in England).

(*g*) Easter Day, succeeding (the usual style in the Netherlands and France).

The styles (*a*) and (*b*) hardly touch the books described.

In style (*c*) the dates from 25th to 31st December might be quoted as (say) 1492/91, the second figure denoting the year in the present style. This mode, however, would affect only a small number of books, and has not, I think, been followed in bibliographies.

In styles (*e*), (*f*) and (*g*) the dates from 1st January to the 31st February, the 24th March, or Easter-Eve, might be quoted as 1491/92. This has been done to a large extent in the description of Netherlandish, French and English books.

It is evident how easily error may arise without detailed investigation of each case, and I plead this excuse in advance. The question is unimportant in our study except in occasional questions of priority in design.

The form 1491–92 implies an issue at dates in both years.

The most convenient reference book for matters of calendar style is A. Cappelli, *Cronologia, Cronografia, e Calendario Perpetuo*, 2nd edition, Milan (Hoepli) 1930, but it cannot, of course, be used for final reference in detail.

THE most frequent abbreviations used are:

S.   for W. L. Schreiber, *Manuel de l'Amateur de la Gravure sur Bois et sur Métal au xvᵉ Siècle* (Vol. V., Parts 1 and 2), and in the case of single cuts, for W. L. Schreiber, *Handbuch des Holz- und Metallschnittes des xv Jahrhunderts.*

H.   for L. Hain, *Repertorium Bibliographicum.*

C.   for W. A. Copinger, Supplements to Hain.

GW.   for *Gesamtkatalog der Wiegendrucke.*

E.   for Prince d'Essling, *Livres à Figures Vénitiens.*

PK.   for Paul Kristeller, *Early Florentine Woodcuts,* and *Die Lombardische Graphik.*

CA.   for Campbell, *Annales de la Typographie Néerlandaise.*

CN.   for Martin Conway (Lord Conway), *Woodcutters of the Netherlands.*

STC.   for A. W. Pollard and G. R. Redgrave, *Short-Title Catalogue of Books printed in England, 1475-1640.*

n.d.   for no date quoted in colophon.

n.p.   no place of printing noted.

n.pr.   no printer named.

Other references, if not given in footnotes, will be readily solved by consultation of the bibliography at the end of each chapter.

CHAPTER V

BOOK-ILLUSTRATION AND CONTEMPORARY SINGLE CUTS IN GERMANY, AUSTRIA AND GERMAN SWITZERLAND

IN the preceding chapter I discussed at some length the obscure question as to whether the block-book might properly be regarded as the 'precursor' or 'prefigurement' of printing from movable type, in the sense intended by the writer in the Cologne Chronicle. The present chapter, dealing with book-illustration in Germany, Austria and German Switzerland during the xv century, only demands the shortest reference to a question of almost equal obscurity, i.e. the exact date and authorship of the introduction of printing from movable type, for it is a matter which has an extensive literature of its own.[1] It will suffice here to say that the discovery must have taken place within a few years of 1450, that JOHANN GUTENBERG (who was working at Strassburg about 1436–44, and at Mainz between 1448 and his death about 1468, except for a short stay at Bamberg in 1457 and 1458) was among the prime movers, if not the actual or sole originator of the new art. The fact that this new art was for some time regarded as secret, and that the earliest printed sheets and books were not signed with the printer's name, preserves the obscurity. A *Calendar* assigned to the year 1448 (preserved in a unique copy at Wiesbaden), various editions of the Grammar (*De Octo Partibus Orationis*) of Aelius Donatus, several Papal Indulgences of the years 1454 and 1455, the 42-line Latin Bible (about 1455),[2] and the 36-line Latin Bible (about 1458) are the chief works hitherto ascribed to Gutenberg, though the 42-line Bible and the 30-line Indulgence are now more generally attributed to JOHANN FUST and PETER SCHOEFFER.[3] The

[1] See p. 208, footnote 2.   [2] Popularly called the Mazarin Bible, as it was Cardinal Mazarin's copy (Collection Mazarine in the Bibliothèque Nationale) to which attention was first drawn.

[3] Johann Fust was originally a goldsmith: he obtained judgment in 1455 against Gutenberg, for the repayment of loans advanced in 1450 and 1452 in connection with printing. Peter Schoeffer, who was a witness in this lawsuit, married Fust's daughter, and was in partnership with his father-in-law until the latter's death in 1467. Fust was evidently the capitalist of the firm, but as a trained goldsmith he may have collaborated with Schoeffer on the technical side as well. But it is noteworthy that verses appended to the colophon of the *Institutiones* of Justinianus (printed by Schoeffer in 1468) while praising both the Johns (i.e. Gutenberg and Fust) for their skill in engraving (*in arte sculpendi*), claim that Schoeffer had surpassed them both in the same field. For early Mainz books see Seymour de Ricci, Gutenberg Gesellschaft, 1911.

type used in the 36-line Bible, and the other works attributed to Gutenberg, came later into the hands of ALBRECHT PFISTER of Bamberg,[1] to whom Gutenberg, when pressed by his creditors, may have sold his stock.

The earliest book, which gives the names of its printers in addition to its date or place, is the *Latin Psalter* issued by Fust and Schoeffer at Mainz in 1457. It is, moreover, the earliest book printed from movable type in which woodcut of any importance occurs. The woodcuts are merely initial letters and not subject illustrations, but such decorative designs always form an important part of the woodcutter's craft, and these early examples are of considerable beauty.

I say 'woodcut', though these initial letters were more probably printed, or stamped, from metal,[2] but the form was no doubt first cut in wood and a mould taken from this to make the metal cast. Throughout the history of woodcut and wood-engraving initial letters, borders and other pieces of decoration have been printed somewhat promiscuously either from the original wood blocks, or from casts,[3] and the very need for constant repetition of initials would incline the printer to preserve the wood, and from time to time to renew his casts. In some examples the appearance of the print may indicate the material to a practised printer, but as in many cases we must be in doubt, it is reasonable to include such casts in a survey of woodcut as if they were woodcuts, just as we have included the relief-cuts in metal. Some of the initials may of course be relief-cuts in metal, but in general casting would probably be the more expeditious method.

The simpler initials in the 1457 *Psalter* are merely stamped or printed in a single colour (generally in red),[4] but the really noteworthy initials are those stamped or printed in two colours. They occur again in the same printers' *Latin Psalter* of 1459, and generally in blue and red, the most remarkable being the large initial B occurring on the first page of both editions. Indentation of the vellum is very clearly marked in the British Museum copy of the 1459 *Psalter*, particularly at the foot of the decorative portion, where the block has been wiped and the stamping is blind to leave

---

[1] See p. 193, for metal-cuts printed with this type.

[2] See G. Mori, *Was hat Gutenberg erfunden? Ein Ruckblick auf die Frühtechnik des Schriftgusses*, Gutenberg Gesellschaft, Mainz 1921 (Beiträge zum 19ten Jahresbericht, 1919–20). Cf. p. 183.

[3] See Index of Subjects (*casts*). The general practice of the Kelmscott Press in the XIX century was to print the decorative pictures from electrotypes, and the subject cuts from the original wood.

[4] Indentation seems to indicate stamping in most cases, but occasionally a letter may be found which looks as if done by stencil (e.g. 1459 *Psalter*, B.M.L., a large I on p. 116).

Fig. 110. Initial B, from the *Latin Psalter*, Mainz 1457.

place for a second and smaller initial. The printers use the blue or the red promiscuously either for the letter itself or the decorative ground.

Similar bichrome initials, in which the decorative portion often borrows suggestion from the Lily of the Valley (*Maiblume*), occur in Duranti's *Rationale*, printed by Fust and Schoeffer, 1459, and in the *Canon of the Mass*, printed by Fust and Schoeffer about the same date (Proctor 68, Oxford), but thereafter they are only found in later reprints of the *Psalter*.

There is an example in a leaf from Schoeffer's reprint of 1490 in the British Museum (IB.259), and the worn condition of such later initials proves that they were done from stamps or blocks and not by the aid of stencils as has been sometimes suggested. The only part of such initials to which the stencil might have been applied with success is the flat surface of the letter itself (like the single-colour initials), not the background of delicate line.

It should be noted that the ornamental part sometimes overlaps the text, which shows that they have been printed separately, and were probably stamped on in the rubricator's shop after the printing of the book. A small letter to guide the rubricator is often visible beneath the initial.

The 42-line *Bible* shows exactly the same kind of bichrome initial, not stamped but done by the hand of the rubricator, a fact which in itself lends some support to the attribution of this work to Fust and Schoeffer. For it is noteworthy that the books generally assigned to Gutenberg, e.g. the 36-line *Bible* and Balbus, *Catholicon* (1460), have no initials either drawn or printed in this style. Apart from the simpler red initials, the more important initials are fully illuminated in the British Museum copies of these works, and certainly show a different illuminator from Fust and Schoeffer's craftsman.

For rather more than a decade after the remarkable essays of the years 1457 to 1459, Fust and Schoeffer and other printers kept to monochrome initials, whether stamped or printed, or drawn by the rubricator with the brush, direct or with the aid of stencil. Then, about 1470, monochrome initials, designed in a style entirely suited to the woodcutter's craft, came into fashion, largely through the influence of the printers of Augsburg and Ulm. To these we shall revert later.

Examples of the same style of bichrome initials as originally used by Fust and Schoeffer, drawn by hand, and often in more than two colours, are occasionally found in the books of other printers. They are sometimes seen in books printed by JOHANN MENTELIN of Strassburg, done by a somewhat coarse hand, e.g. in his *Latin Bible* (about 1460–61), British Museum, King's Library copy. Three examples outside Germany may be noted, i.e. an initial Q in the Grenville Library copy of the *Dyalogus Creaturarum* (Gouda, 3rd June 1480) in the British Museum, initials in a copy of J. de Turrecremata, *Expositio in Psalmos* (about 1482, attributed by Haebler to Paulus Hurus, Saragossa),[1] and another initial Q in a copy of Jean Trechsel's Latin edition of Thomas à Kempis, *Imitation of Christ* (Lyon 1489), in the library of St. Geneviève, Paris.[2]

BAMBERG

The first subject illustrations in printed books are those which were issued from the press of ALBRECHT PFISTER of Bamberg, who, as already noted, had taken over some of Gutenberg's type.[3] Pfister printed in all nine editions of five books, all of extreme rarity, and eight (or at least seven) of these were richly illustrated with woodcuts,[4] as follows:

> (1) Johannes von Saaz, *Der Ackermann aus Böhmen*,[5] 1st edition, about 1460, H. 74. The only copy known, at Wolfenbüttel, is without woodcuts, but it probably had the same as the second edition.
> 2nd edition, about 1463, H. 73. With five full-page cuts (about $8\frac{1}{2} \times 5\frac{5}{8}$ inches). The Wolfenbüttel copy reproduced by the Insel Verlag, Leipzig 1919 (ed. Alois Bernt). Other copies at Paris and Berlin (Print Room). Fig. 111.
>
> (2) Ulrich Boner, *Der Edelstein* (Fables in German). Two editions:

---

[1] See E. P. Goldschmidt, Catalogue viii. No. 96.

[2] Reproduced in A. Claudin, *Histoire de l'imprimerie en France*, vol. iv., 1914, p. 55.

[3] See also p. 193, for a series of metal-cuts printed with the same type.

[4] See Albert Schramm, *Der Bilderschmuck der Frühdrucke*, i., Albrecht Pfister, Leipzig 1922. Pfister's one book without illustrations is Jacobus de Theramo, *Belial*.

[5] See G. Zedler, Gutenberg Gesellschaft, 16 and 17 Jahresbericht.

Dated edition, 1461, with 101 cuts, H. 3578. The earliest dated book in the German language, Wolfenbüttel.[1]

Undated edition, probably about 1464, with 103 cuts, C. 1203. Berlin (Staatsbibl.).[2]

The cuts of the Fables are oblongs about 3 × 4 inches; and at the side of each is placed a small upright cut, about 3 × 1 inches, of a man pointing to the illustration. There is only one 'indicator' cut repeated throughout the first edition, while the second edition has three varieties. The Fable cuts are from the same blocks in each edition. There are illustrated MSS. of Boner's Fables at Munich and Heidelberg (cf. p. 306).

(3) *Vier Historien* (i.e. of Joseph, Daniel, Esther and Judith), 1462, H. 8749. Paris, Manchester. 52 oblong subjects (several being repeated), about $3\frac{1}{8} \times 5\frac{3}{8}$ inches. The carelessness of the printer is shown by the printing of one of the cuts (the *Death of Jacob* on f. 12) upside down, and the illuminator, not unnaturally, omitted to colour this illustration.

(4) *Biblia Pauperum*. Three editions:

(*a*) German (1462). H. 3176. Wolfenbüttel. Paris. Manchester.

(*b*) Latin (1463). H. 3177. Munich (Staatsbibl.). Manchester.

(*c*) German (1464). Pell. 2387. Paris.

On each page there are four cuts: in the upper row, a New Testament subject (about $2\frac{1}{2}$ inches square) flanked by two small blocks with two busts of prophets (oblongs, about $\frac{7}{8} \times 1\frac{5}{8}$ inches); below, two subjects from the Old Testament on one oblong block (about $2\frac{1}{2} \times 5\frac{5}{8}$ inches). In editions (*a*) and (*b*) there are 34 pages of this arrangement; in the second German edition additional cuts appear.

The cuts are largely pure outline, with only a slight use of shading in short parallel strokes. Practically all the copies known are coloured by hand, and the style of the cuts shows that this was the printer's intention, and most copies were probably coloured in his shop. Pfister, with several of the other early printers,[3] may have been his own cutter, but there is no direct

---

[1] Reproduced from the Wolfenbüttel copy by Schramm, with the three additional 'indicator' figures from the undated edition.

[2] Reproduced by P. Kristeller, Graphische Gesellschaft (I. Ausserordentl. Veröffentlichung), Berlin 1908.

[3] Lienhart Ysenhut, who printed at Basle from 1489 to 1507, is recorded in documents as *Briefdrucker, Heiligendrucker, Maler, Briefmaler, Heiligenmaler* and *Kartenmacher*.

evidence in his case. In style of design and cutting the prototype is certainly
to be seen in the Heidelberg *Biblia Pauperum* block-book, but there is more

Fig. 111. Death on Horseback, from *Der Ackermann aus Böhmen*, Bamberg, about 1463.

angularity in the line, and the fingers are shorter, more nearly as in the
Septimia Poenalis block-book. The design and cutting are crude, but as
illustrations the blocks are not wanting in spirit.

After these essays of Pfister between 1460 and 1464, there is an interval of some six years before any other woodcut illustrations appeared in Germany. The woodcutters were still engaged, apart from their single cuts, in making block-books, and there was evidently guild jealousy between the cutters and those parvenus, the printers of books in movable type. The printers had doubtless attempted at first to make their initials and other cuts in their own workshops, and the professional woodcutters were perhaps slow to realise the opportunity that was opening to them in the new rival to their block-books.

The guild jealousy is clearly shown in the experience of Günther Zainer, the printer, on his arrival at Augsburg in 1468, to which we have already alluded.[1] An attempt was first made to hinder the stranger from obtaining citizen's rights and the privilege to print, though these were actually granted on the intervention of the Abbot of St. Ulrich and St. Afra. But at first he was not allowed to decorate his books with initials or other woodcuts, and only obtained this right subsequently, on the express condition that he should only use the woodcutters of the guilds. This points very directly to the probability that either Zainer himself or one of his assistants had intended to cut the blocks.

The early printers would in general have had more than enough to do in perfecting the new craft of printing from movable type, without giving thought to the art of illustration. But even so, it is a natural inference from the Zainer episode to regard guild regulations [2] and jealousies as among the reasons for the interval of some half-dozen years that elapsed between the last of Pfister's woodcuts and the resumption of woodcut illustration, which occurred at Augsburg about 1471.

There are few known artists among the illustrators of xv-century books, and it is only here and there that critics have attempted to group the cuts under anonymous personalities with convenient titles, such as the MASTER OF THE AMSTERDAM CABINET (or the MASTER OF THE HAUSBUCH as he is also called).[3] Such groupings, which have only been consistently carried out in Conway's *Woodcutters of the Netherlands*, are too uncertain and conjectural, and the soundest and most convenient method of describing the anonymous woodcuts of the xv century is still that of classification under the various printers. The woodcutters probably kept for the most part to one town and to special printers, so the division corresponds, at least partially, with grouping according to artist or style.

[1] See pp. 91 and 211.
[2] It must always be remembered that each town had its own regulations.
[3] See below, p. 346.

The appearance of woodcuts by the same hand in various towns need not of course imply a change of habitation in the woodcutter. Wood blocks passed fairly frequently from one printer to another, not only within the country of origin, but sometimes from one country to another. Thus the original blocks illustrating Breydenbach's *Travels* (Mainz 1486) were afterwards printed at Lyon (1489–90), at Speier (1490, lacking one little cut of the *Holy Sepulchre*, which was probably lost in transit) and at Saragossa (1498).[1]

Before continuing further description of German woodcut illustrations according to the method proposed, that of towns and printers, I would add a few general remarks about the beginning of book-illustration.

Occasionally series of woodcuts are found pasted in manuscripts, in spaces left on purpose for the prints, in a way that foreshadows ordinary book-illustration. One of the best examples of this is the *Gulden Püchlein von unser lieben frawen Maria*, dated 1450, preserved in the Graphische Sammlung, Munich.[2] The manuscript contains seventy small cuts, which appear to be copies of a better set, of which examples are known in several collections (e.g. Berlin and Nuremberg, and others once at Maihingen, mostly coming from Swabian convents, at Inzigkofen and Elchingen). An inscription on the back of a drawing of St. Agnes that it was by a 'sister', and the correspondence of a border used in the *Gulden Püchlein* with one that appears on the title of a Codex known to have been written in the Carthusian convent of St. Catherine at Nuremberg in 1451, renders it probable that the book was written and made up with the cuts, collected perhaps from various sources, and coloured in the same convent.

In the above example the prints were pasted in, but another manuscript,

---

[1] See A. W. Pollard, *The Transference of Woodcuts in the XV and XVI Centuries*, Bibliographica, ii., 1896, 343. Numerous examples are cited in Conway's *Woodcutters of the Netherlands*. There are various examples of German dotted prints issued later in France and Spain (see p. 194); the blocks of Grüninger's *Virgil* (Strassburg 1502) were printed by Sacon at Lyon in 1517; those of Rodericus Zamorensis, *Spiegel des menschlichen Lebens*, first printed by Günther Zainer at Augsburg about 1475–76, were issued later by N. Philippi and M. Reinhard at Lyon in 1482, and by Hurus at Saragossa in 1491; those of Boccaccio's *Les Cas et Ruynes des nobles hommes et femmes*, Paris (J. Dupré) 1483/84, appeared later at London in Pynson's *Fall of Princes*, 1494; and a block from Couteau and Menard's *Danse Macabre* (Paris 1492) was used later by Quentell at Cologne (see p. 362).

[2] See Otto Weigmann, *Holzschnitte aus dem Gulden Püchlein von 1450 in der Graphischen Sammlung zu München*, Berlin (Graphische Gesellschaft, xxiv.) 1918. Dr. Erwin Rosenthal has recently recognised that a later series of blocks of the same subjects appeared in Ludwig Moser, *Bereitung zum hl. Sacrament*, Basle, M. Furter, about 1493 (S.4811, C.4368).

a *Dominican Prayer Book*, preserved in the Department of Prints and Drawings at the British Museum (Dodgson, A. 142), and written at Nuremberg before 1461, shows the cuts printed on the vellum page of the manuscript. This example is coloured in the miniaturist's style in body-colour and gold, and one of the illustrations is purely a miniature without woodcut outline, so that the book is a very good instance of how woodcut was first used to save the illuminator the initial labour of making or copying the main elements of his design.

The *Delbecq-Schreiber Passion*[1] is another example of a series of cuts mounted in a manuscript book of devotion (though only preserved in fragmentary form), but this is already nearer the end of the century.

Very few drawings have been recognised as studies for the anonymous xv-century woodcuts. One of the rare examples, a study for the textile print of the *Virgin, Child and St. Anne*, has been noted in an earlier chapter.[2]

But there are a certain number of drawings done somewhat in the style of woodcuts which may possibly be by the hand of a designer or cutter of wood blocks. Such are the drawings in the manuscript *Livre de Genesis* in the British Museum (Add. MS. 39657, from the Curzon Collection), done with the pen in thick outline, with slight parallel shading, and tinted. From its dialect the manuscript is probably Northern French; and from its costume, about 1450, though the pen-work suggests the latter part of the xv century. It has some relation in style to the Netherlandish *Biblia Pauperum*, and in particular to a draughtsman illustrated on plate xix of Paul Durrieu's *Miniature flamande*. In their crude but vivid handling both may be examples of early popular art.[3]

Two drawings in the British Museum, placed for comparison with the early woodcuts, show a style deceptively near to woodcut in character, and apparently contemporary with the style they reflect, i.e. the *Infant Christ in the midst of Flowers* and the *Virgin and Child in a Glory, with Angels* (C. Dodgson, i. pp. 61 and 78). The same deceptive character is seen in the *Angel appearing to Joachim* originally described by Schreiber as a woodcut, but noted as a drawing in his second edition (S. 624).

[1] See p. 582.

[2] See p. 67, footnote 6. Cf. also p. 93, footnote 2. See also Helmut Lehmann-Haupt, *Schwäbische Federzeichnungen : Studien zur Buchillustration Augsburgs im xv* Jahrhundert, Berlin and Leipzig 1929.

[3] They should be compared with the 'Meister des Wavrin', e.g. in the illustrations to the MS. History of Thebes of 1469 in the Dyson Perrins Collection (see F. Winkler, *Vlämische Buchmalerei*, p. 69).

Other good examples of drawings in the woodcutter's style occur in a copy of Gregorius IX., *Novae Compilationes Decretalium Libri V*, Basle (M. Wenssler) 1478, quoted as No. 71 in J. Rosenthal's Catalogue 80, of 1924 (with reproduction). They fill the spaces which had evidently been intended for woodcut illustration.

An early Italian example of a book with spaces left for woodcuts which were never made is Nicolaus de Lyra, *Postilla super Bibliam*, Rome (Sweynheym and Pannartz) 1471–72. A copy is cited in a catalogue of *L'Art Ancien S.A.* (Lugano 1924), No. 2956, in which a series of pen drawings are added in these spaces, in the style of a weak follower of Mantegna. The drawings were possibly commissioned by an owner of the book in North Italy, but it is noteworthy that the maps in the Ptolemy's *Geographia* printed at Rome by Arnold Buckinck in 1478 are engraved in the style of the Ferrarese 'Tarocchi Cards', so that a North Italian artist might have been working for the Roman printers.

In the same way nearly every copy of the French *Valerius Maximus* of about 1476 has the empty spaces at the head of each book filled with miniatures.[1] French woodcut in the xv century is in general rather more nearly related to the style of the illuminators of manuscripts than the woodcut illustrations of other countries, and it is possible that in 1476 the French printer may have originally intended his book to be illustrated with drawings and not with woodcuts.[2]

It is probable that early woodcut book-illustrations are based on miniatures in MSS. more often than we know. Examples in which definite relationships have been established are the *Cologne Bible* of about 1478–79, the Bruges *Ovid* of 1484, and St. Augustine, *Civitas Dei*, Abbeville 1486–87.

It was evidently the aim of the printers in the first two decades of their practice to imitate a manuscript page in type, coloured initials and illustrations. Just as the type economised in scribes, so the outline woodcut saved the illuminator much labour, and the labour of filling in simply outlined spaces with colour could be given to poorer craftsmen than would be re-

---

[1] *Le Livre de Valerius Maximus translaté de latin en françois par Simon de Hesdin*, n.p., n.d., n.pr. (Paris, certainly not later than 1477), Claudin, i. p. 199. Two copies with illuminations are in the Bibliothèque Nationale, another in the Bibl. S. Geneviève, Paris, and a fourth was described in the Fairfax Murray Catalogue (H. W. Davies, 1910, No. 557).

[2] For the relation of the woodcutter to the illuminator see André Blum, *Des rapports des miniaturistes françaises du xvᵉ siècle avec les premiers artistes-graveurs*, Revue de l'Art Chrétien, 1911, p. 357; and R. Kautzsch, *Einleitende Erörterungen zu einer Geschichte der deutschen Handschriften-Illustration im späteren Mittelalter*, Strassburg 1894 (pp. 60-63, 73, 74, 76-80); and *Die Holzschnitte der Kölner Bibel von 1479*, Strassburg 1896, p. 67, note 27, etc.

quired for both drawing and painting a subject throughout. The printer in fact was working in these early years for a public who could not afford the manuscript. Within a short time, however, both type and illustration achieved individual character apart from the scribe and illuminator. From about 1470 woodcut developed its own schemes of shading in line to deal with modelling and tone, and colour gradually became less essential, and by the end of the century had become superfluous.

Fig. 112. Printer's mark of Günther Zainer.

A German example, in which the illustrations are sometimes printed from wood blocks and sometimes purely painted, is Sensenschmidt's *Missale Benedictinum*, Bamberg 1481 (S. 4676, H. 11267). In one of two copies in the British Museum the *Christ on the Cross* (f. 144 b) is a painting, and the pictorial initial T (f. 145 a) a coloured woodcut; in the other the *Christ on the Cross* is a coloured cut, and the T a painting.[1]

[1] The *Christ on the Cross between the Virgin and St. John* is the regular illustration in all missals, occurring at the *Canon of the Mass*, and often described as the *Canon* cut. Missals and breviaries, being the service-books of the Church (the former the office of the Mass, the latter the abridged daily service, excluding the Eucharist) and in constant use, have for the most part been worn out and destroyed, and of most editions only a few (and sometimes only a single copy) are known, often in cathedral or local libraries. In several of the earliest printed Missals single cuts are found pasted in on fly-leaf or in the binding (e.g. a metal-cut of the *Crucifixion*, S. 2338, in the binding of the Oxford copy of a *Canon of the Mass*, printed by Schoeffer, Mainz, c. 1460, Proctor 68). The earliest German Missals with the *Canon* cut printed in the text are those of Bernhard Richel, Basle, 20th January 1480–81 (*Missale Basiliense*, S. 4670, H. 11266), of Sensenschmidt, Bamberg 1481, of Schoeffer, Mainz 1483 (*Missale Wratislaviense*, S. 4777, H. 11333) and Koberger, Nuremberg 1484 (*Missale Strigoniense*, S. 4763, H. 11429, Budapest). From 1485 Erhard Ratdolt of Augsburg was the most prolific printer of liturgical books (see p. 299). Other subjects most commonly found in their illustration are the *Virgin and Child between Saints*, the *Bishops* or their *coats-of-arms*, the *Agnus Dei*, and an initial T figured with *Abraham's Sacrifice*. See W. L. Schreiber, *Christus am Kreuz. Kanonbilder der im Deutschland gedruckten Messbücher des XV Jahrhunderts*, Strassburg 1910. See also in relation to Venice, p. 501, and France, p. 628. The standard catalogue of Missals is W. H. J. Weale, *Bibliographia Liturgica. Catalogus Missalium*, London 1886 (ed. H. Bohatta, 1928).

Several printers later in the century had recourse to various means of economising in their woodcut material, but not without detriment to the appearance of the book. BELLAERT of Haarlem and GRÜNINGER of Strassburg were notable sinners in this respect, applying the same blocks to various situations and often combining several blocks in one subject (e.g. in Jacobus de Theramo, *Der sonderen Troest (Belial)*, Haarlem 1484, and in Grüninger's *Terence* 1496, *Horace* 1498,[1] and *Virgil* 1502).

Similarly DINCKMUT in his edition of *Seelenwurzgarten*, Ulm 1483 (S. 5229, C. 5345), constantly repeats the same cut, one block, representing the tortures of the damned, being used thirty-seven times.

Fig. 113. Jacob's Ladder, from the *Speculum Humanae Salvationis*, Augsburg 1477.

Moreover, one design, or series of designs, would frequently serve several printers. Copies were constantly being made, with or without leave, for copyright hardly existed, and the same printer would often have to replace worn cuts by new blocks in successive editions.

It is not always an easy task to distinguish copy from original. Immediately recognisable as from different blocks are subjects which appear in reverse directions, for the copyist who does not take the trouble to reverse his drawing from the original print, will make a block that will print the subject reversed. If there is uncertainty as to which is the original of two cuts in reverse to each other, a clue may sometimes be given by details

[1] See C. Dodgson, i. p. 232, D. 32.

wrongly expressed (e.g. a sword held in the left hand). But such details are not always decisive, as even the original cutter may be careless of such reversals of the natural order of things in his prints.

Occasionally copies (or later versions of the same originals) may be found better in quality than earlier cuts, so that quality is not invariably the test of an original. The most interesting copies are those like the cuts in the French edition of Francesco Colonna's *Hypnerotomachia Poliphili* (Paris 1554), which reflect the original series in an entirely new idiom.

The bichrome printed initials of Mainz and the woodcut illustrations of Pfister at Bamberg have already been discussed as isolated phenomena which stand rather apart from the main body of German woodcut decoration and illustration of the xv century. In continuing our survey of the chief woodcut illustrations of the period, we shall pursue a course based on chronology, only in so far as we start with *Augsburg* where appeared the earliest illustrated books after Pfister's at Bamberg. Then we shall pursue a course that follows geographical lines, passing from Augsburg to *Ulm*, leaving aside Munich, the present centre of Bavaria, as no illustration of importance appeared there during the xv century. Then we shall find a few works to mention in the neighbouring towns of *Urach*, *Reutlingen* and *Esslingen* before turning south-east to *Basle*, which only developed as an important centre in the last decade of the century. Thence, after a glance at work in other parts of German Switzerland, we shall journey down the Rhine to *Strassburg*, where the most individual work was produced between 1490 and 1500.

From Strassburg proceeding north to the Palatinate, with *Speier* and *Heidelberg* as its centres, and to the Archbishopric of *Mainz*, where illustrations appeared of comparable interest to those of Augsburg and Ulm, though only after about 1480.

Cologne, our next centre, exhibits closer relations to Netherlandish work, and the same may be said of *Lübeck*, both of which towns are notable for their illustrated Bibles of about 1478–79 and 1494 respectively. From Lübeck we turn south again, and after turning aside for some moments to the Cistercian Convent at *Zinna*, to *Leipzig* and to *Würzburg*, we reach *Nuremberg*, the most vital centre of German graphic art in the last decade of the xv century.

Thence via *Passau* and the Danube we may cross the border, and note the few and rare productions of Austria and Bohemia at *Vienna*, *Brünn* and *Prague*.

Alongside book-illustration we shall intercalate, according to known or conjectured locality, some notes on the single cuts of the period. This treatment is the more justified through the fact that, in the second half of the century, book-illustration offers a standard in the development of the art, and the designer and cutter of the single cuts undoubtedly progressed to some extent along lines indicated by the character of book-illustration and the demands of the printers.

I would here mention only one cut, or rather fragment, which I am unable to place in any group, i.e. an *Angel*, apparently from a subject of the *Crucifixion* (S. 1825 x, Oxford). The fragment alone measures about $11\frac{1}{2} \times 8$ inches, so that the whole subject must have been very large. The angel is holding the end of a cloth, and Schreiber refers to it as part of a subject of *Angels holding the Veronica Napkin*, but the aureoles below (of Christ and St. John?) support the title which has been suggested by Mr. Dodgson. It has a fine breadth of style, and from the character of its work probably dates about 1475.

AUGSBURG [1]

We have already spoken of the Augsburg printer GÜNTHER ZAINER,[2] and the difficulties he encountered from the guilds in regard to extra-mural woodcutters. These difficulties settled, he issued a remarkable series of illustrated books from about 1471 (three years after his first printed book) until his death in 1478. The great qualities of his work and of that of several of the other printers of Augsburg and Ulm were first fully recognised by William Morris.[3]

The Abbot Melchior of SS. Ulrich and Afra, who had helped Zainer in his encounter with the guilds, established a press at his monastery in 1472, and obtained a succession of Augsburg printers to direct and instruct his monks. That Günther Zainer was among those so invited is proved by a MS. note in the Fairfax Murray copy[4] of the *Speculum Humanae Salvationis* (S. 5273, H. 14929), showing that it was printed at the monastery with his type in 1473. Baemler and Sorg also printed at the monastery in the same, and succeeding years, with their own types.

The *Speculum* may be taken as typical of the greater part of Zainer's

---

[1] See Hellmut Lehmann-Haupt, *Schwäbische Federzeichnungen. Studien zur Buchillustration Augsburgs im XV Jahrhundert*, Berlin and Leipzig 1929.

[2] Schramm, *Bilderschmuck der Frühdrucke*, ii. *Günther Zainer in Augsburg*, Leipzig 1920.

[3] William Morris, *On the Artistic Qualities of the Woodcut Books of Ulm and Augsburg in the XV Century*, Bibliographica, I., 1895, 437.

[4] Now in the Pierpont Morgan Library, New York.

woodcut illustration, besides presenting one of the finest examples of balance between type and the illustration on the page.

His Gothic type is strong and simple, and the cuts have the requisite strength of line and simplicity of treatment to preserve this balance. The figures are characteristically squat, with large heads on short bodies; the simple outline design is only slightly helped out with some parallel shading, a scheme which the illuminator was still expected to complete with his colour (so that uncoloured copies are rare); the drawing is angular and of little subtlety, but not lacking in expression or vigour.

Like the majority of Augsburg illustrations the cuts of the *Speculum* are enclosed in double border-lines, and are the width of the page of type. In larger books with two columns the smaller cuts are, as a rule, similarly limited by the breadth of a column of type.

Zainer's *Speculum* must have appeared about the same date as the Netherlandish block-book, with its far shorter version of the text, and there is no direct relation between the designs of the two works. The main idea of the *Speculum Humanae Salvationis* (*Spiegel Menschlicher Behältnis*) was the same as that of the *Biblia Pauperum*, i.e. a harmony between incidents of the Old and New Testaments, and of the German type-printed versions some were fairly independent (like Günther Zainer's), and others more directly influenced in design by the *Biblia Pauperum*.[1]

Günther Zainer and his kinsman Johann Zainer (both originally from Reutlingen) had worked in the 'sixties at Strassburg; both are recorded as

Fig. 114. Initial B, from *Plenarium*, Augsburg 1473.

of the Guild of the Painters and Goldsmiths, to which the printers of Strassburg belonged, and it is probable that they learnt their craft, and practised as writers and illuminators, in Mentelin's printing-house. It is also probable from the incidents of his early years at Augsburg that Günther Zainer may have had some part in the designing of initials, if not of other cuts in his books; but we can do no more than indicate the likelihood of such participation in the illustrative side of their publications by Günther and other early printers, for there are no clues to definite attributions. The Augsburg and Ulm printers were particularly happy in their designs of initials decorated with lily of the valley (*Maiblumen*), of which an example is reproduced in fig. 114.

[1] See under the printers B. Richel of Basle (p. 325), and Peter Drach of Speier (p. 346).

Among other books printed by Günther Zainer, with blocks by the same designer as the *Speculum*, or in very similar style, may be noted:[1]

Jacobus de Voragine, *Leben der Heiligen*, 1471, 1472.
>S.4298, H.9968.
>Later Augsburg editions: Baemler, 1475 and later; Sorg, 1478.

Schreiber has noted that in the *Winterteil* (1471) the blocks are printed separately[2] as the text occasionally strays over the border of the cuts. This seems to imply that the blocks were thicker than the depth of the type. This difference was soon adjusted to the economy of book-illustration, and the *Sommerteil* (1472) shows no such anomaly.

Jacobus de Theramo, *Belial*, 1472.
>S.4279, C.5805.
>Later Augsburg editions: Baemler, 1473; Sorg, 1479, 1481.

Ingold, *Das goldene Spiel*, 1472.
>S.4259, H.9187.

Plenarium, 1473.
>S.4945, C.2316.
>Later Augsburg editions: Baemler, 1474; Sorg, 1478.

J. M. Tuberinus, *Geschichte und Legende von dem seligen Kind Simon*, n.d. (about 1475–76).
>S.5258, H.15658.

Schwabenspiegel (*Spiegel kaiserlicher und gemeiner Landrechte*), n.d. (about 1475–76).
>S.4465, H.9868, and S.4466, H.9869.

Johannes Damascenus, *Josaphat und Barlaam*, n.d. (about 1477).
>S.4346, H.5915.
>Later Augsburg edition: Sorg, n.d.

Jacobus de Cessolis, *Schachzabelbuch*, 1477. S.4273, H.4895.

Apart from its smaller cuts the *Plenarium* has an important full-page frontispiece with a representation of *Christ blessing* (fig. 115).[3] It is the

---

[1] Many series of designs for popular books were repeated by one printer after another, sometimes from the same blocks, sometimes from copies. I have aimed at referring to books in their first issues, sometimes appending later editions, without specifying whether the illustrations in these later editions are reprints or copies. Details and dates in Muther can only be accepted after careful checking.   [2] Cf. p. 411.

[3] The passages from the Epistles and Gospels read in the Mass form the chief contents of a *Plenarium*. For further details see Paul Drews, *Realencyklopädie für protestantische Theologie und Kirche*, 3ᵉ Aufl., xv. p. 486.

Fig. 115. Christ blessing, from *Plenarium*, Augsburg 1473.

Fig. 116. Initial U, from the German Bible, Augsburg (G. Zainer), about 1475–76.

earliest issue of a compilation of which numerous editions, with illustrations of the Life of Christ, were published throughout Germany (though chiefly at Augsburg and Strassburg) during the xv century. Similar series of cuts appeared in editions of Guillermus, *Postilla super Epistolas et Evangelia*.[1]

Günther Zainer's large folio *German Bible* demands some notice, as it is one of the three earliest illustrated Bibles printed in Germany, and was probably printed in 1475 or 1476 (S. 3456, H. 3133). The two others of near date are those of PFLANZMANN of Augsburg (S. 3455, H. 3131), and of SENSENSCHMIDT and FRISNER of Nuremberg[2] (S. 3457, H. 3132).

Pflanzmann's Bible has been often conjecturally dated about 1470 (e.g. by Muther), and regarded in consequence as the earliest German illustrated Bible. But the only dated books printed by Pflanzmann belong to the year 1475, so that a date about 1475 or 1476 is the most probable, and it is difficult to decide whether Pflanzmann or Günther Zainer has the priority. Sensenschmidt's Bible was also conjecturally dated about 1472 by Muther, but as it was printed by Sensenschmidt and Frisner (whose partnership occurred between 1474 and 1476), it cannot be before 1474, and is more likely to have appeared about 1476.

In Zainer's and Sensenschmidt's Bibles, the illustrations are chiefly contained in the pictorial capitals, the designs correspond fairly closely, and it is almost certain that Sensenschmidt's blocks, though the more accomplished in cutting, were the later works and based on Zainer's originals.

Pflanzmann's cuts are single column upright blocks, generally occurring at the beginning of each book; those for the prophets are several times repeated, while the New Testament is sparsely illustrated. In cutting,

---

[1] E.g. at Lyon (see p. 604) and Salamanca (see p. 754).

[2] For the general subject of early German Bibles see Richard Muther, *Die ältesten deutschen Bilder-Bibeln*, Munich 1883 (conjectured dates erroneous); Albert Schramm, *Die illustrierten Bibel der Incunabelzeit*, Leipzig 1922.

Fig. 117. Initial U, from the German Bible, Nuremberg (Sensenschmidt and Frisner), about 1476.

they are similar in character to Zainer's blocks (angular design, and slight parallel shading), and one degree poorer in quality. In design, they are for the most part independent, though occasional correspondences occur, which may be the repetition of typical renderings. The two designs of the *Days of Creation* in Pflanzmann similarly have their counterpart in the *Rudimentum Noviciorum*, Lübeck (Lucas Brandis) 1475.

Two other illustrated German Bibles, those of Cologne (about 1478–79) and of Lübeck (1494), both of far more artistic importance than the three just mentioned, will be described later.

Artistically the most attractive of Günther Zainer's books is the undated Rodericus Zamorensis, *Spiegel des menschlichen Lebens* (S. 5102, H. 13948), which was probably issued about 1475–76. The MS., a translation by Heinrich Steinhöwel of the *Speculum Vitae Humanae* preserved in the Munich Library, is dated 1474, and in the *Habsburg Genealogy*, which stands at the head of the printed volume, an event of 1475 is included.[1]

Unlike other illustrations published at Augsburg, the woodcuts are nearly related to Ulm work,

Fig. 118. From the German Bible, Augsburg (Pflanzmann), about 1476.

and the fact that Steinhöwel lived at Ulm and edited various books published in that town (of which more later) renders it probable that

[1] I.e. unless the 1475 given for the Baptism of Maximilian (*b.* 1459, later Emperor) is a misprint.

the blocks were done by an Ulm artist in touch with Steinhöwel, and sent to Günther Zainer for printing.

There were undoubtedly two designers engaged on these illustrations.[1] Some thirteen or fourteen blocks (i.e. ff. 1 a, 3 a, 8 a, 9 a, 48 b, 50 a, 53 a, 63 b, 65 b, 66 b, 69 a, 83 a, 99 b, 135 b) are somewhat more grotesque in their convention than the rest, with a tendency to parallel lines of drapery, and very definitely lined features, and somewhat related in style to work published at Mainz and Speier, e.g. the frontispiece to Schoeffer's *Gart der*

Fig. 119. The Singing Lesson, from *Spiegel des menschlichen Lebens*, Augsburg, about 1475–76.

Gesuntheit (Mainz 1485) and the subject cuts in Breydenbach's *Peregrinationes* (Mainz 1486).[2] The illustration of the *Singing Lesson*, f. 83 (fig. 119), is a good example of this group.

The remaining small cuts are by a more genial, though not more gifted, illustrator; inclining to a less angular style, and to slightly fuller use of parallel shading. The illustration of a *Wedding*, f. 29 (fig. 120), is characteristic of this latter group.

Both groups show taller figures with smaller heads than those of Günther

---

[1] See Erwin Rosenthal, *Die Anfänge der Holzschnittillustration in Ulm*, Halle 1912.

[2] Cf. pp. 352–356. He is more grotesque and formal, and less functional in line and shading, than the designer of the *Spiegel menschlicher Behältnis*, printed by Drach at Speier.

Zainer's *Speculum*, and there is far greater harmony and sense of silhouette
in the design.

The full-page woodcut at the beginning of the book illustrating the
Genealogy of the House of Habsburg is an exceedingly skilful piece of
work, by which a somewhat monotonous material is welded into a most
successful decorative design. Most of the cuts appeared later in editions
issued by Baemler, Augsburg 1479 (S. 5103, H. 13949), by N. Philippi
and M. Reinhard at Lyon 1482 (*Le Miroir de la Vie Humaine*), and by
Hurus at Saragossa 1491 (*Spejo dela Vida Humana*).

Fig. 120. A Wedding, from the *Spiegel des menschlichen Lebens*, Augsburg, about 1475–76.

Like Günther Zainer, JOHANN BAEMLER [1] was known as a scribe for some
years before he worked as a printer, his name appearing as *Schreiber* in
Augsburg records as early as 1453. Moreover, his name in copies of
Eggestein's second *German Bible*, Strassburg 1466 (H. 3037), preserved
at Wolfenbüttel, and of Mentelin's Augustinus, *De Arte Predicandi*, Strassburg, about 1466 (H. 1956), in the John Rylands Library, Manchester,
are among the rare records identifying rubricator's work. On this evidence he seems to have learnt his printing, like the Zainers, at Strassburg.
Two miniature paintings are also known bearing his signature (B. Quaritch,

[1] See A. Schramm, *Bilderschmuck der Frühdrucke*, iii. *Johann Baemler in Augsburg*, Leipzig
1921.

General Catalogue, London 1887, vi. 35777). His activity as a printer in Augsburg extended from 1474 to 1495.

A considerable number of his books contain cuts printed from blocks already used by Günther Zainer, or from copies of Zainer's illustrations. The list of his more important illustrated works here given is chiefly of those of which he was the original publisher:

Eusebius, *Historie vom grossen Alexander* (translated by J. Hartlieb), 1473.
    S. 3132, H. 785.
    Later Augsburg editions: Sorg, 1478, 1480, 1483; Strassburg, M. Schott, 1488 and 1493.
    This and many other books of Baemler contain cuts designed in the same style as G. Zainer's *Speculum*, but generally less well cut.
    The interesting *Portrait Bust* is generally regarded as reproducing Eusebius, but a copy in *Apollonius von Tyrus* (German, by Steinhöwel), Augsburg, Dinckmut, 1495, is labelled *Alexander*.
Gregorius I, *Dialogi* (German), 1473 (printed in the Monastery of SS. Ulrich and Afra).
    S. 4119, H. 7970.
Guido de Colonna, *Historie von Troia*, about 1474.
    S. 4131, H. 5514.
    Several of the battle-scenes repeated from Eusebius, *Alexander*.
    Later Augsburg editions: G. Zainer, about 1476 and 1477; Sorg, 1479 and 1482; Schoensperger, 1488.
    Strassburg: M. Schott, 1489; B. Kistler, 1499.
Jean d'Arras, *Melusina*, 1474 (and 1480).
    S. 4626, H. 11064; S. 4630, C. 3974.
    Later Augsburg edition: Sorg, n.d. (about 1485).
    Another edition, n.d., n.p. (S. 4627, H. 11063), is now attributed to B. Richel, Basle, about 1476. The illustrations suggested by Baemler's edition, but fairly independent.
    Strassburg: Knoblochtzer, n.d., about 1478 (S. 4629, H. 11061); J. Prüss, n.d., about 1481 (S. 4631) (both the latter based on Richel's Basle edition).
Von den sieben Todsünden und von den sieben Tugenden, 1474.
    S. 5354, H. 15535.
    Later editions 1479 and 1482.

Konrad von Megenburg, *Buch der Natur,* 1475.

   S. 3778, H. 4041.

   Later editions, 1478, 1481.

   Numerous later editions by other printers: e.g. Augsburg, Sorg, n.d.; Schoensperger, 1499.

   This is one of Baemler's most individual works, a book on the Essence of Natural Things, human, animal, vegetable, mineral, etc., with twelve full-page cuts, of which one is here reproduced.

Johann Baemler, *Chronica von allen Kaisern und Königen,* 1476.

   S. 3754, H. 9792.

   Generally, but erroneously, known as Königshofen's Chronicle.

Geschichte des Königs Apollonius von Tyrus, 1476.

   S. 3341, H. 1295.

   Later editions: Sorg, 1479, 1480; Dinckmut, 1495. *Buch der Kunst dadurch der weltliche Mensch mag geistlich werden,* 1477.

   S. 3647, H. 4036.

   Later editions, Baemler, 1478 and 1491, and in 1497 by Schoensperger under the title *Ein löblich Büchlin der Gmachelschafft zwischen Gott und der Seele.*

Robertus de Sancto Remigio, *Historie wie die Türken die christlichen Kirchen angefochten,* 1482.

   S. 5391, H. 8753.

   The earliest illustrated book on the Crusades. Some of the cuts repeated from the *Historie von Troia.*

Calendar in German (in book form), 1483.

   S. 4417, H. 9736.

   This may be noted as one of the most interesting of Baemler's illustrated Calendars.

ANTON SORG,[1] who is recorded as *Briefmaler* and *Kartenmaler* soon after the middle of the xv century, became the most prolific of the Augsburg printers, issuing over a hundred illustrated books between 1475 and 1493. Among a great variety of subject, they include the first editions of many romances of considerable literary interest, though their illustration is below the average of Günther Zainer and Baemler in quality of cutting. He frequently followed Günther Zainer and Baemler with later editions of their books, e.g. in his *Spiegel Menschlicher Behältnis* of 1476, with cuts based on Günther Zainer's *Speculum,* while in his *Aesop* of about 1480 he reprinted

---

[1] A. Schramm, *Bilderschmuck der Frühdrucke,* iv. *Anton Sorg in Augsburg,* Leipzig 1921.

the cuts originally issued by Johann Zainer at Ulm. His most richly illustrated book is Ulrich von Reichenthal, *Concilium zu Constanz*, 1483 (S. 5095,

Fig. 121. Studies of Trees, from Konrad von Megenburg, *Buch der Natur*, Augsburg 1475.

H. 5610),[1] but its subject and portrait cuts are of much less value than its wealth of heraldic illustration.

The little cuts in Cyrillus, *Buch der natürlichen Weisheit* (translation of the *Speculum Sapientiae*), 1490 (S. 3650, H. 4047), a popular book of fables, are more generally attractive, though crudely enough cut. The frontispiece (eight figures representing virtues and vices) is cut in an angular style,

[1] Facsimile, ed. E. Voulliéme, Muller & Co., Potsdam.

with strong outline, similar in character of composition to the company of philosophers which appears as frontispiece to the *Gart der Gesuntheit* Mainz (Schoeffer) 1485, and *Hortus Sanitatis*, Mainz (Meydenbach), 1491, and resembling the latter in style of work as well. The following illustrated books printed by Sorg also deserve mention:

> *Die neue Ehe (von der Kindheit und von dem Leiden Jesu Christi)*, 1476.
>> S. 3723, H. 4057.
>> Several of the blocks based on line-engravings, e.g. on IA of Zwolle.
> Hans Schiltberger, *Reisebuch*, n.d. (about 1476).
>> S. 5208, H. 6674.
>> Schiltberger was a prisoner in Turkey, 1395–1417.
>> The book is often found together with the two following works:
> *Historie von Herzog Ernst von Bayern*, n.d. (about 1476).
>> S. 3908, H. 6672.
> *Historie von St. Brandon*, n.d. (about 1476).
>> S. 3533, H. 3718.
> *Historie von Herzog Leuppold und seinem Sohn Wilhelm von Oesterreich*, 1481.
>> S. 4492, H. 11041.
> *Seelentrost*, 1478.
>> S. 5225, H. 14582.
>> Full-page cuts illustrating the Ten Commandments.
> Otto van Passau, *Die verundzwanzig Alten* (or *Der guldin Tron*), n.d. (about 1479) and 1480.
>> S. 4877 and 4878, H. 12128.
>> Later editions, Strassburg, J. Prüss, about 1482; M. Schott, 1483.
> *Passion*, various editions from 1480.
>> S. 3739, H. 12441, etc.
> Mandeville, *Reise nach Jerusalem*, 1481.
>> S. 4798, H. 10647.
> Hans Tucher, *Reise in das gelobte Land*, 1486.
>> H. 15667.
>> The Portrait representing Tucher is copied from the portrait of Marco Polo in the latter's *Reisebeschreibung*, Nuremberg (Creussner) 1477, showing how little actual truth of representation mattered, as the same features serve for both.
>> Cf. edition by Knoblochtzer, Strassburg, 1484 (see below, p. 337).

Suso, *Buch das der Seusse heisst*, 1482.
    S. 5325, C. 5688.
St. Jerome, *Buch der Altväter (Vitas Patrum)*, 1482.
    S. 4217, H. 8605.
Historie von Tristan und Isolde, 1484.
    S. 5381. Facsimile, Hyperion-Verlag, Munich
Boccaccio, *Cento Novelle*, 1490.
    S. 3505, H. 3281.
Ars Memorativa, n.d. (about 1490).
    S. 3369, H. 1827 and 1828.

The illustrations to Flavius Vegetius Renatus, *Von der Ritterschaft*, printed at Augsburg by Johann Wiener, probably about 1476 (S. 5414, H. 15916), were described by Muther with various errors. The book was translated by Ludwig Hohenwang,[1] but there is no reason to infer from the text that he did more than commission the blocks. Even so they are of small artistic interest, as they are almost certainly copied (and in reverse) from the Verona edition of Valturius, *De Re Militari* (1472), and not derived directly from the same original manuscript. The cuts are all placed at the end of the book, with occasional type-printed headings. They were probably printed after the text of the book, and, in view of the quality of the impression, possibly by hand.

LUDWIG HOHENWANG is also known as a printer (though not of this book) at Augsburg in 1477, and at Basle in 1487.

JOHANN SCHOENSPERGER may be noted among the more prolific printers of illustrated books, but most of his illustrations were based on work previously issued by other printers (e.g. his German *Herbarius* of 22nd August 1485, based on Schoeffer's Mainz edition of March 1485, and numerous works following in the wake of the Augsburg printers, Baemler and Sorg). His use of stencil in the colours of his botanical woodcuts in the *Herbarius* contrasts with Ratdolt's method of colour-printing.[2]

Among his more attractive series of cuts are the *Roundels of the Months* (within treble border-line) done for a German Calendar of about 1487 (reprinted 1490) (S. 4420 and 4422, Muther 93, pl. 31-35). Muther speaks of them as the prototype of many other Calendar cuts of the period, but they appear themselves to have a prototype in another series, at Berlin,

---

[1] Muther made another error in relation to Ludwig Hohenwang, and the illustrations of *De Fide Concubinarum* (see p. 334).

[2] See pp. 299 and 462.

which Schreiber attributes to the printer JOHANN BLAUBIRER, about 1485 (S. 4419 a; fig. 122). One of the later series of copies was that printed by Johann Schaeffler, at Ulm, in 1498 and 1499 (Schramm, vol. vii. 348-359). Among the Augsburg printers of the later xv century ERHARD RATDOLT holds a special place, whether as a link between Italian and German printing, or for his practice of printing occasional illustrations from two or more colour blocks.[1] These considerations apart, his illustrations in themselves are of less interest than those of the other Augsburg printers already noticed, and none of his books is richly illustrated.

His work at Venice between 1476 and 1486 will be described with Italian work in a later chapter. He was pressed by two successive Bishops of Augsburg to return to his native city to print liturgical books, yielded to the invitation of the Bishop

Fig. 122. February, from a German Calendar, Augsburg (Blaubirer ?), about 1485.

Friedrich von Hohenzollern in 1486, and issued numerous works between 1487 and 1516. Apart from the liturgical books which formed his chief output,[2] he also specialised, as at Venice, in astronomical and mathematical works.

Much of the type and decorative material used in his Augsburg books were of his Italian period, notably the capital letters with white designs on black ground. Certain black-line pictorial initials were added at Augsburg (e.g. several in the *Psalterium Latino-Germanicum* of 1494, H. 13510). His attractive *printer's mark* (cut in several sizes, and always printed in black and red) is Augsburg work, and so are practically all the cuts of various *Bishops, Patron Saints,* and the *Crucifixion* in his liturgical and

---

[1] See Walter Gräff, *Älteste deutsche Farbenholzschnitte,* Zeitschrift für Bücherfreunde, N.F. i., Leipzig 1919, p. 335.

[2] See Karl Schottenloher, *Die liturgischen Druckwerke E. Ratdolts aus Augsburg 1485-1522,* Mainz (Gutenberg Gesellschaft) 1922.

Fig. 123. Initial B, from the Psalter,
Augsburg (Ratdolt) 1494.

other works printed at Augsburg. Several of these unsigned cuts dating between 1499 and 1502 are now commonly regarded as the work of HANS BURGKMAIR the elder (*b.* 1473), and one has been attributed to him dating as early as 1491.[1] The *Virgin and Child with SS. Corbinian and Sigismund* (Schottenloher, p. 46), in the *Freising Missal* of 1502, is one of these, and certainly by the same designer is the *Virgin and Child between SS. Conrad and Pelagius*,[2] dated in one state 1499 (S. 2022, Schottenloher, pp. 62 and 63), used in the *Constance Breviary*, 1499 (S. 3595, H. 3830), and the *Constance Missal*, 1505. In the 1499 impression St. Pelagius has cap and beard; in the impression reproduced by Schottenloher from the 1505 Missal, the Saint's head is re-cut, beardless and without cap. Schreiber describes these states in the reverse order.

I would also mention here that a few single woodcuts have recently been attributed to another great Augsburg painter, HANS HOLBEIN the elder, e.g. an *Annunciation*, among the blocks of the Derschau Collection at Berlin, which Friedländer dates about 1500,[3] and a *Virgin of Pity* at Basle.[4]

Among the chief editions of Ratdolt's liturgical books issued in the xv century may be noted:

Augsburg Obsequiale, 1487.

S. 4861, H. 11925.

Ratdolt's first Augsburg book. Containing a cut representing Ratdolt's patron, *Bishop Friedrich von Hohenzollern*, printed in black and two or three colours, the first example, apart from Schoeffer's

---

[1] I.e. the *Virgin and Child in a Glory of Flames* (Freising Breviary, 1491; Freising Obsequiale, 1493). See Hans Rupé, *Beiträge zum Werke H. Burgkmairs des Älteren.* Dissertation, Freiburg im Breisgau 1912; Hans Rupé, *H. Burgkmair I. as an illustrator of books.* Print Collector's Quarterly, x (1923) 167.

[2] Dörnhöffer, *Beiträge zur Kunstgeschichte F. Wickhoff gewidmet*, Vienna 1903, p. 116. Dodgson, who formerly attributed this cut to J. Breu (Pr. Jahrbuch, 1900, p. 207), now accepts as Burgkmair.

[3] M. J. Friedländer, Zeitschrift für bildende Kunst, N.F. xxxiii., 1922, 101.

[4] H. Rupé, Münchner Jahrbuch, N.F. iii., 1926, 1. Rupé dates this about 1500; Dodgson inclines to place it about ten years later.

Fig. 124. The Virgin and Child, with St. Hermagoras and St. Fortunatus, from *Aquileia Missal*, Augsburg (Ratdolt) 1494.

stamped capitals, of such colour-printing in Germany. Several of
the cuts noted below are found similarly printed.

Augsburg Missal, 1491.
> S. 4665, H. 11260.
> Includes a cut of the *Virgin and Child, SS. Ulrich and Afra.*

Freising Breviary, 1491
> S. 3600, H. 3842.
> With a cut of the *Virgin and Child within a Glory of Flames*; the
> earliest cut attributed to Burgkmair.

Freising Missal, 1492.
> S. 4699, H. 11303.
> Includes cuts of the *Virgin and Child, King Sigismund and St.
> Corbinian* and of the *Christ on the Cross* (in the *Canon*).

Freising Obsequiale, 1493.
> S. 4866, H. 11930.
> Includes the cut from the *Freising Breviary.*

Brixen Missal, 1493.
> S. 4678, H.C. 11273.
> Includes cuts of the *Virgin and Child, SS. Peter and Paul* and
> the *Christ on the Cross.*

Passau Missal, 1494 (and 1498).
> S. 4741, 4742; H. 11349, 11350.
> With a cut of *SS. Valentine, Stephen and Maximilian* (which
> has been attributed to Burgkmair).

Aquileia Missal, 1494.
> S. 4662, H. 11258.
> Includes cuts of the *Virgin and Child, with SS. Hermagoras and
> Fortunatus* (fig. 124) and the *Christ on the Cross* (in the *Canon*).

Antiphonarium, 1495.
> S. 3337, H. 1156.
> Includes a cut of the *Virgin and Child and two Saints.*

Regensburg Breviary, 1496.
> S. 3622, H. 3885.
> With a cut of *St. Peter.*

Chur Missal, 1497.
> S. 4693, H.C. 11287.
> With a cut of the *Virgin and Child and Saints.*

Constance Breviary, 1499.
> S. 3595, H. 3830.

Apart from the liturgical books may be mentioned his edition of Johannes de Thwrocz, *Chronica Hungarorum*, of June 1488, though its chief cuts are based on the Brünn edition of three months earlier. Original are the little *battle scenes*, with attractive landscape backgrounds, one of which is here

Fig. 125. Battle scene, from Johannes de Thwrocz, *Chronica Hungarorum*, Augsburg (Ratdolt) 1488.

reproduced. The full-page cut representing the *Tartar Inroad into Hungary* is more skilful in drawing than its original, but less vivid in character.

Among Ratdolt's miscellaneous books which contain small cuts of some interest may be mentioned:

Johannes Angelus, *Astrolabium*, 1488.
    S. 3316, H. 1100 (the figures of the *Planets* copied from the cuts in Ratdolt's Venice edition of 1482; the little figures illustrate the horoscopes first used in this book and copied in a Venice edition printed by Emericus de Spira, 1494).
Albumasar, *Flores Astrologiae*, 1488.
    S. 3073, H. 609.
Leopoldus, *Compilatio de Astrorum Scientia*, 1489.
    S. 4493, H. 10042.
Albumasar, *Introductorium in Astronomiam*, 1489.
    S. 3075, H. 612.
Albumasar, *De Magnis Conjunctionibus*, 1489.
    S. 3072, H. 611.

HANS SITTICH should be mentioned for his *Ringbüchlein*, with twenty-one cuts illustrating the art of wrestling, which had been dated by Muther about 1489–90, though it is probably no earlier than 1511 (see p. 261).

HANS SCHAUR, who printed a few books in Augsburg between 1491 and 1500, also issued certain broadsides and books at Munich about 1481 and 1482, e.g. the German popular guide to Rome, *Wie Rom gebauet ward*

(H. 11210), usually known under its later title *Mirabilia Romae*, and a broadside *Zeichen der falschen Gulden*,[1] with a woodcut representing ten coins (S. 4176, *Einbl.*, Kommission für den GW., 1914, No. 1566). A single sheet *Confession Table* in the British Museum dated 1481 (S. 1855) is signed *hanns schawr*, and the cut as well as printing might be his work, and an undated *Virgin with the Rosary* at Nuremberg (S. 1128),[2] which contains a reference to Pope Sixtus IV (regn. 1471–84), also bears his name. Very near in style to the *Confession Table* is a sheet dated 1482 representing the *Ten Ages of Man*, in the British Museum (S. 1881).

HANS RÜST (RIST) is another Augsburg craftsman (recorded as a *Kartenmacher* in various Augsburg documents between 1477 and 1497) who was responsible for a strong but crudely cut representation of *Death* (Munich, S. 1885), and for a woodcut *Map of the World*, to which we shall recur later.[3]

ULM

Ulm had been famous in the late XIV and early XV century as the chief centre for the making and distribution of playing-cards throughout Europe,[4] and its record in the early years of woodcut illustration was as brilliant as that of any other town in Germany. But nearly all its early printers fell on evil days, and were hampered in their publishing by business difficulties, in many cases possibly due to the losses inherent in the frequent visitations of the plague (particularly in the years 1473, 1474, 1483 to 1485, and 1494). Augsburg was a richer commercial centre, and its larger colony of printers would have had more chance of pulling through these years of devastation.

But in the two decades from 1470 to 1490 Ulm possessed illustrators more gifted than any of the same period at Augsburg.[5] That two members of the same family, Günther and Johann Zainer, were printing in Augsburg and Ulm respectively must have to some extent encouraged closer relations, as has been surmised in one instance already noted in

---

[1] See C. Haebler, '*Falsche-Gulden*' *Blätter*, Zeitschrift für Bücherfreunde xi (1907) 219.
[2] S. 1129 is another version of the same subject, bearing an indistinct coat-of-arms (Ulm ?) and dated 1485.　　　　　[3] See p. 315.　　　　　[4] See p. 84.
[5] See Erwin Rosenthal, *Die Anfänge der Holzschnittillustration in Ulm*, Dissertation, Halle 1912; Monatshefte für Kunstwissenschaft, 1913, p. 185; Ernst Weil, *Der Ulmer Holzschnitt im* xv*ten Jahrhundert*, Berlin 1923; Erwin Rosenthal, *Zur Ulmer Formschneidekunst im* xv *Jahrhundert* (Beiträge zur Forschung: Studien aus dem Antiquariat J. Rosenthal), Munich 1930; W. Cohn, *Untersuchungen zur Geschichte des deutsch. Einblattholzschnitts*, Strassburg 1934, p. 22.

which Ulm designs were published in an Augsburg book (Rodericus Zamorensis, *Spiegel des menschlichen Lebens*).

JOHANN ZAINER,[1] who, like Günther, had learnt his craft at Strassburg, must have settled at Ulm about 1472, for his first book (Steinhöwel, *Büchlein der Ordnung der Pestilenz*) was dated 11th January 1473 (S. 5312, H. 15058).[2] Its only woodcut decoration is a half-border and capitals (U with *Martyrdom of St. Sebastian* on the first page, the other capitals being in plain outline without pictures). We have already referred to Heinrich Steinhöwel as the author of the translation from Rodericus Zamorensis, *Spiegel des menschlichen Lebens*, published at Augsburg about 1475–76. Besides being medical officer to the town of Ulm and the writer of various medical books, he was one of the most distinguished humanists of the day. He had travelled in Italy and other parts of Europe, and did much to introduce foreign literature to general readers in Germany by his translations. He was probably as much interested as his printer, Johann Zainer, in directing his illustration.

The first of Johann Zainer's fully illustrated works was Boccaccio, *De Claris Mulieribus*, issued in two Latin editions with some eighty cuts, 1473 (H. 3329 and variant), and in two undated editions with about four cuts less in Steinhöwel's German version (S. 3506, 3507, H. 3333, 3334). To the same year also belongs Petrarch, *Historia Griseldis*[3] (S. 4914, C. 4715), with its ten illustrations in similar style, published as a sort of epilogue to the Boccaccio.

The first page is decorated with a beautiful and entertaining half-border, including the capital letter S (fig. 126). The other illustrations are oblongs about 3 × 4¼ inches in size, full of life and humour, but restrained in action. The figures are longer, smaller-headed and more graceful than those in most Augsburg blocks of the same period, and the compositions are more rhythmical in character. As an example of book-production in fine type, good printing and clear cutting of blocks, the Boccaccio does not reach the same level as Günther Zainer's contemporary books, such as the *Speculum Humanae Salvationis*, but in the gentle and alluring character of its designs it easily surpasses the Augsburg work. The *Procris and Cephalus*

---

[1] See A. Schramm, *Bilderschmuck der Frühdrucke*, v., *Johann Zainer in Ulm*, Leipzig 1923; Johann Wegener, *Die Zainer in Ulm*, Strassburg 1904.

[2] See Karl Sudhoff, *Der Ulmer Stadtarzt und Schriftsteller Heinrich Steinhöwel. Mit Faksimile von Steinhöwels Büchlein der Pestilenz*, Ulm 1473 (issued with A. C. Klebs, *Die ersten gedruckten Pestschriften*, Munich 1926).

[3] Facsimile of the German ed. (C. 4715), ed. E. Vouilliéme, Muller & Co., Potsdam.

Fig. 126. Initial S and half-border, from Boccaccio,
De Claris Mulieribus, Ulm (J. Zainer), 1473.

is a good example of more lively action, while the *Sappho* (fig. 127) shows the more gentle characteristics and an excellent sense of interior composition. The designs were copied a few years later in Sorg's Augsburg edition of 1479, while those of the *Historia Griseldis* were repeated at Augsburg by Sorg (n.d.) and Baemler (1482).

More powerful than the Boccaccio designs are those in Johann Zainer's Aesop, *Vita et Fabulae* (*Das Buch und Leben des hochberühmten Fabeldichters Aesop*), S. 3020, H. 330,[1] which was issued about 1476–77, to which the *Historia Sigismundae* formed a supplement (S. 4487). The original blocks of the *Aesop* were printed later at Augsburg by Günther Zainer about 1477–78 (S. 3025, H. 331),[2] by Sorg soon after 1480, and those of *Sigismunda* by Baemler in 1482 (S. 4490), and the popularity of the work is shown by the fact that the designs were borrowed in some twenty German editions within the xv century.

The book appeared both in Latin and in a German version by Heinrich Steinhöwel. Parts of Aesop had appeared before in German in such popular collections of Fables as Boner's *Edelstein* (see p. 276), and Steinhöwel and his artist no doubt referred to such series, and perhaps to Boner's MSS. such as those preserved

[1] W. Worringer, *Hauptwerke des Holzschnittes*, Munich (Piper & Co.) 1924.
[2] Facsimile ed. E. Voulliéme, Potsdam (Muller & Co.) 1922.

at Munich and Heidelberg. The illustrations to Aesop's Life were entirely original, and show the designer at his best (e.g. *Young Aesop and the Philosopher*, fig. 128). The difference in character in drawing between the *Boccaccio* and the *Aesop* cuts is more than can be explained by a few years' development: it almost certainly shows the hand of another draughtsman. He is more naturalistic in his drawing of the figure; his lines are more functional in their rendering of the varieties of form; they tend to fall in short knots and curves rather than in a continued decorative

Fig. 127. Sappho, from Boccaccio, *De Claris Mulieribus*, Augsburg 1473.

stroke, giving more articulation to the joints and more volume and modelling to face and figure. He shows, moreover, considerably more interest in his landscape backgrounds than most of his contemporary woodcut designers.

In Ulm illustration the *Aesop* master stands alone, and his nearest relation in style is found in the *Spiegel menschlicher Behältnis* printed at Speier about 1478, and in some of the cuts in the *Hortus Sanitatis* and the *Cronecken der Sassen* printed at Mainz in 1491 and 1492 respectively (see pp. 351, 352). In fact so near is the relation that it seems possible that they are the work of the same designer. And the disappearance of this very individual personality from participation in further works at Ulm adds colour to the hypothesis that he left the district. In general character, in the vigour and naturalism of their drawing, there is considerable resemblance in both the *Aesop* and the other works mentioned, to the style of the Master of the Amsterdam Cabinet (the Master of the Hausbuch), but not, I think, sufficient to justify the identification which has been suggested.[1]

One very problematic work should perhaps be quoted in this connection, i.e. Johann Lichtenberger, *Prognosticatio*, n.d., n.p., n.pr. (S. 4499, H. 10080), as the general style of its illustration suggests relationship both to the *Aesop* master and the Mainz cuts mentioned above, and even more to the *Totentanz* (S. 5372), which is now generally ascribed to Heidelberg or Mainz. The *Prognosticatio* is generally assigned to Johann Zainer, about

Fig. 128. Young Aesop and the Philosopher, from Aesop, *Vita et Fabulae*, Ulm, about 1476–77.

1488, but it is by no means certain, and its cuts were printed in 1492 by J. Meydenbach at Mainz (S. 4500, H. 10082). The *Totentanz* itself has been sometimes ascribed to Johann Zainer, Ulm, e.g. by Schreiber, and it would not be surprising if both were found to belong to the region of Heidelberg or Mainz.[2]

There are many beautiful woodcut capitals and pieces of border decoration (generally half-borders, i.e. for the top and left side of the page) in Johann Zainer's books not otherwise illustrated, especially between 1473

---

[1] For book-illustrations printed at Ulm, Augsburg, Esslingen, Urach, Nuremberg, Heidelberg and Speier attributed to this master see K. F. Leonhardt and H. T. Bossert, *Studien zur Hausbuchmeisterfrage*, Zeitschrift, N.F. xxiii., 1912, 132, 191, 239; W. Bühler, *Heinrich Mang der Hausbuchmeister*, Mitteil. der Gesellsch. für vervielf. Kunst, 1931, p. 1. For further bibliography in this relation see notes below in reference to books printed at Speier, Heidelberg and Mainz, p. 346.

[2] Cf. p. 345, for further notes on the *Prognosticatio*.

Fig. 129. Initial O, from Alvarus Pelagius, *De Planctu Ecclesiae*, Ulm 1474.

and 1476. Noteworthy is the half-border with the figure of a fool which appears in several books, e.g. Duranti, *Rationale*, 1473 (H. 6474), Petrus Berchorius, *Liber Bibliae Moralis*, 1474 (H. 2794), and Alvarus Pelagius, *De Planctu Ecclesiae*, 1474 (S. 4904, H. 891). After the later edition of the *Rationale* (18th March 1475, H. 6475), the half-border shows an amusing change and the figure of the fool was cut out and replaced by the figure of a student, appearing thus in Gritsch, *Quadragesimale*, of the 20th October 1475 (H. 8063). One of the most attractive of his pictorial and anthropomorphic capitals, the O from Alvarus Pelagius, *De Planctu Ecclesiae*, is reproduced in fig. 129.

The most interesting of Johann Zainer's later illustrated books is the *Geistliche Auslegung des Lebens Jesu Christi* (S. 3722, H. 2146), which was published without name of place, printer or date. Richard Muther was right in placing the book at Ulm, though his conjectural date of 1470 was certainly too early, and confusion was caused later by one of Robert Proctor's few errors in ascribing the book to the printer Schobser of Augsburg as late as 1494-95. It is now fairly established that it is in the same type of Johann Zainer's, as e.g. Peregrinus, *Sermones*, n.d., about 1485 (H. 12581),[1] with some of the same woodcut capitals which appeared in J. Nider, *Sermones*, n.d., about 1480 (H. 11802), so that a conjectural date of 1480-85 cannot be wide of the mark.

The *Geistliche Auslegung* is a poor piece of book-making, and as far as the illustrations are concerned it is made up in a somewhat haphazard manner, blocks of various sizes and in somewhat diverse state of preservation being fitted into the requisite spaces by the provision of printed rules, for border lines, outside the blocks.

There are two clear groups of cuts by different hands: (1) thirty-two cuts, whose design has sometimes been attributed to Martin Schongauer, of

[1] British Museum *Catalogue of xv-Century Printed Books*, Type 96 b (P. 7), distinct from Schobser 96 (P. 3), in having no tails to its small *f* and *s*.

which fig. 130, from sig. c. 3, verso, the *Flight into Egypt*, is a good example;
(2) forty-eight outline cuts by a designer of more archaic style and less
skill in drawing, of which the *Christ and Peter's Wife's Mother*, from sig. k. 4,
verso (fig. 131), is one of the more interesting subjects.

In addition there are some eight other blocks by one or two other
hands, one of whom has been conjecturally, but not, I think, convincingly,
identified by Weil with
Johannes Schnitzer de
Armszheim.[1]

Fig. 130. The Flight into Egypt, from *Geistliche Auslegung des Lebens Jesu Christi*, Ulm, about 1480–85.

The group of thirty-two
cuts shows a hand of some
naturalistic power of drawing, influenced perhaps by
the designer of the *Aesop*,
and certainly inspired by
the general style of Martin
Schongauer (and in the
Nativity, sig. b. 3, verso,
copying one of his line-
engravings, B. 4, in re-
verse).

The group of forty-eight
cuts has been attributed by
Weil to the author of the
St. Peter and St. Paul with the Veronica Napkin signed H.B. (with crossed
arrows) (Tübingen, S. 1659 a), but not, I think, with any certainty.
The type at the foot of the H.B. cut is the same type as used by Zainer in
the *Geistliche Auslegung*, which fixes the locality, and Schreiber has suggested
the possibility that he may be the HANS BAYER recorded in Ulm documents
in 1461, 1481 and 1484.[2]

As in the *Aesop*, many of the blocks have only partial borders, the
silhouette of the upper part of the subject being regarded as sufficient
termination to the design, though in the *Geistliche Auslegung* this is made
up by the outer border lines of printers' rules.

Later in the 'eighties Johann Zainer fell into debt and was no doubt
forced to sell some of his decorative material, as some of his borders and
woodcut capitals appear in books printed by H. Knoblochtzer at Heidel-

---

[1] I.e. the *Christ carrying the Cross* at f. 114, and five other cuts. See p. 314, for Schnitzer.

[2] Weyermann, *Stuttgarter Kunstblatt*, 1830, Nos. 64-67.

berg (e.g. in the *Totentanz*, S. 5372, about 1489), by Meydenbach at Mainz, after 1491, and by Matthias Hupfuff at Strassburg, after 1498.

He went on printing at Ulm (with intervals of absence) well into the xvi century (the last record being 1523), but his later illustrated books, mostly popular books in German, are comparatively negligible from their artistic quality, and very rare outside German libraries.

One of the exceptions in quality is the little German edition of Thomas à Kempis, *Imitatio Christi* (*Wahre Nachfolgung Christi*) (S. 5346, H. 9115), which probably dates about 1487, with its attractive cut of the *Dead Christ supported by an Angel, the Virgin and St. John*.

Another example above the general average in quality are the six cuts in Ulricus Molitoris, *Tractatus von den bosen Weibern, die man nennet*

Fig. 131. Christ and Peter's Wife's Mother, from *Geistliche Auslegung des Lebens Jesu Christi*, Ulm, about 1480-85.

die Hexen, n.d., about 1490-91 (Schramm, v. 416-421), in which one begins to see some relation to the early style of Dürer. They show the same subjects which appeared in two other books on witches, printed by Michel Greyff and Johann Otmar at Reutlingen about 1489 (Ulricus Molitoris, *Von den Unholden oder Hexen*, or *De Lamiis*), and though they appear to be the later versions, are certainly by far the better drawn and cut. As examples of the cruder type (coarse and angular in cutting) may be mentioned:

Frag und Antwort Künigs Salomon und Marcolfus, 1496.
S. 5191, C. 5248.
Saint Brandons Leben, n.d., about 1499.
S. 3540, H. 3723.
Tondalus ain Riter (*Ritter*) *aus Hibernia*, n.d. (about 1500).
S. 5362 (based on cuts in Schobser's edition, S. 5358, H. 15545).

We have already noted CONRAD DINCKMUT[1] as the printer of a block-book. His earliest type-printed books with illustrations belong to 1482, i.e. *Schwester Demut*, of which only a fragment is known in the Liechtenstein Collection (Schramm, vi. 6-22), and the *Ordnung der Gesundheit* (with only a single cut). In 1483 appeared a *Plenarium* with crude and angular but lively cuts (H. 6733), the *Büchlein genannt der Rosenkranz*, H. 14036 (with three attractive blocks, each containing five roundels, within flower borders, illustrating the Life of Christ), and two editions of the *Seelenwurzgarten* (S. 5229, 5230, C. 5345, H. 14584), and in 1485 the *Erklärung der zwölf Artikel* (S. 4106, H. 6668). The *Seelenwurzgarten* book, with its nineteen blocks repeated so as to offer one hundred and thirty-four illustrations, is an egregious example of an economy of illustrative material frequently practised by the printers of the time.

Dinckmut's best illustrations are contained in two books of 1486, Thomas Lirer, *Chronica von allen Königen und Kaisern* (three editions, one undated with nineteen cuts, two dated 1486 with twenty-three cuts, S. 4507-4509, H. 10116-10118),[2] and Terence, *Eunuchus* (in German). They are the work of a designer and cutter of individual style and sensitive quality, who relied on a delicate outline, with little shading. They are possibly by the same hand as the *Erklärung der zwölf Artikel*, though they show a considerably finer performance. The undated edition of Lirer in the British Museum from which the illustration is taken (fig. 132) shows the line printing more delicately than in the dated edition in the same place, and is undoubtedly the earlier. For the tendency of delicate lines on a block is to be flattened out in the printing, so that later impressions often show a broader line.

The Terence is still better in its drawing and expression than the Lirer, perhaps from the inspiration of a congenial subject. The figures are well drawn, the faces lively in expression and the setting of interest as it no doubt indicates a definite scheme of staging. His edition of Bertholdus, *Andächtig Zeitglöcklein des Lebens und Leidens Christi*, 1493, will be noted under its *editio princeps* at Basle.[3]

Conrad Dinckmut, like Johann Zainer, had his financial difficulties and debts, and these are reflected in the inferior quality of his later illustrations. Steinhöwel's German version of *Apollonius von Tyrus*, 1495 (Schramm, vi. 652-678) is an example, to which we have already alluded under Baemler

[1] A. Schramm, *Bilderschmuck der Frühdrucke*, vi., *Conrad Dinckmut in Ulm*, Leipzig 1923.
[2] Facsimile of ed. 12th January 1486 (H. 10117), ed. E. Voulliéme, Muller & Co., Potsdam.
[3] See p. 328.

for its portrait-bust inscribed *Alexander*. In 1499 Dinckmut left Ulm, and thereafter records cease.

LIENHART HOLLE[1] was another of the unfortunate printers of Ulm,

Fig. 132. From Thomas Lirer, *Chronica von allen Königen und Kaisern*, Ulm, about 1486.

chiefly known for two illustrated books of the year 1482 and 1483, the *Ptolemaeus* and the *Buch der Weisheit*. His edition of Ptolemaeus, *Cosmographia* of 1482 (S. 5031, H. 13539) is an epoch-making work, the earliest

---

[1] A. Schramm, *Bilderschmuck der Frühdrucke*, vii., *Lienhart Holle, J. Reger, J. Schaeffler, and Hans Hauser in Ulm*, Leipzig 1923.

collection of woodcut maps in Germany, and one of the earliest printed editions of Ptolemy's maps (the earlier editions being those of Bologna, 1477, and Rome, 1478, with the maps engraved on copper). The book is

Fig. 133. From Terence, *Eunuchus*, Ulm 1486.

not only interesting in the history of geography, but a really beautiful production with its fine type, woodcut borders and initial letters. The *Map of the World*, which like the rest is double folio in size, is signed *Insculptum est per Johannē Schnitzer de Armszheim*,[1] and Johannes is no

---

[1] Armsheim is situated about eighteen miles south-west of Mainz, west of the Rhine.

doubt responsible for the cutting of all the thirty-two maps. Whether Schnitzer is actually a surname, or merely an indication of his craft, cannot be answered with certainty. Various other cuts have been attributed to JOHANNES DE ARMSHEIM, e.g. Johann Zainer's *Aesop* cuts, by Douce, according to his MS. note in the Oxford copy, the illustrations of Dinckmut's *Seelenwurzgarten* (1483), and of Holle's *Buch der Weisheit der alten Weisen* (1483), and certain of the cuts in Johann Zainer's *Geistliche Auslegung des Lebens Jesu Christi*, by Weil.[1]

The wind-faces are comparable to the full-page portrait figure of Aesop, and in the treatment of the hair at least not unlike the cuts in question in the *Geistliche Auslegung*, but neither here nor in the other cases mentioned is there a sufficient basis for any dogmatic assertion of authorship.

I would interpolate in this place notes on other German woodcut maps of the period, though out of their local order.

In the first place there are three known versions of a *Map of the World*,[2] which shows an earlier stage of knowledge than is seen in Ptolemy's Maps, first introduced to Germany by Holle's edition of 1482, so that in design, and probably in cutting, they are anterior to 1482.

The best version, and perhaps the earliest, is the one signed by HANS RÜST, a craftsman recorded in Augsburg documents between 1477 and 1497, of whom we have already noted another cut (p. 304). The only impression known,[3] now in the Pierpont Morgan Collection, New York (S. 1950 a), came from the binding of a copy of Strabo, *Geographia*, Venice (Vindelinus de Spira) 1472. The two other versions, less carefully cut, are both signed *Hanns Priefmaler* (with the mark of a spur), who is undoubtedly the HANS SPÖRER of Nuremberg who printed two block-books, the *Biblia Pauperum* and *Ars Moriendi* at Nuremberg in 1471 and 1473, and worked after 1487 at Bamberg, and from 1494 until about 1504 at Erfurt. One of these, in the Stiftsbibliothek at St. Gallen, was inserted under the cover of a Latin Bible of Johann Zainer (Ulm 1480); the other, now at Würzburg,[4] was inserted in a copy of Duranti's *Rationale*, Ulm (J. Zainer) 1473. There is no further clue to the dates of these maps, but they were probably all cut within a few years of 1480.

[1] See pp. 304 and 310, and L. Baer, Monatshefte für Kunstwissenschaft, v., 1912, 447.

[2] See H. Hassinger, *Deutsche Weltkarten-Inkunabeln*, Zeitschrift der Gesellschaft für Erdkunde, Berlin 1927, Nos. 9-10.

[3] Reproduced in facsimile, 1924, by J. Rosenthal, Munich, from whom the map was purchased, and in *Einbl.* LXXI., 1929, 31.

[4] S. 1950, the inscription being read *Thomas priefmaler*.

Another map of historical and social interest is the *Pilgrims' Road to Rome from Germany* which is known in several early woodcut versions, e.g.:

(1) Printed by ERHARD ETZLAUB, Nuremberg, about 1492, with title *Das ist der Rom-weg von meylen zu meylen mit puncten verzeychnet von eyner stat zu den andern durch deutzsche lantt.*[1] British Museum, etc.

(2) A different block of the same map. Linz (reproduced, G. Gugenbauer, *Einbl.*, 28, *Linz*, 1912, pl. 25). From the large type used for Nuremberg in the centre of the map, it is probably also a Nuremberg work. S. 1951 m.

(3) Printed by JORG GLOCKENDON, Nuremberg 1510. Liechtenstein Collection. Löbau. A later edition signed *Albrecht Glockendon* 1533 is at Nuremberg (Germ. Museum). S. 1951 n.

Erhard Etzlaub may also have been responsible for drawing the *Plan of Nuremberg and its Environs*, cut by Jorg Glockendon, 1492 (S. 1951 x); Munich Library.

Lienhart Holle's second interesting work, the *Buch der Weisheit der alten Weisen*, 1483 (S. 3484, H. 4029), is one of the earliest European versions of the *Kalīla Wa-Dimna*, by Bidpai, as the author is usually called in Western form.[2] Bidpai is said to have been a wise Brahman of Kashmir, vizier of an Indian ruler of about 300 B.C., and his work a collection of fables, a sort of Mirror for Princes. The book contains a large number of full-page illustrations, about $7\frac{3}{8} \times 6$ inches, crude, but powerful and full of humour, and sometimes, as in the illustration reproduced (fig. 134), evincing real harmony of design. It was evidently a very popular work, for Holle issued several editions in 1483 and 1484.

Another edition was printed at Ulm by Dinckmut in 1485, with the same designs cut down at the sides, the new blocks being about $\frac{7}{8}$-inch narrower.

An earlier edition had been published by Conrad Fyner at Urach about

---

[1] See *Six Early Printed Maps*, British Museum, 1928 (pl. i.); W. Wolkenhauer, *Erhard Etzlaubs Reisekarte durch Deutschland* 1501, Nikolassee bei Berlin 1919. It appears from Wolkenhauer that other variant blocks are known, so that the sheet was evidently printed in large numbers for pilgrims to Rome.

[2] See the *Encyclopaedia of Islam* (ed. by M. T. Houtsma, T. W. Arnold, etc.), London 1913, etc. An English version, 'The Morall Philosophie of Doni', by Sir Thomas North, was published about 1570 (ed. J. Jacobs, London 1888). It is also included in Somadeva, *Ocean of Story* (tr. C. H. Tawney), London, 1924-28, vol. v., with a chart showing all the known versions and editions.

1481–82 (see p. 319), but Holle's designer was fairly independent, and considerably stronger.

In spite of the popularity of the *Buch der Weisheit*, Holle no doubt lost largely through his lavish illustration of this work and the Ptolemy, and his stock was acquired by JOHANN REGER,[1] who printed a second edition of

Fig. 134. From the *Buch der Weisheit*, Ulm 1483.

the *Cosmographia* in 1486 (S. 5032, H. 13540). The chief difference in this edition from that of 1482 is that the maps are provided with headlines, and that the borders to the text on the reverse are omitted.

Holle continued occasional printing at Ulm until 1492, but issued no other illustrated books of note. He was later at Nuremberg, but no longer worked as an independent printer.

Of Reger's original illustrated books may be mentioned the *Walfart*

[1] A. Schramm, *Bilderschmuck der Frühdrucke*, vii., Leipzig 1923.

oder bylgerung unser lieben Frawen, 1487 (S.4586, H.9325; Latin ed.,
Itinerarius, S.4575, H.9323), with title cut and eighteen full-page illus-

Fig. 135. The King entertained, from G. Caorsin, *De Casu Regis Zyzymy*, Ulm 1496.

trations (each divided into three compartments) of the life of the Virgin
and Christ, and the *Schon teutsch Kalender* of 1491 (S.4079), a miniature
calendar with attractive little initials, figures of saints and Passion cuts.

Fig. 136. Initial N, from the *Buch der Weisheit*, Urach, about 1481–82.

But far more important historically and artistically are the two volumes he printed about the Knights Hospitallers (the Knights of St. John of Jerusalem, at Rhodes) written by their Vice-chancellor Gulielmus Caorsin, the *Stabilimenta militum Hierosolymitanorum* of 23rd August 1496 (S. 3669, H. 4364 a) and a volume of various tracts beginning with the *Obsidionis Rhodiae Urbis Descriptio* of 24th October 1496 (S. 3667, H. 4369). The illustrations are all full-page upright cuts, mostly compositions of numerous figures. Those of the *Stabilimenta* are powerful and well composed, but lack the vivacity of some of the others in the volume of tracts. The series of ten plates *De Casu Regis Zyzymy* (from which the reproduction, fig. 135, of *King Zyzymy entertained by the Master of the Order* is taken) are particularly vivacious in handling; one of the subjects, that of Zyzymy riding with his suite, is certainly suggested by the cut of Turkish riders in Breydenbach, *Peregrinationes* (Mainz 1486) and the designer has other qualities in common with Reuwich. The topographical cuts in the title section are also comparable in style to the views in Breydenbach.

Of towns in the neighbourhood of Ulm, a few illustrated books printed by CONRAD FYNER[1] at Esslingen and Urach, and by MICHEL GREYFF[1] at Reutlingen, should be noted.

We have already mentioned Conrad Fyner's[2] edition of the *Buch der Weisheit der alten Weisen* (Urach; n.d.; about 1481–82; S. 3483, H. 4028) as the predecessor of Holle's more remarkable edition. But Fyner's book deserves further notice for its very attractive anthropomorphic initials, full of ingenuity, yet harmonious in design, of which he used seven in this and other books (Schramm, ix. 407-13) (fig. 136), and his *I with Samson and the Lion* (e.g. in Georgius de Hungaria, *De Moribus Turcorum*, n.d., about 1480–81) is another charming example.

Fyner's earlier activity as a printer, from 1472 to 1478, was at Esslingen, and it was here in 1474 that he printed Johannes von Saaz, *Der Ackermann aus Böhmen* (Schramm, ix. 3-5; GW. 197). Beside the half-border on the first page it only contains three little outline cuts (independent of Pfister's designs), and its chief interest is its subject and its rarity, for only one

---

[1] A. Schramm, *Bilderschmuck der Frühdrucke*, ix., Leipzig 1926.   [2] See p. 316.

copy is known (Bamberg; reproduced by A. Schramm, *Deutscher Verein für Buchwesen*, Leipzig 1924).

Apart from the general interest of Fyner's books for their initials, occasional borders, and decorations, two works printed at Urach in 1481 should be noted, the *Plenarium* (S. 4953, C. 2322) and *Leben der Heiligen* (S. 4304, H. 9974), for numerous illustrations of considerable spirit, possibly by the same hand as his *Buch der Weisheit*. An excellent three-sided border occurs in each of these books but in different state: (1) in the *Plenarium*; (2) in the *Leben der Heiligen*, with the upper piece replaced by a new block; (3) in the *Buch der Weisheit*, with the second upper piece reduced in width.

We have already mentioned in relation to Johann Zainer[1] the two editions of a book on witches by Ulricus Molitoris printed at Reutlingen about 1489 under the titles *Von den Unholden oder Hexen* (Michel Greyff) and *De Lamiis* (Johann Otmar).[2] The illustrations in each are from the same blocks, with very little difference in condition, but the edition of Michel Greyff, entitled *Von den Unholden oder Hexen* (H. 11540), probably precedes Johann Otmar's *De Lamiis* (S. 4785, H. 11536).

I would note three other books printed by Michel Greyff at Reutlingen:

Guillermus, *Postilla super Epistolas*, 1494 (suggested by Kesler's Basle edition of 1492).
S. 4150, H. 8287.
Sebastian Brant, *Narrenschiff*, 1494.
S. 3557, H. 3738. The illustrations copied from the first Basle edition of the same year (S. 3555), and
Heinz von Beschwinden, *Gedicht vom Krieg mit Schweizern und Türken*, n.d. (Schramm, ix. 629-633).

The two latter are chiefly remarkable for their borders, rare examples in the dotted manner (white dots on black ground), more characteristic of French books of the period.

Another work where woodcut borders are inspired by contemporary French work printed by Dupré, i.e. Bertholdus, *Andächtig Zeitglöcklein des Lebens und Leidens Christi*, n.d., will be described below under its first dated edition at Basle (see p. 328).

Greyff also issued a considerable number of single-sheet calendars with attractive woodcut decoration.

Before proceeding to Basle and its book-illustration, I would add a few

---

[1] See p. 311.   [2] A. Schramm, *Bilderschmuck der Frühdrucke*, ix., Leipzig 1926.

notes about certain single cuts of Ulm and the neighbourhood, chiefly where names attached to the prints give a definite local clue. The Ulm master, BASTION, and another of the neighbourhood, JERG HASPEL, whose work possibly falls within the first half of the century, have already been mentioned.[1] A small group of cuts belonging to the collection preserved at Ravenna (e.g. the Last Supper, S. 169) has been recently assigned by Dr. Kristeller to Ulm. They show a certain relationship to the Ulm school, but I think it very possible that they may have been done by a German hand in Italy, and reserve their discussion, in consequence, for a later chapter.[2]

MICHEL (or MICHIL) is another name which occurs on other single cuts of uncertain locality, but probably produced in Upper Germany about 1450-70, i.e. on the Christ Child with a Bird, at Halle (S. 782); The Man of Sorrows, at Nuremberg (S. 877); a Pietà (S. 986 m; present locality unknown); St. Bridget, John Rylands Library, Manchester (S. 1289); and a Political Allegory relating to the Meeting of Pope Paul II and the Emperor Frederick III (S. 1956, Munich). The last print is a copy of a Venetian line-engraving,[3] which seems to refer to a meeting which took place between 24th December 1468 and 9th January 1469, and both original and copy probably date soon after the event. The artist may perhaps be identical with a Formschneider of the name of MICHEL who occurs in Ulm records in 1476, though the prints noted would appear to be somewhat earlier.

Another single cut, probably of Upper German origin about the same date, is signed Leinhart, i.e. a St. Ottilia at Graz (S. 1645 b), and Schreiber has conjectured that he may be identical with the printer Lienhart Holle. Two other prints at Graz, Christ on the Cross (S. 417 a), and St. Apollonia (S. 1235 a), are probably by the same hand.[4]

Ludwig mäler ze Ulm 68 is inscribed on a large cut with full-length figures of St. Christopher and St. Anthony (S. 1379, Stuttgart), and he is probably identical with the Ludwig ze Ulm who signed a block-book of the Ars Moriendi (S. ed. VII A). The 68 probably indicates the date 1468, which at least agrees with his style and with the probable date of the block-book, which was copied by Hans Spörer in 1473. He may be identical with either LUDWIG KUCH or LUDWIG FRIESS, who are recorded at Ulm about 1475. Other cuts which have been attributed to him with some probability,[5] i.e. the

---

[1] See p. 128. [2] See p. 424.
[3] A. M. Hind, Catalogue of Early Italian Engravings in the British Museum, p. 276, No. 7.
[4] There is a Lienhart recorded as a Formschneider at Ulm c. 1442, but this would appear to be too early.
[5] See Molsdorf, Schrifteigentümlichkeiten auf älteren Holzschnitten, Strassburg 1914.

Good Shepherd (S. 839, Dresden);[1] *Christ on the Cross* (S. 936a, Dillingen); and *St. Sebastian* (S. 1678), of which an old impression is in the Guildhall Museum, and the original block and two modern impressions in the British Museum. On the reverse side of the *St. Sebastian* block is cut the *Sacred Monogram with the Crucifix and the Four Evangelists* (S. 1812), of which several other woodcut versions exist. It is probably copied from S. 1810 at Berlin. The *St. Sebastian* is a copy of a print at Munich dated 1472 (S. 1679).

Peter mäler ze ulme is another name recorded in a signature, on an *Agony in the Garden* (S. 192) from a *Passion* series (of which ten are preserved at Munich, S. 151, etc.). They appear to be based on an earlier series of cuts, of which a fragment exists at Vienna (Haberditzl 32). An interesting subject of the *Soldiers falling in fear before Christ* (Munich Library, S. 214), is certainly by the same hand, and others near in character are the *Agony in the Garden* (S. 189, once at Maihingen), the *Flagellation* (S. 649, Paris and Salzburg), and the *Holy Trinity* (S. 740, British Museum from St. Gallen). There are Ulm records of a *Peter* 'Kartenmaler' about 1460, and a *Peter Heckenagel* in 1481, and he might be identical with one or the other, or with both.

MICHEL SCHORPP of Ulm is responsible for two cuts of interest for their subjects, a large print of the *Kindred of Christ* signed *Michel Schorpp zu Ulm* (formerly in the Collection Friedrich August II, Dresden, S. 1779a) with inscriptions and names attached to the various members of the Holy Kindred, and a *Byzantine Madonna* signed *Michel Schorpp maler zu Ulm*, 1496 (Paris and Nuremberg, S. 1032, Lemoisne, cxxi.), supposed to have derived from a painting by St. Luke at Rome.

A series of sixteen subjects illustrating the life of *St. Catherine of Alexandria* was recently found by Mr. Campbell Dodgson at Schloss Hohen Liechtenstein (S. VIII, 1315x).[2] They are fragmentary in condition, intended apparently for wall decoration, and originally printed on two double sheets, and the authorship seems fairly certain from the *rpp* which remains of the signature. Their style shows more angularity and less shading than the other two cuts, an indication either of an earlier period of the artist's activity (about 1470–80), or of some lost originals from which they may have been copied.

---

[1] Based on a line-engraving by the Master E.S. (Lehrs 52). There are two copies, S.839a (Paris), S.839b (formerly St. Gallen), and a modified version at Frankfurt (S.839c). It should be compared with the Netherlandish *Good Shepherd* (S.838), which is described and reproduced below (p. 594 and Fig. 347).   [2] See *Einblattdrucke*, No. 75 (1931).

In the case of an inscription with *maler* distinguishing the artist as a painter, it is natural to infer that the design is his, if not the cutting. Michel Schorpp occurs as *Maler* and *Briefmaler* in Ulm records between 1495 and 1500.

HANS HAUSER[1] is responsible for a broadside with a cut of *Death in the Jaws of Hell*, signed *Hanns hauser briefmaler zu Ulme*, the text being in one of Johann Reger's types which points to the probability of a date about 1495 (S. 1894, British Museum).

A woodcut of *Christ on the Cross appearing to a Sick Man* (S. 969, British Museum) signed *Hans husser*, is probably by the same artist, and the different spelling might be an indication of the usage of another district, the southwestern region of Germany, where he might have worked before settling at Ulm.

Fig. 137. Book-plate of Hilprand Brandenburg of Bibrach. S. 2038.

The last name which can be connected with Ulm is that of HANS SCHLAFFER. His name occurs on a *Martyrdom of St. Sebastian* (S. 1682 a, Dresden), of which there is another version at Vienna (S. 1680), a *St. Veronica Napkin* at Lucerne (S. 759 a), and an *Adoration of the Magi* (S. 99, present locality unknown). The signature on the *Adoration* has been read as *Hans Schlaffer von Ulm*, and he is no doubt identical with a craftsman recorded in 1492–1500 at Nuremberg, in 1501 at Ulm, and between 1506 and 1515 at Constance.

Among the small single prints of the region of Ulm which deserves mention is the *Book-plate of Hilprand Brandenburg of Bibrach* (S. 2038), a cut of about 1475-80 and one of the earliest book-plates known (fig. 137). It has interest in relation to our history in indicating provenance from the Carthusian Convent of Buxheim, near Memmingen (to which Hildebrand gave his library), as this was also the original home of the famous *St. Christopher* woodcut of 1423.

Another interesting German book-plate of about the same period is that of *Hans Igler* with its device of a hedgehog (S. 2036), and two other examples worth noting, probably nearer the end of the century, are those of

[1] A. Schramm, *Bilderschmuck der Frühdrucke*, vii., Leipzig 1923.

Niklaus Meyer and Barbara zum Luft, of Basle (S. 2036 e Basle; reproduced Heitz, *Einbl.*, Basel i., 1908, pl. 20), and of the *Carthusian Convent of Thorberg, near Berne,* at Berne (S. 2038 n).

Another book-plate of more problematic origin is that of *Johannes Plebanus,* dated 1407, which is designed in the form of an oval seal (S. 2039). The plate occurs chiefly in incunabula of about 1470-80 in the Munich Library, and the date of the cut can hardly be earlier. Schreiber's explanation is that the date referred to some fund for the purchase of books left by Plebanus, who is known to have been living in 1405.

A certain CLAUS probably belongs to Breisach, on the Rhine, near Freiburg, as the arms of that town appear on a *Christ on the Cross between the Virgin and St. John* which bears his name (S. 947). A *Satire on the Jews* (*Die Juden-Sau*, S. 1961) occurs in several cases on the reverse of impressions of S. 947, and as its size is identical, the subject was probably cut on the back of the same block. Most of the impressions known (e.g. Basle and Augsburg) are considerably later than the date of production. Considering the interpretation of the arms, Nagler's identification with Claus Wolff Strigel of Augsburg is improbable.[1]

One of several versions of a *Crucifix with signs of the Passion* is signed *firabet ze raperswil* (S. 940 m; Zürich, Polytechnicum,[2] and Minnesota Institute of Arts, Minneapolis, from the Herschel V. Jones Collection).[3] A family of the name of Firabet (the local form for Feierabend) was known at the time in Rapperswil on Lake Zürich. Other unsigned versions of about the same date (1460–80) are known (S. 940 n, Graz; S. 941, British Museum; S. 942 a, Boerner Sale, 19th-23rd May 1924, No. 60; S. 944, Darmstadt), and another signed by Caspar (S. 943, British Museum).[4] The British Museum version (S. 941) is stronger and probably earlier than Firabet's, though its faulty inscription makes it probable that it is likewise based on an earlier version. In view of the other existing versions, Firabet is almost certainly the cutter rather than the designer.

The figure of St. John in S. 941 suggests relationship with the style of the Apocalypse block-book, so that the original work may be of Netherlandish design.

Another important woodcut signed by FIRABET OF RAPERSWIL, a *Virgin*

---

[1] Nagler, *Monogrammisten*, ii. 361; W. Bühler, Mitteil. der Gesellsch. für vervielfalt. Kunst, 1925, p. 68.

[2] S. 942 at Sigmaringen is probably a cut impression from the same block.

[3] See *Einblattdrucke*, 73, 1930.

[4] See p. 389.

in Robe decorated with Ears of Corn (Madonna im Ährenkleid) (S. 999 y), has recently been acquired by the Polytechnicum at Zürich.

More attention has no doubt been given to the rare signed prints of the xv century than would be justified by their comparative artistic value in relation to anonymous cuts of the period. But it must be remembered that when such names are also connected with records, they at least offer a definite basis in helping to group anonymous work.

Fig. 138. The Marriage at Cana, from the *Spiegel menschlicher Behältnis*, Basle 1476.

BASLE

In Basle [1] we find a centre definitely poorer in original work than Augsburg and Ulm, and one in which, during the xv century, outside influences were stronger than any indigenous strain. There is at first the marked influence of the schools of Augsburg and Ulm; then an occasional reflection of French modes, and during two brilliant years (1493, 1494) an appearance which is now generally thought to be that of the young Dürer on his *Wanderjahre*.

The most important book of the earliest group is the *Spiegel menschlicher Behältnis* printed by BERNHARD RICHEL, 1476 (S. 5274, H. 14936). The

[1] Werner Weisbach, *Die Baseler Buchillustration des xv[ten] Jahrhunderts*, Strassburg 1896; Weisbach, *Der Meister der Bergmannschen Officin und Albrecht Dürers Beziehungen zur Baseler Buchillustration*, Strassburg 1896; C. C. Bernoulli, *Basler Büchermarken*, Strassburg 1895; A. F. Johnson, *Early Basle Printing*, London 1926. For other Swiss towns see Paul Heitz, *Die Zürcher Büchermarken bis zum Anfang des XVII[en] Jahrhunderts*, Zürich 1895; Paul Heitz, *Genfer Buchdrucker- und Verleger-zeichen*, Strassburg 1908 (Geneva is treated in the French section; see p. 617).

blocks are single column uprights about $5 \times 3\frac{1}{2}$ inches, broad in outline, angular in style, with slight parallel shading.[1] They derive to some extent from Günther Zainer's *Speculum Humanae Salvationis*, but with variations

which show a more direct dependence on the Netherlandish editions of the *Biblia Pauperum* block-book. A later Augsburg edition printed by Peter Berger in 1489 (H. 14937) follows Richel's subjects more nearly than it does Zainer's, and is even more directly influenced by the *Biblia Pauperum*.

The Speier edition of Peter Drach (about 1478) likewise shows numerous points of contact with the *Biblia Pauperum*. It is noteworthy that these type-printed editions of the *Speculum Humanae Salvationis* show no relationship to the Netherlandish block-book of the same title.

In another book published by Richel, Jean d'Arras, *Melusina*, of about 1476 (S.

Fig. 139. From *Die sieben geistlichen Laden*, Basle 1491/92.

4627, H. 11063, Berlin, Munich, etc.), the subjects are again suggested by an Augsburg edition (Baemler, 1474), though they are treated with considerable independence, and, like the *Spiegel*, transformed from small oblongs into larger upright designs. They have something of the same crude strength as the cuts in Holle's Ulm edition of the *Buch der Weisheit* (1483).

Other examples comparable with Augsburg and Ulm work may be noted in the title cuts to St. Augustine, *De Civitate Dei*, 1489 (S. 3393, H. 2064), and Ambrosius, *Opera*, 1492 (S. 3264, H. 896), both printed by JOHANN AMERBACH.

[1] The majority of the original blocks were reprinted in *Le Mirouer de la Redemption*, printed by Martin Huss at Lyon, 1478.

Another work printed by Amerbach, *Die sieben geistlichen Laden*, 27th January, 1491/92 (S. 4462, Berlin Print Room; fig. 139), contains seven cuts of curious subject in which Christ is represented as a pedlar with horse and cart, showing a hermit his wares, the treasures contained in seven boxes. In their vivid style they form something of a bridge between the *Spiegel menschlicher Behältnis* of 1476 and the illustrations attributed to Dürer (see pp. 328–32). But with their straight parallel shading, they belong more to the earlier tradition than to the structural modelling and curved shading of the master of the 'Ship of Fools'.

Among miscellaneous work of poorer quality may be mentioned:

Guillermus, *Postilla in Evangelia et Epistolas*, M. Furter, 1491.
  S. 4146, H. 8273.
  Crude little cuts, copied in an edition of N. Kesler, Basle 1492.
Bernardinus, *Sermones de Evangelio*. N. Kesler, about 1494.
  S. 3428, H. 2828.
  The title cut of St. Bernardino, with an Italian town in the background, is the same subject as the larger single cut (S. 1278 a), which is possibly Italian (see p. 428).
Albertus de Bonstetten, *Passio Sancti Meinradi*. M. Furter, 1496.
  S. 4607, H. 12453.
  Also German editions of about the same date, Copinger 3966, and E. P. Goldschmidt & Co., Catalogue ix., No. 49.
  The cuts probably based on the block-book.
Methodius, *Revelationes Divinae* (ed. S. Brant). M. Furter, 1498.
  S. 4648, H. 11121.
  Crude little cuts in the same style as Furter's *St. Meinrad*.

One of the most attractive printer's marks of the earlier period at Basle is that of JACOB WOLFF of Pforzheim, and the little illustrations in one of Wolff's books, Christoforus Columbus, *Epistola de insulis nuper inventis* (n.d., about 1493, H. 5491), are at least of interest from their subject.[1]

The printer LIENHART YSENHUT has already been mentioned [2] for the variety of crafts under which he figures in records, as *Maler, Briefmaler, Briefdrucker, Heiligenmaler, Heiligendrucker, Kartenmacher*. His *Walfart Marie* (S. 4587, H. 9327) is known to have been issued in 1489 (and there is a Latin edition *Itinerarium Mariae* of about the same date), and he published *Calendars* for 1498 and 1499, but otherwise there is no record

---

[1] The same cuts also occur in an edition by J. Bergmann de Olpe, Basle 1495 (Copinger 1697).
[2] See p. 91.

of the date of his books. They all contain cuts, of no great merit, and he may have been partly responsible for the cutting of the blocks. They include Franciscus de Retza, *De Generatione Christi, seu Defensorium inviolatae Castitatis Mariae* (S.4047, H. 6086), and a German *Aesop* (S. 3034) which is largely based on J. Zainer's Ulm edition.

Fig. 140. From Bertholdus, *Andächtig Zeitglöcklein*, Basle 1492.

An example which very clearly reflects the style of the French *Horae* of Jean Dupré is Bertholdus, *Andächtig Zeitglöcklein des Lebens und Leidens Christi*, printed by Johann Amerbach, 1492 (S.3448, H. 16278; see fig. 140). It is a most attractive little book with occasional subject illustrations and borders to every page, including eight different designs.

There are similar borders, some based on Amerbach's blocks, in editions printed by Dinckmut at Ulm, 1493 (S. 3452, H. 16280), and by M. Greyff at Reutlingen, n.d. (Schramm, ix. 639-683).

Similar French influences will be noted in *Horae* printed about the same time by Marcus Reinhard at Kirchheim and by his brother Johann Grüninger at Strassburg.[1]

By far the most interesting incident in book-illustration at Basle is the visit of ALBRECHT DÜRER between 1492 and 1494.[2] A woodcut of *St.*

[1] See p. 340.

[2] See Daniel Burckhardt, *Albrecht Dürers Aufenthalt in Basel*, 1492–94, Munich 1892

Jerome (Kurth 22; fig. 141) which appeared in an edition of his *Epistles,* printed at Basle by Nicolaus Kesler in 1492 (S. 4227, H. 8561; Basle, Berlin, British Museum, Oxford, etc.; the edition of 1497, S. 4228, H. 8565, contains a copy).[1] Direct evidence of Dürer's authorship is provided by the authentic signature written on the back of the block which is still preserved at Basle. In its angular style it stands so far apart from the earliest of Dürer's woodcuts after his return to Nuremberg in 1494 (e.g. *The Men's Bath,* B. 128; fig. 179), that but for the documentary evidence and the links in development provided by the other works of Basle printers to be mentioned, it might have remained permanently anonymous. It shows distinct

Fig. 141. Albrecht Dürer, St. Jerome. From St. Jerome's *Epistles,* Basle 1492.

relationship to contemporary Basle work, such as the *St. Ambrose in his Study* in Ambrosius, *Opera* (Johann Amerbach, 1492), to which we (reproducing some of Dürer's drawings for an unpublished *Terence*); and Pr. Jahrbuch, xxviii., 1907, 168; H. Koegler, Repert. xxx., 1907, 195; and the works cited above (p. 325) by W. Weisbach; Erich Roemer, *Dürers ledige Wanderjahre,* Pr. Jahrbuch, xlvii., 1926, 118; xlviii., 1927, 77, 156 (with complete reproduction of the *Terence* drawings and cuts); J. Meder, *Dürer-Katalog,* Vienna 1932, p. 13.

[1] See R. Schrey, Mitteil. der Gesellsch. für vervielfält. Kunst, 1908, p. 40.

have referred among the cuts showing the influence of Ulm and Augs-burg.

The other works at Basle attributed to Dürer are the cuts in the *Ritter vom Turn* and the *Narrenschiff* (*Stultifera Navis*). The *Ritter vom Turn*,[1] printed by MICHAEL FURTER in 1493 (S. 5392, H. 5514), contains forty-

Fig. 142. Albrecht Dürer (?). From the *Ritter vom Turn*, Basle 1492.

five cuts each flanked by floral borders, the title cut of the *Knight instructing two Priests and two Writers to compile his book* being repeated, all uniform in style of design, but with a variation in quality of cutting which seems to show two hands. The larger group, including the illustration reproduced (fig. 142), is excellently cut, and the style of all the subjects, both

---

[1] Reproduced and described by R. Kautzsch, Strassburg 1903, and K. Pfister, Munich 1922, Kurth, *Dürer*, 36-48. There is no copy of the original edition in English libraries. The cuts in Schaur's Augsburg edition of 1495 and Furter's edition of 1513 (reprinted by J. Knoblouch, Strassburg 1519) are copies. See p. 265 for further notes.

in figure and landscape, seems the natural source from which the acknowledged works of Dürer sprang.

Sebastian Brant's *Narrenschiff*, first printed by JOHANN BERGMANN DE OLPE on the 11th February 1494 (containing considerably over a hundred cuts), was a most popular work, which passed through more than fifteen editions before the end of the century (see S. 3555 and H. 3736 and following numbers; Kurth, *Dürer*, 49-62).[1] The original series of cuts, with certain variations and additions in different issues, was reprinted in German editions by Bergmann in 1495, 1497 and 1499, and in Latin editions (*Stultifera Navis*) in 1497 (three editions) and 1498. Copies were issued by Peter Wagner at Nuremberg, by M. Greyff at Reutlingen, by J. Schoensperger at Augsburg, and by J. Grüninger at Strassburg, in the year of original

Fig. 143. Albrecht Dürer (?). From Sebastian Brant, *Narrenschiff*, Basle 1494.

publication, and Schoensperger and Grüninger issued several later editions.

There is less uniformity in style throughout this series than in the *Ritter vom Turn*. Some of the blocks are markedly angular in character (fig. 143), while others (fig. 144) have the rounded manner of drawing that characterises Dürer's certainly authentic work. The landscape is throughout in Dürer's style, though the two examples reproduced show considerable difference in the method of coping with details of foliage, which is much more significantly drawn in fig. 144. Granting the prob-

---

[1] See Bibliography, p. 325 (Weisbach), and Hans Koegler, Gesellschaft der Bibliophilen, Weimar 1906, and F. Schultz, Gesellsch. für Elsäss. Literatur, Strassburg 1913, for facsimiles of the original edition of 1494.

ability that the design and cutting of the *Narrenschiff* series were spread over a longer period than the less numerous and more uniform designs of the *Ritter vom Turn*, I think that the development from angu-

Fig. 144. Albrecht Dürer (?). From Sebastian Brant, *Narrenschiff*, Basle 1494.

larity to more sensitive and significant methods of design might easily allow certain sections of the work, apparently divergent in style, to be by the hand of the one artist who was responsible for the *St. Jerome* and *The Men's Bath*.

There may be a proportion of designs by other hands, and if there is uncertainty in the attribution of the main body of the illustrations, it lies rather on the side of the more angular group, for the style of the remainder is entirely in harmony with the drawings preserved on the wood blocks at Basle (of which only a few were cut) for an unpublished edition of *Terence*, which can be accepted for the most part with even less hesitation as Dürer's work (see figs. 145, 146). There are 130 of these blocks, and only a small proportion cut, and these perhaps only cut experimentally at a later period (Kurth, *Dürer*, 23-35). In any case, comparison of the cuts with the drawings show how considerably the original design is coarsened in the process.[1]

---

[1] The opinion that the *Ritter vom Turn*, *Narrenschiff* and *Terence* designs are largely by Dürer is supported by Dr. Burckhardt and Erich Roemer in the works cited above. Dr. Hans Koegler, who shares the same view, has also attributed to the master certain small cuts originally intended as a series for a *Gebetbuch*, but actually only published in various other books (*Repertorium*, xxx., 1907, p. 195, and the Gutenberg Gesellschaft Jahrbuch, 1926; Kurth, *Dürer*, 63-80). The same writers also include in Dürer's work the *Canon* cut from a *Missal* printed by

A few other books published at Basle undoubtedly reflect the influence of the same master's designs, e.g. Johannes Meder, *Quadragesimale novum de Filio Prodigo*, printed by M. Furter, 1495 (S. 4604, H. 13628), three books of Sebastian Brant, printed by Johann Bergmann, *In Laudem Virginis Mariae*, about 1494 (S. 3554, H. 3733),[1] *De Origine et Conversatione bonorum Regum*, 1495 (S. 3574, H. 3735), and *Varia Carmina*, 1498 (S. 3543, H. 3731). Brant's *Varia Carmina* were also issued by Grüninger

Fig. 145. Albrecht Dürer (?). Design for *Terence*. Drawing on the wood block.

at Strassburg in 1498, but one of the subjects (*Ad Divum Maximilianum*) appeared in the work of 1495, and it seems probable that the Basle designs are the originals throughout. Certainly the portrait in the Basle edition is more convincing, as if based on a drawing from the life, than the more conventionalised Strassburg cut.

Grüninger at Strassburg in 1493, and the much-debated illustrations to the *Revelationes Sanctae Brigittae*, printed by Koberger at Nuremberg, 1500. A summary of this view is given in Dr. F. Winkler's edition of Dürer in the Klassiker der Kunst series. Divergent views are held by other critics, such as Dr. Röttinger, who once attributed the group largely to Hans Wechtlin (Vienna Jahrbuch, xxvii., 1907, Heft 1), but now in part to Peter Vischer 1. (*Dürer's Doppelgänger*, Strassburg 1926), and by Hans Tietze and E. Tietze-Conrat (*Der junge Dürer*, Augsburg 1928).

[1] Two of its cuts are repeated in Jacob Wimpheling, *De conceptu Mariae*, J. Bergmann, 1494 (S. 5473, H. 16171).

Sebastian Brant was one of the most distinguished of the humanists of the day, and exerted an immense influence through his original writings and translations, which were printed by Bergmann at Basle, and Grüninger at Strassburg.[1] His interest in the illustration of his works is recorded, and he appears to have controlled his designers in detail in their interpretation of his ideas.

Before leaving Basle, I would mention a book published in the early years of the xvi century, and therefore strictly outside my province, i.e.

Fig. 146. Albrecht Dürer (?). Design for *Terence*. Woodcut.

Paulus Olearius, *De Fide Concubinarum*, first issued without date or name of place or printer. Muther (No. 380) describes this first edition under the authorship of Jacob Wimpheling, and attributes it to the printer LUDWIG HOHENWANG, who he thought might also be the designer of the illustrations, three statements which all need correcting. It appears to have been printed at Basle between 1501 (a date which occurs in the text) and 1505, when a reprint was issued by Froschauer at Augsburg. There seems no doubt that its interesting cuts are by the Basle master, who is only known by the monogram D.S., which occurs on certain of his other works.[2]

---

[1] See G. R. Redgrave, *The Illustrated Books of Sebastian Brant*, Bibliographica, ii., 1896, 47.

[2] For description and reproduction of his work see E. Bock, *Die Holzschnitte des Meisters D.S.*, Berlin 1924; cf. C. Dodgson, Pr. Jahrbuch, xxviii. (1907), 21.

FREIBURG IM BREISGAU

Two books printed by FRIEDRICH RIEDRER at Freiburg im Breisgau deserve mention, as containing cuts now attributed to Dürer, i.e. the *Septem Horae Canonice Virginis*, about 1493 (S. 4574; Kurth, *Dürer*, 82) with a cut of the Virgin adored, by A. Bonstetten, and Riedrer's own *Spiegel der wahren Rhetorik*, 1493 (S. 5096, H. 13914; Kurth, *Dürer*, 83, 84), with an excellent title-cut and an interesting rendering of the *Fall of Icarus*.

Fig. 147. From Jean d'Arras, *Melusina*, Strassburg, about 1478.

STRASSBURG

The earliest book-illustrations printed at Strassburg[1] are those of the press of HEINRICH KNOBLOCHTZER[2] between 1476 and 1484. Knoblochtzer afterwards left Strassburg, and is known to have been at Heidelberg in 1489, and may have already been there in the intermediate years.

His illustrations and the earlier Strassburg cuts in general, like those of Basle, reflect the style and often repeat the subjects of Augsburg and Ulm books, but with considerable originality of treatment. For example, his cuts to Jean d'Arras, *Melusina*, n.d., about 1478 (S. 4629, H. 11061, S. and S. 7; see fig. 147), and 1481 (S. 4632, S. and S. 18), derived originally from Baemler's Augsburg edition of 1474, though immediately from Richel's Basle edition of about 1476 (the subjects being upright in form), are treated

---

[1] See Paul Kristeller, *Die Strassburger Bücher-Illustration im XV und in Anfang des XVI Jahrhunderts*, Leipzig 1888; P. Heitz and K. A. Barack, *Elsässische Büchermarken*, Strassburg 1892.

[2] Karl Schorbach and Max Spirgatis, *H.K. in Strassburg* (1477–84), Strassburg 1888.

in bold and vivacious style, with an occasional effective use of white on black (e.g. in the fifth illustration). The cuts in his edition of Jacob de Theramo, *Belial,* 1477 and later editions (S. 4281, C. 5808, S. and S. 1, etc.) are equally broad in treatment, and almost entirely in outline. Simple rounded forms are characteristic of two large cuts in Hans Erhard Tusch, *Burgundische Historie,* 1477 (S. 5398, H. 6664, S. and S. 3), and the *Historie von Peter Hagenbach* of the same year (S. 4182, H. 8345, S. and S. 4), a battle-scene, which occurs in both, and *Religious Procession at Strassburg Minster* (possibly the earliest print of the Cathedral) from the latter book.

His Aesop, *Vita et Fabulae,* n.d. (S. 3021, S. and S. 37; see fig. 148), and his *Historia Sigismundae,* n.d. (S. 4488, C. 2885), both between about 1478–81, are based on Johann Zainer's Ulm editions, and his Pius II, *De Duobus Amantibus* (Aeneas Sylvius, *Euryalus und Lucrecia*) (S. 3017, H. 242, S. and S. 10) is equally in the Ulm manner.

Single cuts of interest may be noted in Maphaeus Vegius, *Philalethes,* n.d., about 1478–80 (S. 5416, H. 15926, S. and S. 11),

Fig. 148. Border from *Aesop,* Strassburg, about 1480.

Fig. 149. Initial D, from Jean d'Arras, *Melusina*, Strassburg, about 1478.

which is a copy (and improved rendering) of the same subject in the Nuremberg edition of Johannes Regiomontanus (of about 1474), and in Hans Tucher, *Reise zum heiligen Grabe*, 1484 (S. 5385, S. and S. 31),[1] with its pretended portrait of Tucher standing against a tapestry background. How little consideration is paid to truth of portraiture at this period is shown by the fact that Knoblochtzer's cut is copied (with no change of feature) from a supposed representation of Marco Polo, printed by Friedrich Creussner at Nuremberg in an edition of his *Travels*, 1477.

Knoblochtzer's work is distinguished by good ornament in borders, and initials. A two-sided border (of leaf, flower and bird) occurs in *Melusina* and various other books, and an excellent complete border of similar character on the front page of his *Aesop* (fig. 148). He follows Ulm and Augsburg in his *Maiblumen* initials, and copied an *Initial I with Samson and the Lion* from a block of Conrad Fyner of Urach,[2] using it in his 1483 edition of Jacobus de Theramo, *Belial* (S. 4288, C. 5813, S. and S. 15), and in Jacobus de Cessolis, *Schachzabelbuch*, 1483 (S. 4276, H. 4897, S. and S. 40).

An *Initial D with St. John the Baptist, and other Figures*[3] is in the style of Fyner's anthropomorphic initials, but it is actually copied from the engraved alphabet of the Master E.S. (Lehrs, 286). It occurs in the *Lucidarius*, n.d., n.p., n.pr. (S. and S. 17), described by Kristeller as printed by Martin Schott, but rightly assigned by Schorbach and Spirgatis, and in the British Museum Catalogue, to Knoblochtzer.

Apparently his own are the set of twelve *Calendar Initial D's with the occupations of the Months* (see fig. 149), issued complete in his *Calendar* of 1483 (H. 9734) and imitated later in a German Calendar by Johann Schaeffler at Ulm, 1498 (Schramm, vii. 360-371).

And in the broad style of his own early cutter is the large *Pictorial Initial A with Christ washing the Disciples' Feet*, which occurs in Thomas Ebendorfer de Haselbach, *Sermones*, 1478 (S. 5344, H. 8370).

The work done for Knoblochtzer is easily the most important part of the earlier Strassburg woodcut illustration, but certain other books deserve mention for one reason or another.

The numerous illustrations in Sir John Mandeville, *Itinerarius*, 1483

---

[1] Cf. edition, Augsburg, Sorg, p. 297.   [2] See p. 319.

[3] Reproduced Kristeller, *Strassburger Bücher-Illustration*, Abb. 2, and S. and S., p. 72.

(S. 4801) and 1484 (S. 4802, H. 10649), printed by JOHANN PRÜSS, crudely and angularly cut, are interesting for their subject, though based on the better cuts in an undated edition (about 1481) of Bernhard Richel of Basle (S. 4799, C. 3833). Moreover, the book is among the few in which the headlines are also cut.[1] To the same printer should also be assigned the edition of Otto von Passau, *Die vierundzwanzig Alten* (or *Der guldin Tron*), n.d. (about 1482) (S. 4879, H. 12127, Muther 6), which Muther attributed to an unrecorded 'Sebastian Pfister' of Bamberg. It contains twenty-six illustrations, made by repetition from four blocks, two of which were based on an edition printed by Sorg, at Augsburg, about 1479 and 1480 (S. 4877 and 4878, H. 12128).

Another Strassburg edition of the same work, printed by MARTIN SCHOTT in 1483 (S. 4881, C. 4541), is chiefly notable for a good three-sided border with scroll work and wild folk in the lower piece, which also occurs in the same printer's edition of Guido de Colonna, *Historie der Stadt Troia*, 1489 (S. 4138, H. 5518). Martin Schott's woodcuts in the latter book, and in his Eusebius, *Historie vom Grossen Alexander*, 1488 (S. 3138, H. 791), are largely based on Baemler's Augsburg edition.

Printed in type used by both Prüss and Grüninger (and left unassigned in the British Museum Catalogue) are the works of Joannes Gerson, 1488 (S. 4101, H. 7622). A large cut of *Gerson as Pilgrim* occurs at the beginning of each of the three volumes. It was copied in the edition of Nicolaus Kesler, Basle, 1489 (S. 4102, H. 7624), in which a single border-line immediately distinguishes it from the original. A third edition, also of 1489, which has also been regarded as a Strassburg issue, now generally assigned to Georg Stuchs at Nuremberg (S. 4103, H. 7623), contains a cut in which the same subject is treated quite independently, and is possibly one of the earliest works of Albrecht Dürer (fig. 177). Finally, an additional fourth volume of the first Strassburg edition, printed by the younger Martin Flach in 1502, contains a further independent version, which is attributed by Passavant to Wechtlin (P. iii. 334,59).

Of other books issued by Johann Prüss, one of the richest in illustration (with over 200 cuts) is *Das Heldenbuch, oder Wolfdieterich*, of about 1483 (S. 4197, H. 8420), and one of the more interesting, though only for a single cut of *Tubal Cain*, is Hugo Reutlingensis, *Flores Musicae*, issued in 1488, and in two undated editions (about 1490 and 1492) (S. 5270, 5271, and 5271a, H. 7174 and 7173).

A rare book of very individual character is the *Directorium Statuum, seu*

---

[1] Cf. Josephus, *De Antiquitate Judaica*, Lübeck (Lucas Brandis), n.d. (about 1475) (S.4402, H.C. 9450).

Tribulatio Seculi printed by Johann Prüss for Peter Attendorn, about 1489 (S. 3831, H.C. 6274).[1] It contains three cuts illustrating treatises dealing with the morals of the lower clergy and university students, the two latter sections on the inebriety and prodigality of students being lectures delivered before Heidelberg students in 1489. The woodcut of a *Students' Drinking-bout* (fig. 150) certainly reproduces the sketch of an artist of considerable gifts, with a vivid touch comparable to that of the Master of the Amsterdam Cabinet, and with something of the spirit of the young Dürer, or whoever was responsible for the cuts of the *Narrenschiff* at Basle.

Fig. 150. A Students' Drinking Bout, from *Directorium Statuum*, Strassburg, about 1489.

Of considerable originality in its decorative setting is the frontispiece to the *Evangelien und Episteln*, 1488, the only book printed at Strassburg by THOMAS ANSHELM. It also contains numerous small oblong illustrations, of less interest, which are sometimes made up from more than one block, a practice of which we shall find Grüninger constantly taking advantage.

JOHANN (REINHARD) GRÜNINGER[2] was not a maker of beautiful books; he was too devoted to such economies as the combination and repetition of various blocks in different subjects not to sacrifice harmonious design in the process, but he is of great interest in our history for the new character of woodcut which appears to have been introduced in his workshops. It con-

---

[1] For a full note on the book see E. P. Goldschmidt & Co., London, *Catalogue IX.*, No. 24.

[2] Called Grüninger from his birthplace of Grüningen. See Paul Heitz, *Zierinitialen in Drucken des Johann Grüninger*, Strassburg 1897.

sisted in a close system of parallel lines of shading, straight or curved, according to the requirements of form, which approximated more nearly than woodcut had hitherto done to the richer tonal character of line-engraving. The resemblance is more apparent than real, for cross-hatching of lines (which causes infinite labour to the cutter) occurs only little, and much less than in the style of woodcut developed by Albrecht Dürer.

Fig. 151. April, from a Roman *Horae*, Kirchheim, about 1490.

One of the earliest books he printed with any cuts of artistic value, the *Cursus beatae Mariae Virginis*, n.d. (about 1494), is in a different vein and modelled on the style of French *Horae*. Its immediate source is a German Book of Hours (*Die sieben Zeiten unser lieben Frauen*) printed by Grüninger's kinsman, MARCUS REINHARD, at Kirchheim (Alsace) in 1491, though the blocks are largely different. Reinhard himself had issued a Latin edition about 1490 (*Horae secundum usum Ecclesiae Romanae*), which again was composed for the most part of different blocks. The most attractive section of this edition of 1490, which is not repeated, is the Calendar, from which the *Month of April* is here reproduced (fig. 151). Except for the Calendar, most of the borders in this edition show a plain black ground (but not dotted as usually in French *Horae*). In the edition of 1491 most of the borders are in black line and only the *Dance of Death* on a black ground. Grüninger's edition is in black line throughout.[1]

¹ For a study of these three *Horae* (all in the British Museum) see Robert Proctor, *Marcus Reinhard and Johann Grüninger*, Bibliographical Essays, 1905, pp. 19-38. Proctor is wrong in

THEATRVM

Fig. 152. The Theatre. Frontispiece to *Terence*, Strassburg 1496.

Another book printed by Grüninger before the appearance of his more
characteristic cutter, the *Missale Speciale* of 1493 (S. 4758, H. 11250),
contains a *Canon* cut which is now generally accepted as by Dürer
(Kurth 85).

The Latin *Terence* of 1496 (S. 5331, H. 15431; German edition, 1499,
S. 5333, H. 15434) is the first important work with cuts in the new style.

Fig. 153. Illustration to *Heautontimoroumenos*, from *Terence*, Strassburg 1496.

Apart from the practice of making up his smaller illustrations from various
stock pieces, the marginalia to his text militate in this and his other editions
of the Roman classics against a harmonious page. There is an amusing
fantasy in the frontispiece, the *Theatre of Terence* (fig. 152), and a full-page
cut preceding each play, while the various characters, properties and backgrounds reappear in a variety of combinations in the smaller composite
illustrations (one reproduced in fig. 153 being made up of five different
blocks).[1]

The two other classical editions which followed the *Horace* of 1498
(S. 4240, H. 8898) and the *Virgil* of 1502 were produced in the same style,
with the same wealth of illustration. The *Virgil*, edited by Sebastian Brant,

stating that the borders are largely the same blocks in each edition. Marcus Reinhard had printed
at Lyon with N. Philippi, 1477–82, before returning to his native Alsace.

[1] There are numerous earlier examples of the practice of making up illustrations from various
blocks, especially in Holland (e.g. Jacobus de Theramo, *Der sonderen Troest*, printed by Bellaert,
Haarlem 1484, see p. 574).

Fig. 154. The First Eclogue, from *Virgil*, Strassburg 1502.

is the finest book of the three, and the printer did not resort to the ugly economy of composite blocks as in the two preceding works. Moreover, there is more embellishment in the nature of pictorial capitals, used in different sizes for text and marginal notes. Brant did not escape abuse from his contemporaries for the unclassical fantasy of his illustrator's works. The illustration to the apocryphal *De Copa et Hortulo* is an attractive anticipation of the style of Augsburg illustration of about 1520–30 (e.g. that of Hans Weiditz). The *C A* on the cartouche has sometimes been interpreted as the artist's initials, but it is probably only the beginning and end of COPA.

Other cuts of a similar character occur in several medical works of Hieronymus Braunschweig, printed by Grüninger, i.e. the *Chirurgia (Wundartzny)* of 1497 (S. 3642, H. 4017), the *Liber de Arte Distillandi (Distillirbuch)* of 1500 (S. 3644, H. 4021), the *Liber Pestilentialis (Buch der Vergift der Pestilenz)* of the same year (S. 3645, H. 4020), and Boethius, *De Consolatione Philosophiae*, 1501.

A cut of *Master and Pupils* occurs in these, and was borrowed by Johann Prüss for his edition of the *Hortus Sanitatis*, n.d., about 1497 (S. 4284, H. 8941), in which the numerous other illustrations were based on Meydenbach's Mainz edition of 1491.

Good examples of the same style occur in Grüninger's Frater Petrus, *Legenda de vita S. Catherinae*, 1500 (S. 4291, H. 12850), both in the illustration and in the delicately cut initials, and in Jacob Wimpheling, *Adolescentia*, which was printed by MARTIN FLACH in 1500 (S. 5471, H. 16190). Similar but less well cut are the illustrations in Johann Lichtenberger's *Prognosticatio*, printed by BARTHOLOMEUS KISTLER in 1497 (S. 4505, H. 10088),[1] and small examples of the same character of engraving are the cuts in the *Hortulus Animae* (the German counterpart of the French *Horae*) printed by WILHELM SCHAFFENER, in 1498 and 1500 (S. 4242, H. 8936).

HEIDELBERG

We have already mentioned Knoblochtzer's removal from Strassburg to Heidelberg, and he is now generally thought to have printed at this place about the year 1489, or within the preceding four years, the Dance of Death, entitled *Doten dantz mit figuren clage und antwort* (S. 5372).[2]

---

[1] Based on the Ulm blocks of about 1488 (J. Zainer) (S. 4499, H. 10080), which were used later by J. Meydenbach, Mainz 1492 (S. 4500, H. 10082).

[2] Facsimile, ed. Albert Schramm, Leipzig 1922; L. Baer, *Der Heidelberger Totentanz und die Mittelrheinische Buchillustration des XV Jahrhunderts*, Gutenberg Gesellschaft, 1925, p. 269.

This first edition, containing forty-one cuts, has woodcut initials from the stock of Johann Zainer of Ulm, and it is not surprising that the book itself has been sometimes ascribed to Zainer (e.g. by Schreiber).

Moreover in style of design it has considerable relationship to another book issued *sine nota*, but commonly assigned to Johann Zainer of Ulm, about 1488, Johann Lichtenberger's *Prognosticatio* (S. 4499, H. 10080), though the cuts in the latter are somewhat cruder and less sensitive.[1] But it is not beyond the bounds of possibility that the *Prognosticatio* itself (whose

Fig. 155. From the *Doten dantz*, Mainz, about 1492.

cuts were printed later by J. Meydenbach at Mainz in 1492, S. 4500, H. 10082) may have been printed by Knoblochtzer at Heidelberg.

A second edition of the *Doten dantz*, with forty-two illustrations (one cut being repeated), without the woodcut capitals, was issued by Jacob Meydenbach at Mainz, about 1492 (S. 5373, C. 3733; fig. 155).[2] The *Totentanz*, as already noted,[3] has a very definite resemblance in style to the cuts of the Ulm *Aesop*, and an equally close relationship to certain Mainz cuts, more particularly to the frontispiece in Meydenbach's edition of the *Hortus Sanitatis*, and to various cuts in Schoeffer's *Cronecken der Sassen*.

SPEIER[4]

The earliest of the books of this middle Rhine group to share the char-

---

[1] See p. 308.

[2] It is curious that Low German characteristics which appear in the text of the first edition, e.g. *Doit* for *Dot*, disappear in the second. [3] See p. 308.

[4] See Albert Schramm, *Bilderschmuck der Frühdrucke*, xvi., Leipzig 1933.

acteristics which have suggested attribution of their designs to the Master of the Amsterdam Cabinet is the *Spiegel menschlicher Behältnis,* printed by PETER DRACH of Speier, about 1478 (S. 5276, H. 14935, Berlin; fig. 156).[1]

Fig. 156. The Marriage at Cana, from the *Spiegel Menschlicher Behältnis,* Speier, about 1478.

The treatment of the subjects derives more closely from Richel's Basle edition of 1476 than from Günther Zainer's *Speculum Humanae Salvationis* (Augsburg 1473), showing variations which are sometimes more nearly allied to the Netherlandish block-book of the *Biblia Pauperum.*[2]

The best of the plates are extraordinarily vivid in draughtmanship, with a rounded and sensitive line, far more expressive of form than most contemporary woodcuts, and it has already been suggested that they may be by the hand of the designer of the Ulm *Aesop.*[3] A small proportion of the plates are more angular and less sensitive in character, e.g. the *Baptism of Christ* (Naumann, pl. 50), which denotes a second designer, as the difference seems too much to be explained by the varying skill of cutters.

[1] See Hans Naumann, *Die Holzschnitte des Meisters vom Amsterdamer Kabinett zum Spiegel menschlicher Behältnis* (Speier, Drach), Strassburg 1910. I keep to the title 'Master of the Amsterdam Cabinet' as the author of the engravings of which the largest collection is at Amsterdam, rather than 'Master of the Hausbuch', as only the Planets series in the Hausbuch are generally accepted as by the engraver, the rest being by an assistant. Naumann reserves the title 'Master of the Hausbuch' to this assistant, and it seems a necessary distinction. For further literature on the attribution of cuts to the Master see W. F. Storck, Monatshefte, iii., 1910, 285; E. Flechsig, Monatshefte, iv., 1911, 95, 162; W. F. Storck, Kunstchronik, N.F. xxii., 1911, 407; K. F. Leonhardt and H. T. Bossert, Zeitschrift, N.F. xxiii., 1912, 133, 191, 239; W. Bühler, *Heinrich Mang der Hausbuchmeister,* Mitteil. der Gesellsch. für vervielf. Kunst, 1931, p. 1.

[2] Cf. pp. 326 and 230.   [3] Cf. p. 307.

A very attractive little cut by the same hand showing the *Bishop of Speier adoring the Virgin and Child* occurs at the head of an Episcopal

Fig. 157. The Bishop of Speier adoring the Virgin and Child, from an Episcopal Proclamation, Speier 1483.

Proclamation for Advent 1483, printed by Peter Drach of Speier (British Museum, C.D., A 134, S. 2021; fig. 157), and on an *Ordo Hyemalis* for 1484 of the same printer (British Museum, Proctor 2355).

Another interesting book printed by Peter Drach in both Latin and German editions, in and about 1493, is Petrus de Crescentiis, *Opus Ruralium Commodorum* (S. 3788, 3789, 3790, H. 5826, 5833, 5834). Its text and numerous cuts are a wonderful storehouse of country lore (illustrating agricultural work, sports, animals, plants, etc.). In style they are nearly related to Drach's *Spiegel menschlicher Behältnis,* and to Meydenbach's *Hortus Sanitatis* (1491), but for the most part cruder and more angular in design, and poorer in quality (see fig. 158).

One of Peter Drach's later books, the *Reformation der Stadt Worms,* 1499 (S. 5054, H. 13719), is note-

Fig. 158. From Petrus de Crescentiis, *Opus Ruralium Commodorum,* Speier, about 1493.

worthy for the woodcut arms of Worms, designed by NICOLAUS NYFERGALT.

Of other illustrated books printed at Speier, German and Latin editions of *Tondalus der Ritter* (*De Raptu animae Tondali*), printed by JOHANN and CONRAD HIST, about 1483 (H. 15540, 15541), barely deserve mention for their crude little cuts.

MAINZ[1]

The earliest books with woodcut decoration printed at Mainz by Fust and Schoeffer have already been described.[2] Fust appears to have died from the plague on a visit to Paris about 1466, and from 1467 Schoeffer continued printing alone until the end of the century, but only issued three books of importance for their woodcuts, the *Herbarius Latinus* (1484), *Gart der Gesuntheit* (sometimes called *Herbarius zu Teutsch*) (1485), and the *Cronecken der Sassen* (1492).

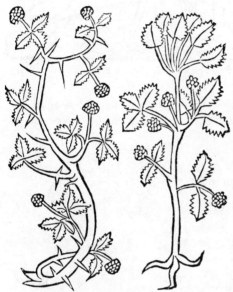

Fig. 159. Mulberry, from *Herbarius Latinus*, Mainz 1484.

Except perhaps for the *Herbarius* of Lucius Apuleius, printed in Rome, and described below,[3] Schoeffer's *Herbarius Latinus* was the earliest of a series of Herbals, with text compiled from a variety of sources, very popular in the xv century, and still of great interest for their woodcut illustrations.[4] These woodcuts must in part have been based on earlier drawings in manuscripts, but a considerable number were undoubtedly newly and faithfully designed

---

[1] See Albert Schramm, *Bilderschmuck der Frühdrucke*, xiv. and xv., Leipzig 1931, 1932.

[2] See p. 274. For Mainz books in general see Paul Heitz, *Frankfurter und Mainzer Drucker- und Verlegerzeichen*, Strassburg 1896. [3] See p. 402.

[4] See Dr. J. F. Payne, Bibliographical Society, vol. vi.; Arnold C. Klebs, Papers, Bibliographical Society of America, Chicago, xi., 1917, p. 75, and xii., 1918, p. 41; *Hortus Sanitatis Deutsch*, Mainz, Schoeffer, 1485: Facsimile (with text by W. L. Schreiber, on the Herbals of the xv and xvi centuries), Munich 1924.

Fig. 160. Group of Thirteen Physicians. Frontispiece to the *Gart der Gesuntheit*, Mainz 1485.

from nature, and all are cut with a charming simplicity and true decorative quality.

The first work, the quarto *Herbarius Latinus* of 1484 (S. 4203 and variants 4204 and 4205, H. 8444), contains descriptions and figures of 150 plants. The second book, of 1485, is not merely a German version of the Latin Herbal, but a far more comprehensive work in folio, in 435 chapters, with 381 illustrations (from 380 blocks), including the frontispiece (fig. 160), the *Physician with a Woman* at the beginning of Part V. (on urines), 369 plants (all different blocks from those in the 1484 *Herbarius*, and mostly in larger scale), and 9 animals (the *elephant* being repeated). Like many xv-century books, it has no title-page, but in his preface the author (Dr. Johann Wonnecken von Cube of Frankfurt) calls it *Gart der Gesuntheit*, and this is certainly a better description than the *Herbarius* of its colophon. It is not a mere herbal, but a book of medical science, which has a short section on urines, and includes the properties of a few animals as well as the more numerous plants. In spite of correspondence of title, the Latin *Hortus Sanitatis*, printed by Meydenbach, 1491, is an independent work, though of course largely derived from its greatest predecessor in the same field. Schoeffer's *Gart der Gesuntheit* is a smaller folio than Meydenbach's book, and they are also occasionally referred to respectively as the 'smaller' and the 'larger' *Hortus*.

The frontispiece to the *Gart der Gesuntheit* is a most vividly rendered *Group of Thirteen Physicians* and has all the characteristics of Erhard Reuwich's draughtsmanship, as seen in his illustrations to Breydenbach, and is almost certainly by his hand.[1] And the same may be said of the second figure subject.

A passage in the preface of the *Gart der Gesuntheit* refers to a noble personage, accompanied by a wise and skilful painter, who procured information and drawings of the rarer herbs and plants, and the route they followed on their journey makes it at least possible that the reference was to Breydenbach and Reuwich. Breydenbach's journey was completed January 1484, so there would have been ample time for Reuwich to develop his designs before the *Gart der Gesuntheit* (March 1485). There is nothing in the style of the plants to compare with the known illustrations of Reuwich, but some of the animals, e.g. *elephant* (cap. 172 and 371), *gazelle* (cap. 272) and *stag* (cap. 292), are more evidently compatible with his style.

Schreiber speaks of the *Herbarius* of Lucius Apuleius, printed at Rome by J. P. de Lignamine (H. 1322), as of about 1493 and based on the

---

[1] As has been suggested by L. Baer, Gutenbergfestschrift, 1925. Cf. p. 354.

Herbarius Latinus, but it is more probably contemporary or even earlier than the Mainz *Herbarius,* and perhaps the earliest of the printed herbals.[1]

The *Hortus Sani-tatis,* printed by JACOB MEYDENBACH at Mainz in 1491 (S. 4247, H. 8944), is a more extensive work than Schoeffer's *Gart der Gesuntheit,* having a second part supplementary to the herbal, dealing comprehensively with beasts, birds, fishes, stones, and urines. The cuts of plants are based on Schoeffer's, and equally good but even more interesting are the new designs to the second part, numerous illustrations with figures, of which we have already spoken as probably in part by the hand of the Master of the Ulm *Aesop,* and the Speier *Spiegel menschlicher Behält-nis.* Later editions of the *Hortus Sanitatis* of 1491, with newly

Fig. 161. Illustration to the Chapter on Stones, in *Hortus Sanitatis,* Mainz 1491.

cut designs, were issued by Johann Prüss at Strassburg, about 1497 (S. 4248, H. 8941) and about 1499 (S. 4249, H. 8942).

Dr. Arnold Klebs's studies in the Papers of the Bibliographical Society

[1] See p. 402.

of America, with his lists of incunabula, give a clear picture of the comparative popularity of the three chief herbals during the xv century. Of the *Herbarius Latinus* (Mainz 1484) there are about eleven later editions, three printed by Veldener at Culenborg and Louvain, four by J. Petri at Passau, and others by J. and C. Hist at Speier, by Leonardus Achates and Gulielmus of Pavia at Vicenza, by Bevilaqua at Venice and Jean Bonhomme at Paris. Of the *Gart der Gesuntheit* (Mainz 1485) there are some fourteen later editions, nine printed by Schoensperger at Augsburg, two by Grüninger at Strassburg, and others by Dinckmut at Ulm, by M. Furter at Basle, and Steffen Arndes at Lübeck (the last with additions from the *Hortus Sanitatis*). Of the *Hortus Sanitatis* (Mainz 1491) there are only four later editions, three printed by J. Prüss at Strassburg, and one by Vérard at Paris, about 1500 (see p. 670). There is also a French work largely based on the *Gart der Gesuntheit*, of which the only xv-century editions known are (*a*) *Arbolayre*, probably printed by P. Metlinger, Besançon, about 1487–88, and (*b*) *Grant Herbier en françois*, printed by P. Le Caron, Paris, between 1495 and 1500 (see p. 672).

To return to Schoeffer's books, the *Cronecken der Sassen* of 1492 (S. 3531, H. 4990) contains a large number of interesting cuts, views of towns with their founders and patron saints, genealogical, heraldic and portrait illustrations and the like. Such cuts as that of *Two Men bartering* (sig. a 8, rev.) and *Otheberne* (sig. v 8, rev.) are entirely in the manner of the *Portrait of Aesop* in the Ulm *Aesop*, and can hardly be due to any other designer. Many of the other illustrations are cruder in execution than the Aesop cuts, but their vivid mode of expression seems to derive from the same source. The *Wedekind Duke of Saxony and his Duchess*, on sig. d 8, is a fine example of heraldic decoration.

Perhaps the most interesting of all the Mainz books of this period is Bernhard von Breydenbach's *Sanctae Peregrinationes* (Journey to the Holy Land), which was illustrated and printed by ERHARD REUWICH in 1486.[1] Erhard Reuwich was an artist of Utrecht, and though this is the only book in which he is noted as the printer, there is no direct evidence to support Voulliéme's suggestion that he was helped in this capacity by Schoeffer except the fact that the types used corresponded with two of the latter's founts. Breydenbach was a man of noble family, and Dean of Mainz, who according to his own account lived somewhat loosely in his youth, and undertook the pilgrimage in 1483–84 as a sort of penance. There were

[1] See H. W. Davies, *Bernhard von Breydenbach and his Journey to the Holy Land*, 1483–84. A Bibliography, London 1911.

Fig. 162. Frontispiece to Breydenbach, *Sanctae Peregrinationes*, Mainz 1486.

altogether some 150 members of the pilgrimage, including Felix Fabri, who also wrote an account of the journey.[1] Apart from his journal of the pilgrimage, Breydenbach included in his work a description of Palestine, a Life of Mahomet, accounts of the sieges of Constantinople and Rhodes, and notes on the laws and manners of the inhabitants of the Holy Land.

Erhard Reuwich went as Breydenbach's official artist, and was responsible for all the 'embellishment' of the book. No other designs are recorded as his, but to judge from its style he very probably designed the frontispiece to Schoeffer's *Gart der Gesuntheit*, 1485, and possibly also the other illustrations of the same book.[2]

The style of his figures has very definite relation to the woodcuts in various Dutch books of the period, especially to those by the Delft designer, who has been identified conjecturally with the Master of the Virgo inter Virgines.[3]

The work must have been exceedingly popular, for it was issued in thirteen editions between 1486 and 1522, of which the following summary is taken from Davies:

A. *Editions with the Original Cuts*

MAINZ (REUWICH). 11th February 1486. Latin text. S. 3628, H. 3956.
MAINZ (REUWICH). June 21st 1486. German text. S. 3630, H. 3959.
MAINZ (REUWICH). 1488. Flemish text. S. 3633, H. 3963.
LYON (ORTUIN). 1489–90. French text.
SPEIER (DRACH). 1490. Latin text. S. 3629, H. 3957.
SPEIER (DRACH). About 1495. German text. S. 3632, H. 3958.
SARAGOSSA (HURUS). 1498. Spanish text (with a new cut, a view of Rome, added).

B. *Editions with Copies of the Original Cuts*

AUGSBURG (SORG). 1488. German text. Copies A. S. 3631, H. 3960.
LYON (TOPIÉ and JACOBUS OF HERRNBERG). 1488. French text. Copies B (the folding plates now engraved on copper).
SPEIER (DRACH). 1502. Latin text. Copies C.
SPEIER (DRACH). About 1505. German text. Copies C.
PARIS (N. HIGMAN for REGNAULT). 1517. French text. Copies D.
PARIS (N. HIGMAN for REGNAULT). 1522–23. French text. Copies D.

The cuts of the original edition included a frontispiece, seven folding plates of views (*Venice, Parenzo, Corfu, Modon, Candia, Rhodes* and

---

[1] MS. in the Stadtbibliothek, Ulm, 1st ed., 1843. See p. 84, for another work by Fabri.
[2] See p. 350.   [3] See p. 572.

Fig. 163. Part of the View of Venice, from Breydenbach, *Sanctae Peregrinationes*, Mainz 1486.

Jerusalem), two cuts printed on the reverse of the *Jerusalem*, i.e. *Animals seen in the Holy Land* (including a Unicorn!), and the *Holy Sepulchre*; and the following illustrations in the text: the *Church of the Holy Sepulchre*, six plates illustrating various races (*Saracens, Jews, Greeks, Syrians, Abyssinians* and *Turks*; see fig. 164), and seven plates of Alphabets in various languages. The little cut of the *Holy Sepulchre* does not appear in the Speier edition of 1490, so it was probably lost on the journey from Lyon.

Fig. 164. Mounted Turks, from Breydenbach, *Sanctae Peregrinationes,* Mainz 1486.

The frontispiece is one of the finest pieces of allegorical and heraldic decoration produced in Germany during the xv century. It was evidently a model for decorative work in the frontispiece to the *Nuremberg Chronicle* (1493), which also borrowed from its views of towns. The views are perhaps the earliest cuts of any importance which can definitely be regarded as based on genuine topographical studies, and the lively figure designs are equally interesting as examples of studies from nature, at a period when 'historical' illustrations were mostly imaginary fictions added to please the reader's eye.

Another illustrated book printed at Mainz has already been described in the section devoted to Dotted Prints (Turrecremata, *Meditationes,* 1479).[1]

COLOGNE

Descending the Rhine from Mainz to Cologne,[2] and coming to other

[1] See p. 194.
[2] See Paul Heitz and O. Zaretzky, *Die Kölner Büchermarken*, Strassburg 1898; E. Voulliéme, *Der Buchdruck Kölns bis zum Ende des xv^{ten} Jahrhunderts*, Bonn 1903; A. Schramm, *Bilderschmuck der Frühdrucke*, viii., Leipzig 1924.

towns of North Germany, one is immediately struck by the comparative dearth of fine illustrated books; in fact there are only three works of outstanding importance for their cuts, i.e. the *Cologne Bible* of about 1478–79, the Lübeck *Dance of Death* of 1489, and the *Lübeck Bible* of 1494. We shall need, however, to describe, or refer to, certain other books for various other reasons beside their artistic virtues.

Fig. 165. Noah's Ark, from *Fasciculus Temporum*, Cologne (Gotz), about 1473.

The earliest book of historical importance illustrated with woodcuts at Cologne is Werner Rolewinck, *Fasciculus Temporum*, which was issued in numerous editions (with many varieties of cuts) by printers at Cologne and elsewhere from 1473 or 1474 onwards. The earliest dated editions printed at Cologne, by NICOLAUS GOTZ (S. 5105, H. 6917) and ARNOLD THER HOERNEN (S. 5106, H. 6918), belong to the year 1474. The *Fasciculus Temporum* was the first and most popular of the printed Epitomes of History, being quickly followed by the anonymous *Rudimentum Noviciorum* of Lübeck, 1475 (translated into French as *La Mer des Hystoires*), and at a longer interval by the much more valuable *Weltchronik* of Hartmann Schedel, Nuremberg 1493. Apart from the circles of the genealogical tables, there are only a few unimportant diagrams and illustrations in the various editions of the *Fasciculus*, which generally include a *Noah's Ark*, a *Rainbow*, the *Tower of Babel*, the *Temple at Jerusalem*, a *Christ on the Cross*, a *Christ blessing*, and some views of towns (invariably in the Cologne editions, a *View of Cologne*).

The Gotz edition, though undated, probably precedes that of Ther Hoernen, but it has fewer cuts (five in all) and is without the subject of the *Christ blessing*. Ther Hoernen's edition may be regarded as the type followed with modifications in most of the later issues of the book in Germany and elsewhere.

Of the later editions, that of Quentell (first issue 1479, S. 5110, H. 6923) is among the best, the view of Cologne being an interesting variation on Ther Hoernen's version.

In the section on Dotted Prints we have already mentioned Nicolaus Gotz's printer's mark, which occurs in various editions of the *Fasciculus Temporum*.[1]

The earliest of Cologne printers, ULRICH ZEL, whose publications extend from 1466 to 1507, was not the first in the field with illustrated books. His earliest illustrated work was Nicolaus de Lyra, *Postilla in Universas Biblias*, n.d., about 1485 (S. 4844, H. 10368), but the cuts are even less important than those in the *Fasciculus Temporum*, being chiefly diagrams, illustrations

Fig. 166. View of Cologne, from *Fasciculus Temporum*, Cologne (Ther Hoernen) 1474.

of the Temple and its Treasure, and the like. The only other illustrated work of any note that he printed during the xv century has already been mentioned in the section on Dotted Prints (Bertholdus, *Horologium Devotionis*).[2]

The great *Cologne Bible*, printed by HEINRICH QUENTELL about 1478–79,[3] is perhaps the most epoch-making of all contemporary Bibles for the influence its woodcuts had on Bible-illustration in general for generations. It is a large folio, printed in two columns, issued in two editions: I. in *Low Saxon* dialect (S. 3465, H. 3142, GW. 4307); II. in *West Low German*, the Cologne dialect (S. 3466, H. 3141, GW. 4308). The bulk of the woodcuts are some hundred illustrations to the Old Testament, the *Creation* $7\frac{1}{2}$ inches square, the rest oblongs extending to the breadth of the

[1] See p. 195.   [2] See p. 194.
[3] R. Kautzsch, *Die Holzschnitte der Kölner Bibel von 1479*, Strassburg 1896; W. Worringer, *Die Kölner Bibel*, Munich 1923.

page, $4\frac{3}{4} \times 7\frac{1}{2}$ inches, all being within double border-line. Then four similar oblongs illustrating the four evangelists, two small column cuts of a messenger and letter repeated in the Epistles, and finally nine oblong cuts to the Apocalypse. The last eight of the Apocalypse cuts (Schramm, figs. 465-472) and the second of the Epistle cuts (Schramm, fig. 463) only appear in Edition II, and there are also a few differences in the Old Testament cuts in the two editions.

In addition to the subjects there is a four-sided border composed of three blocks, one block a for the top and left, alternatives b1 and b2 for the right side, and alternatives c1 and c2 for the lower member.

The variant blocks may be distinguished as follows: (b1) with a jester and five other figures (Schramm, figs. 357 and 464), (b2) with an archer, dragon and standard-bearer (Schramm, fig. 473), (c1) the *Adoration of the Magi* (Schramm, figs. 357, 464 and 473), (c2) nude men and woman supporting two shields.

In the British Museum copy of Edition I borders occur: (1) f1, with a, b2 and c1 (see fig. 167); (2) Genesis I, with a, b2 and c2; (3) Proverbs I, with a, b2 and c2; (3) Apocalypse, with a, b2 and c2.

In the British Museum copy of Edition II (imperfect; only to end of Kings, with 2 leaves, including Genesis I, wanting) the only border, f1, is composed of a, b1 and c1.

The dating and even the order of the two editions (neither of which bear dates) have been matters of considerable conjecture. The order given above is now generally accepted, and the *Gesamtkatalog* dates them both about 1478. The borders occur in various forms in other books printed by Quentell and the *Adoration of the Magi* appears as a separate illustration in his *Fasciculus Temporum* of 1479. Comparison of the condition of the blocks of the borders in the British Museum copies of the two editions seems to support the order given above, though I can only state that the impression in Edition I is generally clearer. On the other hand, comparison with dated editions of other works in which the border occurs proves that both Editions I and II precede 31st August 1479, as neither of them show the break in the middle of the rim of the hat of the top figure in b1 which occurs in Astesanus, *Summa de Casibus Conscientiae*, 31st August 1479 (H.1894, GW. 2755, Pr. 1236, B.M.L. IC. 4362). Therefore, even if some copies of either edition might have been printed later,[1] the first printings of both editions must have been made before 31st August 1479, and the date 1478-79 is therefore probable for both.

[1] Mr. Dyson Perrins's copy of Edition I has a contemporary MS. date of 1480 at the end.

Fig. 167. Page with border, from the *Cologne Bible*, about 1478–79.

The subject blocks which appeared in those editions were reprinted, with certain variations and omissions, by Koberger in his *German Bible*, Nuremberg 1483 (S.3461, H.3137).

The design of the woodcuts is Netherlandish in character, an influence very marked in the *Abraham and Melchisedek*, which is one of the best of the cuts in figure and expression. But it is probable that they are based on miniatures done in Cologne, where the Netherlandish influence was strong, and Kautzsch is probably right in referring to the miniatures in MS. 516 in the Berlin Library as the originals used by the designer, or if not these

Fig. 168. Jacob's Blessing, from the *Cologne Bible*, about 1478–79.

actual drawings (they are done in the pen, some being lightly tinted), at least some unidentified series of the same school. For the most part the cuts are without much subtlety of expression, heavy in outline and hard and angular in linear style.

Shading is in straight parallels and parallel series of short strokes are often used for the ground as in Netherlandish woodcuts of the period. The style is nearer to that of the weaker *Biblia Pauperum* block-books than to the majority of Netherlandish book-illustrations, which are generally treated with a lighter and more mobile touch. The resemblance sometimes noted to the style of French cuts (e.g. to that of Vérard's book-illustrations) consists more in the blunter expression of the Netherlandish modes, common to both, than in any intrinsic relationship. The borders used in Quentell's *Missale Itinerantium*, n.d. (S. 4714, C. 4140), are certainly French in inspiration, though the influence probably came through the Low Countries. Quentell must however have had relation with Paris printers, for he actually borrowed a large French block of a *Student in his Chamber*, and used it in several of his books, e.g. as a portrait of *Albertus Magnus*, in Aristotle, *De Anima, cum Commentario Alberti Magni*, n.d. (S. 3349, H. 1711, Schramm 493). The block had originally belonged to Gillet Couteau and Jean Menard and was first used in their *Danse Macabre* of 1492 (see Claudin, *Histoire de l'imprimerie en France*, ii. p. 176).[1]

Other examples near in style to the cuts of the *Cologne Bible* are a *Scene in a Court of Justice* in the *Sachsenspiegel*, printed by BARTOLOMAEUS DE UNKEL, 1480 (S. 5169, H. 14081), a *Crucifixion* in the *Missale Coloniense*, printed by CONRAD WINTERS DE HOMBORCH, 1481 (S. 4683, C. 4114), and the illustrations in Otto von Passau, *Die vier und zwanzig Alten*, printed by JOHANN KOELHOFF THE ELDER, 1492 (S. 4882, C. 4543). Still in the same tradition but rather more allied to the harder French manner, are the cuts in the *Cologne Chronicle* (*Die Cronica van der hilliger Stat van Coellen*) printed by JOHANN KOELHOFF THE YOUNGER in 1499 (S. 3753, H. 4989), which we have already quoted for its passage on the invention of printing.[2] There are over fifty woodcuts, but they are of far less importance in illustration than the *Cologne Bible*, and poorer in quality.

Blocks originally belonging to Knoblochtzer of Strassburg were reprinted by Johann Koelhoff the elder (e.g. in his Low German *Aesop*, 1489, S. 3039, C. 118), and many of the cuts used by Ludwig von Renchen go back to the same source. But a greater number of contemporary Cologne illustrations derive from the Netherlands, and Koelhoff the elder actually borrowed Antwerp blocks to illustrate his edition of the *Historia Septem Sapientum Romae*, 1490 (S. 5139, H. 8725). The blocks were originally printed by Claes Leeuw in his Flemish edition of 1488 (H. 8739, CA. 954), and later by Gerard Leeuw in 1490 (CA. 950).[3]

One other book printed by Koelhoff the elder deserves mention for its attractive floral border design (leaves and flowers on a black ground), i.e. Gerardus de Vliederhoven, *Die Vijer Vijssersten*, 1487 (S. 4095).

The last of the Cologne printers to whom reference might be made is HERMANN BUMGART, but only for the cut of the *Adoration of the Magi* in an architectural setting which he used in various books before the end of the xv century as his printer's mark.

[1] See p. 647.   [2] See p. 207.   [3] See p. 579.

Lübeck

Lübeck[1] was a far less important centre than Cologne in the printing of books, but it can boast one designer (the author of the cuts in the *Dance of Death* of 1489, and Steffen Arndes's *Bible* of 1494) of greater individuality than any of the Cologne illustrators.

One of the earliest illustrated works issued at Lübeck, the *Rudimentum Noviciorum* printed by LUCAS BRANDIS, 1475 (S. 5159, H. 4996),[2] is notable among early printed Universal Histories, following within about a year the first dated Cologne edition of Rolewinck's *Fasciculus Temporum*. This compilation, intended for the instruction of young ecclesiastics, had an even greater vogue in its French translation, under the title of *La Mer des Hystoires*, in the fine editions printed by Pierre Le Rouge in Paris, 1488-89, by Jean Dupré at Lyon, 1491,[3] and in various later issues.

The numerous cuts of the Lübeck edition include genealogical tables (in the forms of chains, the round links sometimes filled with figure subjects), maps of the world and of the Holy Land; little upright cuts of stock subjects (for repetition on various occasions) such as the storming of a city, the building of a town, and typical representations of emperor, pope, saints and philosophers; and numerous Bible subjects, including a full-page woodcut in compartments illustrating the Passion of Christ.

The designer, who generally uses shading in parallel series of short strokes, is either from the Low Countries or directly under Netherlandish influence. The cuts are of no great quality, but possess certain characteristics of vivid representation.

Certain of the decorative cuts in the *Rudimentum* had appeared earlier (it seems) in the same printer's Josephus, *De Antiquitate Judaica*, n.d. (S.4402, H. 9450), i.e. the *Initial I with the portrait of Josephus* (fig. 169), and a three-side scroll border, with lions supporting a shield at the foot. The *Josephus* has already been noted for its woodcut headlines,[4] and is remarkable too for its large pictorial initials in which a few subjects are printed from separate blocks within different letters.

A *Psalter*, of about 1483, printed by Lucas Brandis without date (S. 5026, H. 13520), is also chiefly attractive for its initials and border decoration. Two other works of the same printer, *Die Nye Ee und dat Passional van*

---

[1] A. Tronnier, *Die Lübecker Buchillustration des XV Jahrhunderts*, Göttingen Dissertation (1904), Strassburg 1904; A. Schramm, *Bilderschmuck der Frühdrucke*, x., xi., xii., Leipzig 1927, 1928, 1929.
[2] See p. 569.   [3] See pp. 632 and 612.   [4] Cf. p. 338.

Ihesus und Marien (several editions, in and about 1478 and 1482, C. 3349 and H. 4061)[1] and *Spiegel menschlicher Behältnis*, n.d., about 1483 (S. 5283, H. 14941), contain some hundreds of illustrations, but crude and angular, chiefly in outline, and far less individual than those of the *Rudimentum*.

An undated work printed by Lucas's brother, MAT-THAEUS BRANDIS, Meister Stephan, *Dat Schaekspel* (S. 5318, H. 4898), contains crude but amusing cuts illustrating the various classes and occupations of mankind.

The *Revelationes Sanctae Brigittae*, printed by BARTHOLO-MAEUS GHOTAN, 1492 (S. 3502, H. 3204), is a far more important work for its full-page woodcuts, designed and cut with considerable force, and interesting also for its pictorial initials.

The *Lübeck Bible*, in Low Saxon, printed by STEFFEN ARNDES in 1494 (S. 3467, H. 3143),[2] was probably less epoch-making than the *Cologne Bible* in its influence on other designers, but it certainly stands higher for the individual genius of its chief illustrator. Herein lies its real virtue, for as a book it cannot compare in beauty with the best works issued by the Zainers at Augsburg and Ulm. Most of the illustrations are oblong, covering the two columns of the text. There is a large square cut of *St. Jerome* at the beginning and a smaller one of the same saint repeated in various other places; a *Roundel of the Creation* at the beginning of Genesis; four cuts of the *Evangelists*, and one of an *Apostle handing a messenger a letter*, used at various places throughout the Epistles, these five already issued in a *Plenarium* printed by Arndes in the previous year (S. 4985, H. 6753).

Most of the large oblong cuts are in the earlier portion of the Bible, and of these the better part are at the beginning. There are certainly two designers, as Romdahl first contended: the better and more individual hand (Master A)

Fig. 169.
Initial I,
from
Josephus,
Lübeck,
about 1475.

[1] Cf. p. 569.
[2] A. L. Romdahl, *Zeitschrift für Bücherfreunde*, 1905–06, p. 391; Hans Wahl, *Die 92 Holzschnitte der Lübecker Bibel*, Weimar 1917; M. J. Friedländer, *Die Holzschnitte der Lübecker Bibel zu den 5 Büchern Mose*, Berlin 1918; M. J. Friedländer, *Die Lübecker Bibel*, Munich 1923.

shows characteristic circular strokes and shading, a great command of human expression and of the rendering of solid form, and the use of types both of figure and architecture which seem to betoken knowledge of Italy (see fig. 170); the second designer (Master B) has a more angular method, with harder outline and straighter shading. General characteristics of design and treatment show that he was inspired by the Master A, though he was far more limited in power, and more Gothic in style.

Practically all the illustrations to the Pentateuch (with the possible exception of Genesis iii., Leviticus x. and Numbers xiii., and the few cuts

Fig. 170. Jacob's Ladder, from the *Lübeck Bible*, 1494.

of other forms than oblong are designed by Master A; from the First Book of Kings (our 1st Samuel) onwards nearly all are by the Master B, with two exceptions from the Pentateuch which are repeated as different subjects. Sometimes the second designer's work is powerful and spirited in design (e.g. the *Death of Absalom*, 2nd Book of Kings, i.e. 2nd Samuel xviii.), but it has none of the subtle qualities of the chief designer. I refer to two designers, as I hardly think the distinction could be caused by the difference in merit of two cutters: it is a definite difference in the character of the drawings cut.

In general style of figure and landscape composition both derive from the Netherlands, even if they are not by Netherlandish designers, and the peculiar touch of the chief illustrator has much in common with the early work of Jacob Cornelisz and Lucas van Leyden. This comparison was rightly suggested by Dr. Max Friedländer in his

Fig. 171. The Burgomaster, from the Lübeck *Dance of Death*, 1489.

edition of the Lübeck *Dance of Death* (*Des Dodes Dantz*), issued by an unknown printer in 1489 (S. 5375),[1] where cuts of Death and members of the various classes of mankind are certainly designed by the same hand. The book is very rare, the first edition being only known at Nuremberg and Linköping (Sweden), the second Lübeck edition of 1496 (S. 5376) at Wolfenbüttel, and xvi-century editions at Oxford (Lübeck 1520) and Copenhagen (in Danish, Copenhagen 1536). The text is based on the inscriptions attached to a series of wall-paintings of the subject in the Marienkirche at Lübeck.

The earlier Lübeck editions bear the colophon mark of *Three Poppies on a Shield*, and books with this mark are generally assigned to 'the Poppy Printer', who has been generally identified with Matthaeus Brandis. But recent researches by Swedish authorities tend to regard such books as by several printers (e.g. Matthaeus Brandis, Johann Snel, and Steffen Arndes) issued under the literary and commercial direction of HANS VAN GHETELEN. The relations of Lübeck printers with Denmark and Sweden render the study of their publication by students of Scandinavian bibliography of great importance.

Occasional impressions from blocks of the *Dodes Dantz* occur in other books, e.g. *Death with a Scythe* in the *Navolghinge Jesu Christi* (*Imitatio Christi*), Lübeck ('The Poppy Printer') 1489 (S. 5349);[2] the *Pope, Cardinal* and *Bishop* in the *Speygel der Leyen*, Lübeck ('The Poppy Printer') 1496 (S. 5284), and the *Nun* in the anonymously printed *S. Birgitten Openbaringe*, Lübeck 1496 (S. 3501, H. 3206).

[1] M. J. Friedländer, Graphische Gesellschaft, xii., Berlin 1910 (facsimile of the Nuremberg copy).

[2] In very good impression in British Museum Library copy, before the breaks in the border seen in the 1st ed. of *Dodes Dantz*.

Considering that the style of the chief designer of the *Lübeck Bible* (1494) is fully developed in the *Dance of Death* of 1489, I cannot agree with Schreiber's suggestion that the cuts in Ghotan's *Revelationes S. Brigittae* of 1492 (S. 3502), with their much less mobile touch, are by the same hand. Schreiber also attributes to the same master the cuts in the *Life of St. Jerome*, Lübeck (Ghotan) 1484 (S. 4229, H. 6723), the *Heiligenleben*, issued by an anonymous printer, Lübeck 1487 (S. 4322, H. 9989), and the *Upsala Breviary*, Stockholm (Johannes Fabri) 1496 (S. 3627).

Confusion as to other attributions has been caused by regarding the whole series as by one designer, and Romdahl was on the right track in estimating the relationship of other Lübeck cuts (apart from the *Dodes Dantz*) as nearer to the Master B rather than to the Master A. And if Goldschmidt's suggestion that the Lübeck painter BERNT NOTKE may be the designer is correct,[1] he is more probably the designer B than the other remarkable but somewhat alien personality who disappears from Lübeck after 1494 (and may perhaps have died in the course of the work, as its completion by another would suggest). The nearest of the related cuts appear to me to be the illustrations added in the second edition of Steffen Arndes' *Heiligenleben*, 1492 (S. 4324, H. 9991), but several other works, e.g. Ghotan's *Revelationes Sanctae Brigittae*, 1492, already mentioned, might be noted as possibly from the same workshop.

Comparison was first made by Dr. Kristeller between the *Lübeck Bible* and the *Terence*, printed by Trechsel at Lyon in 1493, and Friedländer suggested identity of authorship. There is undoubtedly kinship in general style between the better cuts of the *Lübeck Bible* and these *Terence* illustrations, though the latter are cut with all the characteristic precision of certain French woodcutters. The kinship might come from common education in some German atelier, for Trechsel's designer might have gone with Trechsel himself from Mainz to Lyon. Something peculiar to both the Lübeck Master and Trechsel's designer might have found inspiration in the lively style of the Utrecht painter who designed and printed Breydenbach's *Peregrinationes* at Mainz in 1486.

ZINNA—LEIPZIG—WÜRZBURG

Turning southwards from Lübeck in our survey, I would mention a curious book of about 1494, the only work printed at the Cistercian Convent of Zinna, i.e. Hermann Nitzschewitz, *Novum beatae Mariae Psalterium*

[1] A. Goldschmidt, Zeitschrift für bildende Kunst, 1901, pp. 33, 55.

(H. 11891, S. 4859). Nitzschewitz, who was chaplain to the Emperor, had appealed to Frederick III for funds for the publication, and these were granted by his son and successor Maximilian I in 1494. Thus the two full-page blocks on the first and second pages show the *Virgin and Child supported by the two Emperors, and adored by four Ecclesiastics* and the *Two Emperors adoring the Virgin and Child*, while the series of cuts illustrating the life of the Virgin and of Christ are flanked by border-pieces which again represent the two Emperors in adoration. This latter part of the book, with its subject cuts at the head and borders at the outer sides and foot of each page, shows a richness of woodcut illustration comparable with French *Horae*, though far below the best of these in quality. The most attractive decorative feature in the book is the large floral border and initial letter occurring at signatures a ii and a v. It is probable that the convent obtained the collaboration of some Leipzig printer such as CONRAD KACHELOFEN.

We then pass Leipzig itself,[1] which is only notable in xv-century book-illustration for Kachelofen's block-book calendars,[2] and Böttiger's *Auslegung der Messe* of 1495 with its dotted prints,[3] and turning aside to note the Missals and Breviaries of Würzburg and Eichstätt printed by GEORG and MICHAEL REYSER,[4] though these are chiefly remarkable for the occurrence of line-engraving[5] instead of the usual woodcut in illustration, we may come without further delay to our last important centre of German book-illustration, i.e. Nuremberg.

NUREMBERG

Woodcut work produced at Nuremberg and the not far distant towns of Nördlingen and Regensburg has already been noted in the block-books issued by Hans Spörer, Friedrich Walther and Hans Hurning, Johannes Eysenhut and the Master Lienhart, between about 1470 and 1473. And we have already described one of the earliest illustrated Nuremberg books, i.e. Sensenschmidt's *German Bible*, n.d., about 1476 (S. 3457, H. 3132), in relation to the *Bibles* of Günther Zainer and Pflanzmann of Augsburg.[6]

Reference has also been made to a cut in Maphaeus Vegius, *Philalethes*, printed by JOHANN MÜLLER about 1474, and to a supposed *Portrait of Marco Polo* in an edition of his *Travels* printed by FRIEDRICH CREUSSNER,

---

[1] See A. Schramm, *Bilderschmuck der Frühdrucke*, xiii., Die Drucker in Leipzig und Erfurt, 1930. [2] See p. 262. [3] See p. 195.
[4] See A. Schramm, *Bilderschmuck der Frühdrucke*, xvi. Leipzig 1933.
[5] See M. Lehrs, *Geschichte und Kritischer Katalog*, vi. pp. 124 and 155.
[6] See p. 290. For notes on single cuts assigned to Nuremberg see W. Cohn, *Untersuchungen zur Geschichte des deutschen Einblattholzschnitts*. Strassburg 1934, p. 37.

Nuremberg 1477 (S. 5002, H. 13245), in describing copies issued by Knoblochtzer of Strassburg.[1] And of Creussner's early books we may mention two more, Tuberinus, *De Puero Simone*, n.d., about 1476 (S. 5260, H. 15654), for its large and crude cut of the notorious *Ritual Murder of St. Simon of Trent* (S. 1967),[2] which took place in the year 1475, and the *Auslegung des Amts der Heiligen Messe*, n.d., about 1482 (S. 4643, H. 2143), for its charmingly naïve rendering of the *Visitation*, with its round and angular conventions for trees.

Fig. 172. The Visitation, from *Auslegung des Amts*, Nuremberg, about 1482.

Three other books printed by Johann Müller may be mentioned for their initials of strapwork on a black ground based on those used by Sweynheym and Pannartz at Rome (e.g. in the *Suetonius* of 1470), i.e. Basilius, *Opusculum ad Juvenes*, n.d., about 1474 (H. 2683), Marcus Manilius, *Astronomica*, n.d. (H. 10703), and J. Müller, *Tractatus contra Cremonensia*, n.d., about 1475 (H. 13805, S. 4374). It appears probable that the German initials may be casts from the Italian blocks.[3]

Of the other earlier Nuremberg printers, HANS FOLZ, a barber-surgeon, holds a somewhat special place for the variety of popular poems he wrote

---

[1] See pp. 336 and 337.

[2] The cut, which occurs as a separate print in Paris (Bouchot 125), appears in the Munich and Bamberg copies of the book.　　　　　　　　　　　　　　　[3] See p. 398.

and issued in the few years succeeding 1479, each illustrated with one crude cut. But books of this character, which are of great rarity outside German libraries, are of far less interest for their woodcuts than for their illustration of social history.

And a *Salzburg Missal* printed by GEORG STUCHS in 1492 (S. 4755, H., C. 11420) deserves mention for a powerful frontispiece, a full-page *Portrait of Bishop Friedrich von Schaumburg, standing behind his Coat-of-arms*.[1]

By far the most important of Nuremberg books are those issued by ANTON KOBERGER,[2] the most famous of the printers of his day. He was a man who had made himself a great position in Nuremberg; who was reputed even in 1470 (i.e. the year before his first book was issued) to have had a hundred craftsmen and twenty-four presses at work, and who more than any of his contemporaries developed extensive international relations in printing and book-selling. The records of his work and establishment which are preserved throw much valuable light on the methods of publication at the period.

The illustrations to an edition of Nicolaus de Lyra, *Postilla super Bibliam*, of 1481 (S. 4843, H. 10369), recut in smaller scale in his *Latin Bible* of 1485 (S. 3472, H. 3166), are chiefly diagrams and plans of little artistic interest. They certainly served as models for the *Latin Bibles* (*cum postillis N. de Lyra*), Venice, 1489 and 1495. And his *German Bible* of 1483 merely reprinted the blocks of the great *Cologne Bible* of about 1478–79.

His first illustrated book of individual interest was Jacobus de Voragine, *Passional* (*Leben der Heiligen*), 1488 (S. 4313, H. 9981), containing many cuts very closely resembling the style of the illustrations in Lirer's *Chronica* and Terence, *Eunuchus*, printed at Ulm in 1486.

It is difficult to believe that such a print as *St. Helena finding the Cross* (f. xxv) is not by the author of Lirer's illustrations, and the *Salome with the Head of John the Baptist* (f. xlviii; fig. 173) not the work of the Terence Master; in fact they may all be by the same designer.

The lively style that originated in this Ulm designer must have been an important factor in the development of Dürer's genius, if the early illustrations which have recently been attributed to the great painter and engraver

---

[1] Reproduced, Rosenthal, Catalogue 80 (1924), No. 190. The Rosenthal copy is now in the collection of Mr. Campbell Dodgson.

[2] O. von Hase, *Die Koberger, Buchhändler Familie zu Nürnberg. Eine Darstellung des deutschen Buchhandels*, Leipzig 1869; *Die Koberger, ein Darstellung des buchhändlerischen Geschäftsbetriebes in der Zeit des Überganges vom Mitlelalter zur Neuzeit*, Leipzig (2ᵉ Auflage) 1885; Albert Schramm, *Bilderschmuck der Frühdrucke*, xvii. *Die Drucker in Nürnberg*. (1) *Anton Koberger*. Leipzig 1934.

are actually his design. To these we shall return after some survey of the work of Dürer's master, Wolgemut, and that of Wolgemut's stepson, Wilhelm Pleydenwurff.

MICHEL WOLGEMUT (1434–1519)[1] is the earliest painter, whose work is recognised in this capacity, known also as a designer of book-illustrations, for Erhard Reuwich is only a name to us outside the cuts he designed for Breydenbach's *Peregrinationes* (1486). As a painter Wolgemut was the head

Fig. 173. Salome with the Head of St. John the Baptist, from the *Passional*, Nuremberg 1488.

of a flourishing workshop, but the quality of the pictures that issued from this source is so variable that no certain estimate has been formed of his individual powers.

The only direct evidence of his participation in woodcut design is contained in the colophon of Schedel's *Nuremberg Chronicle*, 1493, where both he and WILHELM PLEYDENWURFF are described as painters and the authors of the illustrations, and in the contracts for the illustrations of the work.[2] Of Wilhelm Pleydenwurff little is known; he was the son of a painter Hans Pleydenwurff, whose widow Wolgemut married in 1473; the date of his birth is unknown; the only documentary evidence is limited to the

[1] For the most valuable notices on Wolgemut as designer of woodcuts see: Valerian von Loga, *Beiträge zum Holzschnittwerk M. W.'s.* Pr. Jahrbuch, xvi., 1895, 224; C. Ephrussi, *Étude sur la Chronique de Nuremberg de H. Schedel*, Paris 1894; C. Dodgson, *Some Rare Woodcuts by W.*, Burlington Magazine, iv., 1904, 245; Franz J. Stadler, *M. W. und der Nürnberger Holzschnitt im letzten Drittel des xv Jahrhunderts*, Strassburg 1913.

[2] A. Gümbel, *Die Verträge über die Illustrierung und den Druck der Schedelschen Weltchronik*, xxv. (1902), 430.

years 1490–95, and he died before the 6th February 1495. There is no direct evidence that he collaborated with Wolgemut in the *Schatzbehalter*, though it is often assumed that he did.

Attempts have been made to distinguish the hands of Wolgemut and Pleydenwurff in the *Chronicle*, but the difficulty of unravelling Wolgemut's style as a painter from that of his workshop, the entire lack of knowledge of Pleydenwurff's painting, and the evident variety of cutters who took part in the work and no doubt modified to varying degrees the designers' styles, would vitiate any dogmatic conclusions. The large W which appears on banners in half a dozen of the *Schatzbehalter* cuts has sometimes been interpreted as Wolgemut's signature, but letters A and G similarly occur on another cut, so that the explanation is hardly probable, and, in consequence, a dangerous basis for a distinction.

The *Schatzbehalter* by Father Stefan Fridolin, issued by Koberger on the 18th November 1491 (S. 5202I, H. 14507), is a folio printed in double column with ninety-six full-page illustrations from ninety-one blocks. The book according to its second title is a 'Treasury of the true Riches of Salvation', and apart from a few allegories, the cuts are entirely subjects from the Bible.

A certain proportion of the subjects are suggested by earlier prints, but there is a considerable residue of original invention, showing at the lowest estimate the virtues of lively humour and vivid expression, while an occasional subject, such as the *Annunciation*, contains elements of real beauty. The design is intensely Gothic in its angular conventions, enhanced by the curled beards and hair which are so characteristic of the Wolgemut cuts. Here and there a design lacks the characteristic verve, but on the whole the quality of both design and cutting is fairly regular throughout.

One of the subjects (No. 66, the *Virtues of Christ and The Wickedness of his Enemies symbolised by divers birds and beasts*) occurs in a separate print at Munich, with a border containing the arms of Nuremberg and the signature *Wolfgang* (S. 1216, described wrongly as a *Temptation of St. Anthony*), and it seems possible that a WOLFGANG HAMER, to whose prints we shall refer later, might have been one of Wolgemut's cutters.

A sketch-book containing over a hundred drawings, probably by Wolgemut, several being original studies for the *Schatzbehalter's* subjects, once in the possession of Rosenthal, Munich (Catalogue 90 of 1892, No. 4), was later in the collection of Professor V. Goldschmidt at Heidelberg. Von Loga noted that one of the drawings was very near a cut

Fig. 174. The Finding of Moses, from the *Schatzbehalter*, Nuremberg 1491.

of *St. Jerome* signed *Wolfgang* (S. 1530, Munich), which is further support to the suggestion made above.

Hartmann Schedel's *Weltchronik* (commonly called the *Nuremberg Chronicle*), issued in July 1493 in the Latin edition (*Liber cronicarum ab inicio mundi*,

Fig. 175. Part of the View of Salzburg, from Schedel, *Weltchronik*, Nuremberg 1493.

S. 5203, H. 14508), and in December of the same year in a German translation by Georg Alt (*Buch der Chroniken*, S. 5205, H. 14510),[1] is a much larger folio than the *Schatzbehalter*, and contains a far greater number of illustra-

---

[1] Later editions with new blocks copied from Koberger's were issued at Augsburg by J. Schoensperger, in German, 1496 (S. 5206, H. 14511), in Latin, 1497 (S. 5204, H. 14509). On the question of binding see E. P. Goldschmidt, *Gothic and Renaissance Bookbindings*, London 1928, vol. i. p. 165, No. 38.

tions. From an analysis made by Sir Sydney Cockerell,[1] it appears that the number of separate blocks (with certain unimportant exceptions) is 645; and that with repeats, the total number of illustrations comes to 1809. The contract for the illustrations to be supplied by Wolgemut and Pleydenwurff was made in December 1491, but references in the contract to blocks already cut, and the date 1490 in Wolgemut's original drawing for the title-cut in the British Museum, prove that the work was in hand some time earlier.

The cuts include numerous scriptural and other subjects, genealogical trees and portraits, maps and many views of towns.[2] There is little historical value in the portraits, and only a beginning of faithful topography in the views (though these are by far the most valuable part of the illustration). Kristeller has aptly said that the illustrations were more often finger-posts to the ordinary reader wishing to find his place in a voluminous text, than any definite attempt at actual illustration. Blocks of the greatest variety of subject and shape scattered almost haphazard, as it seems, over the large areas of type (views often extending over a complete opening), entirely stultified any attempt at making a harmonious page. Moreover, there are far fewer subjects of attractive individual invention in the *Chronicle* than in the *Schatzbehalter*, and far greater diversity of quality in the cutting. The extensive character of the project carried through within so short an interval after the *Schatzbehalter* was enough to damp the invention of far greater talents. The *Roundel with Angels* (f. 2) and the *Roundel with the Creation of the Birds* (f. 4, verso) are graceful examples among many instances of clumsy or awkward design.

We have referred to the sketch-book which contains designs of the *Schatzbehalter*, but by far the most important of Wolgemut's original drawings is his design for the frontispiece of the *Chronicle*, dated 1490, in the British Museum.[3] The pen-drawing is in a style very near in linear conventions to the woodcut; but it differs considerably in details (of shading, etc.), and is in the same direction as the print. It is natural to infer that a transfer drawing on the surface of the block must have intervened, and the question arises whether the painter himself made this final drawing for the cutter to follow in facsimile, or whether another assistant, or the cutter himself, made the drawing on the block from this original of Wolgemut.

---

[1] S. C. Cockerell, *Some German Woodcuts of the xv Century*, London (Kelmscott Press) 1897.

[2] V. von Loga, *Die Städteansichten in H. Schedel's 'Weltchronik'*, Pr. Jahrbuch, ix., 1888, 93, 184.

[3] See Sidney Colvin, Pr. Jahrbuch, vii., 1886, 98.

That Wolgemut having made a drawing in this detail should make another on the block seems unlikely, and the inferiority of the cut to the drawing in many painter-like characteristics rather supports this theory. But it would be dangerous to dogmatise, or to infer a general practice from this one case. In fact, as it seems to be the only important study for the *Chronicle* existing, it is more likely that as a general rule the painter made his own finished drawing on the block.

In discussing the general question of designers and cutters[1] we quoted at length from an account of the costs of another large project of book-illustration which was never published (for Peter Danhauser, *Archetypus Trimphantis Romae*), covering the years 1493–97. The first agreement in this relation occurred in July 1493, only a few days from the publication of the first edition of the *Chronicle*. Sebald Schreyer was chiefly responsible for this work, as for the *Chronicle*, so that, although the painters are not mentioned by name, it seems almost certain that they were Wolgemut and Pleydenwurff. Pleydenwurff, however, can have taken little part, as he died in January 1494. It seems almost certain that a series of allegorical cuts only known in comparatively modern impressions (e.g. at Berlin and Vienna)[2] is a small remnant of the *Archetypus*. Besides miscellaneous allegories, it includes copies after the Ferrarese 'Tarocchi' engravings, and after the *Triumphs of Petrarch* in the 1490 Venetian edition of Pietro de Plasiis Veronese (H. 12771).[3]

The actual woodcutter of the *Archetypus* blocks, SEBALD GALLENSDORFER, is mentioned, so that it is probable that he worked on the earlier books as well. It is interesting to note that he receives much larger fees than the painters. This must imply that the work of cutting so many blocks engrossed the majority of his time, while the painters undertook their designs for book-illustration very much as side-issues from their larger works.

It has sometimes been categorically stated that Wolgemut was a woodcutter as well as a painter,[4] and considerable confusion has been caused by the vague statements of C. G. von Murr in his articles on *Formschneiderkunst* and *Versuch einer Nürnbergischen Kunstgeschichte* in his *Journal zur Kunstgeschichte* (Nuremberg 1766), and by the haphazard way in which he placed painters in his lists of *Formschneider*, without any documentary basis.

---

[1] See p. 90.   [2] Described by von Loga, Pr. Jahrbuch, xvi., 224.

[3] Which are in their turn free renderings of the Florentine Broad Manner engravings (A. M. Hind, *Early Italian Engravings in the British Museum*, B. ii. 1-6).

[4] E.g. W. von Seidlitz, in the article on Wolgemut in the *Deutsche Allgemeine Biographie*, lv. (1910), p. 118.

Fig. 176. Frontispiece to Schedel, *Weltchronik*, Nuremberg 1493.

The best available reference for Nuremberg documents on artists is Albert Gümbel, in the *Repertorium für Kunstwissenschaft*, xxviii., xxix. and xxx. (1905–07), and there no painter is found noted in contemporary records as *Formschneider* as well. Confusion of thought goes back through statements of Heinecken (*Nachrichten*, II Theil, 1769, p. 100), to Sandrart (*Teutsche Akademie*, 1676, p. 216, II Theil, III Buch) and Karel van Mander (*Het Schilderboeck*, 1604, part i. f. 204 b); but the original statement of Karel van Mander that *meest alle Plaet-snyders oock Schilders waren*, certainly refers to line-engravers, though two of the masters he cited designed woodcuts. Bartsch in his introduction to the work of Dürer (*Peintre Graveur*, vol. vii.) strongly contests the statements that Dürer and painters generally were also cutters. Since his day the battle has raged on either side of the controversy, and the old error is by no means extinct. For the whole question see E. Flechsig, *Dürer*, 1928, to whom I owe various references, and to my Chapter III., pp. 90–92.

Apart from the works already mentioned, there is only a comparatively small number of other woodcuts attributed to Wolgemut. The most attractive of these is undoubtedly the *Virgin as Queen of Heaven* (S. 5152 a), known in two states, the first, dated 1492, on a broadside printed in Koberger's types (Graphische Sammlung, Munich), the second in which the cut is surrounded by a scroll border with two angels (Munich Library, in a copy of the *Nuremberg Chronicle*, which belonged to Schedel himself). It has much the same gracious character as the *Annunciation* in the *Schatzbehalter*.

The earliest cut attributed with any certainty is the frontispiece to the *Reformation der Stadt Nürnberg*, printed by Koberger, 1484, S. 5051, H. 13716 (the *Arms of the Empire and Nuremberg flanked by SS. Sebald and Lawrence*), and one of the latest, the *St. Sebald* which occurs on a broadside, Conrad Celtis, *Sapphic Ode to St. Sebald*, printed by Bergmann von Olpe at Basle, about 1494–95 (S. 1673, H. 4844). Another cut used outside Nuremberg was done for the 1493 edition of the *Würzburg Missal* (S. 4707, H. 11312), replacing a copper engraving by A.G. in earlier editions, appearing again in the edition of 1495 (S. 4708, H. 11313) but replaced by another woodcut in 1497.

Kristeller mentions the cut in Isocrates, *Praecepta*, printed by Creussner, n.d. (a *Knight beheading a Lady*), as possibly early work of Wolgemut. But the type used seems to place the book nearer 1497, and the work, though resembling Wolgemut in landscape and general style, seems from a certain refinement to be rather that of a follower. And by 1489 Wolgemut was certainly doing better work than the *Deathbed Scene* in *Versehung von Leib Seele Ehre und Gut*, printed in that year by Peter Wagner (S. 5423, H. 16019).

ALBRECHT DÜRER (1471–1528)[1] found in woodcut the most perfect medium for the expression of his genius, and is perhaps the greatest figure in the whole history of the art. But the greater part of his production falls within the XVI century, so that his work cannot be treated adequately within the limits of our study, and an estimate of his achievement is more appropriately left to a history dealing with the later period.

The early work, of which we shall give a short survey, formed the climax of the Gothic spirit, yielding, as the century waned, to the Renaissance influences which moulded the development of his later years.

Dürer entered Wolgemut's studio on the 1st December 1486, and his apprenticeship was over on the same day in 1489. Wolgemut's serious participation in designing book-illustration only began with the *Schatzbehalter*, which was issued nearly two years after Dürer had left his studio, while the *Weltchronik* takes us nearly two years later still. So that the assumption, often made, that he might have helped Wolgemut in preparing the designs of one or other of these works is not very convincing; and it is unlikely that block-cutting would have formed any part of his education. On the other hand, he may have followed his master in these early years in making occasional designs for book-illustration, if the cuts attributed to him by Dr. Kurth, which nearly all belong to the period of his apprenticeship, are actually his work, e.g. illustrations in:

> Nicolaus von der Flühe, *Brüder Claus*, Nuremberg (Marx Ayrer) 1488 (S. 4839, H. 5380, K. 1-5; later edition, n.d., printed by Peter Wagner).

[1] H. W. Singer, *Dürer Bibliographie*, Strassburg 1903; J. Heller, Bamberg 1827; M. Thausing, *Leben*, Leipzig 1876 and 1884 (English ed., 1882); William Martin Conway (Lord Conway of Allington), *Literary Remains of Albrecht Dürer*, Cambridge 1889; D. Burckhardt, *Aufenthalt in Basel*, Munich 1892; H. Woelfflin, Munich 1905; W. Weisbach, *Der junge Dürer*, Leipzig 1906; the Dürer Society, London 1898–1911; C. Dodgson, *Catalogue of Early German and Flemish Woodcuts in the British Museum*, vol. i., 1903; M. J. Friedländer, *Albrecht Dürer: der Kupferstecher und Holzschnittzeichner*, Berlin 1919; Erich Roemer, *Dürers ledige Wanderjahre*, Pr. Jahrbuch, xlvii., 1926, 118; xlviii., 1927, 77, 156; Willi Kurth, *The Complete Woodcut Work of Albrecht Dürer*, London 1927; E. Flechsig, Berlin 1928; Hans Tietze and E. Tietze-Conrat, *Der junge Dürer, Verzeichnis der Werke bis zur venezianischen Reise 1505*, Augsburg 1928; F. Winkler, *Dürer* (Klassiker der Kunst), Stuttgart 1928; F. Stadler, *Dürers Apocalypse und ihr Umkreis*, Munich 1929; Joseph Meder, *Dürer-Katalog*, Vienna 1932 (the most detailed catalogue of Dürer's prints). For special bibliography on work done at Basle see p. 328.

Philipp Frankfurter, *Die Geschichte des Pfarrers von Kalenberg*, Nuremberg (Peter Wagner), about 1490 (S. 4410, K. 6-12).

Bertholdus, *Horologium Devotionis*, Nuremberg (Creussner, 1489) (S. 3441, H. 8934, K. 13, 14).

Ein allerheilsamste Warnung vor der falschen Lieb dieser Welt, Nuremberg (Wagner), before 1490 (S. 5455, H. 16150, K. 15-17).

Oratio Cassandre Venete, Nuremberg (Wagner), about 1489 (S. 3675, H. 4553, K. 18).

Wie der Würffel auff ist kumen, Nuremberg (M. Ayrer), 1489 (S. 5490, K. 19).

Johannes Gerson, *Opera*, Nuremberg (G. Stuchs), 1489 (S. 4103, H. 7623, K. 20; see fig. 177).[1]

Alexander Gallus, *Prima Pars Doctrinalis*, Nuremberg (Creussner) 1491 (S. 3079, H. 682, K. 21).

Dürer left Nuremberg on his *Wanderjahre* soon after Easter 1490, returning after Whitsun in 1494. He married Agnes Frey in July of the latter year, and Flechsig very reasonably suggests that his visit to Italy took place in the same autumn (i.e. after the completion of his *Wanderjahre*), and that both this Italian visit and the second of 1505 were in part due to a desire to avoid the plague by which Nuremberg was severely ravaged in those years. The actual course of Dürer's wanderings between 1490 and 1494 has been much debated, for no word from the master himself is preserved to enlighten us, apart from the period of departure and return. The one definite clue is the block of *St. Jerome* designed by Dürer for a Basle book of 1492, which we have already discussed in the section on book-illustration at Basle. We have also described other cuts done at Basle, Freiburg im Breisgau, and Strassburg, attributed to Dürer. The arguments in favour of Dürer's authorship on the side of style are very strong. The weak points are the entire lack of reference in Dürer's writings to so important a series of cuts as those of the *Narrenschiff*, and the fact that a young painter on his *Wanderjahre* could hardly be expected to undertake so extensive a commission as this implied. But in spite of these *a priori* objections, no more plausible solution has yet been found for the authorship of the Basle series. And granting that the *Terence* subjects are by Dürer, it would be difficult not to accept so kindred a design as the woodcut of *Gerson as Pilgrim* (fig. 177), with its background of town and lake in so similar a rhythm to that of *Terence writing* (fig. 145). Both the Terence and many of the earlier

[1] Cf. p. 338.

Nuremberg cuts attributed show how direct is the descent in style from the Ulm designer of Lirer's *Chronica* and Terence, *Eunuchus*, a relation which we have also noted in Koberger's *Passional* cuts of 1488. Perhaps this very family likeness in other Nuremberg cuts should induce some further hesitation in accepting all the work noted above as by Dürer.

The *St. Jerome* is somewhat isolated in a certain formal Gothic character of design, in the midst of other cuts attributed, both before and after its date of 1492. But this difference may depend to some extent on the cutter in the same way as the woodcut frontispiece to the *Nuremberg Chronicle* is so much stiffer than Wolgemut's own original drawing.

There is something peculiarly attractive about these presumed beginnings of Dürer's work. But if it were not for later developments there would be little in it to disclose any greater

Fig. 177. Albrecht Dürer (?). Title-cut to Joannes Gerson, *Opera*, Nuremberg 1489.

personality than the anonymous Master of the Amsterdam Cabinet, or even the designer of the Ulm Terence. For the world at large it would matter little if his woodcuts remained unrecognised before those signed with his well-known monogram and produced after the return from his first visit to Italy, which undoubtedly inspired him to the nobility of style that characterised all his work thereafter. His Gothic traditions were never wholly shed, but they were gradually mellowed by the influence of the great Venetian masters of composition.

In subjects like the so-called *Hercules* of about 1496 (B. 127, K. 99)[1] the

---

[1] The original block of B. 127 is in the British Museum, which also possesses the block of

dependence on Italian modes, especially on Mantegna, is evident, while in others such as many of the *Apocalypse* series, the Gothic character persists in company with an enhanced sense of dignity in both form and composition, which undoubtedly derived from Italian inspiration.

The complete series of fifteen large cuts of the *Apocalypse* was published with text in Koberger's type in both German and Latin editions in 1498; so that Dürer had probably begun their design considerably earlier. The titles, *Die heimlich offenbarūg iohñis* and *Apocalipsis cū Figuris* respectively, are cut in ornamental Gothic letters on separate blocks, and in the second Latin edition of 1511 a cut of *St. John with the Virgin and Child* (B. 60) is added beneath the title. There is only one German edition.

The text occurs on the reverse of the woodcuts, each cut on the right-hand page being faced by text on the left.[1] There are also proofs without text, generally with the 'Reichsapfel' water-mark (the imperial orb, Hausmann 24, Meder 53), the same water-mark which is most frequently found on other proofs of the large woodcuts done between about 1495 and 1500. These (unless they show indication of flaws in the blocks, not seen in the 1498 edition, but corresponding to the 1511 edition) may be regarded as

B. 117 (*Martyrdom of the Ten Thousand Christians*). Two other large original blocks are in the Metropolitan Museum, New York, i.e. B. 2 (*Samson and the Lion*) and B. 120 (*The Martyrdom of St. Catherine*). The British Museum also possesses thirty-five of the original blocks of Dürer's *Small Woodcut Passion*, i.e. all but the title-cut, and *Christ taking leave of his Mother* (B. 16 and B. 21).

[1] The following are the subjects, and a few of the distinguishing marks in text between the 1498 (I) and 1511 (II) Latin editions (first given fully by Cornill d'Orville, Naumann's *Archiv für die zeichnenden Künste*, Leipzig, ix., 1863, p. 204; cf. Meder, 163-78):

    (1) Title B. 60. I, Title only; II, title cut added.
    (2) The Martyrdom of St. John. B. 61. Line 1 ends: I, *beati 10*; II, *beati.*
    (3) The Seven Golden Candlesticks. B. 62. Line 2 ends: I, *pphetem*; II, *pphetem do.*
    (4) The Four and Twenty Elders. B. 63. Line 15 ends: I, *se*; II, *sedis.*
    (5) The Riders on the Four Horses. B. 64. Line 28 ends: I, *inter*; II, *in.*
    (6) Stars falling from Heaven. B. 65. Line 4 ends: I, *quatuor*; II, *quattu.*
    (7) Angels restraining the Winds. B. 66. Line 24 ends: I, *septimi*; II, *septi.*
    (8) The Seven Angels with Trumpets. B. 68. Line 31 ends: I, *cū*; II, *cum.*
    (9) The Four Destroying Angels. B. 69. Line 12 ends: I, *fro*; II, *fron.*
    (10) St. John swallowing the Book. B. 70. Line 5 ends: I, *magnu* ⩟ ; II, *magnum.*
    (11) The Dragon with Seven Heads. B. 71. Line 3 ends: I, *dece* ⩟ ; II, *decē.*
    (12) Michael and Angels fighting the Dragon. B. 72. Line 6 ends: I, *descē*; II, *descen.*
    (13) The Beast with Lamb's Horns. B. 74. Line 8 ends: I, *magna* ⩟ ; II, *magnam.*
    (14) The Adoration of the Lamb. B. 67. Line 13 ends: I, *gē*; II, *gen.*
    (15) The Whore of Babylon. B. 73. I, dated 1498; II, dated 1511.
    (16) The Angel with the Key of the Pit. B. 75. Blank on reverse.

Fig. 178. Albrecht Dürer. The Riders on the Four Horses, from the *Apocalypse*.

before the edition of 1498. If there are intermediate impressions without the text, these would more probably be on paper with the 'bull's head' water-mark.

The *Great Passion* series of twelve woodcuts corresponding in size with the *Apocalypse* (i.e. about 15 × 11 inches) was first published complete with Latin text in 1511, but seven of the subjects were certainly done about 1497–1500, for their style is of this period, and proofs without text are on the 'Reichsapfel' paper which was most generally used at this time. These early subjects are the *Agony in the Garden* (B. 6), the *Scourging of Christ* (B. 8), *Christ shown to the People* (B. 9), *Christ bearing the Cross* (B. 10), the *Crucifixion* (B. 11), the *Lamentation* (B. 13) and the *Entombment* (B. 12). The later subjects are dated 1510, i.e. *The Last Supper* (B. 5), the *Betrayal of Christ* (B. 7), the *Descent to Hell* (B. 14) and the *Resurrection* (B. 15), while the title-cut, *Christ crowned with Thorns* (B. 4), was no doubt added about the same time for the edition of 1511. Impressions without the text are also known later than 1511, e.g. from the reprint without text of Jakob Koppmayer, Augsburg 1675 (with water-mark of the Augsburg arms, a fir-cone on a base).

Dürer issued the two series, the *Apocalypse* and the *Great Passion*, with the *Life of the Virgin* (whose production falls entirely in the xvi century), as a single book from his own printing-press in 1511. The double-column black-letter text of the *Apocalypse* (printed in the same form in the 1498 and the 1511 editions) makes a good balance to the cuts. On the other hand, the single-column Roman type text of the *Great Passion* and the *Life of the Virgin*, with its short-lined verses, is far less harmonious, presenting pages inadequate in weight to the powerful cuts they face.

In addition to the *Hercules* (B. 127, K. 99) already mentioned, the other large woodcuts of the early period, corresponding in form with the *Apocalypse* and the *Large Passion*, are the *Martyrdom of the Ten Thousand Christians* (B. 117, K. 98), the *Holy Family* (B. 102, K. 104), the *Knight and Man-at-Arms* (B. 131, K. 100), the *Men's Bath* (B. 128, K.101; fig. 179), the *Martyrdom of St. Catherine* (B. 120, K. 102) and *Samson and the Lion* (B. 2, K. 103).

All these examples, in varying degrees, are stronger in cutting than three large and rare unsigned prints, the *Lamentation* (K. 87, British Museum and Berlin), the *Crucifixion* (K. 88, British Museum and Berlin) and the *Martyrdom of St. Sebastian* (K. 90, British Museum, etc.). The designs of the latter are certainly by Dürer, and the difference in quality is probably

Fig. 179. Albrecht Dürer. The Men's Bath.

explained by the poorer skill of a cutter, working perhaps away from the master's supervision.

The great strength of the *Apocalypse* woodcuts has inclined Friedländer[1] to the view which I have already combated in regard to Wolgemut, and would equally combat in the case of Dürer and other painters of the period who designed for woodcut, that he cut some of the blocks himself. The strength of the cut seems to me to depend entirely on the design, and on a craftsman skilful enough to cut a true facsimile. Granting a good design on the block, it is even more likely that a successful result would be achieved by the cutting of an experienced craftsman than if the painter should turn his own hand to the negative labours entailed.[2] Nor is the inference from Dürer's own words in his 'Bücher von menschlicher Proportion',[3] that the artist occasionally cut his own blocks, entirely indisputable, for his use of the words *Eiselein* and *versticht*, for the usual *Messer* and *schnitt*, would hardly fall from one accustomed to the craft of woodcutting, if indeed it does not, as Flechsig suggests, refer to sculpture in wood.

On the other hand, it is more than probable that difference of quality in the cutting of his designs depended partly on whether Dürer actually made the drawing on the surface of the block, or merely gave a design on paper for a woodcutter to transfer. In the latter eventuality, even a good cutter might have lost the subtle qualities of the original in transferring to the block; in the former case, a good craftsman would have no reason to blunt the artist's design. And in the best of Dürer's work it is fairly certain that

---

[1] *Der Holzschnitt*, Berlin 1921, pp. 56-57.

[2] Dürer has himself left a reference to his own drawing on a block in the Diary of his Netherlands journey (Antwerp, 3rd September 1520), *Item die zween herrn von Rogendorff haben mich geladen. Ich hab einmal mit ihren gessn und ich hab ihr wappen gross auf ein holz geriessen das mans schneiden mag* (J. Veth and S. Muller, *Dürers niederländische Reise*, Bd. I., *Die Urkunden*, Berlin and Utrecht 1918), a passage rendered by Conway (*Literary Remains*, p. 103): 'The two Lords of Rogendorf invited me. I dined with them once and drew their arms large on a woodblock for cutting'. The only known impression of this cut is in the German National Museum, Nuremberg.

[3] Nuremberg 1528, Bk. III., Sig. T ii; the British Museum MS. (slightly differing from the printed text) transcribed in K. Lange and F. Fuhse, *Dürers schriftliche Nachlass*, Halle 1893, p. 221, and translated in Conway, *Literary Remains*, p. 244. The MS. reads: *Daraus kummt, dass manicher etwas mit der Federn in eim Tag auf ein halben Bogen Papiers reisst oder mit sein. Eiselein etwas in ein klein Hölzlein versticht, dass würd künstlicher und besser dann eins Andern grosses Werk, daran derselb ein ganz Jahr mit höchstem Fleiss macht*, and is translated by Conway: 'For this reason a man may often draw something with his pen on a half-sheet of paper in one day or engrave it with his tool on a small block of wood, and it shall be fuller of art and better than another's great work whereon he hath spent a whole year's careful labour'.

he not only drew on the block, but supervised the cutting as well as the printing.

In addition to the large unsigned cuts of inferior cutting already mentioned, the other chief examples which come under the same category are the four unsigned blocks of the *Albertina Passion*, so called as the Albertina, Vienna, is the only collection which possesses impressions of all four. The subjects are *Christ crowned with Thorns* (K. 94), *The Scourging of Christ* (K. 95), *Christ bearing the Cross* (K. 96) and *Christ on the Cross* (K. 97). Somewhat similar in quality of line, and weaker than the signed and certainly authentic woodcuts, are the numerous illustrations to the *Revelationes S. Brigittae*, printed by Koberger, 1500 (H. 3205, K. 128-142), the two frontispieces to the *Opera Hrosvite* (edited by Conrad Celtis) (P. 277 a and b, K. 143-44), two of the twelve blocks in Conrad Celtis, *Quattuor libri Amorum* (H. 2089; P. 217 and B. 130; K. 145-146), the Celtis books printed respectively in 1501 and 1502 for the Sodalitas Celtica, at Nuremberg, and a series of small cuts used in two Nuremberg prayer-books of about 1503, one being a *Salus Animae* printed by H. HÖLZEL (K. 147-66).[1] But though some of the designs were done within the XV century the detailed discussion of their authorship must be left to the historian of the XVI century. Suffice it to say here that the designs of the two latter books are more certainly Dürer's than the St. Bridget illustrations; and that even in this case the greater distance from Dürer's more convincing draughtsmanship of the same period might have depended on the craftsman employed by the printer to cut the artist's design.

One other attractive little woodcut of the early period, which has only been recently recognised as by Dürer, is the *Head of a Man with Phrenological Notes* (K. 93) from Ludovicus de Prussia, *Trilogium Animae*, printed by Koberger in 1498 (H. 10315, at f. 77 a). As a portrait it bears very direct resemblance to Dürer's friend Willibald Pirkheimer.

I would add here note of a woodcut peculiarly interesting for its subject, and clearly influenced by Dürer's work, which appeared on the title-page of Jacobus Issickemer, *Büchlein der Zuflucht der Maria*, printed at Nuremberg by Caspar Hochfeder, 1497 (S. 4271, H. 9319; fig. 180). It represents an Altar hung with offerings to the Virgin of Alt-Oetting, in the shape of

---

[1] See C. Dodgson, *Holzschnitte zu zwei nürnbergischen Andachtsbüchern aus dem Anfange des XVI Jahrhunderts*, Graph. Gesellschaft, xi., Berlin 1909. For other views on the authorship of the group see H. Röttinger, *Hans Wechtlin*, Vienna Jahrbuch, xxvii. (1907), Heft 1.; and *Dürers Doppelgänger*, Strassburg 1926. In the last-named work Röttinger attributes to Peter Visscher I. part of the group which he had earlier ascribed to Wechtlin.

casts of human figures and limbs for which healing was sought, and a man broken on the wheel, a cripple, and three kneeling figures before the altar.

Before leaving Germany we would make some reference to certain single cuts of Nuremberg and neighbouring regions, of whose designers or cutters occasional record is preserved.

Fig. 180. From J. Issickemer, *Buchlein der Zuflucht der Maria*, Nuremberg 1497.

In the first place, there are several cuts, mostly large representations of saints, signed WOLFGANG, or WOLFGANG HAMER, e.g. the *St. Minus* (S. 1632, British Museum, Basle, and the block in the Derschau series at Berlin) and the *Kindred of Christ* (S. 1779, Munich) with the full name, and a *St. Jerome* (S. 1530, Munich) signed *Wolfgang*. We have already referred to one of Wolgemut's *Schatzbehalter* cuts occurring within a border signed *Wolfgang*, and to the similarity of a supposed Wolgemut drawing to the *St. Jerome* cut,[1] and it appears a very probable inference that Wolfgang Hamer was one of the Nuremberg cutters. His name has not been found in Nuremberg documents, but several others of the family are recorded among Nuremberg *Briefmaler* and *Karten-maler* in the XVI century.

Various other large anonymous cuts of saints have been attributed to his hand, e.g. a *St. Sebald* at Munich (S. 1672), and the same type of work is seen in several other full-length figures of saints, e.g. a *St. Jerome* in the British Museum (S. 1527 a), a popular subject, to judge from the existence of two other versions at Magdeburg (S. 1527) and Weimar (S. 1527 b).

[1] See pp. 372, 374.

Another name which occurs on even cruder cuts is that of HANS PAUR, e.g. on a large and amusing sheet, the *Stock in Trade of a Married Couple* (S. 1991, Munich), on the *Creed, the Apostles and Prophets* (S. 1852, Stuttgart), while the *Lord's Prayer* of 1479 signed *h.p.* (S. 1851, Munich) is probably by the same hand, which is more likely to be the cutter than the designer.

JORG GLOCKENDON is another Nuremberg craftsman who signed various woodcuts which date about the turn of the xv and xvi centuries (if indeed there are not actually two cutters of the name), e.g. the *Virgin and Four Saints* (S. 1162, Berlin, with the original block from the Derschau Collection), *The Youth and Death* (S. 1898, Bamberg), the *Vision near Constantinople* (S. 1944, Munich Library), the *St. Christopher and St. John Baptist* (Metropolitan Museum, New York, from the McGuire Collection; Heitz, *Einbl.*, vol. lxv., pl. 23) and two maps and plans already noted.[1]

The name of CASPER (or CASPAR) occurs on other cuts of the same period, and is probably that of a Regensburg or Nuremberg cutter.[2] A *Virgin and Child and St. Anne* at Stockholm (S. 1191) and the *Influence of Venus* (S. 1975 a, Berlin) are signed *Casper*, while on a *Crucifix with Signs of the Passion* (S. 943, British Museum)[3] and a *St. Francis and the Stigmata* (S. 1423 a, Munich Library) the signature is spelt *Caspar*. Dr. Rosenthal has noted a further signed cut, *St. Florian*, and its unsigned pendant, *St. Wolfgang*,[4] and has made various probable attributions. The variety of style shown in the signed cuts renders it almost certain that he was a cutter and not a designer. A variety of dialect shown on the various cuts again probably implies that he was following text as well as designs supplied him as a journeyman cutter.

An earlier cutter, definitely belonging to Regensburg, LIENHART (WOLFF?), has already been noted among the authors of block-books.[5]

LANDSHUT

Of considerably greater interest than the five craftsmen just mentioned is MAIR OF LANDSHUT. He has been generally called Nicolaus Alexander

---

[1] See p. 316. See also p. 265 for an undescribed series of cuts by Jorg Glockendon.

[2] See Erwin Rosenthal, *Casper* (Beiträge zur Forschung: Studien aus dem Antiquariat J. Rosenthal), Munich 1929.

[3] Another version was signed by Firabet ze Raperswil (see p. 324).

[4] The *St. Florian* and *St. Wolfgang* now in the Metropolitan Museum, New York, from the McGuire Collection, and reproduced on pls. 25 and 30 of Heitz, *Einbl.*, vol. lxv.

[5] See p. 257.

Mair, but the most recent study of his work [1] finds no grounds for his identification with the painter of that name, though he was himself probably also a painter, and identical with the *Mair Maler von Freising* who occurs in the Munich 'Stadtsteuerbuch', 1490, and the painter of a work in Freising Cathedral. The *Alexander* might also be based on a confusion with Alexander Mair, a later Augsburg engraver (1559–1620). Only three woodcuts bearing his name are known, *Christ disputing with the Doctors* (dated 1499), *The Scourging of Christ* (fig. 181) and *St. Barbara*, dated 1499, the first known in two impressions (Paris and the British Museum), the other two only in the British Museum.[2] There is also a fourth woodcut after Mair's design, and only known in the British Museum impression, the *Reception at the Door of a Gothic House* (the same design as Mair's line-engraving, P. 13),[3] which is signed by the woodcutter HANS WURM, whom we have already mentioned for his block-book of the *Art of Wrestling*.[4] It is very probable that Mair's fellow-citizen, Hans Wurm, may also be the cutter of the three other subjects. In three of the cuts considerable portions of the background are left black: and the same practice of printing on tinted paper and heightening with white is found as in the case of Mair's line-engravings. In fact the *St. Barbara* is the only uncoloured impression. Mair's style of design has a certain mannered simplicity, his figures archaic in flavour for their date (and reminiscent of such designs as those in the Ulm *Buch der Weisheit*, printed by Lienhart Holle, 1483),[5] and his architecture that of doll's houses.

A woodcut *Pedigree of the Counts Palatine and Dukes of Bavaria*, belonging to a book entitled *Chronik und Stamm der Pfalzgrafen bei Rhein und Herzoge in Bayern*, printed by N. Wurm at Landshut, 1501,[6] is of a similar character and possibly also cut by Hans Wurm, though there is no reason to regard him as the designer of this subject any more than of the *Art of Wrestling* block-book. Mair may quite possibly be his designer in each case.

[1] Franz Schubert, *Mair von Landshut*, Landshut 1930. Cf. Max Lehrs, *Geschichte und Kritischer Katalog des Deutschen Kupferstiches*, vol. viii., 1932, p. 282.

[2] See Dodgson, *Catalogue of Early German and Flemish Woodcuts in the British Museum*, vol. i. p. 148, A. 143-45.

[3] See Dodgson, vol. ii. p. 263.   [4] See p. 261.

[5] Cf. e.g. *Reception at the Door of a Gothic House* with *Buch der Weisheit*, Sig. i. iii. (reproduced Schramm, vii. fig. 84).

[6] Edited by G. Leidinger, Strassburg (Heitz) 1901. Leidinger attempts to identify the printer N. Wurm with Hans Wurm. Schreiber regards him as probably Hans Wurm's father.

Fig. 181. Mair of Landshut. The Scourging of Christ.

PASSAU

The last German town which we shall pass in our survey before crossing the borders of Austria is Passau[1] on the Danube. But there is nothing of greater note than the cuts in two works printed by JOHANN PETRI, the

plants in his *Herbarius* of 1485 (S. 4206, H. 8445), copied from Schoeffer's Mainz edition of 1484, and a stiff design of Leopold, Duke of Austria, in J. F. de Pavinis, *Defensorium Canonisationis S. Leopoldi,* n.d., about 1490 (S. 4903, H. 12536).

On Austrian territory (according to the old borders) the first printer to interest us is ALBRECHT KUNNE (of Duderstadt, near Göttingen), who printed books for the publisher HERMANN SCHINDELYP of Trent about 1475–76, not for any actual book-illustration, but for

Fig. 182. Portrait of Mahomet II. S. 4557.

a single cut with accompanying text, a *Portrait of Mahomet* (S. 4557, Munich), probably intended for Mahomet II., the conqueror of Constantinople.[2] The text, of which a part is preserved, is a supposed letter

[1] See Albert Schramm, *Bilderschmuck des Frühdrucke,* xvi., Leipzig 1933.

[2] The patterned background should be compared with the pavement design in a curious cut of *Two Monkeys doing Circus Tricks on Horseback* (with revolving monkeys) at Zürich (S. 1985 n), of which there is another, perhaps earlier, version without the pattern at Nuremberg (S. 1985 m).

of the Turkish Emperor, in a type of Italian character, used by Schindelyp and probably printed by Albrecht Kunne. It was probably issued originally as a broadside, or folding sheet, but it is preserved with the incomplete text printed on the reverse of the cut.

It is possible that the Munich sheet may have been printed by Kunne in Italy, and at least certain that the design came from an Italian source. The portrait should be compared with the Florentine engraving *El Gran Turco* at Berlin,[1] and for the Venetian type of design with the *Portrait of Scanderbeg* in M. Barletius, *Historia Scanderbegi*, Rome, n.d., though the latter is a considerably later work belonging to the early xvi century.[2]

Another contemporary woodcut of the *Sultan*, lettered *der türgisch Kayser* (S. 2008, British Museum), seems more fanciful as a portrait if intended to represent Mahomet II. It is probably Upper German work of about 1480.

From about 1480 Albrecht Kunne was settled for some years at Memmingen, and issued a small portrait of the author in his edition of Paolo Attavanti, *Breviarium Decretorum*, 1486. But this is only a copy from the original cut in the Milanese edition of 1479.

VIENNA

Apart from Kunne's *Mahomet* there are few cuts of any interest issued on Austrian territory during the xv century.[3] One of the earliest is an illustration in the *Legend of St. Roch*, issued without printer's name at Vienna, 1482 (Gollob, *Verzeichnis*, No. 226), only known in the copy at the Abbey of Melk.

Most of the other occasional cuts in Viennese books of the end of the xv century were printed by JOHANN WINTERBURGER, e.g. a *Sick-room with two doctors and two patients* in Steber, *A Malafranczos morbo Gallorum Praeservatio*, n.d. (Gollob 242), and the *Author writing at his desk* in Augustinus Datus, *Elegantiae Minores*, 1499 (Gollob 81). But in these early years of his press, the best woodcuts used by Winterburger are the initials and borders, generally in white on black ground after the Venetian style of

---

Bear-baiting and bull-baiting in Elizabethan times frequently ended with the 'pleasant sport of the horse and the ape' (see *Shakespeare's England*, Oxford, 1917, ii. p. 430), and the prints may represent a diversion of the same kind.

[1] See Lippmann, Pr. Jahrbuch, ii. 215, for reproduction, and notes of other portraits.

[2] Reproduced by Essling, part ii. No. 2317, as a Venetian cut.

[3] See Hedwig Gollob, *Der Wiener Holzschnitt in den Jahren von 1490–1550*, Vienna 1926; *Systematisches Verzeichnis der mit Wiener Holzschnitten illustrierten Wiener Drucke*, 1482–1550, Strassburg 1925.

Ratdolt and others. The title border to his *Practica auf dis jar 1497* (Gollob 216) is an attractive floral design on black ground.

BRÜNN—OLMÜTZ

We have already mentioned the cuts in Johannes de Thwrocz, *Chronica Hungarorum*, printed by CONRAD STAHEL and MATHIAS PREUNLEIN at Brünn, 20th March 1488, in relation to the other blocks of the same subject in Ratdolt's edition of three months later.[1] The illustration of the *Tartars marching into Hungary in the time of Bela IV.* is a clumsy but spirited piece of work.

A woodcut of *St. Wenceslas* which appeared in the *Olmütz Psalter*, printed by Conrad Stahel alone, Brünn 1499 (S. 5029, H. 13503), of which there are other versions in Grüninger's *Olmütz Breviary*, Strassburg 1499 (S. 3611), occurred later on the title of Augustinus Moravus, *De Secta Waldensium*, printed by CONRAD BAUMGARTEN, Olmütz 1500 (S. 3397, H. 11614).

KUTTENBERG—PRAGUE

A *Bohemian Bible*, printed at Kuttenberg by MARTIN OF TISCHNIOWA, 1489 (S. 3468, H. 3162), and a *Bohemian New Testament*, printed anonymously at Prague about 1497–98 (S. 5336), are both illustrated with cuts, but they are crude works and only merit a passing notice.

BIBLIOGRAPHY

BURLINGTON FINE ARTS CLUB. Catalogue of a Collection of Woodcuts of the German School, xv and xvi Centuries. London 1882.

MUTHER, Richard. Die ältesten deutschen Bilder-Bibeln. Munich 1883.

MUTHER, Richard. Die deutsche Bücher-illustration der Gotik und Frührenaissance (1460–1530). 2 vols. Munich and Leipzig 1884.

BARACK, Carl August. Elsässische Büchermarken. Strassburg 1892.

SCHORBACH, Karl. Seltene Drucke in Nachbildungen, mit einleitendem Text. 5 vols. Leipzig and Halle 1893–1905.

    i. Die Historien von dem Ritter Beringer. Strassburg 1495 (S. 3427, Nuremberg).

    ii. Dietrich von Bern. Heidelberg (Knoblochtzer) 1490 (S. 3822, Berlin).

    iii. Ecken Auszfart. Augsburg (H. Schawr) 1491 (S. 3885, Berlin).

    iv. Laurin. Strassburg 1500 (S. 5152, *Rosengarten König Laurins*; Berlin).

    v. Die Geschichte des Pfaffen vom Kalenberg. Heidelberg 1490 (S. 4409, *Kalenberg-Pfaffe*; Darmstadt).

---

[1] See p. 303. For Bohemian and Moravian books in general, see J. Volf, *Geschichte des Buchdruckes in Böhmen und Mähren*, Weimar 1928.

COCKERELL, S. C. Some German Woodcuts of the xv Century. London 1897.

HEITZ, P., and SCHREIBER, W. L. Die deutschen Accipies und Magister cum Discipulis Holz-schnitte als Hilfsmittel zur Inkunabel-Bestimmung. Strassburg 1908.

HEITZ, P., and SCHREIBER, W. L. Christus am Kreuz. Kanonbilder der in Deutschland ge-druckten Messbücher des xv[ten] Jahrhunderts. Strassburg 1910.

WORRINGER, Wilhelm. Die altdeutsche Buchillustration. Munich 1912 (3rd ed., 1921).

MURRAY, C. Fairfax. Catalogue of a Collection of Early German Books in the Library of C.F.M. 2 vols. London 1913.

EINBLATTDRUCKE DES xv[ten] JAHRHUNDERTS. Ein bibliographisches Verzeichnis. Herausgegeben von der Kommission für den Gesamtkatalog der Wiegendrucke. Halle 1914.

VOULLIÉME, E. Die deutschen Drucker des xv[ten] Jahrhunderts. Berlin 1916 (2nd ed., 1922).

SCHRAMM, Albert. Der Bilderschmuck der Frühdrucke. Leipzig, fol.

    i. Die Drucke von Albrecht Pfister in Bamberg. 1922.

    ii. „   „   Günther Zainer in Augsburg. 1920.

    iii. „   „   Johann Baemler in Augsburg. 1921.

    iv. „   „   Anton Sorg in Augsburg. 1921.

    v. „   „   Johann Zainer in Ulm. 1923.

    vi. „   „   Konrad Dinckmut in Ulm. 1923.

    vii. „   „   Lienhart Holle, Johannes Reger, Johann Schaeffler and Hans Hauser in Ulm. 1923.

    viii. Die Kölner Drucker. 1924.

    ix. Die Drucker in Esslingen, Urach, Stuttgart, Reutlingen, Tübingen, Blaubeuren. 1926.

    x. „   „   in Lübeck. (1) Die beiden Brüder Brandis. 1927.

    xi. „   „   „   (2) Steffen Arndes. 1928.

    xii. „   „   „   (3) Ghotan; (4) Mohnkopfdrucke. Die Drucker in Magde-burg. 1929.

    xiii. „   „   in Leipzig and Erfurt. 1930.

    xiv. „   „   in Mainz. (1) Fust und Schoeffer; (2) Johann Numeister; (3) Peter Schoffer. 1931.

    xv. „   „   „   (4) Erhard Reuwich; (5) Jacob Meydenbach; (6) Peter Fried-berg. 1932.

    xvi. „   „   in Speier, Würzburg, Passau, München, Ingolstadt, Zweibrücken, Freis-ing, Memmingen. 1933.

    xvii. „   „   in Nürnberg. (1) Anton Koberger. 1934.

SCHRAMM, Albert. Die illustrierten Bibel der Inkunabelzeit. Leipzig 1922.

SCHRAMM, Albert. Illustrierte Gebetbücher des xv[ten] Jahrhunderts. Wolfenbüttel 1928.

WEIL, Ernst. Die deutschen Druckerzeichen des xv[ten] Jahrhunderts. Munich 1924.

JUCHHOFF, Rudolf. Drucker- und Verlegerzeichen des xv[ten] Jahrhunderts in den Niederländen, England, Spanien, Böhmen, Mähren und Polen. Munich 1927.

JAHN, Johannes. Beiträge zur Kenntnis der ältesten Einblattdrucke. Strassburg 1927.

GEISBERG, Max. Die Deutsche Buchillustration in der ersten Hälfte des xvi Jahrhunderts. Munich 1930, etc. (in progress).